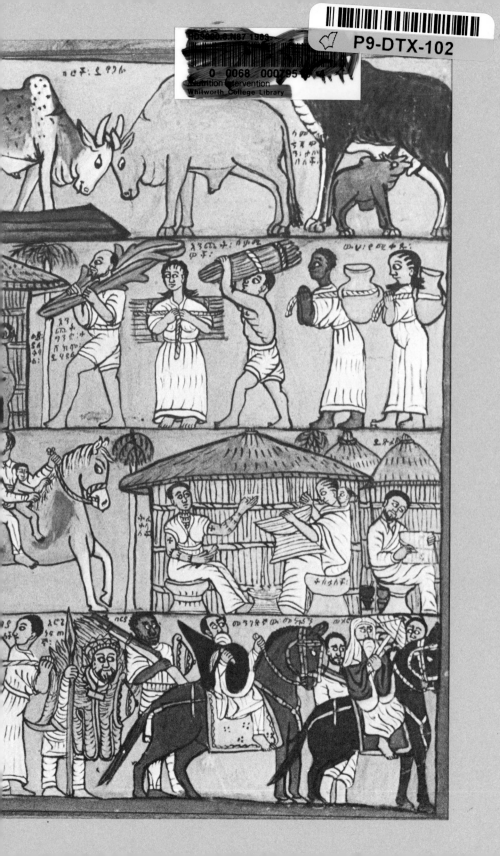

Agricultural village scenes vividly depict complex of socio–cultural influences that limit the production, distribution, and use of food — hence nutritional status — in nonindustrialized societies. Unknown Ethiopean artist; collection of William J. Darby.

Nutrition Intervention Strategies in National Development

THE NUTRITION FOUNDATION

A Monograph Series

Nutrition Intervention Strategies in National Development

Edited by

BARBARA A. UNDERWOOD

Department of Nutrition and Food Science
International Food and Nutrition Program
Massachusetts Institute of Technology
Cambridge, Massachusetts

1983

ACADEMIC PRESS

A Subsidiary of Harcourt Brace Jovanovich, Publishers

New York   London
Paris   San Diego   San Francisco   São Paulo   Sydney   Tokyo   Toronto

ACADEMIC PRESS, INC.
111 Fifth Avenue, New York, New York 10003

United Kingdom Edition published by
ACADEMIC PRESS, INC. (LONDON) LTD.
24/28 Oval Road, London NW1 7DX

Library of Congress Cataloging in Publication Data
Main entry under title:

Nutrition   intervention strategies in national
    development.

    (Nutrition Foundation series)
    Includes index.
    1. Food supply--Government policy. 2. Nutrition
policy. 3. Income distribution--Government policy.
4. Agriculture and state. I. Underwood, Barbara A.
II. Series: Monograph series (Nutrition Foundation)
HD9000.6.N87 1983   363.8'56   82-20588
ISBN 0-12-709080-0

PRINTED IN THE UNITED STATES OF AMERICA

83 84 85 86   9 8 7 6 5 4 3 2 1

Contents

I
Nutrition Interventions in General

II
Socioeconomic Strategies

III
Supplementary Feeding Programs

IV
Strategies for Treatment of Protein Energy Malnutrition

16. Rehabilitation of Protein Energy Malnutrition in Young Infants: Hospital and Community Based Programs in Chiang Mai, Thailand

OUSA THANANGKUL, DAMRI DAMRONGSAK, VICHARN VITHAYASAI, TASANAWAN VANIYAPONG, AND JURAI CHAMNAN

17. Nutrition Recovery Centers: The Chilean Experience

FERNANDO MONCKEBERG AND JOSE S. RIUMALLO

V

Nutrition–Infection Cycle as Related to Intervention Techniques

VI
Nutrient-Specific Interventions

VII
Nutrition Education

Contributors

Numbers in parentheses indicate the pages on which the authors' contributions begin.

E. *Alvarez*[1] (287), Instituto de Nutricion de Centro America y Panama, Guatemala City, Guatemala, Central America

Mirna Amar (273, 315), Instituto de Nutricion y Tecnologia de los Alimentos, Universidad de Chile, Santiago, Chile

Antonio Arteaga (91), Departamento de Nutricion, Facultad de Medicina, Universidad Catolica, Santiago, Chile

G. H. Beaton (67), Department of Nutritional Sciences, Faculty of Medicine, University of Toronto, Toronto M5S 1A8, Canada

Marisol Cayazzo (315), Instituto de Nutricion y Tecnologia de los Alimentos, Universidad de Chile, Santiago, Chile

Patricia Chadud (273, 315), Instituto de Nutricion y Tecnologia de los Alimentos, Universidad de Chile, Santiago, Chile

Jurai Chamnan (179), Research Institute for Health Sciences, Chiang Mai University, Chiang Mai 50 002, Thailand

Lincoln C. Chen (227), The Ford Foundation, New Delhi 110003, India

Neville Colman (343), Veterans Administration Medical Center, Bronx, New York 10468, and Mount Sinai School of Medicine, New York, New York 10029

James D. Cook (257, 285), Division of Hematology, Department of Medicine, University of Kansas Medical Center, Kansas City, Kansas 66103

Damri Damrongsak (179), Research Institute for Health Sciences, Chiang Mai University, Chiang Mai 50 002, Thailand

Johanna Dwyer[2] (117), Frances Stern Nutrition Center, New England Medical Center Hospital, Boston, Massachusetts 02111

Rafael E. Ferreyra[3] (393), Magdalena 160, Casilla 13970, Santiago, Chile

[1]Inter-Country Project—Nutrition, Nutrition—W.P.R.O., World Health Organization, Suva, Fiji.

[2]Present address: Department of Medicine, Tufts Medical School, and New England Medical Center Hospital, Boston, Mass. 02111.

[3]Present address: San Juan 1561, Barrio Caseros, Cordoba 5000, Argentina.

Guillermo Figueroa (241), Instituto de Nutricion y Tecnologia de los Alimentos, Universidad de Chile, Santiago, Chile

Rodolfo F. Florentino (165), Nutrition Center of the Philippines, Makati, Metro Manila, Philippines

Nicolás González (101, 241), Consejo Nacional para la Alimentacion y Nutrition, Ministerio de Salud, Santiago, Chile

Abraham Horwitz (387), National Library of Medicine, National Institutes of Health, Bethesda, Maryland 20014

Antonio Infante (101), Instituto de Nutricion y Tecnologia de los Alimentos, Universidad de Chile, Santiago, Chile

Pablo Lira (265), Departamento de Hematology, Facultad de Medicina, Universidad Catolica, Santiago, Chile

Sandra Llaguno (315), Instituto de Nutricion y Tecnologia de los Alimentos, Universidad de Chile, Santiago, Chile

Ines López (315), Instituto de Nutricion y Tecnologia de los Alimentos, Universidad de Chile, Santiago, Chile

John I. McKigney (363), Office of Nutrition, U.S. Agency for International Development, Washington, D.C. 20523

Josip Matovinovic (324), Department of Internal Medicine, The University of Michigan Medical School, Ann Arbor, Michigan 48109

Martín Miranda (397), Instituto de Nutrition y Tecnologia de los Alimentos, Universidad de Chile, Santiago, Chile

Sergio Molina (47), Naciones Unidas Comision Economica Para America Latina, Santiago, Chile

Fernando Monckeberg (13, 31, 101, 189, 241), Instituto de Nutricion y Tecnologia de los Alimentos, Universidad de Chile, Santiago, Chile

Jose Obdulio Mora[4] (79), Instituto Colombiano de Bienestar Familiar, Bogotá, Colombia

Manuel Olivares (273, 315), Instituto de Nutricion y Tecnologia de los Alimentos, Universidad de Chile, Santiago, Chile

Oscar Pineda (287), Instituto de Nutricion de Centro America y Panama, Guatemala City, Guatemala, Central America

Fernando Pizarro (273, 315), Instituto de Nutricion y Tecnologia de los Alimentos, Universidad de Chile, Santiago, Chile

Ernesto Ríos[5] (273), Instituto de Nutricion y Tecnologia de los Alimentos, Universidad de Chile, Santiago, Chile

Jose S. Riumallo (189), Instituto de Nutricion y Tecnologia de los Alimentos, Universidad de Chile, Santiago, Chile

Roberto Rueda-Williamson (111), Contesen Internacional de Colombia, Bogotá, Colombia

[4]Present address: Medicine Comunitaria, Escuela Colombia de Medicina, Bogotá, Colombia.

[5]Present address: Pediatrics-Hematology Clinic, Hospital Calvo-MacKenna, Universidad de Chile, Santiago, Chile.

Liana Schlesinger (241), Instituto de Nutricion y Tecnologia de los Alimentos, Universidad de Chile, Santiago, Chile

Carlos Schlessinger (101), Instituto de Nutricion y Tecnologia de los Alimentos, Universidad de Chile, Santiago, Chile

Nevin S. Scrimshaw (201, 209), International Nutrition Program, Massachusetts Institute of Technology, Cambridge, Massachusetts 02139

M. Teresa Segure (241), Instituto de Nutricion y Tecnologia de los Alimentos, Universidad de Chile, Santiago, Chile

Marcelo Selowsky (23), The World Bank, Washington, D.C. 20433

John B. Stanbury (324), International Nutrition Policy and Planning Program, Massachusetts Institute of Technology, Cambridge, Massachusetts 02190

Abraham Stekel (273, 315), Instituto de Nutricion y Tecnologia de los Alimentos, Universidad de Chile, Santiago, Chile

Ousa Thanangkul (179), Research Institute for Health Sciences, Chiang Mai University, Chiang Mai 50 002, Thailand

Ernesto Tironi (51), Centro de Estudios del DeSarrollo, Santiago, Chile

Benjamin Torún (287), Program of Physiology and Clinical Nutrition, Instituto de Nutricion de Centro America y Panama, Guatemala City, Guatemala, Central America

Ricardo Uauy (397), Instituto de Nutrition y Tecnologia de los Alimentos, Universidad de Chile, Santiago, Chile

Barbara A. Underwood[6] (3, 57), Department of Nutrition and Food Science, International Food and Nutrition Program, Massachusetts Institute of Technology, Cambridge, Massachusetts 02139

Alberto Valdés (41), International Food Policy Research Institute, Washington, D.C. 20036

Tasanawan Vaniyapong (179), Research Institute for Health Sciences, Chiang Mai University, Chiang Mai 50 002, Thailand

Fernando E. Viteri[7] (287), Division of Human Nutrition and Biology, Instituto de Nutricion de Centro America y Panama, Guatemala City, Guatemala, Central America

Vicharn Vithayasai (179), Research Institute for Health Sciences, Chiang Mai University, Chiang Mai 50 002, Thailand

Jorge Weinberger (241), Instituto de Nutricion y Tecnologia de los Alimentos, Universidad de Chile, Santiago, Chile

[6]Present address: National Eye Institute, National Institutes of Health, Bethesda, Maryland 20205.

[7]Present address: Division of Disease Prevention and Control, Pan American Health Organization, Washington, D.C. 20037.

Foreword

Improvement of health and quality of life on a national level requires the broadest possible range of attacks, no one of which, initiated in isolation, is likely to be maximally successful. Planning for the elimination of malnutrition and the betterment of nutritional status cannot be separated from multiple policy considerations for national development. The burden of malnutrition affects socioeconomic development; conversely, socioeconomic factors affect the state of nutrition in a country.

It is difficult, even impossible, to assign a specific return to most developmental measures. Reduction in incidence or eradication of a disease, either of infectious or deficiency origin, are returns for which an increasing number of effective measures can be credited with confidence.

This work presents recently adduced evidence concerning nutritional measures that can be effective components of health programs without broad policy planning for national development.

Prevention of widespread disease by planned controlled change in the quality of diet eaten by a large segment of the population is a health measure of long-recognized effectiveness. It is not of recent origin. James Lind's demonstration in 1747 of the curative value of lemons in ship scurvy eventually resulted in issuance of a daily ration of citrus juice to prevent this disease in the British Navy. Admiral Takaki, a Japanese naval physician, in 1882 increased the allowance of vegetables, meat, and fish and displaced some of the polished rice with barley in ships' rations, thereby eliminating beriberi in the Japanese Navy. At approximately the same period, the proposal was made to increase the amount of iodine in the diet by adding it to salt in goiterous regions. Where properly introduced, the measure proved effective in preventing endemic goiter and associated cretinism. Pronounced reduction in incidence of nutritional deficiency diseases in infants followed the introduction in infant feeding of regular supplements of particular foods or concentrates that are antiscorbutic, antirachitic, or antixerophthalmic. Shortly thereafter, supplements of brewer's yeast were distributed in pellagarous areas in order to reduce endemic pellagra, especially during periods of disasters that would compromise food supply. Fluoridation of water was introduced to reduce dental caries. Each of these measures might well be considered as mass "preventive therapy" aimed at control of a specific disease.

Despite long recognition of the benefits of such measures in combatting particular diseases, it was not until the 1940s and 1950s that there arose the concept of nutritionally designing foods to meet the needs of major segments of the population. "Enrichment" or "restoration" was then introduced in the United States, the Philippines, Newfoundland, and elsewhere as a broadly applicable public health technique. Interest in nutritional measures in public health programs was intensified by the suddenly increased awareness of the severe toll of kwashiorkor or "protein–calorie malnutrition" among toddlers in lesser developed countries. This awareness stemmed from the dramatic descriptions of Cecily Williams and Hugh Trowell from Africa and others and was intensified by reports generated from WHO–FAO sponsored studies initiated with the Brock–Autret report on "Kwashiorkor in Africa" and work in several centers in Central and South America and Southeast Asia. The agencies of The United Nations (WHO, FAO, UNICEF) then gave varying support to the employment of iodinization and of cereal enrichment with selected B vitamins and iron, in addition to encouraging national production, distribution, and the use of protein-rich foods. Initially expressed opposition to enrichment slowly diminished and the use of it has gradually spread.

Interest in and action on the more broadly conceived notion of employing a wide variety of different techniques of "nutritional intervention" was focused by the 1974 World Food Conference. At the opening session of this conference, the then Secretary of State of the United States, Henry Kissinger, called not only for maximum food production with farmer incentives but for intensified utilization of effective intervention strategies that would reduce or eliminate specific deficiency syndromes such as vitamin A deficiency xerophthalmia and preventable blindness, nutritional anemia, and the like. This call was promptly followed by the development and publication by The Nutrition Foundations of Sweden, Britain, and the United States of "Proposed Nutritional Guidelines for the Use of Industrially Produced Nutrients."

These and other developments focused on *applicable* techniques of *demonstrated* effectiveness in reducing health impairments due to nutritional deficits or imbalances. Evaluation or demonstration of the effectiveness of intervention schemes as applied in the field were undertaken. Variations in existing intervention measures or newly designed ones suitable for differing sociocultural societies have been promoted. Consequently, experience with a wide variety of evaluated public health procedures now allows objective determination of estimation of cost effectiveness and permits the design of effective intervention techniques that are applicable in varied sociocultural situations.

This Nutrition Foundation treatise summarizes such experiences that will provide guidance to health workers concerned with nutrition intervention programs in widely differing settings. The Nutrition Foundations in the United States and in Chile have joined in sponsoring the preparation of this book as a part of their commitment to the "advancement of nutrition knowledge and to its effective application in improving the health and welfare of mankind." This volume, concerned as it is with research on and appraisal of targeted *application* of nutrition knowledge in public health, is fittingly timely as the thirteenth volume in the Nutrition Foundation Monographs series, published during the past nine years, dealing with varied aspects of nutrition research.

This volume is not intended to be all-inclusive. Existence of excellent up-to-date works concerning some of the older intervention measures, such as iodinization and goiter or fluoride and dental caries, makes unnecessary detailed treatment of these subjects here. Also, many supplementary details of the technology of intervention strategy for prevention of vitamin A deficiency and resultant blindness and of nutritional anemia, especially iron deficiency, are accessible in reports of the International Vitamin A Consultative Group (IVACG) and the International Nutritional Anemia Consultative Group (INACG). These reports are available from The Nutrition Foundation.

We are indebted to those scientists who have generously labored to bring to fruition this valuable resource; particularly, we are grateful to the editor, Dr. Barbara A. Underwood, whose broad experience in the laboratory as well as in the field provides a rare balance of sensitive appreciation of the needs that realistically can be fulfilled within an accomplishable time frame and at affordable costs.

William J. Darby
Department of Biochemistry
Vanderbilt University School of
Medicine
Nashville, Tennessee

Fernando Monckeberg
Instituto de Nutricion y
Technologia de los Alimentos
Universidad de Chile
Santiago, Chile

Preface

Staggering numbers are generated by pundits who attempt to estimate the number of people in the world who are malnourished, both those overfed and those underfed. Figures for undernutrition range from 450 million to 1 billion, depending on the criteria selected to define malnutrition.[1,2] These widely varying numbers have caused many development planners to conclude either that the figures are simply "guesstimates" and meaningless for program-planning purposes or that the problem is too large and complex to tackle by specific nutrition intervention strategies.

Regardless of which criteria one uses, there is consensus that there are an unconscionable number of undernourished people in the world and that the vast majority are children and their families from poor homes. Apart from the suffering this situation imposes on individuals and their families, it is a deterrent to worldwide human, as well as economic, development. Some feel that intervention strategies to reach those most in need should center on improving economic and social development generally, nutritional problems being solved in the process. Others argue that the time span is too long before social and economic development will "trickle down" benefits to the poor[3] and that much can be done in the interim through specific nutrition intervention programs that include the high risk groups.

[1]Overcoming World Hunger. "The Challenge Ahead." Report of the Presidential Commission on World Hunger, March, 1980.
[2]"World Development Report 1980," World Bank. Oxford University Press, New York, 1980.
[3]Berg, "Malnourished People, A Policy View." Poverty and Basic Needs Series. World Bank, 1981.

This book compiles the work and thoughts of individuals who are actively participating in developing and implementing strategies to reduce worldwide malnutrition. Some contributors are laboratory scientists and medical doctors; others are economists and education specialists. They present a spectrum of strategies. Some approach the problem from a critical analysis and synthesis of what has been attempted and failed or succeeded and others share their experience in specific ongoing research and evaluation projects.

I am grateful for the help of the Advisory Committee—Dr. Sam Middleton, Dr. Fernando Monckeberg, Dr. Ricardo Uauy, Dr. C. O. Chichester—in bringing this volume to fruition and for the assistance of Dr. Vivian Beyda of the Nutrition Foundation for her help with some of the editing and necessary but time-consuming technical support. Gratefully acknowledged is the translation assistance given by Dr. Oscar Brunser of INTA.

Barbara A. Underwood

I Nutrition Interventions in General

1 Some Elements of Successful Nutrition Intervention Strategies

BARBARA A. UNDERWOOD

Through the years there have been many attempts to design intervention strategies to reduce the prevalence of undernutrition. Many of these have been relatively small scale pilot projects, and some have been successful as long as they remained limited in size and scope. Only a limited number of nutrition intervention strategies have been transferable from successful pilot projects to successful, sustainable national programs. Limited success when pilot programs are expanded is true of many kinds of development programs, but in the health field it is especially true of those that are preventive rather than curative in orientation. From an analysis of the few national "successes," some guiding elements can be extracted that appear critical, universal, and thus deserving of special emphasis (Table I). Undoubtedly other elements are critical on a more micro scale when considering specific community programs applied in specific locations. Some of these are shown in Table II. One obvious weakness of past programs has been the lack of well established viable inkages between the macro or national and the micro or local programs.

CONCEPTUALIZATION

The first critical element for "success" is an explicit conceptualization of the program and its principal objectives. Ideally the conceptualization and objectives should evolve as a combined effort of those politically, as

3

NUTRITION INTERVENTION STRATEGIES IN NATIONAL DEVELOPMENT

TABLE I

Elements of Success (Macro or National View)

---

1. Clear conceptualization of program and of principal objectives
2. Clear commitment to program and objectives
3. Administrative structure for implementation: stability, visibility, multisectoral coordination
4. Means of monitoring and evaluating effectiveness

---

well as fiscally and physically, responsible for implementation. The conceptualization should be based on available factual information obtained nationally and locally on the existance of a problem, its magnitude, and its suspected causes. Too frequently, and for understandable reasons, political leaders who make decisions and allocate resources at national, regional, and community levels are not involved in the conceptualization stages and, therefore, have limited exposure to the range of factors contributing to the problem, amenable to change and soluble within the local resource constraints (Fig. 1). As a consequence, at a later date, they may allocate limited resources inappropriately.

Program failure on expansion can often be traced to an inadequate diagnosis prior to conceptualization of an expanded program and of the extent of regional and local variations that contribute to the problem. Undernutrition as a problem may be universal, but there exist markedly regionally specific variations in the differential contribution of various causal factors. Recognition of and accommodation to these local factors can determine the likelihood of a successful intervention. This underlines the importance of establishing regional linkages to national programs even during the conceptualization stage (Fig. 1).

TABLE II

Elements of Success (Micro or Community View)

---

1. Clear conceptualization, commitment, a structure for implementing, monitoring, and evaluating
2. Needs oriented
3. Feasible
     Economically
     Ecologically
     Stable resources
4. Locally managed
     Responsibility
     Accountability
5. Culturally and socially adapted
     Translatability of concepts
     Participation of family units

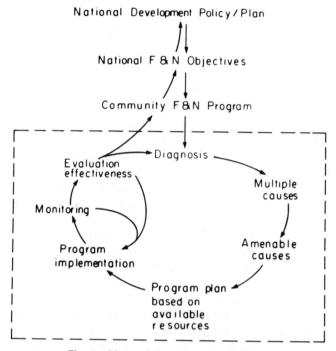

Fig. 1. National development policy/plan.

Personnel, of course, change during the implementation of a program. Failure in programs in many cases can be traced to inadequate orientation of new personnel who did not participate in the original conceptualization. For example, many nutritional rehabilitation or mother-craft centers have failed because the original concept of simplicity and community self-reliance was lost by well-meaning latecomers wanting to advance program services beyond those perceived by the community as needed and sustainable (1). If perceptions of program objectives vary, this leads to different or confused interpretations of how well a program is progressing and may disenchant political leaders from continuing their support.

COMMITMENT

A second element for success is an extant, clear commitment to the program and its stated objectives. For a broad coverage national program, particularly one using public funds or donated foods, this commitment must be obvious at all levels of decision making. In some instances it may be facilitated by a government sponsored decree, legislation, or public campaign. Examples of governmental action taken by some countries include Law 27 enacted in 1974 in Colombia that calls for the creation of Centers for Integrated Attention for Preschool Children that include a feeding component (2), or the Presidential Decree 491, The Nutrition Act of the Philippines, that declared nutrition to be a priority of the government and to involve all branches of the government in implementing an integrated program to include a food assistance component (3). There is also the early social security legislation in Chile that entitles working mothers to receive milk for their infants whom they are unable to breast-feed because of employment (4). Another example is the legislation that created the Woman, Infant, and Children (WIC) Program in the United States that is described in detail elsewhere in this volume. Legislation of this type focuses public attention on nutrition as a national priority and facilitates political commitment and program implementation at successively lower levels by virtue of the "orders down" aura. Legislation, of course, must be accompanied by the commitment of money and the resources necessary for program implementation. It is essential that the political commitment as well as a portion of the monetary and other resources be decentralized and under the control of the implementors at lower levels of the hierarchy. Some flexibility in program selection, implementation, and budgetary allocation at the community level is critical to allow for culturally and socially appropriate adaptations (Table II).

MULTISECTORIAL, VISIBLE, AND STABLE INFRASTRUCTURE

A third element important to success is a stable, visible administrative structure for program implementation that allows for coordination of the activities in food and nutrition with those of other community projects. The causes of malnutrition are many, and solutions must be sought that consider the total ecological context within the community and family. Figure 2 is an attempt to illustrate some of the many interrelated factors that act synergistically to trap poor families into a web of deprivation contributing to the malnutrition problem. Integrated national programs adapted to local conditions can help to break into this web from several possibly vulnerable points. Vertical programs that provide a food supplement or financial incentives or educational components in isolation from the context of the malnutrition-deprivation web, with few exceptions, have repeatedly failed to become institutionalized at the national

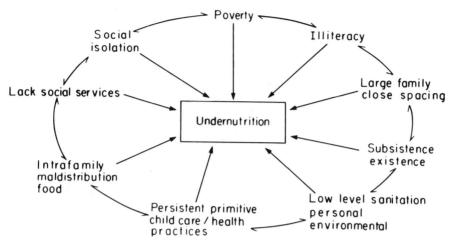

Fig. 2.   Deprivation web (family level).

or local levels. To overcome this, sustainable, publicly supported nutrition programs need to be horizontal or multisectorial in their planning and implementation. They should be viewed as having objectives beneficial politically to several ministries, departments, and community projects. To achieve this, representatives from sectoral groups must be involved in setting the objectives and must be familiar with the policies and program plans for meeting those objectives. Although it is easy to gain acceptance of this idea, it is not easy to implement (5). It is, however, critically important to success because policies and programs that are established on a broad base are less likely to be toppled by the political and resource vicissitudes that often affect narrowly conceived programs.

   An administrative structure that allows for multisectoral participation increases program visibility both nationally and within communities. Visibility must be recognized as an important political component for continued commitment. It is not enough to pass legislation or to incorporate food and nutrition goals into 5-year development plans, and then to retreat into a vertically oriented action plan. Rather, continued broad-based visibility during the implementation period is essential to sustaining the multisectorial commitment that is necessary to ensure program stability.

   National food and nutrition programs must be coordinated with community endeavors that have nutritional implications and that relate directly to family priorities and recipient needs (Fig. 3). Supplementary feeding programs should be linked, for example, to agricultural development projects designed to stimulate local production of nutritious

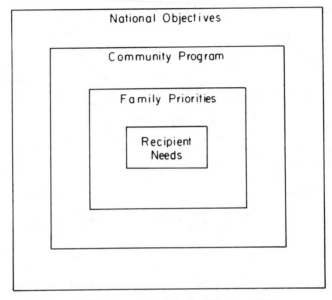

Fig. 3. Linkages critical to "success."

foods. Feeding programs that are curative in focus should be linked also to health development projects, including primary health care, to facilitate delivery to those likely to be most in need not only of food, but also of preventative and curative health services. Important linkages must also be made to educational programs, to income-generating and redistribution schemes (particularly for women), and to programs that facilitate social involvement and interactions. Although these linkages to other community programs designed to meet specific local family and individual needs are important to maximize opportunities for synergistic supports, care must be taken not to piggyback nutrition intervention programs onto other ongoing programs in such a way that the system becomes overloaded. For example, it is very tempting to use health center personnel as implementers of food distribution programs and to expect them to provide monitoring and nutrition education as well. In many systems, however, health personnel are already overutilized and will be resentful and reluctant participants in a program that further adds to their work responsibilities. A similar example can be drawn from the overuse of community school teachers to serve as data collectors for program monitoring. Successful programs stem from willing and committed personnel, not overburdened, resentful professionals from a discipline not closely linked to nutrition.

FEEDBACK FOR PROGRAM ADJUSTMENTS

A fourth element of durable, successful programs is a means of ongoing surveillance to provide program feedback and evaluation of progress locally and nationally toward achieving stated objectives (Fig. 1). The collection of interesting but superfluous data can overload the system and increase costs; it must be avoided. Additionally, the national program must be sufficiently flexible to allow for program adjustments, as indicated from regional and local surveillance systems, in order to correct operational problems inhibiting progress toward meeting objectives. Also important is that "success" or "failure" not be judged prematurely. Although flexibility in regional and local program implementation is important, stability of agreed upon objectives is equally important. Stated in other terms, the goals must remain unchanged, whereas flexibility is needed in the means of achieving them under local conditions. Furthermore, demonstrable benefits may occur within different time frames for different kinds of programs. Evaluations to judge "success" or "failure" must take this into account.

NEEDS ORIENTED

National nutrition objectives are achieved through community-based programs. Community programs should be designed to meet the nutritional needs of local recipients (who are specified by the national program objectives). These programs should recognize the local cultural and social context in which the target population lives and those local factors that contribute to malnutrition (Table II). To be effective, community programs must also recognize the family context in which the intended recipient or recipients live because this can determine intrafamily food distribution patterns. The community and family context will vary from region to region and within regions. It is important, therefore, to establish the supportive linkages of local programs to national objectives while retaining flexibility in local program implementation. From a community viewpoint, therefore, it is important that appropriate community leaders be involved in diagnosing local nutritional problems, in identifying the causes of the problems and in deciding which ones are likely to be amenable to change (Fig. 1). They must be involved in the design of programs appropriate to bring about change and should decide which of these programs has priority, in their view, for the use of available resources. Lasting programs are those that place responsibility on community leaders for diagnosing local problems and selecting programs appropriate for their solution. Such programs also should hold community leaders accountable for achieving agreed upon nutritional objectives with the national resources made available (Table II). This is why the community must be involved in program management, implementation, monitoring, and evaluation. The underlying principle is that of promoting community self-reliance (6). Ideally, nutrition intervention programs should be considered within this hierarchical context that allows communities to determine how programs will be implemented and how local resources will be utilized to reach national objectives (Fig. 3).

COMMUNITY PARTICIPATION

Successful community programs tend to be those that maximize community participation, that is, they are oriented to locally identified needs, are feasible within the community context, are locally managed, and are adapted to the existing cultural and social conditions. Applied to nutrition intervention programs that have more than a political objective, this means that the community must decide how this program fits into the larger picture of social and community development, particularly as it applies to interrupting the complex etiology of the deprivation web (Fig. 2).

Different countries and different communities will vary in their ability to enter into this level of community participation in program planning and implementation. Most will need external help in learning how to plan and manage. It is in this context that support from external sources is especially needed and through which the needed linkage can be made to professionals in the national program (7).

Communities also will vary in the availability of local resources to apply toward their nutritional problems, and some may choose to emphasize programs other than those directed specifically toward nutrition. For example, some communities may need an improved road system to gain access to markets where food can be obtained, sold, or exchanged, or improved irrigation to increase crop yields, or improved sanitation to provide potable water and to facilitate elimination of excreta. External assistance in providing access to needed resources, including appropriate supplementary foods, should be used effectively to supplement, not replace, local supplies. For example, supplementary feeding programs that include foods not available locally should at least have access to a local alternative to cover periods common to all such programs, when the external source is unavailable. Erratic supplies lead to erratic participation, and usually such programs have minimal, if any, long-term nutritional, educational, or social benefits.

CONCLUSION

Although there have been few examples from the developing world of "successful" national nutrition intervention programs that involve voluntary compliance, there are some guiding principles for programs planners extractable from other types of successful development programs. Nutrition planners need to carefully consider the appropriate application of these elements in their attempts to design and implement intervention strategies with the specific objective of reducing the prevalence of undernutrition.

REFERENCES

1. Fougere, W., and King, K. W. Capitulation as a key ingredient to eradication of severe malnutrition in children. *J. Trop. Pediatr. Environ, Child Health* **21,** 240 (1975).
2. Pollitt, E. "Poverty and Malnutrition in Latin America. Early Childhood Intervention Programs," Chapter 6. Praeger, New York, 1980.
3. Solon, F. Nutrition and government policy in the Philippines. *In* "Nutrition and National Policy" (B. Winikoff, ed.), p. 233. MIT Press, Cambridge, Massachusetts, 1978.
4. National Food and Nutrition Council. "Food and Nutrition Policy in Chile." CONPAN, 1977.
5. Wallerstein, M. B. "Interdisciplinary Dialogue on World Hunger," Report of a workshop on the goals, processes and indicators of food and nutrition policy. IPDHW-1/UNUP-229. United Nations University, 1981.
6. Shah, P. M., and Shah, K. P. Community diagnosis and management of malnutrition. A realistic approach to combat malnutrition at the grass-roots level. *Food Nutr.* (*FAO*) **4,** 2–7 (1978).
7. Pines, J. M. The language of nutrition planning. *Food Nutr.* (*FAO*) **3,** 19–21 (1977).

2 Nutrition Intervention: Basic Concepts

FERNANDO MONCKEBERG

Although the nutritional situation of the world population on the average has improved in the last decades, there have never been so many malnourished individuals. In Latin America alone, 40% of the population receives less calories than the FAO/WHO recommendations. Stated differently, 55 million people on this continent are ingesting 250 calories per day less than the standards established by these international organizations.

The factors that have led to this situation vary in different countries. Some examples include inadequate food production, deficiencies in the food chain, failure of the educational system, and local beliefs and taboos. In the last 10 years, experts in nutrition have demonstrated that many individuals are malnourished not because they do not know what to eat or because an adequate variety of foodstuffs is not available in the market, but because they do not have the means to purchase enough food. There is a direct relationship between calorie and/or protein intake and income (1). At least in Chile, and I believe the same happens in most less developed countries, low family income is the first restricting factor that limits the quality of the diet. In Latin America, as an average, almost 70% of income is spent on food. Food expenditure, however, should not exceed 30%. Studies carried out in Chile demonstrated that when less than 30% of family income is spent on food, selection of the types of food prefered becomes possible. When choice is possible, families make correct selections and eat diets adequate in quantity and quality. When income is low and more than 30% is spent for food, the diet becomes distorted. Man's first requirement is to satisfy hunger. If income is low, individuals are forced to buy the largest volume possible at

13

NUTRITION INTERVENTION STRATEGIES IN NATIONAL DEVELOPMENT

the lowest cost. Seen in this context, the habit of the Chilean populations to eat large quantities of bread, spaghetti, or potatoes appears as
an adaptation to a harsh economic reality. The dietary pattern of the
poor Chilean fulfills the primary objective of quelling hunger at the
lowest cost. Americans and Europeans, on the other hand, spend an
average of 17% and 24% of their incomes, respectively, on food; this
means that they have the possibility of choice.

The need for income redistribution so that all families will have similar
possibilities to improve their diet has been long stressed. However, this
approach offers no solution if applied as an isolated measure. Our studies in Chile show that even if total, homogenous redistribution of income were achieved, the problem would not be solved. Rather, under
these circumstances, everyone would fall below the desired minimum.
In most poor countries, or in the less developed countries, not even the
most homogenous redistribution of income would achieve the goal of
providing an adequate diet. For example in the United States in 1970 the
average per capita expenditure for food was 600 dollars, an amount that
exceeded the per capita income of most Latin American countries at that
time.

Many experts insist on propounding palliative measures to solve the
problem of undernutrition while forgetting that the basis of the problem
is social and economic underdevelopment. It is obvious that malnutrition is intimately linked to poverty and that neither of them can be
eliminated unless a more equitable income distribution is coupled to a
much faster generation of income. In other words, malnutrition and
poverty cannot be eradicated if significant and parallel economic and
social developments do not occur. The nutritional interventions directed
to target groups might be useful, but they only constitute palliative
measures.

On first view, one might conclude that it is enough to devote all
efforts to economic development and generating greater and greater
wealth would benefit progressively more individuals, eventually reaching the entire population. However, two questions arise immediately.
The first is how long it would take under the best of circumstances for
this to occur, taking into account the realities existing in poor countries.
Poor countries are without adequate technologies and without possibilities of either generating or acquiring them, have inefficient basic
structures, are without trained workers, and have low saving capacity
and little capital. The logical answer is economic development, which
will take a long time, probably many generations in most poor countries.

The second question is whether it is possible to have significant and
persistent development when in some countries from 30 to 60% of the

population has had its capacity to express its full genetic potential limited for many generations. The logical answer is again negative. A country in which all risks are high, in which one-half of the deaths occur before 15 years of age, where most of the survivors have a disability in one form or another, and will become useful elements of a modern society only with the greatest difficulties, has almost no possibilities of economic development.

The main resource needed for economic development is the human resource; it is therefore mandatory to preserve it. To adequately preserve human resources means that adequate social development must be achieved with haste. Social development includes the concept of income redistribution. Governments have direct and indirect means to bring about a better distribution of incomes. An example of a direct mechanism is adequate labor legislation that guarantees reasonable salaries and protects the rights of the workers vis-à-vis capital employers. An example of an indirect mechanism is the organization of efficient basic services. The latter operates through taxation of the groups with higher incomes. The use of the resources thus obtained should be applied to develop services that will be used by all the population especially by the less privileged: health, education, nutrition, housing, and environmental sanitation.

In spite of efforts to promote social development by many governments using direct and indirect mechanisms, the aims have not been achieved. Experience shows that although these measures undoubtedly benefit the middle strata, they do not reach the lowest strata who remain marginally touched despite all efforts.

The marginality in which those of extreme poverty live is difficult to penetrate. They are not benefited by wage policies because they are frequently jobless, hold only occasional short-term jobs, or are self-employed with very low income. In a study to elucidate who are the fathers of infants with advanced undernutrition, we found that the employment characteristics of 92% fitted into one of the above-mentioned groups. Only 8% of the malnourished infants were offspring of workers with stable jobs. People living in extreme poverty have no capacity to become organized, and they do not and cannot exert political pressure to obtain favourable wage legislation. For practical purposes, they are marginated from the economic system.

At the same time those of extreme poverty are also difficult to reach with the basic services that governments provide. They were born in extreme poverty, and they have persisted in this condition for many generations. It is for them the normal ambience, and they do not feel any urgency to change these conditions; change is not one of their priorities. They have no expectations, and they do not perceive what advantages they could obtain from basic services provided by the government. In practical terms, the conventional methods of income redistribution are inefficient in reaching the lower strata of society. Increased marginality determines almost subhuman living conditions and high risk. Alternative strategies are needed that will effectively reach marginated groups and improve their living standards. Specific forms of economic intervention must be developed so that these people can generate their own income and thus benefit from the advantages of a modern society. With some frequency, experts tend to consider nutrition as separate from all the other factors that condition extreme poverty. As a result, programs of nutritional intervention have been designed as isolated actions. The final effect is that they end up becoming another charitable activity that will not produce any permanent benefit. This is obviously a mistake. The problem will not be solved by simply giving away food to the hungry. The only definitive solution is to incorporate these people into the socioeconomic system.

Evidence is accumulating that suggests that the high frequency of psychomotor retardation detected in the groups living in extreme poverty is due to the deprived environment they live in, and especially to malnutrition and lack of sensory-affective stimulation.

All the intervention activities designed for these groups must take into account all the factors that condition extreme poverty. The objectives will be to rescue these individuals from this situation and to prevent the damage it causes, using the family as the basic unit. The interventions must, directly or indirectly, improve self-esteem, raise human dignity, and generate new expectations. Charity and paternalism are of little help; on the contrary, they reinforce dependent tendencies and decrease self-esteem. Initiative must be stimulated and individuals must be encouraged to develop efforts aimed at adequate goals, while at the same time, adequate mechanisms and legal instruments must be provided. Priority must be given to the search for mechanisms that will specifically allow these groups to gain real access to basic services and will enable them to improve their living conditions and to maintain these gains. If the mechanisms thus far available have proved to be inefficient, then new ones have to be devised for these marginal groups. Perhaps government, international organizations, or the population should create semiautonomous organizations or semiprivate agencies with these marginal groups as their sole aim. Their actions should complement those already in effect.

All these activities should have broad coverage, with the aim of preventing the damage caused by extreme poverty in the new generation and, at the same time, recovering those already living in this situation.

There are many types of activities that may be planned, but among them the following must be included:

1. Family planning and structuring, since in those groups living in extreme poverty, especially in the periurban belts, the structure of the family is very distorted or does not exist. A study of the families of severely undernourished infants revealed that 63% of the mothers were unmarried. In 32% of the cases, the mother was less than 18 years of age. There is a high frequency of prostitution. Illiteracy reaches 42% in this group, whereas the national average was 6%. It is necessary to give a legal basis to these family groups to make them more stable. Family planning programs must be launched to encourage responsible parenthood.

2. Nutritional intervention programs aimed at the high-risk groups: pregnant and lactating mothers, infants, and preschool age children.

3. Comprehensive educational programs aimed at eradicating parental illiteracy and teaching principles of hygiene, adequate feeding practices, child nutrition, and care. People should receive information leading to better use of the already existing basic services: health; preschool education in kindergartens; elementary, high schools, and technical education. Training should also be provided on food production at the family level making use of small plots of land attached to each house by means of family-garden programs. Job training should be encouraged to improve possibilities in the labor market.

4. Programs of subsidized credit to allow families to build their own homes or to improve them, especially their sanitary facilities.

It is evident that nutritional intervention cannot be separated from other forms of intervention whose objective is to improve the well-being of these groups.

The strategies for these groups must operate from the bottom upward in the social scale. (The usual measures operate in the opposite direction.) They will have to be different in every country depending on social and economic realities. They will depend on degrees of development, cultural and educational levels, political structure, percentages of urban and rural population, its density, and numerous other economic and social factors, which may even differ in the various regions of the same country.

There is general agreement about the need for social and nutritional interventions aimed at the groups exposed to the highest risks. However, it is not the experts who in general have the power to make the decisions to implement them and to transform them into realities. This means that a political decision is required, and this fundamental step is in the hands of others. It is important to pause for a few moments and ponder this, because in the end this is the stage that decides whether a program will or will not be implemented. Political factors are issues that as a general rule nutrition experts try to avoid. To design nutritional policies is rather easy, and most countries have accumulated enough basic data to plan specific interventions of unquestioned nutritional benefit.

However, their implementation is not simple because a decision to carry them out is required first, and for this to occur, they must be politically attractive. The School Lunch or the Food Stamp programs were not implemented in the United States simply because they were needed but because they were found to be politically appealing. In many of the less developed countries where nutritional programs have been implemented, these have been discussed beforehand in political caucases. The Five-Year Plan in India, which sets specific goals in food nutrition, is evidently a political document. The widespread milk distribution programs in Chile, for example, have also been political tools and on more than one occasion they have been used as slogans by power-hungry groups. The same happens at the international level. PL-480, the Food-for-Peace Program launched in 1954, was the answer to domestic political problems in the United States related to agricultural surpluses. At the same time, it proved to be a useful tool in international politics.

The need for adequate nutritional planning is therefore quite important, but the ultimate decision to implement depends on political decisions. This is a reality that must be accepted and taken into account.

To obtain a political commitment to carry out nutrition intervention programs, however, is not an easy task. Support for a program will be obtained from decision makers only if they perceive political benefits will result. The first priority of politicians is to achieve power. On the basis of these antecedents, support for interventions is obtained only when definite benefits will accrue to its political supporters. Hence, it is necessary not only to calculate the nutritional cost/benefit relationship of a given program but also the political cost/benefit. Only those professionals who, having calculated the nutritional cost/benefit of a given program, have been capable of translating it into a political equation will see their program implemented. Once this is achieved, the program has a good chance of being implemented if it receives the support of those who make the decisions. The important thing is to operate within the framework of the realities in which we live.

To reach the political-decision levels, the first and fundamental step is to create a consciousness of a need for a nutritional program within the community. Only when the community has become aware of its problem and the possible solutions developed by the expert will the people and the politicians become interested. The politicians aiming at gaining power will then be ready to use the program for their political purposes. Awareness is not enough; it is necessary to present feasible solutions that in most situations have to be of a technical nature.

This second part is of paramount importance. If only consciousness about the need for a nutritional problem is achieved, it is highly probable that erroneous actions with considerable showiness, but little nutritional effect, will result. In Chile some of these stages have already been reached, and if an enhanced social sense about nutrition exists, it is because over many years it has been possible to create awareness about these problems. Although the measures undertaken have sometimes been used for propaganda purposes, technical criteria have slowly gained ground. In the 1970 presidential election, all the candidates had programs aimed at eradicating malnutrition as part of their partisan platforms.

Once the decision to implement a program is reached, all efforts must be made to ensure its success. This is a stage that presents high risks to the professional and to those whose responsibility it is to carry it out. Every political system or government has its supporters and its enemies, both in the country and abroad, and the programs, with their successes and failures, will necessarily come to be identified with the government in power. The professionals who are responsible for the programs will therefore also come to be identified with the government. The crucial point for the profession is to reach an acceptable balance between his involvement and his moral responsibility.

Summarizing, it seems obvious that there is an urgent need for countries to develop nutritional policies that take into account all these concepts and facts and that concentrate on the solution of the problems entailing the highest risk for the population. Such policies should necessarily be part of and congruent with the strategies for socioeconomic development at the national level. This requires a rational flexibility to adapt the nutritional components to the "rules of the game" imposed by the national policies and strategies. Nutritional policies should, therefore, be designed within this context.

It appears most important, furthermore, that our actions not be restricted to the mere design of interventions. We must, also, prove effective in persuading the decision levels of the government not only to approve nutritional interventions as a matter of policy but to actually implement them.

REFERENCE

1. Reutlinger, S., and Selowsky, M. "Malnutrition and Poverty. Magnitude and Policy Options," World Bank Staff Occas. Pap. No. 23. Johns Hopkins Univ. Press, Baltimore, Maryland, 1976.

II Socioeconomic Strategies

3 The Economic Effects of Early Malnutrition: Economic Considerations for Nutrition Intervention Programs

MARCELO SELOWSKY*

JUSTIFICATION FOR INVESTMENT IN ALLEVIATING EARLY MALNUTRITION

What are the economic justifications for a higher investment in nutrition? What are the economic consequences for a country of having one-fifth of its children with caloric deficiency? Should the will for action depend on the answers, or should we simply accept that ethical justification is sufficient and that these questions are rather academic or, at best, only relevant from a tactical point of view if they can influence action?

As economists we are often faced with these issues. My reaction is rather pragmatic: There is evidence that the hypothetical possibility of malnutrition producing economic effects has made governments and international organizations more receptive to the need for action. If we can show that these effects are more than hypothetical possibilities and this encourages action, then all the better.

The economic effects of improving children's nutrition can be traced through two major mechanisms: first, it can have a *resourse savings* effect in other sectors of the economy. Second, it is one type of investment in *human capital* to the extent that it influences the future economic productivity of an individual.

*The views are those of the author and should not be attributed to the World Bank or its affiliated organizations.

NUTRITION INTERVENTION STRATEGIES IN NATIONAL DEVELOPMENT

RESOURCE SAVINGS EFFECT

The first mechanism is based on the notion that better infant nutrition can save resources presently being invested in related sectors. Governments are already devoting economic resources to achieve particular minimum social targets (which we may call "outputs") in sectors such as health and education. If infant nutrition is one of the several "inputs" determining these "outputs," the economic question becomes what is the optimal combination of inputs that will minimize the cost of reaching these outputs or social targets. If the total cost of achieving a particular target goes down with improved children's nutrition, a "resources savings" benefits arises. Improved nutrition has released resources—spent previously in other sectors—of a higher value than the cost of the nutrition improvement. It will become clear that the evaluation of these resource savings requires quite a bit of interdisciplinary cooperation inasmuch as the relation between these "inputs" and "outputs" is basically a biological and/or psychological phenomena.

Let us use two examples to illustrate this point. First, let us assume that a country has the objective of reducing infant mortality due to infectious disease. For this purpose a given amount of public resources is invested in drinking water and sewage system services. Since the incidence of infectious diseases in children not only depends on the accessibility of water and sewage services, but also on their nutritional status, there exists an optimal combination of these interventions. The optimal intervention in water, sewage systems, and nutrition is the one that minimizes the cost of reaching the mortality goal. The possibility of an overinvestment in water and sewerage relative to nutrition arises when additional investment in nutrition diminishes the cost of reaching the goal. This will occur when the nutrition intervention releases resources in the other sectors of a higher value than the cost of the nutrition intervention. The difference might be called the resource savings generated by the intervention. This benefit is strictly economic; however, its computation requires a large amount of interdisciplinary research involving economists, physicians, and public health specialists.

A second example is in education. Let us assume that the educational objective is to reach a minimum standard of literacy in children at the fourth year of primary schooling. If learning depends not only on school inputs (quality of teachers, school books, etc.), but also on the nutritional status in infancy and at school age, there will be an optimal mix of interventions minimizing the cost of this educational objective. Again there may exist an overinvestment in education relative to nutrition; in such a case the nutritional intervention will release resources in the educational sector of a higher value than the cost of the intervention.

HUMAN CAPITAL EFFECT

The second mechanism by which infant nutrition can generate economic benefits is by increasing the future economic productivity of the individual. Nutrition becomes one type of capital—human capital. This notion is consistent with the present way of looking at the economic growth of countries, which depends on the accumulation of an all inclusive concept of human and physical capital. Thirty years ago education did not play a role as human capital; today it is widely accepted and thoroughly studied by economists. Why can we not treat nutrition similarly?

To the extent that families are conscious of the productivity effect of nutrition, one would expect society to automatically invest in nutrition. The reason for a possible underinvestment stems from the asymetry between human capital and physical capital. There are no capital markets to finance investment in human capital: It is hard to borrow or invest in nutrition since the individual receiving the investment cannot be used as collateral. This feature of capital markets generates an underinvestment in human capital in the lowest income groups of the population.

The relationship between infant nutrition and the productivity of the individual at adulthood is still hypothetical. The medical literature tends to show a relationship between early malnutrition and the mental development of children. The issue is how to use these findings to go one step forward, to trace the economic impact of these deficits in the mental development of children. I would like to suggest some ideas on interdisciplinary collaboration on this issue.

APPROACHES TO STUDY THE ECONOMIC EFFECTS OF EARLY MALNUTRITION

The effect of early malnutrition on the productivity of an individual as an adult can only be studied through a long-term follow-up of individuals. This follow-up would include measurements of all variables (genetic, environmental, and medical) characterizing the individual from birth until the age he enters the labor force. By using multivariate analysis techniques, one could isolate the net effect of early malnutrition, i.e., by controlling the effect of the other variables. Even in developed countries this kind of data is not available. The challenge is how to use shorter follow-ups presently being studied, so as to replicate these follow-ups that are presently unavailable. In other words, how can we "paste" or put together these shorter follow-ups so as to simulate the longer (unavailable) follow-up.

As economists we can join this kind of collaborative research from the opposite direction, namely going from adulthood to infancy. We can ask ourselves what are those particular abilities at adulthood that influence the economic performance of an individual in a particular labor market. These can be identified by using a battery of tests through which a large set of different abilities are separately measured. Having identified these particular abilities (for example by simultaneously regressing wages on *all* abilities), we can ask how these particular abilities are "produced." Possibly they have been influenced by heredity, education, home environment, nutrition, etc. This relationship can be broken into subrelationships: the particular abilities at adulthood (let us say at age 30) can be expressed as a function of an index of abilities at age 15 and of all variables to which the individual was exposed between ages 15 and 30. Abilities at age 15 are a function of abilities at age 10 and of the effect of other variables affecting the individual between 10 and 15, and so forth. One can "paste" together these short follow-ups attempting to trace the effect of early malnutrition on the future economic performance of the individual.

This framework was followed in an early study conducted on a sample of Chilean children (1). Researchers at the R. del Rio Hospital provided us with data on children who had experienced early malnutrition and were then followed until 4 years of age. The sample included the degree of early malnutrition, socioeconomic characteristics of the family, and the performance in a Terman Merril (TM) test at age 4. With this sample, it was possible to separate statistically the effect of early malnutrition on the TM test. In a second stage we contacted a group of psychologists to find out what test for adults could be highly correlated with the TM test given at age 4. The manual component of the Wechsler-Bellevue (WB) test was suggested. This test was administered to a sample of workers so as to derive a relationship between work performance and performance in the test. At this stage we had two relationships: a relationship between early malnutrition and the TM score at age four and a relationship between the WB score in workers and their work performance. The difficult task is to relate the TM score at childhood with the WB score at adulthood. Relationships found in other countries were used so as to conduct a sensitivity analysis. This is our main gap in knowledge, resulting from the lack of long follow-ups of individuals in developing countries.

THE CASE OF LATIN AMERICA

Latin America can certainly finance programs to alleviate its caloric deficit and I would even go one step further and say that it can finance such programs without sacrificing long-term efficient economic policies, i.e., those policies that increase growth and employment in the long run even though their short-term nutritional effects may prove negative.

The reason for the coexistence in Latin America of efficient economic policies, aggressive distributive policies, and nutritional policies in particular, is the use of policy instruments that are expensive from a fiscal point of view. It is possible to demonstrate that low prices for poor consumers may coexist with high prices to producers (so as not to act as a disincentive to domestic production) if there is a capability to finance a policy of subsidies.

There are several examples showing that efficient policies and aggressive distributive policies can coexist if the fiscal cost is accepted. Many countries, however, cannot finance policies that are expensive from the fiscal point of view. Such is the situation in Bangladesh and India. In Latin America the case is different.

What features of the Latin American situation support this view? First, the nutritional problem in Latin America is basically distributive: The distribution of calorie consumption parallels the distribution of family income. The caloric deficit is not a problem of lack of production of food. I want to emphasize this because it is often mentioned in public and professional forums. The mean per capita calorie availability in Latin America is 10% higher than the estimated requirement. Nevertheless, 36% of the population consumes less than they require while 32% consume at least 130% of the per capita requirements. Clearly in Latin America this is a distributive problem, not a problem of an aggregate deficit of food as is the case in Africa and Asia. One can calculate the caloric deficit of all income groups having a per capita consumption below requirements and compute the equivalent value of this deficit in terms of cereals. The deficit is less than 1% of Latin America's GNP and equal to 2.9% of the total consumption of cereals; in other words the macro economic magnitude of the caloric deficit is extremely small.

The data on income distribution in Latin America (the richest 10% of the population accounts for 40% of the GNP) support the assumption that an additional income tax of 2.5% to the highest income group would finance the calorie deficit of the region. This redistributive policy does not require a sacrifice of other economic policies that are efficient for long-term growth. The key proposal the nutritionists could make to the economists is the following: We are prepared to support you in implementing your monetary policies, foreign trade policies, and all of your long-term efficient economic policies that increase the growth rate, but we want from you a tax reform giving us 1% of the GNP to finance nutritional programs. The cost of such a tax on the highest income group in terms of a lower growth rate can be estimated. The growth rate (if one-half of the tax comes from savings of this income group) would go down by only one-tenth of 1% (from 6 down to 5.9% per year, for example). The conclusion is that in Latin America the nutritional problem can be solved by sacrificing the growth rate of output.

If the caloric deficit is equal to 1% of the GNP, very probably the fiscal cost of inducing an increase in consumption equal to this 1% would be much higher. In this sense the fiscal cost of solving the problem has been underestimated. If we want to increase the caloric consumption of the poorest groups through a general subsidy, a very inefficient policy instrument, other income groups will also benefit and the fiscal costs will be larger than 1%. The problem becomes still more complex in that even those programs that reach exclusively a specific target group can have a much higher fiscal cost. The reason is that in addition to administrative costs, such programs generally operate like an equivalent income transfer. It is very difficult to design food programs in which the additional effect on consumption is different from giving the family an equivalent subsidy in cash. For example, if the marginal propensity for food expenditure is 0.5 (i.e., for an income increase of $100, households spend an additional $50 for food) we would have to distribute 2% of GNP in terms of food programs in order to get one percent of the GNP actually used to increase food consumption in the target group. In this respect economists interested in nutrition have to support the research of our colleague nutritionists so that other economists will not say: "Well, if the program you have designed simply operates like an income transfer, the cost of solving the nutritional deficit is going to be twice this 1% of the GNP you mentioned earlier." Therefore, we should begin to identify programs that have an effectiveness larger than an equivalent income transfer.

We would like to increase the interest of physicians in this subject. Physicians, however, appear more interested in foreign trade, in monetary policies, and similar economic matters than on elaborating on intrafamily nutrition behavior. There is far too little discussion, for example, of the problem of how much of the milk being distributed to a family through social programs will be consumed by the infant, how much by children from 6 to 8 years, and how much by others.

The problem is the difficulty in designing programs whose effectiveness is different from an equivalent income transfer. Let us look closely at some target-group oriented programs. Many of these programs either substitute previous levels of consumption or end up being diverted toward adults within the family. The net effect can be larger, equal, or smaller than an equivalent income transfer. Which types of programs operate like an income transfer? Generally, those that distribute food in volumes smaller than the amount previously consumed without the program. To illustrate, assume that the marginal propensity to spend for milk is 0.1. If a family was consuming $100 worth of milk and the program distributes $20 worth of milk, the family will diminish purchases of milk by $18. Therefore, the increase in consumption due to the program is $2 and not $20. To put it in a different way, if the family feels richer by $20 it will consume two additional dollars worth of milk. The effect on consumption is equal to having given the family $20 in cash.

On the other hand, if food is distributed in excess of what the household voluntarily wants to consume the response is to resell. The family will try to become liberated from having to consume an excessive food transfer; it will try to maintain its freedom of choice. The problem is how to analyze these behaviors and identify programs that are more effective than an equivalent income transfer.

Programs that operate differently are those that induce a substitution among foods. This takes place when the family cannot resell the food due to institutional restrictions or when the food being distributed is a new food. Under these circumstances the new food will substitute for previously consumed foods; the characteristics of this substitution is fundamental to predict the net effect on the consumption of calories. Let us consider some examples. Imagine a program that only subsidizes the price of wheat purchased by a particular income group, and resale is not possible. The caloric intake would increase due to a higher wheat consumption; however, households may purchase less rice. Substitution will take place, and if rice provides substantially more calories per dollar than wheat the total calorie consumption will decline. This will depend on how the family substitutes wheat for rice. If the family does not think exclusively in terms of calories but in terms of taste and texture as well, the net effect on calories could be negative.

This could even happen with direct on-site feeding programs for children, i.e., school feeding programs that can operate like an income transfer. For example, if a child receives a glass of milk at school and he was previously consuming milk at home, it might well happen that the mother stops giving him at home an equivalent amount and will redistribute that food to the rest of the family. A more complicated but not less realistic case occurs when the family was not previously consuming milk. Here again the net effect on calories could be negative. Let us suppose that children do not consume milk at home and that when they receive 10¢ worth of milk at school the mother withdraws from them 2¢ worth of cereal at home and redistributes this cereal to the rest of the family. If, as available data indicate, cereals have substantially more calories per dollar than milk, the effect on the child's calorie intake could be negative. What is fundamental is how the mother substitutes these foods. Understanding of this intrafamily behavior is basic to the identification of programs of greater efficacy.

The Achilles' heel of nutritionists in relation to supplementary feeding programs is the insufficient knowledge of the recipient families nutritional behavior. This knowledge is of fundamental importance to increase the efficacy of this type of nutritional intervention.

CONCLUSION

The reason for entering into such details and examples is my conviction that the only method of studying the economic effects of malnutrition is at the level of the individual. It cannot be done at the aggregate level, for example, by using cross-sectional data relating the level of development of a country (i.e., its per capita income) with the nutritional status of its population. In such analyses many other variables confound the nutrition variables preventing the possibility of finding a causal relationship. Further, I am convinced that we need more knowledge of family level food behavior to design economically efficient and nutritionally effective intervention programs.

REFERENCE

1. Selowsky, M., and Taylor, L. The economics of malnourished children: An example of disinvestment in human capital. *Econ. Dev. Cult. Change* October (1973).

4

Socioeconomic Development and Nutritional Status: Efficiency of Intervention Programs

FERNANDO MONCKEBERG

During the last few years, experts have become aware that, in the less developed countries, individuals are undernourished not because they do not know what to eat, nor because there are not adequate varieties of food available, but mainly because they lack the economic means to assure an adequate daily diet. In poor countries there is a direct correlation between income and the amount of calories consumed (1). Those groups of population with higher incomes receive more calories. By studying the lower strata of society, it becomes evident that there is an association between lower incomes, decrease in caloric intake, and a deterioration of dietary quality.

It is true that the causes of malnutrition are varied: lack of adequate knowledge, deficient sanitation, inadequate food production, excessive postharvest losses, inadequate food preservation, and marketing, etc. Nevertheless, poverty appears always as the main factor; the low income of the family group makes it impossible to purchase adequate amounts of food.

It is for this reason that in the poor countries the severity of malnutrition is directly linked to the degree of economic and social development. The Institute for Social Development of the United Nations has created an indicator of development based on 80 items (kilowatts consumed per person, kilometers of paved roads, number of TV sets per person, number of schools per person, etc.). This index of development correlates

NUTRITION INTERVENTION STRATEGIES IN NATIONAL DEVELOPMENT
Copyright © 1983 by Academic Press, Inc.
All rights of reproduction in any form reserved.
ISBN 012-709080-0

quite well with the nutritional status of the infant population. Figure 1 correlates these factors in selected countries. The infant and preschool child mortality rates have been selected as indicators of nutritional status. When malnutrition disappears as a cause of infant death in a developed country, there is a rate of 1/20 to 1/25 between preschool child and infant mortality rates. This means that in developed countries, for each preschool child that dies, 20 to 25 infants will also die of a variety of causes. In underdeveloped countries, where malnutrition is an important cause of death, from 5 to 10 infants die for each preschool child. This suggests that the ratio of infant mortality/preschool age mortality may be considered a good indicator of the nutritional status of the population. Figure 1 shows that there is a good correlation between the degree of development of a given country and the prevalence of malnutrition in the first 4 years of age among its population. Of course, it is difficult to demonstrate a good cause/effect correlation, but there seems to be good agreement between both.

This indicates that it is·very difficult to eradicate malnutrition unless social and economic development are strongly accelerated. Food production is also to a large extent dependent precisely on economic and

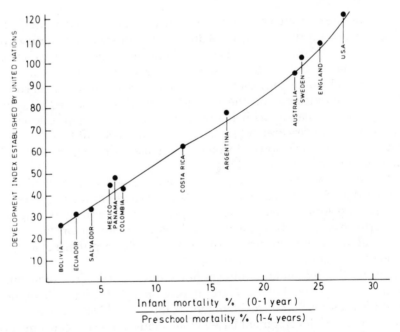

Fig. 1. Correlation between nutritional status of children below 6 years of age and degree of development in selected countries.

social development. It is difficult for poor countries to increase food production through partial solutions. Food production only increases in parallel with socioeconomic development. Low food production is then another manifestation of underdevelopment.

When the income of most of the population is low, it becomes almost impossible to increase food production. All improvements in agricultural production and productivity require investments (machinery, fertilizers, pesticides, irrigation, etc.). Often it appears as if farmers resist the implementation of new tachnologies when the reality is different: They have adapted to the realities of the local market. New technologies tend to increase expenditures that may not be profitable. They may be able to produce more, but in order to sell more, they would have to lower their prices. This may not be feasible for them from the economic point of view. This is what occurred in India during the "Green Revolution." Wheat production was increased, but farmers had to increase their investments (the new seeds require more water, more fertilizers, etc.). Because the internal market did not grow due to the low income of the population, India was forced to export wheat to other countries.

The increase of food availability in the less-developed countries depends ultimately on the possibilities for economic and social development. If family income and purchasing power increase, a series of events will be triggered that will make it possible to increase food production efficiently. Food production depends on demand. Demand, in turn, depends on purchasing power. Purchasing power, in turn, depends on income, and income depends on social and economic development.

Thus, malnutrition and inadequate food production are only a final consequence of social and economic underdevelopment. This also means that it is very difficult to increase food production and eradicate malnutrition independently of economic and social development. Because of this holistic approach, many experts think that nutritional intervention programs of necessity can have only limited success.

On the other hand, many people thought that all that was needed was economic growth and that the resources thus created would permeate the different strata of society and improve the lot of more individuals. Nevertheless, facts have proved this concept to be mistaken. This is especially evident in Latin America where, during the last 20 years, economic development has led to widening social differences. Thus, while the poorest 20% of the population has not increased its per capita income, the richest 10% increased its income by about 400 dollars in stable currency (2). This clearly indicates that in less developed countries economic development per se does not result necessarily in improved life conditions. Economic development is necessary, but the active intervention of government is also required to attain better distribution of income and of resources, to improve social development, and to increase the quality of life.

To improve living standards, it is necessary that individuals be protected from the moment they are born, or even before, by means of adequate nutrition, sanitation, health care, education, and housing. Income redistribution per se probably would not attain all the results desired in the sense of improving living standards if, at the same time, some services that satisfy some needs of the population were not provided. Better income distribution, creation of basic services, and economic development are the three components that must be well coordinated because these are interrelated and interdependent.

Adequate nutrition is one of the most basic needs and one of the most difficult to fulfill because of the complexity of the problem. Infants and preschool children are more severely affected by malnutrition in all underdeveloped countries. Children have nutritional requirements that are high and specific because of their rapid growth. Infectious diseases are also quite damaging during the first years of life. In addition, children depend on others for their food. Quite frequently their parents lack either the economic means or the educational level required to provide satisfactory nutrition for their children or they lack an adequate sense of responsibility (3). As a consequence, in evaluating the nutritional situation of a country, the possible deficiencies appear magnified in children under 6 years of age. Requirements are lower for adults. Futhermore, they can feed themselves and therefore suffer less from decreased food availability. A number of intervention programs have been implemented to improve the nutritional situation of the infant population. However, very few of them have shown significant and sustained success. This has raised questions about the usefulness of nutritional intervention programs.

However, when these programs are closely scrutinized, it becomes apparent that those that fail have very specific limitations. Either they are unilateral and do not take into account all the factors that condition the appearance of malnutrition, or their coverage is inadequate or not long enough to induce significant changes in the nutritional status of the infantile population. At times, it becomes apparent that they are not supported by even a minimum of health or educational infrastructures that will penetrate all the strata of society. Simply stated, the programs do not reach those who need them the most.

There are some instances in which these programs are successful.

Therefore, it is important to analyze the reasons for this success. As previously stated, there is a close correlation between the degree of development of a country and the nutritional status of its infant population (Fig. 1). However, in two Latin American countries, Chile and Cuba, this situation is not observed. In both countries the nutritional status is significantly better than what their economical development would suggest. Both countries, each with an intermediate degree of development and a population of about 11 million people, have developed long-range, wide-coverage health and nutrition programs.

Both countries have had for several years a state-operated National Health Service whose coverage includes most of the population (Table I). For this purpose they have an adequate number of hospitals and health centers. Cuba has 35,000 hospital beds and Chile 34,000. Chile has 1422 Health Centers and Cuba 1232. Births take place in hospitals in 96% of the cases in Cuba and 92% in Chile. Milk or weaning foods are distributed in both countries to children below 6 years of age. In Chile, families with malnourished children receive food suplements. Pregnant and nursing mothers receive milk supplements. Both in Chile and Cuba there are special homes for pregnant mothers who live in the countryside. Through this program, mothers who live far from hospitals arrive at the home 15 days before delivery and remain for an additional

TABLE I

Comparison of Nutrition and Health Programs in Chile and Cuba

Program	Cuba	Chile
National Health Service		
Number of hospital beds	35,000	34,000
Health Centers	1,232	1,422
In-hospital deliveries (percentage of total deliveries)	96	92
Free distribution of milk and weaning foodstuffs (0 to 6 years of age)		
(Percentage of total population)	96	93
Homes for pregnant mothers from rural areas (number of homes)	63	42
Centers for recovery of severely malnourished infants (number of beds)	1,010	1,320
Kindergartens for preschool children (total number)	725	630
Programs of health and nutrition education	Yes	Yes
Family planning program	Yes	Yes

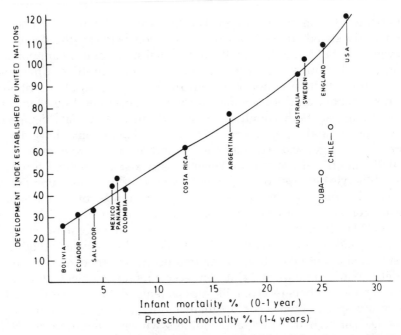

Fig. 2. Correlation between nutritional status of children below 6 years of age and degree of development in selected countries.

15 days after delivery. There they receive medical care and education and training on infant care.

Both countries operate centers for the recovery of infants (under 1 year of age) suffering from severe malnutrition. In the case of Cuba this program was organized by the government. In Chile it was organized by a private foundation (CONIN) receiving government support. The number of beds available is comparable in both countries. Both countries have instituted extensive nutrition education and breastfeeding programs using the health structures. Both countries also operate family planning programs through the health structures. This has resulted in drastic reductions of the population growth rates. Finally, both countries have implemented programs of preschool education in kindergartens. Children below 6 years of age, who live in poor areas receive, besides psychomotor stimulation, daily food that covers their nutritional requirements. Both countries also operate wide scale programs for school breakfasts and lunches for children from 6 to 15 years of age.

In the case of Chile the budget of the National Health Service is 1,000 million dollars per year. The nutritional programs have an additional cost of 180 million per year. There are no data available for Cuba.

When the results of these programs are evaluated through some bio-demographic indicators, it becomes clearly apparent (Table II) that they are entirely comparable in both countries and that they are far above the Latin American average (Fig. 2). In the case of Chile, the health and nutrition programs were launched in 1951 and have been continuously expanded and improved. Figure 3 shows the evolution of economic growth and nutritional status throughout the years. In 1940 the correlation between both factors was as expected: a country with precarious economic development and a very high incidence of childhood malnutrition. Subsequent economic growth was slow, whereas the nutritional status of childhood was substantially improved. At present, the nutritional status exceeds that expected for the degree of economic development. These results seem to indicate that nutritional intervention programs may be quite useful provided they are wide reaching and provided they include health and education components.

Chile and Cuba are two countries with different economic systems. Cuba has a centrally planned economy, whereas Chile has a free market economy. It is quite interesting to notice that two countries that pursue different political and economical systems have developed strategies of intervention that are comparable and similarly successful. This indicates that, whatever the political system in a country, it is possible to successfully prevent malnutrition when there is a political decision to implement programs if the necessary resources are allocated and if they are implemented with scientific and technical criteria.

TABLE II

Nutrition and Health Strata in Chile and Cuba, 1980

	Cuba	Chile
Infant mortality rate (%)	26	31
Preschool age mortality rate (%)	1.2	1.2
Malnourished children below 6 years of age		
Mild malnutrition (%)	NA[a]	10
Moderate malnutrition (%)	NA	0.8
Severe malnutrition (%)	NA	0.2
Birth rate	18	21
Eradication of *Tetanus neonatorum*, malaria, and poliomyelitis	Yes	Yes
Life expectancy (years)	66.0	67.3

[a] Information not available.

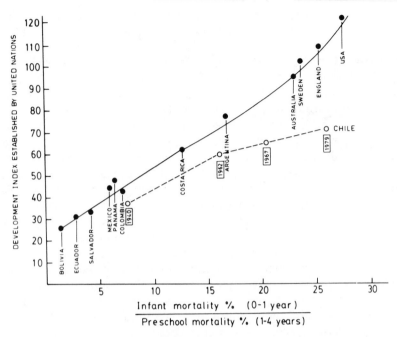

Fig. 3. Correlation between nutritional status of children below 6 years of age and degree of development in selected countries.

Both Chile and Cuba are countries with intermediate degrees of development and both have been able to create and perfect rather efficient health and education infrastructures. The low rate of illiteracy in both countries is another parameter of the success of these programs. The possibilities of success in countries that are less developed and that have little or no infrastructure is more remote. The setting of such infrastructure may well be first priority for these countries.

GENERAL COMMENTS

During the last few years, doubts have been raised about the real benefit of the nutritional intervention programs in developing countries. Several failures and partial results have discouraged governments and international agencies. All indications show that without fundamental changes in the social and economical structure it is very difficult to prevent malnutrition, because this is the consequence of underdevelopment. However, what has been noticed in Chile, Cuba, and other countries seems to show the opposite. The reasons for failure can be explained by analyzing several programs of intervention: either their approach has been unilateral, their scope has been limited, not enough time was allotted to produce significant changes, or, finally, there was a lack of scientific and technical support in terms of its outline, implementation, or execution.

The success achieved in decreasing and preventing malnutrition in some countries brings promise for the usefulness of intervention programs. The results achieved are the consequence of many years of intervention supported by some of the following basic elements:

1. The political decisions were maintained over changes in Government which allowed implementation of the necessary resources over a long period.
2. The holistic approach of interventions, coordinating health, education, sanitation, and nutrition programs.
3. Development of efficient infrastructures, specially in the areas of health and education, which allowed the achievement of broad coverage as well as adequate penetration to reach the lowest strata of society.
4. Scientific support through basic applied and operational research that allowed programs to develop and be evaluated with an efficient cost–benefit relationship.

If these four conditions are met, it is possible to succeed in programs of nutritional intervention. Thus, positive changes can be attained even before any significant economic and social development has occurred.

REFERENCES

1. Reutinger, S. "Malnutrition: A Poverty or a Food Problem?" 4th Annual James Memorial Lecture. North Carolina State University, Raleigh, 1977.
2. Terra, J. P. Situación de la Infancia en Latino América y el Caribe. *Annu. Meet. UNICEF, Mexico,* 16–18 May, 1979.
3. Donoso, G., and Monckeberg, F. Desnutrición infantil. Consideraciones generales y epidemiología. *Rev. Chil. Pediatr.* **36**(5), 301 (1965).

5 Integrating Nutrition into Agricultural Policy

ALBERTO VALDÉS

Food production in Latin America has grown more slowly than effective demands and continues to be an area of fundamental concern. Moreover, there is consensus that production of food crops in most of Latin America is far smaller than its economic potential. At the same time, increasing attention is being given to alleviating malnutrition among the poor. Nutritional well-being has become an explicit objective of the social policy of most countries. Within this context, we may ask ourselves how can agricultural policy help achieve that objective? Should and could nutritional objectives be included among agricultural policy objectives? Of course, in a sense this is a normative question. However, the answer not only depends on the norms one is willing to accept, but also on the opportunity cost of using agricultural policy for nutritional objectives.

In fact, nutritional goals are found in the agricultural policies of very few countries. Although they usually do make reference to the need for reasonable consumer prices, the focus of agricultural policy in most developing countries is on agricultural production, and it encompasses other, broader objectives such as contributing to overall economic growth or supplying foreign exchange. (In many industrial countries, the focus of agricultural policy is on farmer's income.) Even a rapid expansion of food production is not likely to solve nutrition problems. Nevertheless, a national agricultural policy will most decidedly affect the nutrition of the poor. Agricultural policy is not synonymous with food policy, which is directly concerned with food supply and consumption objectives through a combination of procurement, imports (including food aid), rationed distribution, and consumer pricing interventions.

NUTRITION INTERVENTION STRATEGIES IN NATIONAL DEVELOPMENT
Copyright © 1983 by Academic Press, Inc.
All rights of reproduction in any form reserved.
ISBN 012-709080-0

Typical parts of agricultural policies are:

1. Government expenditures on agriculture, such as irrigation, roads, and agricultural research. Decisions on government expenditures in health, education, and nutrition in rural areas of Latin America usually do not fall under the ministry of agriculture or under other specialized agencies dealing with agriculture, and these agencies are usually excluded from the so-called "agricultural development plans."

2. Structure of incentives policies, including exchange rates, taxes, and subsidies in addition to direct price policies. We will discuss this later, because the relationship between food price policy and food consumption patterns is particularly relevant to our topic.

3. Land tenure policies and land reform, with its concomitant effects on income distribution. Land reform surges to the forefront of agricultural policy in a country once in perhaps a century, for 5 to 7 years, and then subsides, taking an inactive role rather than remaining an active policy instrument.

The link between agricultural policy and nutrition is indirect, and this is not the capricious result of narrow-minded policies. Most LDCs are not closed economies. Food imports, particularly cereals, add to domestic supply in meeting consumption demand, and the relative prices paid for food are not set locally—and it is not certain that they should be. Import and export markets affect the structure of domestic prices and supply. Thus, shifts in domestic production should not necessarily affect domestic prices. Barring the risk of export embargoes from all sources of supply, in countries with a highly diversified food consumption pattern such as is the case in South America, efforts to define how much to produce domestically to meet nutritional requirements could be limited to nontraded foods such as some root crops, perishables such as vegetables, or to "closed" economy situations, such as isolated regions. Price manipulation by governments usually deal with "nominal" prices of some key commodities, and this action sets in motion changes in the relative price structure, usually beyond the effective control of the government.

Nutrition can be improved very little by manipulating domestic agricultural production in middle income countries where a large fraction of the population is found in urban areas because chronic malnutrition is essentially a result of low income and not of inadequate supplies of food. We should remember that most food is not produced by malnourished farmers.

Thus, although most governments do find political support for their efforts to reduce malnutrition, it becomes evident that reducing malnutrition is a complex task when the cost of dealing with the nutritional problem by intervening in food production is considered. For example, food subsidies that avoid disincentives to agricultural production may result in budgetary pressures that conflict with monetary and fiscal policy. Efforts to stimulate agricultural production through economic incentives without increasing the fiscal burden can collide with the desire to reduce the price of food. Again, how is it possible to accelerate the growth in agricultural production and simultaneously attain specific nutritional objectives at a reasonable cost?

The principal question is defined by the effects of alternative policies on the price structure of basic foods. These prices affect the production and the consumption of those foods that are the major source of calories for the lowest income groups. For this discussion, we are defining the most vulnerable groups as the urban and landless rural groups. If we were discussing a largely rural society, such as Bangladesh or parts of West Africa, our concern would be focused on the vulnerable groups of the rural sector, a large proportion of which are agricultural producers. The conflict between efficiency and welfare would then be less complex.

Chile provides an illustration of the food price dilemma faced by many developing countries. Throughout the 1950s and 1960s, the country experimented with what was known as the "cheap food policy." Food prices were artifically kept lower than import prices through a combination of exchange rate policy, intervention prices, and export quotas (1). But intervention in food pricing was used primarily as part of an unsuccessful effort to control inflation and in consideration of the role of food as a wage good in the industrialization process, rather than for nutritional objectives. Fiscal expenditure was avoided, as there were no important direct subsidies, although, as expected, foreign exchange expenditures on food imports increased.

If the government had pursued a more open trade policy, food prices in general would have been higher than they actually were. This would have provided an economic environment more conducive to investment in agriculture and would probably have led to an expansion in domestic agricultural production. But in the short run at least, elimination of distortions (that is, overvaluation of the exchange rate, export controls, and official prices) would have raised the cost of wage goods consumed by the lowest income groups, who spend a high proportion of their incomes on food. This would have aggravated the problems of income distribution and malnutrition in urban areas. In the long run, whether or not the loss of purchasing power of the lowest income groups would have been totally compensated for by increases in employment opportunities and real income is an open question for which we do not have empirical evidence. But evidence does suggest that under an open economy trade policy, most LDCs become more export oriented, and export goods tend to be more labor-intensive than import substitutes (2). This probably applies to agriculture as well.

If agriculture is open to foreign trade, as it is now in Chile, it should be complemented by policies designed to consider the food needs of vulnerable groups. Otherwise, low-income families would be vulnerable to wide fluctuations in real income and, consequently, in food consumption. International prices of food products are now relatively low in real terms. There is less conflict between an open economy and urban welfare. If the strong inflationary tendencies in world prices of the period 1973 through 1975 should recur and if the export prices of wheat were set at 30 to 40% above current prices, we would be much more concerned about a conflict between agricultural policy and the nutrition of a large part of the population.

Some countries, such as India, Sri Lanka, and Bangladesh, have established dual price systems that offer an incentive price for the producer but keep a lower price for the consumer. The government absorbs the difference between these prices by greater fiscal expenditure. Under this two-price system, the need for incentives to accelerate agricultural growth is recognized, but the government allocates a large amount of fiscal resources to reduce the price to the consumer so that a minimum consumption level for the lower income groups is guaranteed (3–5). These consumer food price subsidies have unquestionably raised the food intake of part of the urban population.

A problem with general food subsidies in the form of lower prices, such as the cheap food policy in Latin America, is that they transfer income to all types of consumers, rich and poor, adults and children, and the fiscal cost effectiveness could be low. If the nutrition problem lies fundamentally with the mothers in poor families and with their children, the leakage from a program of subsidized food prices could be high. Moreover, although food price manipulation certainly affects the real income of households, cheap food becomes an income transfer to the family, and as we know from household behavior studies in low- and middle-income countries, the family will spend only a fraction of the transfer on low-cost calories. In spite of unmet energy needs, people choose to spend the remaining part of the transfer (perhaps two-thirds of it) on high-cost calories, consumer durables, and other nonfood items. Thus, the effectiveness of every dollar spent under a general food subsidy on total calorie intake could be much lower than expected. (For a discussion of food subsidies and the household preference function, see Chapter 3, this volume.)

So far, this chapter has concentrated on the effect of policies on the levels of prices and has ignored the impact on poor families of price instability and reliability of supplies. A widely accepted objective of food security is to avoid significant year-to-year shortfalls in the supply of basic foods. These could cause food prices to jump and could reduce the real income of poor families. Although the loss of actual income may be temporary, it can cause malnutrition, with perhaps permanent physical effects in addition to the suffering it inflicts. The basic source of food supply instability is variation in domestic production (due to climate and uncontrollable conditions). This need not destabilize domestic supply if the country concerned has the capacity to vary its food import volume to compensate for the variability in products. However, its ability to do so could be limited by sudden increases in world prices for food imports and/or decreases in export revenues (6). Thus foreign exchange availability could be the most crucial factor in determining whether or not a country can import enough to stabilize food consumption.

As an example, within an open economy such as the present-day policy in Chile, what would happen to the food intake of the most vulnerable part of the population if the world price of a basic staple such as wheat rose to $220 a ton? What would happen to food consumption without a nutrition intervention program that would attempt to conpensate for the loss of income caused by such a factor that is beyond the control of a family, or for that matter, the country? Food prices in world markets have fluctuated considerably in real terms, although they do not show an upward long-run trend (6). A combination of imports and stocks designed to reduce the volatility of food prices would reduce consumer's vulnerability. We must try to anticipate and evaluate the effects of these phenomena of instability on the vulnerable groups, assessing the effectiveness of alternative approaches. This is badly needed in Latin America.

It comes as no surprise that to satisfy nutritional objectives, middle-income countries with relatively well-developed infrastructures for information and delivery systems choose to adopt targeted food distribution systems rather than modify their agricultural policies. It is attractive to think that some agricultural price policy would favor the poor, but manipulation of farm prices is rather ineffective in improving nutrition and often produces contradictory results. The interdependence of agricultural policy and macroeconomic goals makes it difficult to adjust the former to specific nutritional aims. It is our hope that agricultural policy can be spared a principal role in solving nutritional problems and that targeted food management systems can be expanded, according to the absorptive capacity of the system, to cope with nutritional objectives.

REFERENCES

1. Valdés, A. Trade policy and its effects on the external agricultural trade of Chile, 1945–1965. *Am. J. Agric. Econ.* **55,** (1973).
2. Krueger, A. *et al.* "Trade and Employment in Developing Countries, National Bureau of Economic Research." Univ. of Chicago Press, Chicago, Illinois, 1981.
3. Gavan, J. D., and Indrani Sri Chandrasekera. "The Impact of Public Foodgrain Distribution of Food Consumption and Welfare in Sri Lanka," Res. Rep. No. 13. IFPRI, Washington, D.C., 1979.
4. Ahmed, R. "Foodgrain Supply, Distribution, and Consumption Policies within a Dual Pricing Mechanism: A Case Study of Bangladesh," Res. Rep. No. 8. IFPRI, Washington, D.C., 1979.
5. George, P. S. "Public Distribution of Foodgrains in Kerala - Income Distribution Implications and Effectiveness." Res. Rep. No. 7. IFPRI, Washington, D. C., 1979.
6. Siamwalla, A., and Valdés, A. Food insecurity in developing countries. *Food Policy* **5,** (1980).

6 Comments on Economic Growth, Income Distribution, and Human and Social Development in Latin America

SERGIO MOLINA

GROWTH, DISTRIBUTION, AND POVERTY

From 1950 until 1975 the economies of the Latin American countries grew at a rate never before seen. During this period the annual per capita income increased an average of 2.6%, whereas the population grew by 2.8%. This growth surpassed the figures of almost all other regions of the world. Estimates for the decade of 1960 to 1970 made by the Economic Commission for Latin America (ECLA) show that the poorest 20% of the Latin American population increased its per capita income by 2.9% during this period. This is equivalent to 2 dollars in 1970.

Recent studies about levels of critical poverty in Latin America reveal that in 1970 around 40% of the population, i.e., nearly 115 million people, had an annual income below the poverty line (estimated for that year to be around 200 dollars). The indigency line, i.e., the income that buys a "food basket" that provides the minimum amount of calories and proteins needed by a subject to grow, fluctuated around 100 dollars, and 19% of the Latin American population (i.e., around 55 million people) was below this line.

NUTRITION INTERVENTION STRATEGIES IN NATIONAL DEVELOPMENT

FACTORS DETERMINING DISTRIBUTIVE INEQUALITY

The uneven distribution of income in Latin America has been determined by several factors. Among these, the great inequalities in the use of human resources and in the ownership of capital stock (land, physical and financial capital) and certain negative characteristics of the economic system when applied to the poor are worthy of mention. To these should be added the weak action of governments in this area.

Estimates of income distribution at the regional level made by the ECLA indicate that, in 1970, the richer 5% of the population obtained 30% of the income, whereas the poorer 20% received only 2.5%. Therefore, as an average, the per capita income of the first group was nearly 50 times that of the second group.

The differences in income per worker account for little more than one-half of the income inequalities between poor and nonpoor homes. The rest is basically explained by differentials in the rates of participation (ratio between the number of employed persons in the household) and dependency (ratio between number of minors/number of individuals in the household).

Despite the close relation between unemployment and poverty, it is necessary to point out that the great majority of the heads of indigent and poor families are employed. However, a high percentage of them are underemployed, and they work less that 39 hours per week. They explicitly declare their will to work longer hours.

MAGNITUDE AND DIFFICULTIES OF REDISTRIBUTION

To rescue the poor from their poverty, it would be necessary to transfer to them nearly 12% of the income of the richest 10% of the population, or 6% of the total disposable income. These figures, together with the average income reached by a sizable part of the Latin American countries, indicate that the problem of poverty is basically a question of income distribution and, to a lesser extent, a problem of low average income.

From the point of view of available resources, a solution to the problem of poverty seems possible in several Latin American countries. Attempts undertaken so far, however, have shown limited success. The causes of this failure are, among others, the lack of will and/or political capacity to undertake the task to eradicate poverty, the weakness and/or inadequacy of the administrative structure, and the inadequate approach due to the lack of a previous accurate diagnosis. The latter has hindered the appropriate selection of the proper instruments. The belief that growth by itself will solve the poverty problem and higher priorities given to other objectives (stability, international equilibrium, growth, etc.) may be mentioned as other causes of failure.

THE FREE MARKET: DOES IT SOLVE THE DISTRIBUTIVE INEQUALITIES?

Mere growth has not solved the problem of poverty. The play of the free market is inadequate to orient the resources toward meeting the needs of the poorest groups. Only factors external to the mechanism of the market, acting through or besides them, will reorient resources to satisfy the needs of the poorest groups, changing the prevailing trend of development, which is characterized by efforts to meet the needs of the medium and especially the highest income groups.

The task of eradicating poverty is so complex and of such a magnitude that it is of the utmost importance for the government to act to promote and implement policies and activities for this purpose.

AREAS OF STATE INTERVENTION

1. *Global Character.* (a) Areas which affect the accumulation and growth rates and by this means, employment and work income. Growth facilitates the application of redistributive measures. This is also related to the levels of saving and the amount and quality of investments. (b) Areas which affect the productive structure through policies of taxation, exchange rates, prices and investment, to balance it with the availability of resources. (c) Areas which influence the market of factors and goods. The market of factors relates principally to the degree of integration and intensity of their use. With regard to the market of goods, it must tend to eliminate concentration of the surplus originated in existing oligopolies and monopolies.

2. *Transfer.* These policies have the specific aim of reducing poverty and, in general, are linked to certain focal groups. They may imply a redistribution of income, consumption, the existing assets, or the new investments.

3. *Organization and Participation.* The success and continuity of a policy of poverty eradication is linked to the social and political support received from the groups it favors. This means that a strategy to eradicate poverty must take into account the promotion of economic, social, and

political organization and the participation of the groups which thus far have not benefited from growth.

4. *Demographic.* Within the broad development context the fight on poverty will affect, among other variables, the income levels of the poor, their mortality and morbidity indices, and their educational level. All this will weigh on the demographic behavior of the poor homes, probably reducing the number of wanted children.

7 Role of the Government in Income Distribution and Nutritional Improvement: The Chilean Case

ERNESTO TIRONI

Discussion among economists has centered mainly on the question of whether or not government should play an active role in regulating income distribution, improving nutritional conditions, and eradicating extreme poverty. If the answer is yes, then the next important question is *how* should government fulfill these objectives. This second question is particularly important because it provides the actual answer to the former, beyond the demogogic official statements that nearly always assert that government has as one of its prime roles the eradication of poverty and malnutrition.

The common reply given to the question of "how" to intervene nutritionally is that the State should follow a long-run strategy aimed at maximizing economic growth while in the short term it implements some assistance or corrective social programs. Nevertheless, it is well known that such a strategy does not necessarily lead to the solution of the problem, because maximum growth is no guarantee for the eradication of extreme poverty (See Chapter 6, this volume.)

However, the latter approach is often also based on the claim that government interventions in social and economic matters are inefficient and tend to be (or have been) regressive, i.e., lead to a deterioration in income distribution. The contention is that government programs do not reach extreme poverty groups, but rather favor the medium and high socioeconomic strata.

NUTRITION INTERVENTION STRATEGIES IN NATIONAL DEVELOPMENT

The Center for Economic Research on Latin America (CIEPLAN) carried out an exhaustive investigation of whether this assertion was valid in Chile (1). More than 140 different public programs in social and economic areas were analyzed. They included most official lending programs, the Social Security system, the educational system, the health services, public transport systems, and many others.

The results revealed that some specific public programs were regressive, but this did not apply to all programs. In fact, because the progressive programs were relatively more important, the *overall* action of government was strongly progressive in the years covered by the study (1969–1970). Total expenditures increased the average income of the poorest 30% of the Chilean households by over 90%. This is of the utmost importance, because it has been usually argued that governmental actions are regressive in order to underrate the role of the Government in the economy. The CIEPLAN study proved, however, that that argument was not supported by the empirical evidence in the Chilean case up to the early 1970s.

The most progressive programs were those in the social area, particularly in health. Thus, the poorest 30%, which received around 8% of national income, benefited from over 33% of government expenditure in health care services. This implied that the total *real* income or welfare of that group increased as a consequence of public expenditure in health.

One example of a regressive government intervention was that in higher (university) education because the poorest 30% of all households benefited from less than 7% of public expenditure in that subsector. But government outlays in higher education accounted for only about one-fourth of all expenditure in education so that it came out that the government's participation in the whole educational system was progressive.

It must be stressed that the evaluation of the progressive or regressive nature of government programs was done by considering also their financing by the different income groups. The financing of some of them was regressive, but since their benefits were distributed more evenly the net result was finally progressive. An example of a case such as that appeared in the Social Security system. The poorest 30% of the population contributed more to the total financing of the system than their share of the national income would warrent. Therefore, from the point of view of "who pays the bill," it is true that the Chilean Social Security system was regressive. But with respect to the delivery of benefits, it was progressive. The income of the poorest group increased by at least 22% through the benefits received from government's expenditure in Social Security. Therefore, in net terms the latter favored the lower income group.

In summary, the argument about the regressiveness of public programs is not really a valid justification for a decreased government action on redistributive matters. On the contrary, it justifies a strengthening of such actions.

On the other hand, it is frequently stated that government intervention is convenient and necessary for the eradication of extreme poverty, but it should be exerted for only a limited time and carried out through precise actions aimed at specifically identified groups. In other words, attention should be targeted on the specific recipient group to be assisted by public funds and on the distribution of these funds to this group.

The above considerations imply a partial view of the phenomenon. On the one hand, they ignore that malnutrition results from complex and numerous variables, especially socioeconomic. On the other hand, it disregards that government actively manages and controls a wide group of economic policies that affect nearly all those variables. There are numerous ways and means by which the Government affects income and consumption of different social groups, especially the poor. Therefore, in order to attain the objective of eradicating poverty and eliminating malnutrition, it is necessary to analyze the impact on poverty of several economic policy variables.

It is not sufficient to channel public funds to this end. It is necessary to consider especially the impact on poverty of government policies about employment, salaries, and social security. In some cases foreign trade and credit policies, as well as monetary and fiscal anti-inflationary policies, should be included. In an economy like that found in Chile, policies leading to increases in unemployment may have an impact on malnutrition that is practically impossible to compensate through social expenditure and other specific public policies. It is simply a problem derived from the magnitude of the effects: a 10% increase or 10 additional points of unemployment in Chile would result in approximately 350,000 additional people without work, affecting around 200,000 families. How many children in these families suffer malnutrition due to this situation or have a higher risk of becoming malnourished? Monckeberg (see Chapters 2 and 4, this volume) has stated that 92% of the malnourished children in Chile have unemployed parents. This underscores the importance of the linkages that we have outlined between malnutrition and macroeconomic policies.

There are strong economic reasons for considering economic policies and social programs in a broader perspective. Although social expenditure programs may partially compensate for some of the negative effects of other economic policies, the cost of doing so by following this approach may be much higher than otherwise. Many experts try to justify economic policies involving high social costs on the basis that those costs prevail for a short initial period, whereas their benefits prevail over a long-term period. For instance, some policies may initially generate unemployment but may later lead to improvement in the economic system. When this occurs, workers would presumably obtain higher salaries, and the country as a whole would increase its income level. These policies would then act, in a way, like a vaccine that may produce initial pain (it has a cost), but the benefits produced (by the immunity created) are maintained over many years acting as compensation for the initial pain. It should not be forgotten, however, that many short-term policies may generate harmful effects of long duration, effects such as having more handicapped workers because they were malnourished as a child when their parent became unemployed. Consequently, the actual costs of policies that generate unemployment may last for many years and be much higher than the short run loss of production while the unemployment lasts.

REFERENCE

1. Foxley, Aninat y Arellano, ¿Quiénes se benefician de los gastos públicos? *Estud. CIEPLAN* N°10 (1977).

III *Supplementary Feeding Programs*

8   Success or Failure of Supplementary Feeding Programs as a Nutritional Intervention

BARBARA A. UNDERWOOD

SUPPLEMENTARY FEEDING PROGRAMS AS NUTRITIONAL INTERVENTION

Supplementary feeding programs traditionally have been the most popular form of intervention for correcting undernutrition. Distributing food frequently is the easiest pallative and most politically satisfying way of dealing with the problem by statistics, i.e., tons of food distributed. The underlying causes of undernutrition as a public health problem, however, are far more complex; they go beyond what can be corrected by distributing food alone. These causes are rooted in the physical, biological, economic, and sociocultural environment in which man lives, particularly among the impoverished. Supplementary feeding programs if not attached to other basic socioeconomic programs can be simply a Band-Aid approach covering an underlying ulcer; the ulcer will still be there when the Band-Aid is removed unless appropriate healing measures are applied while the surface protection is in place.

Hence, supplementary feeding programs should be viewed as short-term means for achieving specific nutrition and health objectives, while long-range programs are being put into operation to attack the root causes of undernutrition. Program "successes" or "failures" should be judged within the context of short- and long-range goals. Supplementary feeding programs should not be open-ended, nor should they

NUTRITION INTERVENTION STRATEGIES IN NATIONAL DEVELOPMENT

create a welfare-type of dependency that is vulnerable to political and economic vicissitudes.

NATURE OF SUPPLEMENTARY FEEDING

Most feeding programs are based on a food product, or products, being provided either at no cost or at a subsidized price through private, government, or, occasionally, commercial channels (1). Frequently, the primary supplementary food is from external supplies sometimes extended by the addition of local products. Often the primary food supplement is a processed or blended mixture of cereal and legumes nutritionally well balanced, but unrecognizable as being derived from products available within the context of the recipient. Examples include mixtures such as corn–soya–milk (CSM), wheat–soya blend (WSB), and fish protein concentrate (FPC)—all of which are based on foreign imports—or alternately Incaparina, Fortesan, Bal-Ahar, and many other mixtures produced from local and/or imported commodities (2). The food supplement may be consumed "on-site" or distributed through "take-home" programs. Supplementary feeding programs based on culturally unfamiliar and unrecognizable mixtures usually require educational campaigns to acquaint recipients with the product and its merits. Promotional programs frequently have resulted in high acceptance of processed blends as long as these are provided at no cost. However, the blended products have failed to generate a demand sufficient to create a sustained commercial market when sold, even at a subsidized price (2).

Conversely, other supplementary feeding programs have used recognized and accepted foods, usually milk, in one form or another or bakery products such as buns or cookies, but have relied on external supply and distribution systems. These programs are subject to many uncertainties in supply that are difficult to predict and control. Too often such programs have not included contingency plans to provide alternatives when the primary food becomes unavailable or the delivery system fails.

Recently, a new type of supplementary feeding program has emerged based on indigenous foods provided in a natural or simply processed, recognizable form. This is the basic concept followed by most of the existing mothercraft or nutrition rehhabilitation-type feeding centers. It is the concept behind the "Nutripak" approach promoted in the Philippines and elsewhere.

Supplementary feeding programs have sometimes provided a contributed food for "on-site" consumption, either alone or as part of a total meal, or have periodically distributed a "take-home" food supplement.

Programs of both types occasionally include educational health and or sensory-stimulation components, the latter consisting of programmed play and social interaction. Each program combination has merits to be achieved at certain costs, as well as disadvantages. Before the approach most likely to succeed can be selected for a given situation (3), the benefit-cost trade-offs must be considered carefully within the context of program objectives, available resources, and alternative uses of those resources for achieving objectives.

JUSTIFICATION FOR SUPPLEMENTARY FEEDING PROGRAMS

Supplementary feeding programs may legitimately have political, health and nutritional, and/or behavioral and social objectives. Any one or a combination of such objectives may justify a program as long as the objectives are explicit. Political objectives are an inevitable part of any broad program involving public funds, but such objectives are seldom openly expressed. Hopefully even programs that are basically political will have explicit nutritional objectives as well. In any case, the objectives must be clearly perceived by those involved in implementing a program because the objectives will largely determine the nature of the program and will certainly provide the yardstick to determine the program's "success" or "failure." For example, if the objective is purely political (e.g., to demonstrate government concern and action), then a program that offers the broadest coverage is called for, and a scheme that monitors the number of people receiving the supplement is adequate for evaluation. "Success" in this case is not dependent on demonstrating a physiological benefit. On the other hand, if the objectives are both political and nutritional (e.g., to decrease the number of cases of second- and third-degree malnutrition in a particular population in a specified time), then the feeding program must be designed to locate the target malnourished population, deliver the food supplement to them, and evaluate periodically the physiological response. In this case "success" is determined by demonstrating a reduced incidence of malnutrition.

Similar examples could be cited for supplementary feeding programs that have behavioral and social objectives, such as to increase the number of mothers who utilize community services, to change child feeding practices to prevent young children from developing malnutrition after weaning, or to stimulate participating children through social interactions. The schemes for implementing, monitoring, and evaluating such programs obviously will increase in complexity and cost as the objectives broaden. This benchmark information must be established at the onset of a program so that "success" or "failure" can be assessed appropriately at a later date.

TYPES OF SUPPLEMENTARY FEEDING PROGRAMS

School feeding programs for political and logistical as well as health reasons, were most popular up to the early 1970s. School children are a visible, captive population for whom there exists a delivery system to achieve broad coverage and that can be tapped at a reduced operational cost. The assumption is that a nutritious food supplement fed to this group will have nutritional and health benefits. Notably lacking in many school feeding programs are the statistics to validate this assumption.

Sometimes school feeding programs are aimed at children from the low socioeconomic strata who are most likely to be at risk of marginal health and poor nutritional status and to those identified as underweight or retarded in growth. These "targeted" programs usually result in improved weight gain in recipients. Seldom do school feeding programs, even targeted ones, include parent education, and therefore, may have minimal lasting carry-over value to the home environment. Nutrition education of the school-aged recipient is of limited immediate significance since most at this age do not control their own food supply. Although targeted school programs are an efficient way to use supplementary foods to meet real needs, they carry a stigma for some children that may limit both the participation of those most in need and the effectiveness of the program in achieving long-range nutrition education goals.

From a physiological point of view, the nutritional impact and, hence, the "success" of untargeted feeding of school-aged children to reduce the prevalence of malnutrition are limited. It is unusual to find the seriously undernourished child routinely attending school. This is not to imply that school feeding programs might not offer more subtle social benefits for those moderately or mildly undernourished, but these benefits are difficult to demonstrate. From a political viewpoint, school feeding programs frequently are popular and thus "successful" and likely to continue.

In the late 1960s and early 1970s, emphasis turned toward the needs of the less accessible toddlers and preschoolers. At this time, malnutrition became widely recognized as an underlying contributor to morbidity and mortality from infections (4,5) and to other chronically debilitating and permanent effects on physical, social, and mental development (6). As a result, program planners striving to reach this population were faced with a new set of logistical problems. Many small-scale and a few large-scale projects emerged to test different delivery systems for their operational and physiological cost effectiveness. These included forms of "on-site" programs, many of which included an educational component and sometimes direct participation by mothers, as in the Nutritional Rehabilitation Centers (7,8). Problems developed, however, in transferring the lessons learned from "successful" pilot projects to programs with broad coverage that were sustainable economically and logistically (9).

The alternative approach, using "take-home" supplementary foods, reduced costs and increased outreach (10) but raised many questions as to whether supplementary food alone can effect lasting improvements in terms of health and development for toddlers and preschoolers (11–13). Furthermore, intrafamily distribution and other "leakages" from a "take-home" food supplement program prolong the time needed to demonstrate nutritional improvement. Yet, expanding the scope of a "take-home" program beyond simply supplying food increases operational costs. Given the budgetary limitations of most countries with a high prevalence of malnutrition, this decreases the number of people that can be reached. Consequently, few supplementary feeding programs for preschoolers have been successfully replicated on a national scale (14).

The importance of adequate nutrition for women during their childbearing years and especially during *pregnancy and lactation* is well recognized. However, efforts to provide high coverage to this group through food supplementation are recent. The long-range benefits of decreasing infant and child morbidity and mortality by providing improved nutrition for pregnant and lactating women is receiving added and worthwhile consideration in many countries. Again, however, there are operational problems in reaching those women who are seriously malnourished and most in need of a food supplement. Often they are the ones who, for economic and social reasons, do not participate in public programs. There are also problems in determining the real nutritional and health significance of a food supplement when given in amounts that are economically feasible in broad coverage programs (12).

Broad coverage supplementary feeding programs for workers, the elderly, and other nutritionally vulnerable populations are, for the most part, a luxury affordable only by affluent nations or large-scale corporate employers. As worthy as these programs may be, they are not priority concerns in the less-developed nations, which have to deal with under-employment and limited resources for combating serious and wide-spread health and nutritional problems. Certainly a valid case can be made that decreased productivity of the work force caused by subclinical malnutrition is a deterrent to national development. When resources are limited, this argument must be balanced against the vast wastage of human life and the diversion of human monetary and other resources necessary to combat the consequences of high maternal, infant, and child morbidity and mortality.

EVIDENCE OF SUCCESS IN REDUCING THE PREVALENCE OF MALNUTRITION

Pregnant and Lactating Women and Their Suckling Infants

The rationale for providing a food supplement to pregnant and lactating women is curative with respect to grossly malnourished poor women and preventative with respect to the developing fetus or suckling infant. Studies in Guatemala (15), Colombia (16), and Mexico (17) demonstrated that a dietary increase of at least 150–190 kcal daily in the last trimester of pregnancy resulted in fewer babies being born weighing less than 2500 g, and less subsequent growth retardation during the first 3 years of life (13).

A minimum of an additional 15,000 to 20,000 kcal in the maternal diet during the last trimester of pregnancy was needed to achieve a maximum birth increment of 100 g. However, the impact in Colombia was greatest among those women who were most underweight and who, because of intrafamily distribution, consumed only 150 kcal daily of the 850 kcal take-home supplement provided. From a purely nutritional perspective, these programs might be deemed successful. But, from a cost viewpoint, this is a very expensive intervention to achieve a small physiological increment, the biological importance of which remains to be demonstrated for both mother and offspring (12).

Some evidence suggests that the duration of lactation may be affected both by the amount of weight gained during pregnancy and by the amount retained postpartum (18). The volume of breast milk may be influenced by maternal nutrition as well. This, in turn, would influence the optimum time, from a preventive perspective, when supplementary feeding programs for toddlers might be introduced to provide maximum physiological benefits in the most cost-effective way.

In many developing countries, underweight women, who fail to gain adequate weight during pregnancy and who lose weight during lactation, may constitute 20–30% of the population in the fertile age range. The cost of providing this large number of potential recipients with sufficient supplementary food from nationally provided resources to meet their needs does not seem feasible when the associated intrafamily dilution effect is also considered. On the other hand, a program focused on providing food from community resources, through community services and more appropriate intrafamily distribution, may be practical (19).

One example of a community-based preventive program for pregnant women of projected national scope is being established in the Philippines through agricultural extension workers (20). The program is basically educational and relies on community food resources, identified by the program implementer, but supplied insofar as possible by the recipient herself, who is shown how to utilize the foods effectively. In the Philippines, the program begins during pregnancy and continues for the first 6 months of the child's life. When the infant is 3 to 4 months old, nursing mothers are helped to identify, prepare, and feed their infant appropriate foods to supplement breast milk. Early evaluations suggest that the program has decreased the number of infants who develop third- and second-degree malnutrition in the first year of life. Additional evaluations are needed to determine whether this approach is sustainable and to assess the impact of this kind of community-centered supplementary feeding program on maternal and child morbidity and mortality and on the adequacy and duration of the mother's lactational capacity.

Weaning Period: 3 to 36 Months

During the period when foods are introduced to complement and finally replace breast milk, children are particularly vulnerable to diarrhea and infection (21). It is also the period when poor mothers tend to be least adept at providing food from family resources appropriate in quantity and kind to supplement their milk. Supplementary feeding programs for children in this weanling crisis period, therefore, are likely to have the greatest nutritional and health impact, provided that they include not only food, but also access to preventive and curative health services. Normal growth increments are realized and possibly lasting deficits avoided when both nutritional and health needs are attacked concurrently. For these reasons, it is important, where possible, to link supplementary feeding programs during the weaning period with a health care system to maximize the potential for success.

Preschool Period: 36 to 60 Months

There are numerous examples, mostly from nutrition rehabilitation or day-care centers or hospitals, of the successful, curative effectiveness in terms of weight gain and prevention of morbidity and mortality of some supplementary feeding programs for severely malnourished pre-schoolers. Examples of success, as indicated by health and nutritional measurements, for normal or mildly malnourished children enrolled in supplementary feeding programs are less numerous (22). Indeed, one study in the Philippines showed a weight deterioration among children who were not originally severely malnourished, possibly because the food provided replaced, rather than supplemented, that consumed at home (23).

When "success" is judged by changed behaviors and developmental objectives, as well as by growth, feeding programs must be combined with sensory stimulation for effective beneficial change (11,12). Day-care centers that simply provide food and baby-sitting services do not accomplish the desired goals, although they are less costly to operate because fewer high-level professiónal staff members are required (12).

CONCLUSIONS

In contrast to institutionally based supplementary feeding programs, there are few examples of broad-coverage supplementary feeding programs for women in their reproductive years or for toddlers or pre-schoolers that have endured for long periods of time. One notable exception is the milk distribution program in Chile, which has been in operation for many years (24). Other national programs, such as the National Nutrition Program of the Phillipines (25), the ones in Chile, Colombia, and elsewhere (12) that have a food assistance component, are too new to judge for viability and success. These programs need to be carefully monitored to extract from them those elements critical to success and that are sustainable within the economic, social, and political constraints of developing nations (26).

REFERENCES

1. Anderson, M. A., Austin, J. E., Wray, J. D., and Zeitlin, M. F. "Nutrition Intervention in Developing Countries. Study 1: Supplementary Feeding." Oelgeschlager, Gunn & Hain Publishers, Inc., Cambridge, Massachusetts, 1981.

2. Orr, E. The contribution of new food mixtures to the relief of malnutrition. *Food Nutr. (FAO)* **3,**2–10 (1977).
3. Gordon, J. E., and Scrimshaw, N. S. Evaluating nutrition intervention programs. *Nutr. Rev.* **30,** 263 (1972)
4. Scrimshaw, N. S., Taylor, C. E., and Gordon, J. E. "Interactions of Nutrition and Infection." World Health Organ., Geneva, 1968.
5. Puffer, R. R., and Serrano, C. B. Patterns of mortality in childhood. *Sci. Publ.—Pan Am. Health Organ.* **262** (1973).
6. Scrimshaw, N. S., and Gordon, J. E. "Malnutrition, Learning and Behavior." MIT Press, Cambridge, Massachusetts, 1968.
7. Fougére, W., and King, K. W. Capitulation as a key ingredient to eradication of severe malnutrition in children. *J. Trop. Pediatr. Environ. Child Health* **21,**240 (1975).
8. Beghin, I. Centers for combating childhood malnutrition. *In* "Nutrition in the Community" (D. S. McLaren, ed.), p. 169. New York, 1976.
9. Scrimshaw, N. S. Myths and realities in international health planning. *Am. J. Public Health* **64,** 792 (1974).
10. Gopaldas, T., Srinivasan, N., Varadarajan, I., Shingwekar, A. G., Seth, R., Mathur, R. S., and Bhargave, V. "Project Poshak: An Integrated Health-nutrition Macro Pilot Study for Preschool Children in Rural and Tribal Madhya Padresh," Vols. 1 and 2. Care India, New Delhi, 1975.
11. McKay, H., Sinisterra, L., McKay, A., Gomez, H., and Llorida, P. Improving cognitive ability in chronically deprived children *Science* **200,**270 (1978).
12. Pollitt, E. "Poverty and Malnutrition in Latin America. Early Childhood Intervention Programs." Praeger, New York, 1980.
13. Brozek, J., Coursin, D. B., and Read, M. S. Longitudinal studies on the effects of malnutrition, nutritional supplementation, and behavioral stimulation. *Bull. Pan Am. Health Organ.* **11,** 237 (1977).
14. Beaton, G. H., and Ghasseni, H. "Supplementary Feeding Programs for Young Children," *Am. J. Clin. Nutr. (Suppl.)* **35,** 864–916 (1982).
15. Klein, R. E., Arenales, P., Delgado, H., Engle, P. L., Guzman, G., Irwin, M., Lansky, R., Lechtig, A., Martorell, R., Pivaral, V. M., Russell, P., and Yarbrough, C. Effects of maternal nutrition on fetal growth and infant development. *Bull. Pan Am. Health Organ.* **10,** 301 (1976).
16. Mora, J. O., de Paredes, B., Wagner, M., de Navarro, L., Suescun, J., Christiansen, N., and Herrera, M. G. Nutritional supplementation and the outcome of pregnancy in Colombian women: Preliminary report on birth weight. *Proc.—West. Hemisphere Nutr. Congr., 4th, 1974* (as reviewed in references 11 and 12).
17. Chavez, A., Martinez, C., and Yuschine, T. The importance of nutrition and stimulation on child mental and social development in early malnutrition and mental development. *Proc. Symp. Swed. Nutr. Found., 12th, 1977,* p. 211 (as reviewed in references 11 and 12).
18. Whitehead, R. G., Hutton, M., Muller, E., Rowland, M. G. M., Prentice, A. M., and Paul, A. Factors influencing lactation performance in rural Gambian mothers. *Lancet* **2,** 178 (1978).
19. Arole, M., and Arole, R. A comprehensive rural health project in Jamkhed (India). *In* "Health by the People" (K. W. Newell, ed.), p. 70, World Health Organ., Geneva, 1975.
20. Department of Agriculture, Bureau of Agricultural Extension Malnutrition Prevention Projects: Implementing Guidelines, Manila, 1977.

21. Gordon, J. E., Chitkasa, I. D., and Wyon, J. B. Weanling diarrhea. *Am. J. Med Sci.* **245**(3),345 (1963).
22. Rao, D. H., and Naidu, A. N. Nutritional supplementation—whom does it benefit most? *Am. J. Clin. Nutr.* **30**,1612 (1977).
23. Asia Research Organization, Inc. Evaluation of the Targeted Maternal Child Health Program in the Philippines, Manila, 1976.
24. Hakim, P., and Solimano, G. Supplemental feeding as a national intervention: The Chilean experience in the distribution of milk. *J. Trop. Pediatr. Environ. Child Health* **21**,186 (1976).
25. National Nutrition Council. The Philippine Nutrition Program, 1978–1982, Manila, 1977.
26. Newell, K. W., ed. "Health by the People." World Health Organ., Geneva, 1975.

9 Supplementary Feeding Program in Pregnancy and Lactation: Consideration for Intervention Programs

G. H. BEATON

INTRODUCTION

That the level of nutrition of the fetus and newborn affects physical growth and development during these periods is now beyond question. The relationship has been repeatedly demonstrated in experimental studies in animals and has been supported by observational studies in humans. The available evidence suggests that severe nutritional deprivations during early development may have lasting effects upon growth and functional development. The long-term effects of "less than severe" malnutrition remain uncertain (1).

On the basis of this growing body of knowledge, scientific groups and governments in many parts of the world agree that the maintenance of adequate nutrition for the fetus and the newborn must have a high health priority. Unfortunately, however, this consensus does not necessarily translate into a high priority for operational programs in all settings.

The remarks that follow are confined to those situations in which the maternal organism is interposed between the dietary environment and the infant either in the uterus or suckling at the breast. Artificial feeding of infants is not considered. This situation of maternal imposition provides important biological advantages and poses an important practical problem. Of clear advantage is the physiological role of the mother in

NUTRITION INTERVENTION STRATEGIES IN NATIONAL DEVELOPMENT

converting foods to forms that are suitable to the rapidly growing infant. Another clear advantage is the buffering effect provided by maternal tissues that in the event of dietary shortfalls may be utilized to maintain nutrient supplies to the infant. Thus, while the infant develops *in utero* or suckles at the breast, important homeostatic mechanisms operate to protect it, in part at least, from environmental changes (2).

THE LIMITS OF ADAPTATION

The practical problem that arises for nutrition intervention programs is in defining the limits of adaptability provided by maternal homeostatic mechanisms. Dietary interventions are aimed at the mother and only indirectly affect the infant. What are needed are functionally relevant descriptions of maternal nutritional status as predictors of dietary inadequacies or excess that may exceed the limits of adaptability (1, 2). Although concerted effort has been expended to establish indicators at the biochemical and physiological levels (3), few studies have carefully attempted to relate these to functional outcomes.

For example, the problem of nutritional anemia and indices for the assessment of nutritional status with regard to iron, folic acid, and vitamin B_{12} have been thoroughly discussed by other contributors to this volume. The evidence is convincing that severe maternal anemia, associated with a serious depletion of maternal iron stores, presents a situation in which the homeostatic processes cannot be maintained. Yet, although it seems probable that a severe maternal anemia might detrimentally affect fetal growth *in utero*, evidence to establish this relationship is sparse. There is increased probability, however, of anemia in the infant occurring within the first few months of life.

Analogous situations probably exist for most of the other minerals and vitamins. Severe deficiencies may interfere with fetal development *in utero*; on the other hand, the infant may be functionally normal at birth but be predisposed to deficiency at a later age if the maternal milk contains inadequate amounts of a given nutrient due to continuing maternal dietary inadequacy. Two clear examples of this process are widely cited: (1) the age of onset of keratomalacia may be determined by the level of vitamin A secreted in milk (4); (2) infantile beriberi may occur in association with low levels of thiamine in the milk of mothers who themselves show only marginal clinical signs of thiamine deficiency (4, 5).

Less attention has been directed toward potential adverse effects of excessive intakes of nutrients during pregnancy and lactation. Animal studies have demonstrated that a number of nutrients taken in gross excess can have teratogenic effects on the fetus. In the human, excess intake of vitamin D by young children is known to produce growth failure and, in some infants, irreversible mental damage. It has been suggested that these effects may begin *in utero* (6). Excessive intakes of other vitamins, such as ascorbic acid, during pregnancy may lead to the development of dependency states in the newborn (7, 8).

The main point of these remarks is simple. In our concern about possible effects of nutritional inadequacies, we must not establish intervention approaches that might create other problems attributable to excessive intake levels. There are limits to nutritional adaptability in both directions.

PREGNANCY AND LACTATION AS A CONTINUUM

In the design of intervention programs, pregnancy and lactation need to be considered as a continuum. This point deserves special emphasis. Attention to now has focused on vitamin and mineral nutrition. The relationship between energy (or protein intake) and fetal growth as marked by birth weight must now be assessed.

Epidemiologic studies have provided indication of maternal variables that associate with birth weight. Strong associations are found between maternal weight gain and birth weight and between prepregnancy weight and birth weight (9–11). Data from England, but not from the United States, showed prepregnancy height was strongly associated with birth weight as was also relative maternal weight for height (9). These are not the only, or the most important, variables associated with birth weight. However, they are of particular nutritional interest because one can rationalize that prepregnancy weight reflects nutritional status of the mother before pregnancy and perhaps even during her own growth and development during pregnancy. Similarly, weight gain during pregnancy may reflect the relative state of energy balance during the pregnancy. Thus, these parameters of nutritional status may be more directly associated with a functional outcome, i.e., fetal growth.

Associations observed in epidemiologic studies, however, do not necessarily reflect cause and effect relationships. Experimental data from animals suggested that, indeed, there is a causal relationship between the level of maternal feeding and fetal growth, and two human studies provide strong suggestive evidence.

During the World War II there was an acute period of severe famine in an area of Holland. Because medical records were maintained with care, it has been possible to examine the effect of this famine on birth weight and to compare the data with areas of Holland not affected by the famine. The women were relatively well nourished prior to pregnancy. The data suggest that severe food deprivation during the pregnancy significantly reduced mean birth weight, whereas women who became pregnant immediately after the famine had babies of normal birth weight. Hence, the effects of acute food shortage in the mothers did not persist (12). This natural experiment created as a result of political conflict can be viewed as a negative intervention that had the predictable effects.

On the positive experimental side, the most widely cited intervention studies are those described by Lechtig and his colleagues carried out in Guatemala (13). Women considered to have been chronically undernourished prior to pregnancy were offered food supplements, and their voluntary intake was recorded. The data revealed a strong positive relationship between the voluntary intake of supplemental energy sources and birth weight.

Thus, these two situations, one negative and one positive in direction, seem to substantiate the inference of the epidemiological data. There is a causal relationship between energy intake (and presumably energy balance), weight gain of the pregnant women, and birth weight of the baby.

However, there have been other studies that do not appear to fit this pattern. A supplementation study in Harlem, New York, conducted among women predicted to be at high risk of delivering low birth weight babies failed to show a positive relationship between the provision of a food supplement and birth weight. When the supplement was primarily an energy supplement providing about 10% of the energy as protein, there was a small positive effect. When protein was added to this supplement (also providing additional energy), there was no further improvement and indeed, there may have been a detrimental effect on mean birth weight (13, 14).

It is difficult to draw comparisons between the Harlem study and the Guatemalan experience. There may have been major differences in the genetic makeup, nutritional status, and obstetrical history of the populations. There was an important methodologic difference. In Guatemala, the extent of consumption of the supplement was voluntary, i.e., the individual woman controlled her own intake. In the New York study, a prescribed supplement was given to women allocated to the particular experimental groups. Every effort was then made to encourage and to monitor compliance. The voluntary choice of these women was not in the amount of supplement consumed but in the amount of food consumed in addition to the supplement.

An important lesson may be found here. Until we better understand the factors operating in these two studies, it would be wise to recognize a distinction between making supplementary food available for voluntary consumption and supplementing all subjects with a fixed amount of food. At present, the former approach would seem to be preferred.

Not all populations or all women within single populations can be expected, of course, to show equal benefit from supplementary feeding. The baseline plane of nutrition and the effective demand for food would be important variables in predicting cost–benefit relationships of supplementation programs. Also assumed is that the supplementation must affect the total food intake (diet + supplement) to bring about a significant change in energy balance and weight gain.

The quantitative relationship between energy intake, weight gain, and birth weight are of interest to consider. More correctly, energy balance should be examined; appropriate data are not available. Working with data from Guatemala and from Baltimore, Beaton (2) has offered the following calculations.

Lechtig et al. (13) found an average increase of 29 g in birth weight per 10,000 kcal of additional supplement consumed (the change in food intake, if any, was not recorded). Taking into account the probable costs of depositing proportionate increases in placenta, uterus, blood, and other pregnancy-related tissues (9), this would imply that some 34,000 kcal of energy entered maternal stores, or was otherwise expended, for a 100 g increase in birth weight.

Eastman and Jackson (10) provided data on the relationship between maternal weight gain and birth weight. Over the linear portion of this response, a 100 g difference in birth weight was associated with a 6.8 lb difference in weight gain. Again taking into account proportional changes in pregnancy-related tissues, it seems probable that maternal stores increased by some 3 kg in association with a birth weight difference of 100 g. If this store is adipose tissue, as suggested by Hytten and Leitch (9), some 23,000 kcal of energy would have been deposited in reserves to accomplish a 100 g change in birth weight. Importantly, in the Baltimore series the relationship between maternal weight gain and birth weight was relatively independent of prepregnancy weight.

These observations have important implications for intervention programs. If food is offered to the pregnant woman with the primary objective of increasing birth weight, the process must be seen as being very inefficient. Much of the additional food will be diverted to maternal stores rather than to the fetus per se. Presumably this is in keeping with the homeostatic mechanism operating during pregnancy. However, the adipose tissue accrued is to be seen as a reserve to subsidize the energy demands of lactation (9,15). In the continuum of pregnancy and lactation, the most important effects of supplementary feeding may not be apparent until a few months after birth when the adequacy of milk production is of critical importance.

The relationships discussed in this chapter have been derived from rather crude studies. Although we are interested in patterns of growth and development, the present studies give us only birth weight as a marker. Hopefully future studies will include some measures of intrauterine growth using new technologies such as ultrasound and incorporating these measurements into careful epidemiologic studies and in association with intervention programs (16). Such studies should shed important light on the relationships between nutrition, maternal weight gain, and fetal growth patterns.

At the present time, the most practical index of nutritional status would seem to be weight gain during pregnancy and weight loss during lactation. Epidemiologic studies have given us reasonable normative data for the former in relation to birth weight as a functional outcome. There is need for data relating maternal weight change during lactation to the growth rate of breast-fed infants. The previous discussion has assumed that energy balance is the major independent variable. The Guatemalan data suggest that indeed this is the case. However, it would be expected that this might vary depending upon the indigenous diet of the population and the particular dietary practices during pregnancy and lactation. In operational programs it would seem unwise to provide supplements of energy sources alone. Rather, the composition of supplements should be reasonably balanced with regard to energy sources, including protein, and the vitamins and minerals. There may be specific indication for particular nutrient supplements (17).

MATERNAL WEIGHT AND WEIGHT GAIN
AS INDICES OF RISK

Earlier in this presentation I described the relationship between maternal weight gain and birth weight as had been observed in a population of women living in Baltimore (10). The data suggested that both prepregnancy weight and maternal weight gain during pregnancy were associated with birth weight. Importantly, the relationships seem to be independent of each other. That is, a small thin woman with low weight gain during pregnancy is certainly at risk of having a low birth weight baby. A relatively large woman who exhibits a low weight gain during the pregnancy is also at risk—the presence of absence of energy stores at the beginning of pregnancy (and maternal growth during her own development) affects the outcome of pregnancy but does not negate the effect of energy intake and energy balance during pregnancy.

The point, then, is that weight gain during pregnancy is the best index now available of what is happening, or likely to be happening, during the pregnancy. I hope that we may be able to refine our knowledge and our clinical monitoring by using noninvasive techniques, such as ultrasound to assess and follow fetal growth during the pregnancy. At present this is a research and advanced diagnostic tool.

In predicting risk situations prior to pregnancy, it seems that low maternal weight is an indicator of increased risk. In British studies both small maternal stature (height) and low weight for height contribute to this risk. This would suggest that undernutrition or other impairment of the growth and development of the mother (height), as well as the mother's current nutritional state (weight for height), may affect the course of the pregnancy. This would represent a linkage across generations.

The hypothesis that links prepregnancy weight and weight gain during pregnancy with fetal growth is important. Most are prepared to assume that it is valid. It is important to recognize that it is based largely upon observed associations rather than clear experimental evidence. Because of this, there remains a need for well-designed studies that will test the validity of the hypothesis and perhaps expand our understanding of the linkages.

The issue of maternal diet and fetal development may be addressed by dividing it into three separate questions and commenting on each.

1. Does maternal nutrition affect fetal growth?
2. Should nutrition intervention be expected to improve fetal growth and birth weight?
3. What else might be affected, and should be measured, in a nutrition intervention?

DOES MATERNAL NUTRITION AFFECT FETAL GROWTH?

Unquestionably, yes. It must be stressed, however, that this relationship is conditioned by maternal physiological mechanisms that operate homeostatically to maintain the environment of the developing fetus. These mechanisms mitigate against major effects of undernutrition and permit the development of a viable infant even under very adverse dietary conditions and even at the expense of maternal tissues. Howev-

G. H. Beaton

er, the homeostatis is imperfect. There are subtle, important, effects on fetal growth and development as noted above. This relationship, to me, is quite surprising.

In developing models of the composition of weight gain during pregnancy, Thompson and his co-workers decided that, in normal English women gaining an average of 12.5 kg during pregnancy and producing infants with an average birth weight of about 3400 g, a maternal store of about 3.5 kg of adipose tissue was deposited. When they considered a series of Indian women exhibiting a weight gain of only about 7 kg and giving birth to viable infants of mean weight 2900–3000 g, they concluded that a major difference in maternal weight gain was in adipose tissue. In their model, some was deposited during the first two trimesters but the gain was then utilized to meet the increasing needs of fetal growth in late pregnancy; the net deposition of adipose tissue was very small. If these models are compared they suggest that for, a difference in growth rate that represented an average birth weight difference of about 400 g, there was a difference of about 5.5 kg in maternal weight gain and about 3.5 kg in adipose tissue storage. Protective homestatic mechanisms were in operation. If adequate energy were available, both maternal stores and fetal growth increased. The partitioning of this energy between maternal stores and fetal growth was strongly toward maternal stores. These stores would normally be used to meet part of the energy requirements of lactation and hence to continue the "homeostasis" to postnatal growth and development. Data from the Baltimore study portrayed this range of situations—a relatively large change in maternal weight gain in association with a relatively small increment in birth weight.

As we probe these models further, subpopulations can be found in which women show no weight gain during pregnancy yet give birth to a viable, albeit smaller, infant. Over the period of the pregnancy, there has actually been a loss of maternal tissue to support fetal growth.

Clearly the partitioning of energy utilization between maternal and fetal tissues depends upon the levels of maternal feeding (actually maternal energy balance reflecting energy intake and energy expenditure) and maternal nutritional status.

WOULD NUTRITION INTERVENTION BE EXPECTED TO INCREASE BIRTH WEIGHT?

The answer probably depends upon where you start. In the severe case portrayed above, a modest increment in food intake might result primarily in improvement of maternal status with little effect on birth weight. At a somewhat higher plane of nutrition, where maternal status is better, there might be a close relationship between energy balance and birth weight. At still higher levels of intake, the effect might be predominantly on maternal adipose tissue stores with lesser effects on birth weight. Ultimately, it could be assumed that virtually all of the additional energy finds its way into maternal adipose tissue with very little effect on the baby (it would be expected to be somewhat "fatter").

In many human populations, perhaps those in most of the developing countries, we are operating in that middle ground where improvement in energy balance is likely to improve fetal growth. In this situation, the expectation would be a fairly strong association between energy balance and maternal weight gain and between maternal weight gain and birth weight. The potential change in mean birth weight is probably not large (perhaps 100–200 g) but in terms of newborn risk, it is significant.

There are two important conditions that can be put on this prediction. First, I would wish assurance that, for the population in question, the limiting factor in fetal growth is indeed food intake and energy balance. As discussed earlier, there are many factors that affect fetal growth; maternal feeding is only one of these. It is quite conceivable that in some populations, factors other than nutrition really limit fetal growth, and nutrition intervention, by itself, would have minimal impact. This would argue for two things—the need for pilot studies before national programs and the need for a comprehensive approach to prenatal programs, an approach in which nutrition is an important *part* rather than the *sole* component of the program.

Second, I would wish assurance that the nutrition intervention actually affected the energy balance and nutrient supply of the mother. There are two aspects to this. If supplementation is under consideration, then it is obvious that intrafamily distribution of the supplemental food must be considered and controlled (or sufficient given that the mother's intake still increases even after sharing with others). But another consideration is whether or not the mother is in a condition to consume and benefit from the extra food. An obvious problem would be anorexia—the food made available to her might be rejected. An analogous situation holds if the mother consumes the food offered but decreases her intake of home foods, for whatever reason. A third situation would be that in which additional feeding is accompanied by additional work. The issue here is that it is not food intake per se that is important, it is the net effect on energy balance. I suspect that some studies have missed the relationship between maternal nutrition and fetal growth because they have measured energy intake (or even worse, intake of supplementary foods) rather than energy balance. We do not have good measures of energy expenditure that would permit reliable calculation of energy balance. It might be suggested that body weight change, reflects the energy balance and may be a better parameter than intake by itself.

That this is largely hypothetical, should be recognized. In the earlier part of this discussion paper, some studies were cited that give credibility to the hypothesis, but it remains far from proved. There is a need for well designed studies that will put the hypothesis to the test.

WHAT ELSE MIGHT BE AFFECTED? WHAT ELSE SHOULD BE MEASURED?

Emphasis has been on factors affecting fetal growth and birth weight as a convenient marker. If indeed a substantial amount of adipose tissue is being deposited as a part of a "normal" pregnancy and persists beyond the end of the pregnancy, as the model implies, then this energy reserve must be available for use during lactation. A part of the beneficial effect of a nutrition intervention during pregnancy would be expected in lactation and might be reflected in early growth and development of the infant.

In the design of an intervention trial and in the evaluation of the effects of an intervention, we must ask ourselves very specifically "What are the objectives we expect to accomplish?" Surely the objective is to have a woman proceed through the cycle of pregnancy and lactation in such a manner that a healthy, well-developed, infant is produced and that the woman is in at least as good nutritional status as when the cycle began. In many settings, she is in better nutritional status at the end than at the beginning, and this may be a specific objective of the intervention design. It is not enough to look at birth weight; this is a midway marker, not the end of a process. It is not enough to consider growth and development in the first year or two (though this would be an important part of any study). I believe that we must also look at the woman and measure, as best we can, the net effect of the cycle of pregnancy and lactation, and of the intervention, on her nutritional status. Only then will we be in a position to begin fitting the pieces together in a realistic perspective.

In this discussion emphasis has been placed on energy and energy balance. This should not be taken to imply either that individual nutrients are unimportant or that intervention can be considered on the basis of energy alone (e.g., providing sucrose, fat, or other energy-rich nutrient-poor supplements). In most settings in developing countries, the total intake of food appears to be more limiting than the intake of specific energy sources, such as protein, but any supplementary feeding program or other intervention design *must* consider the nutritional composition of the existing diet and that of the probable composite diet if the intervention succeeds in changing total intake. When individual nutrients appear to be in short supply, they should be provided as part of the intervention [i.e., they must be considered in selecting foods (17)].

CONCLUSIONS

In the design and implementation of any food supplementation program, it should be decided whether the primary objective is really a health benefit or whether the intervention is intended as a social-welfare program with tangential health benefits. This is a perfectly acceptable goal, although it implies different assessment techniques. Regardless of the immediate objective, the long-term goal must be improvement of the underlying conditions of the population such that there is effective demand for, and adequate supply of food to permit, adequate nutrition of the population. This is clearly a social goal. The implementation of a supplementation program as an expedient measure must not be allowed to direct attention away from the proper goals.

REFERENCES

1. Food and Nutrition Board, Committee on International Nutrition Programs. Summary Report: Workshop on the Need for Research on Nutrition and Function, Washington, 1977.
2. Beaton, G. H. Nutritional needs of the pregnant and lactating mother. *Symp. Swed. Nutr. Found. XIV* pp. 26–34.
3. Food and Nutrition Board, Committee on Nutrition of the Mother and Preschool Child. "Laboratory Indices of Nutritional Status in Pregnancy." Nat. Acad. Sci., Washington, D.C., 1978.
4. Report of a Joint FAO/WHO Expert Group on Requirements of Vitamin A, Thiamine, Riboflavine and Niacin. *W.H.O. Tech. Rep. Ser.* **362** (1967).
5. Committee on Nutrition of the American Academy of Pediatrics. The prophylactic requirement and the toxicity of vitamin D. *Pediatrics* **31**, 512 (1963).
6. Fraser, D. The relation between infantile hypercalcemia and vitamin D. Public health implications in North America. *Pediatrics* **40**, 1050 (1967).
7. Cochrane, W. A. Overnutrition in prenatal and neonatal life: A problem? *Can. Med. Assoc. J.* **93**, 893 (1965).
8. Norkus, E. P., and Rosso, P. Changes in ascorbic acid metabolism of the offspring following high maternal intake of this vitamin in the pregnant guinea pig. *Ann. N.Y. Acad. Sci.* **258**, 401 (1975).
9. Hytten, F. E., and Leitch, I. "The Physiology of Human Pregnancy," 2nd ed. Blackwell, Oxford, 1971.

10. Eastman, N. J., and Jackson, E. Weight relationships in pregnancy. I. The bearing of maternal weight gain and pre-pregnancy weight on birth weight in full term pregnancies. *Obstet. Gynecol. Surv.* **23,** 1003 (1968).

11. Hardy, J. B., and Mellitg, E. Relationship of low birth weight to maternal characteristics of age, parity, education and body size. *In* "The Epidemiology of Prematurity" (D. M. Reed and F. J. Stanley, eds.), p. 105. Urban & Schwarzenberg, Munich, 1977.

12. Susser, M., and Stein, Z. Prenatal nutrition and subsequent development. *In* "The Epidemiology of Prematurity" (D. M. Reed and F. J. Stanley, eds.), p. 177. Urban & Schwarzenberg, Munich, 1977.

13. Lechtig, A., Habicht, J. P., Delgado, H., Klein, B. E., Yarbrough, C., and Martorell, R. Effect of food supplementation during pregnancy on birth weight. *Pediatrics* **56,** 508 (1975).

14. Rush, D. Studies of prevention and intervention. *In* "The Epidemiology of Prematurity" (D. M. Reed and F. J. Stanley, eds.), p. 291, Urban & Schwarzenberg, Munich, 1977.

15. Report of a Joint FAO/WHO Ad Hoc Expert Committee on Energy and Protein Requirements. *W.H.O. Tech. Rep. Ser.* **522** (1973).

16. Solari, P. Ph.D. Proposal, University of Toronto (personal communication).

17. Beaton, G. H., and Bengoa, J. M. Distribution of vitamin and mineral supplements. *W.H.O. Monogr. Ser.* **62,** 313 (1976).

10 Supplementary Feeding during Pregnancy: Impact on Mother and Child in Bogota, Colombia

JOSE OBDULIO MORA

The relationships between maternal nutrition during pregnancy and fetal growth and development continue to be the subject of concern and study. Although research in animals seems to demonstrate a close relation between nutritional deprivation during pregnancy and fetal growth retardation, studies in humans have yielded contradictory results. On the one hand, the model of deprivation commonly used in animal research cannot be used in humans for ethical reasons. On the other hand, differences between species make generalization of the findings in animal research of limited value in humans.

Relevant information, therefore, drawn from three types of human studies is as follows:

1. The so called *natural experiments* in which disaster situations from war unintentionally replicate in humans the conditions seen in animal models of deprivation (1, 2).

2. *Epidemiological studies* of the relation between diet during pregnancy and fetal growth and development (3–7) in large samples of population.

3. Small-scale *clinical studies* (8–10).

Despite some inconsistencies, the following general broadly accepted conclusions have emerged from these studies:

NUTRITION INTERVENTION STRATEGIES IN NATIONAL DEVELOPMENT

1. Severe nutritional deprivation during the second-half of pregnancy results in retardation of fetal growth and increased perinatal mortality; similar effects do not seem to appear when nutritional deprivation occurs only during the first-half of pregnancy.

2. When significant deficits in calorie and/or protein intake exist in pregnant women, it is possible to demonstrate a defined relation between intake and fetal growth.

3. The most accepted index of fetal growth, that is, weight at birth, is clearly related to perinatal mortality and with the growth and development of the child (11–15).

4. A high intake of calories and/or proteins during the second-half or the last 3 months of pregnancy can increase the weight of infants at birth in mothers exposed to deficient diets during the first-half of pregnancy.

These conclusions justify supplementary feeding programs during pregnancy as a means to improve fetal growth in populations in which malnutrition is highly prevalent. However, prospective studies have not always demonstrated the effectiveness of these interventions. The results from studies of prenatal supplementary feeding on birth/weight do not allow one to conclude that such an intervention will always result in increased fetal growth (16–19). This fact has caused a certain amount of justifiable skepticism among many scientists.

There is always the risk of rejecting nutritional interventions because of apparent inconsistencies in the results of field studies. This makes it necessary to consider some aspects related to the effectiveness of nutritional supplementation which evaluate the conditions under which such interventions are truly effective. It is worthwhile to note that the apparent failure of some prenatal supplementation programs to induce significant effects on birth weight does not imply absence of a direct relation between maternal nutrition and fetal growth. Moreover, in the analysis of the problems inherent to the design of interventions or the evaluation of programs, it is important to consider two practical aspects of great relevance that partly explain the divergencies in their observed effects.

INITIAL NUTRITIONAL STATE

It seems logical to assume that any nutritional intervention will produce demonstrable effects only when directed to correct deficiencies which actually exist in the target population. Consequently, supplementation should be directed to pregnant women with proved nutritional insufficiencies. Unfortunately, there are no indexes of relative nutritional status of pregnant women with adequate validity and reliability that can be used under field conditions. The search for sensitive, simple indicators to be used for the evaluation of the nutritional status of pregnant women in community programs is urgently needed. Solution of this problem should have priority in nutritional research.

The differences in effects of prenatal supplementation can be partly explained by the fact that the target populations have variable levels of nutritional deficiency whose magnitude is not always clearly defined. Thus, for example, ambiguous or discouraging results have been frequently observed in industrialized countries in groups with marginal or unproved nutritional deficiencies. Likewise, some studies in developing countries have supplemented specific nutrients either without previous data to document the prevalence of specific deficiencies or have given the specified nutrients to pregnant women with multiple deficiencies that are so frequent in developing societies. The type of initial deficiency would explain why some studies report increased birth weight by calorie supplementation and others by increased protein intake.

ACTUAL LEVEL OF SUPPLEMENTATION

The effects of supplementation will be in direct relation to the level of initial nutritional deficiency being corrected, the level of supplementation provided, and its actual consumption and the behavior of beneficiaries in relation to their usual dietary intakes.

1. *Quality and quantity of supplements* are important in relation to the type and magnitude of the deficiencies that they are intended to correct. Several studies have provided variable amounts of foodstuffs with different nutritional content. These have covered variable proportions of existing nutritional deficiencies.

2. *The intake of supplements* can change according to the quantities and qualities supplied, its congruence with the feeding patterns of the population, the distribution and control systems, and the concurrent education in nutrition. Also, intake of supplement seems to depend on the perception that mothers have of their feeding needs in relation to the other members of the family. Undoubtedly when supplements are distributed for home consumption, frequent distortions occur in their use, particularly dilution within the family, sale, bartering, etc. Problems of intake are minimized when supplements are consumed directly in *ad hoc* centers. This system is not usually feasible, however, when programs have wide coverage. Intake problems notoriously increase when coupon distribution systems are used.

3. *The behavior of the beneficiaries with respect to their usual diet* is generally characterized by the replacement of foodstuffs from the regular diet by those supplied as supplements. These then become substitutive instead of supplementary. Replacement is a problem frequently underestimated and affects substantially the results of programs. Distortions in the use of supplements and replacement among them suggest biological adaptation of chronically undernourished populations to relatively low levels of nutrient intake. However, it is more frequently considered as a sociological phenomenon related to the cultural patterns and perceptions that families have of their needs. The end result is that supplementary feeding programs in fact may not be nutritional interventions. Through changes induced in the distribution of the family income, these programs may become actions that increase family income but with marginal nutritional effects.

IMPACT OF SUPPLEMENTARY FEEDING DURING PREGNANCY ON MOTHERS AND CHILDREN IN BOGOTA

The preceding concepts have been underscored by results of studies carried out in Metropolitan Bogota, as part of a Program of Longitudinal Research on Nutrition, Stimulation and Mental Development implemented jointly by the Instituto Colombiano de Bienestar Familiar (Colombian Institute of Family Welfare) and Harvard University. The study was carried out on 456 pregnant women of low socioeconomic level whose children under 5 years of age were malnourished and were randomly assigned to two experimental groups as follows: control group, 230 women; supplemented group, 226 women.

Random assignment produced groups comparable in relevant socioeconomic and biological variables, such as family size, income, expenditures in food, age, height, weight and gestational age of mothers at the time of enrollment, initial calorie and protein intake, number of previous pregnancies, and educational level (Table I).

The program consisted of supplying weekly natural foodstuffs to be consumed at home in quantities sufficient to cover a significant proportion of the recommended nutrient intake for all the members of the family. Quantities delivered for daily consumption by the women, as well as their calorie and protein content, are shown in Table II. Some measures were taken to avoid alterations in the family distribution of the habitual diet as well as substitution of the supplements. All the families received health care. Measurements were carried out blindly by trained staff and were carefully standardized.

TABLE I

Relevant Socioeconomic and Biological Variables at Entry of the Control Group and of the Group to Be Nutritionally Supplemented

Variable	Control group (N = 230)	Supplemented group (N = 226)
Family members (number)	5.8 ± 2.5	5.2 ± 2.0
Rooms in the household (number)	1.7 ± 0.9	1.6 ± 0.9
Built area (m² per person)	3.2 ± 1.8	3.5 ± 1.9
Monthly family income (US$)	50.9 ± 25.4	46.9 ± 20.5
Monthly per capita income (US$)	9.7 ± 6.1	9.9 ± 4.8
Family expenditures in food (US$)	27.7 ± 13.4	26.2 ± 12.6
Maternal characteristics		
Age (years)	26.6 ± 6.1	25.8 ± 5.4
Height (cm)	149.9 ± 5.3	149.9 ± 5.5
Daily calorie intake	1621 ± 655	1623 ± 635
Daily protein intake (g)	37.0 ± 22.9	35.6 ± 19.2
Previous pregnancies (number)	4.2 ± 3.2	3.6 ± 2.6
Years of education (median)	2.96	3.01

Impact upon Maternal Diet

The average daily calorie and protein consumption by pregnant women before and after the program are shown in Tables III, both in absolute quantities and as percentages of adequacy. The women consuming low intakes (around 1600 calories and 36 g of protein) in the control group did not change in their consumption patterns during the program. In

TABLE II

Composition of Nutritional Supplement Provided to Mothers during the Last Trimester of Pregnancy[a]

Supplement	Grams	Calories (no.)	Protein (g)	Vitamin A (I.U.)	Iron (mg)
Powdered skim milk	60	214	21.6	18	0.4
Enriched bread	150	466	16.8	6	2.6
Vegetable oil	20	176	—	—	—
Vitamin and mineral supplement	—	—	—	6000	15.0
Total	230	856	38.4	6024	18.0
Percentage of recommended allowances	—	40	60	100	100

[a] Quantities per capita per day.

Jose Obdulio Mora

TABLE III

Daily Average Intake of Calories and Protein of Pregnant Women before and during
Supplementation

	Calories		Protein (g)	
Group	Before	During	Before	During
Control	1621 ± 655	1573 ± 656	37.0 ± 22.9	35.5 ± 21.2
Supplemented	1623 ± 635	1773 ± 568	35.6 ± 19.2	56.2 ± 22.0
Percent of adequacy	74.8 ± 28.6	80.9 ± 25.9	56.1 ± 30.3	86.3 ± 34.0
Percent increase	—	6.1 ± 29.5	—	30.2 ± 37.7

the supplemented group, total intake increased only by 150 calories and
20.6 g of protein per day despite the fact that 856 calories and 38.4 g of
protein were supplied. In terms of meeting the recommended intake,
the net increase was only 6% for calories and 30% for proteins (20).

The results of the program are summarized in Fig. 1, where the origin
of the calories and proteins consumed is indicated. Supplementation
was much lower than expected due to a lesser consumption of the sup-

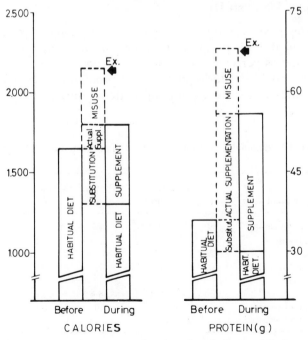

Fig. 1. Daily calorie and protein intake of mothers before and during supplementation. Ex, expected level of intake.

plements and to replacement in the common diet. Replacement was less for proteins than for calories, indicating that foodstuffs of low protein content were replaced by protein-rich supplemented foodstuffs. In this program the low intake of the supplements by the pregnant women was due more to inadequate use than to dilution, since foodstuffs were supplied for all the family. The level of replacement was highly correlated with the initial calorie ($r = .71$, $p < .001$) and protein ($r .67$, $p < .001$) intake.

Impact on Maternal Weight Gain

Supplementary feeding produced a significant effect on maternal weight gain during the last 3 months of pregnancy; the effect was greatest in those mothers who participated in the program for 13 weeks or longer (Table IV). On the other hand, weight gain correlated significantly with birth weight for the control group ($r = .18$, $p < .001$), as well as for the supplemented group ($r = .23$, $p < .001$) and in the total sample ($r = .24$, $p < .001$). Likewise, in the supplemented group the duration of supplementation had a significant correlation with maternal weight gain ($r = .18$, $p < .01$).

Impact on Infant Birth Weight

Supplementary feeding for 13 or more weeks induced a significant effect on the weight of infants at birth: the difference from the control group was 90 g (Table V). Supplementation for less than 13 weeks did not produce significant effects on birth weight. The difference between the supplemented group as a whole and the control group was only 63 g (19). The duration of the supplementation was significantly correlated

TABLE IV

Body Weight Gain during the Last Trimester of Full-Term Pregnancies in Control and Supplemented Groups

Group	N	Body weight gain (kg) (Mean ± SD)	p^a
Control	183	3.46 ± 1.73	—
Supplemented	190	4.20 ± 1.76	.0005
Less than 13 weeks	75	3.94 ± 1.94	.025
13 or more weeks	115	4.38 ± 1.62	.0005
Total sample	373	3.84 ± 1.78	—

[a] T test (one tail) for difference with control group.

TABLE V

Birth Weight of Full Term Newborns by the Control and Supplemented Groups

Group	N	Birth weight (g)		p^a
		Mean	SD	
Control	165	2940	318	—
Supplemented	177	3003	354	0.05
Less than 13 weeks	76	2967	344	N.S.
13 or more weeks	101	3030	364	0.025
Total sample	342	2973	338	—

[a] T test (one tail) for difference with control group.

with the weight at birth ($r = .19$, $p < .01$). The dose–response ratio in terms of calorie supplementation was approximately 50 g of increased birthweight per 10,000 calories; this ratio is higher than the 30 g per 10,000 calories found in a similar study in Guatemala (18), and it falls within the range estimated for different calorie–protein intakes (21). It is worth noting that supplementation was proportionately higher for proteins than for calories in a group with more severe deficiency of protein (45%) than of calories (25%).

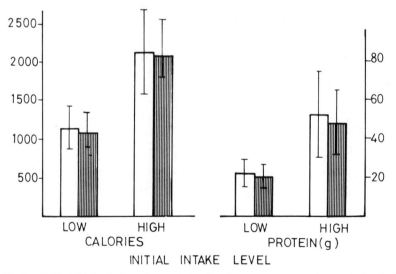

Fig. 2. Daily initial calorie and protein intake of pregnant women by intake levels. □ controls; ▤ supplemented.

To study the effects of supplementation in pregnant women with different initial levels of intake, the sample was divided in subgroups of high and low initial intake, using a dividing point of 1500 calories and 30 g of protein (22). Figure 2 shows that the initial average intake in the two subgroups were not different between supplementation groups. The groups with low intake had an initial average intake of approximately 1100 calories and 20 g of protein; for the groups of high consumption, intake was 2100 calories and 50 g of protein.

The first interesting finding is the absence of differences in average intake of supplements between the initial high and low subgroups. The second interesting finding shown in Fig. 3 was that when the low intake subgroup was supplemented, a significant increase of intake occurred up to about 1600 calories and 50 g of protein; the high intake subgroup increased protein (up to 60 g) but no calorie intake, due to considerable replacement in the diet (Fig. 3).

Finally, there were significant differences in birth weight between the control and the high intake subgroup of the supplemented group. This effect on birth weight was associated with an increased intake of protein without a significant increment in calorie consumption. This apparent

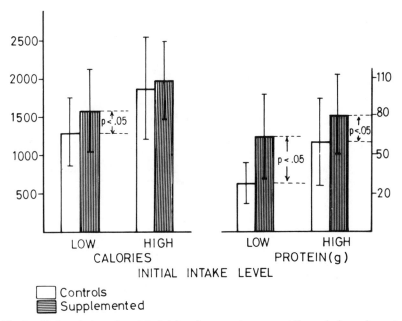

Fig. 3. Daily calorie and protein intake of pregnant women at the end of supplementation, by initial intake. □ controls; ▤ supplemented.

discrepancy compared with the findings of the Guatemala study (18) may be attributed to the relatively more severe protein deficiency in Bogota (daily consumption 45 g for Guatemala versus 36 g for Bogota) than calorie deficiencies, which were comparable in the two studies (intake around 1600 calories per day).

Despite the fact that calorie and protein supplementation was achieved, the absence of effects on fetal growth in the lowest intake subgroup suggests that a minimum threshold of intake must be exceeded before any effects on fetal growth become detectable. In our study this threshold may be somewhere between 1600–2100 calories and 50–60 g of protein per day. Although the gain of weight of the mothers was greater in the high intake subgroup, the differences between the control and supplemented groups were significant in both subgroups. This is in accordance with suggestions that the nutritional supplementation of chronically undernourished pregnant women will initially restore the mother's reserves before it becomes reflected in an increase in fetal growth.

Impact on Perinatal Mortality

The most important differences between newborns from supplemented and nonsupplemented mothers were observed in peri- and neonatal mortality rates (23). In effect, these rates were at least 2 times higher in the latter group as compared to the former (Table VI). Perinatal as well as neonatal mortality were, in general, 10 times higher in prematures than in those born at term. Both rates were nearly 3 times lower in prematures from supplemented mothers (Table VII).

In summary, there are few doubts about the direct relationship be-

TABLE VI

Stillbirths, Perinatal, and Neonatal Deaths in the Control and Supplemented Groups

	Control group		Supplemented group		Totals	
	N	Rate	N	Rate	N	Rate
Stillbirths[a]	8	36.0	2	9.0	10	22.6
Perinatal deaths[a]	14	63.1	7	31.7	21	47.4
Neonatal deaths[b]	9	42.1	5	22.8	14	32.3

[a] Rate per 1000 pregnancies.
[b] Rate per 1000 live births.

TABLE VII

Perinatal and Neonatal Mortality of Premature and Full-Term Newborns in Control and
Supplemented Groups

	Control group		Supplemented group		Totals	
	N	Rate	N	Rate	N	Rate
Perinatal deaths[a]						
Prematures	9	360.0	3	136.4	12	255.3
Full-term newborns	5	28.6	4	21.4	9	24.9
Totals	14	63.1	7	31.7	21	47.4
Neonatal deaths[b]						
Prematures	6	285.7	2	95.2	8	190.5
Full-term newborns	3	15.5	3	15.2	6	15.3
Totals	9	42.1	5	22.8	14	32.3

[a] Rate per 1000 pregnancies.
[b] Rate per 1000 live births.

tween prenatal nutrition (expressed as maternal calorie and protein intake) and fetal growth, as well as about the effectiveness of food supplementation during pregnancy in women with nutritional deficiencies. It is of considerable practical importance to determine the most effective means to achieve adequate calorie and protein intakes for pregnant women who compose the masses of the nutritionally marginal populations in developing countries.

The response to this issue must consider not only possibilities of paliative interventions but, what is more important, the search for solutions to the underlying problem of poverty affecting these population groups.

REFERENCES

1. Antonov, A. N. Children born during the siege of Leningrad in 1942. *J. Pediatr.* **30,** 250 (1947).
2. Smith, C. A. Effects of maternal undernutrition upon the newborn infant in Holland (1944–1945). *J. Pediatr.* **30,** 229 (1947).
3. Burke, B. S., Beal, V. A., Kirkwood, S. B., and Stuart, H. C. The influence of nutrition during pregnancy upon the condition of the infant at birth. *J. Nutr.* **26,** 569 (1943).
4. Ebbs, J. The influence of prenatal diet on the mother and child. *J. Nutr.* **22,** 515 (1941).
5. McGanity, W. R., Cannon, R. O., Bridgeforth, E. B., Martin, M. P., Densen, P. M.,

and Darby, W. J. The Vanderbilt Cooperative Study on Maternal and Infant Nutrition. Relationships of obstetric performance to nutrition. *Am. J. Obstet. Gynecol.* **67,** 501 (1954).

6. Sontag, L. W., and Wines, J. Relation of mother's diets to status of their infants at birth and in infancy. *Am. J. Obstet. Gynecol.* **54,** 994 (1947).

7. Thomson, A. M. Diet in pregnancy. III. Diet in relation to the course and outcome of pregnancy. *Br. J. Nutr.* **13,** 509 (1959).

8. Kasius, R. V., Randall, A., Tompkins, W. T., and Wiehl, D. G. Maternal and newborn studies at Philadelphia Lying-in Hospital. Newborn studies. I. Size and growth of babies of mothers receiving nutrient supplements. *In* "The Promotion of Maternal and Newborn Health," pp. 153. Milbank Memorial Fund, New York, 1955.

9. Venkatachalam, P. S. Maternal nutritional status and its effect on the newly born. *Bull. W.H.O.* **26,** 193 (1962).

10. Iyenger, L. Effects of dietary supplements late in pregnancy on the expectant mother and her newborn. *Indian J. Med. Res.* **55,** 85 (1967).

11. Churchill, J. A., Neff, J. W., and Caldwell, D. F. Birth weight and intelligence. *Obstet. Gynecol.* **28,** 425 (1966).

12. Wiener, G., Rider, R. V., Oppel, W. C., and Harper, P. A. Correlates of low birth weight: Psychological status at eight to ten years of age. *Pediatr. Res.* **2,** 110 (1968).

13. Yersushalmy, J. Relation of birth weight gestational age and the rate of intrauterine growth to perinatal mortality. *Pediatr. Clin. North Am.* **17,** 114 (1970).

14. Puffer, R. R., and Serrano, C. V. Patterns of mortality in childhood. *Sci. Publ.—Pan Am. Health Organ.* **262,** (1973).

15. Davies, P. A., and Stewart, A. L. Low birth-weight infants: Neurological sequelae and later intelligence. *Br. Med. Bull.* **3,** 85 (1975).

16. Committee on Maternal Nutrition, Food and Nutrition Board, National Research Council. "Nutritional Supplementation and the Outcome of Pregnancy." Natl. Acad. Sci., Washington, D.C., 1973.

17. Blackwell, R. Q., Chow, B. F., Chinn, K. S. K., Blackwell, B. N., and Hsu, S. C. Prospective maternal nutrition study in Taiwan: Rationale study design, feasibility, and preliminary findings. *Nutr. Rep. Int.* **7,** 517 (1973).

18. Lechtig, A., Habicht, J. P., Delgado, H., Klein, R. E., Yarbrough, C., and Martorell, R. Effect of food supplementation during pregnancy on birth weight. *Pediatrics* **56,** 508 (1975).

19. Mora, J. O., de Paredes, B., Wagner, M., de Navarro, L., Suescún, J., Christiansen, N., and Herrera, M. G. Nutritional supplementation and the outcome of pregnancy. I. Birth weight. *Am. J. Clin. Nutr.* **32,** 455 (1979).

20. Mora, J. O., de Navarro, L., Clement, J., Wagner, M., de Paredes, B., and Herrera, M. G. The effect of nutritional supplementation on calorie and protein intake of pregnant women. *Nutr. Rep. Int.* **17,** 217 (1978).

21. Lechtig, A., Yarbrough, C., Delgado, H., Habicht, J. P., Martorell, R., and Klein, R. E. Influence of maternal nutrition on birth weight. *Am. J. Clin. Nutr.* **28,** 1223 (1975).

22. Christiansen, N., Mora, J. O., de Navarro, L., de Paredes, B., and Herrera, M. G. Effects of nutritional supplementation during pregnancy upon birthweight: The influence of pre-supplementation diet. *Nutr. Rep. Int.* **21,** 615 (1980).

23. Mora, J. O., Clement, J., Christiansen, N., Suescún, J., Wagner, M., and Herrera, M. G. Nutritional supplementation and the outcome of pregnancy. III. Perinatal and neonatal mortality. *Nutr. Rep. Int.* **18,** 167 (1978).

11 Nutrition Intervention Programs in Chile for Pregnant Women and Nursing Mothers: The Issues

ANTONIO ARTEAGA

Although the importance of nutrition during pregnancy has long been recognized, there is no agreement on the actual relationship between nutrition and gestation. Analysis of past and present supplementation programs for pregnant women reveals contradictory results that impede the establishment of definitive criteria (1–6). The planning of feeding intervention programs for pregnant women should consider biological, social, and medical objectives. Because fetal malnutrition may substantially influence subsequent development of the child, primary objectives should be to prevent fetal undernutrition by ensuring the best nutritional status of the mother and by eventually fostering adequate lactation.

Because of severe limitations of resources in developing countries, nutrition intervention programs for pregnant women must reach maximum efficiency, and at the same time they must avoid the waste resulting from ineffective or unnecessary actions.

SELECTION OF RECIPIENT POPULATIONS

In planning supplementation programs, one of the first issues to confront is how to select the target population. A first alternative would be total coverage of all pregnant women, based on the universally accepted

NUTRITION INTERVENTION STRATEGIES IN NATIONAL DEVELOPMENT

assumption that their nutritional requirements are increased and that a large proportion of the population of developing countries receives deficient diets. This type of program has high costs in relation to its potential benefits. It would be ineffective in population groups in which food supplementation would lead to intakes in excess of requirements and unnecessary in those groups that have the economic capacity to independently supplement their diet. It could be even adverse for some beneficiaries, because supplementation leading to positive calorie balance beyond the requirements of pregnancy is prone to cause obesity. Further, indiscriminate intervention could fail to provide effective protection for pregnant women at highest risk.

A second alternative would be to restrict coverage to the lowest socioeconomic groups of the population, based on the subjective observation that in poor countries the majority of pregnant women belonging to this group suffer from a certain degree of undernutrition. This observation is not entirely valid in developed countries where in fact a minority of the lower social strata is undernourished. There is evidence that the proportion of undernourished women in the poor sector varies markedly in relation to the degree of development of the country analyzed. There is also information showing that within a given sector of the population, the nutritional status among subjects of the same social group may differ (7–9).

The other programatic alternative is to limit coverage to undernourished pregnant women. The rationale for this would be the close association between maternal undernutrition, fetal development retardation, and the observation that fetal growth is linked more to prepregnancy maternal stores than to actual dietary intake during pregnancy. This implies that undernourished pregnant women with low nutritional stores would be unable to maintain adequate fetal growth unless their food intake is substantially increased.

ASSESSMENT OF NUTRITIONAL STATUS

To implement this type of program, a health organization capable of evaluating the nutritional status of pregnant women is required. This underlines the need for targeted programmed health care. The nutritional status of pregnant women can be evaluated through the record of their food intake, anthropometric measurements, and biochemical evaluation, the latter being difficult to perform under field conditions. The weight–height ratio is accepted as the most reliable anthropometric indicator of current status and furthermore is easily determined with the usual tools available to health teams. Prepregnancy weight or the weight corresponding to a certain stage of gestation, which is corrected by the expected weight increase for this period, can also be used. The desirable weight should be selected from patterns established within the environment under study.

A deficient calorie–protein intake can be estimated from the dietary history. Another way to assess this deficiency is by measuring *the weight gain during pregnancy,* which in our opinion, is a useful parameter to evaluate caloric balance. Investigations in this respect have shown a close parallel between weight gain during pregnancy and weight of the newborn (10, 11). Furthermore, it has been established that maternal nutritional status and weight gain during pregnancy may vary independently but when they change in the same direction, their effects on fetal growth are additive.

A criterion useful to select beneficiaries of remedial actions may be to detect undernourished women through the weight–height ratio in the initial examination and/or by comparing weight gains in successive controls. In our country where the prepregnant weight is usually not available and there is a delay in the first medical appointment, we recommend the use of the modified weight–height ratio or corrected index, that is,

$$\text{Corrected index} = \frac{\text{actual weight}}{\text{desirable weight} + \text{expected weight increase for gestational week}}$$

Based on our experience we think that this indicator correlates closely with fetal development, is easy to calculate, is applicable at any age of gestation, permits an early evaluation of the pregnant women's nutritional status, and is a rational basis for nutritional intervention.

Figure 1 presents the relation we found between the corrected index during pregnancy and the average newborn's weight, height, and cranial circumference in 130 pregnant women from a low socioeconomic population. The average value of the three parameters was significantly lower in those women with a lower than normal corrected index (weight $p < .01$, height $p < .05$, cranial circumference $p < .05$). The newborn from the underweight pregnant women, weighed 331 g less than that of infants whose mothers were of normal weight.

SELECTION OF TYPE OF SUPPLEMENT

A second issue is the type of supplementation to be used, based on quantity and quality. This will depend on the requirements of pregnancy per se, on the physiologic adaptation of the fetoplacental unit, and on

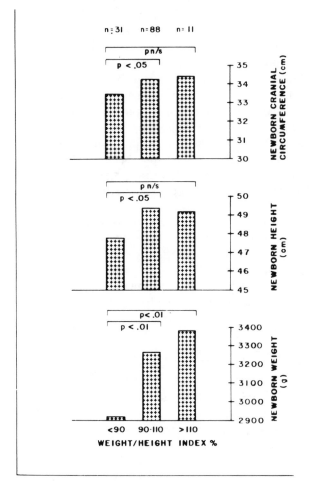

Fig. 1. Pregnant weight–height index and average newborns anthrometrics measurements. Date from Catholic University, Santiago, Chile, 1974–1977.

the nutritional status of the population to be supplemented (in relation to their reserves as well as nutrient intake during pregnancy). Hence, no universal rules can be formulated, and specific actions will have to be planned based on local realities.

There is no agreement as to the effects of maternal vitamin and mineral deficiencies on the fetus. However, deficiencies can be easily solved by therapeutic administration or through fortification programs.

In the case of calorie–protein deficiencies, which are the most common problems, the supplements will have to be adapted in quantity and quality to the local needs. Protein intake has been traditionally stressed, due to observations in animals which showed that protein deficit may retard fetal development (12). Also, malnourished pregnant women retain more nitrogen than expected (13). However, attention has recently been centered on caloric intake. Better understanding of the relation of protein and calorie intake to nitrogen retention has shown that calorie supplementation is as effective as protein in promoting fetal growth. Moreover, available evidence suggests that supplementation with large amounts of protein to women not protein deficient may produce negative effects on fetal growth (3).

WHEN TO SUPPLEMENT

The third issue focuses on when to provide supplementation. Evidence in humans is still inadequate. However, observations on Dutch women exposed to a limited period of extreme caloric deprivation during World War II indicated that the most critical period was the second half of pregnancy (14). More significant were observations suggesting that maternal nutritional stores at the beginning of pregnancy were a factor determining fetal growth (12). Obese women or those with a normal nutritional status were capable within limits of maintaining adequate fetal growth even when their dietary intake becomes deficient during pregnancy. On the other hand, undernourished women with low stores appeared to be unable to maintain adequate fetal growth unless, as already noted, they receive substantial dietary supplementation. We must be aware that preconceptional nutritional intervention may prove necessary for pregnant women to acquire satisfactory nutritional reserves. This observation does not contradict studies showing fetal development retardation under extreme deprivation conditions during pregnancy, which would affect the fetus once a critical maternal reserve level is reached.

Based on the above assertion and on our own epidemiological observation, we believe that, to effectively avoid maternal malnutrition, food supplementation should be provided as early in gestation as possible.

Figure 2 shows the correlation between the daily caloric intake during pregnancy, measured by a weekly recall technique, and the pregnant weight–height index in 122 pregnant women from a low socioeconomic level. No significant correlation was found ($r = .0025$). This illustrates that the adequacy of weight in our pregnant women is not a consequence of the caloric intake during pregnancy and suggests the influence of the prepregnant diet.

Further evidence is given in Table I that the incidence of newborns with low weight (less 2500 g), insufficient weight (2500–3000 g), small

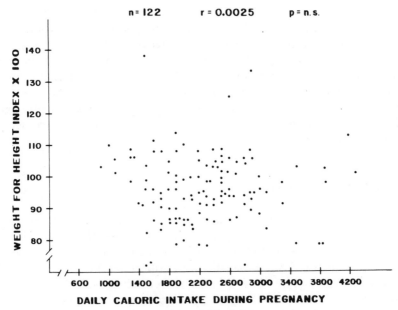

Fig. 2. Correlation between the daily caloric intake during pregnancy and the pregnant weight–height index. Data from southeast health area, Santiago, Chile, 1974–1977.

for gestational age, and premature of low and normal weight for height pregnant women. The incidence of newborns with insufficient weight and "small for date" in the pregnant women with a low weight–height index (45.5 and 15.5%, respectively) is significantly greater ($p < .005$) than in the group with a normal weight–height index (13.7 and 1.1%). No significant difference was found in the incidence of premature and low birth weight newborns. These two findings suggest that the planning of food intervention must be preferentially oriented to obtain an adequate food intake prepregnancy or at least in the early part of pregnancy. Furthermore, the significant correlation found between the low maternal weight for height index and the delay in fetal growth suggest that this group of pregnant women are at the highest nutritional risk and deserve the highest priority for food supplementation.

EVALUATION OF PROGRAM EFFECTIVENESS

Another issue is how to evaluate the effectiveness of nutrition intervention programs during pregnancy. This is fundamental to ensure the maximum efficiency of programs and to introduce modifications when

TABLE I

Maternal Nutritional Status (Weight–Height Index) and Incidence of Insufficient and Low Birth Weight of Small and Premature Newborns[a,b]

Maternal nutritional status	Number of cases	Insufficient birth weight (2500–3000 g)	Low birth weight (< 2500 g)	Small for date	Premature
A. Low weight–height index (less than 90)	33	15 (45.5%)*	4 (12.2%)[†]	5 (15.5%)[‡]	3 (9.15)**
B. Normal weight–height index (90 to 110)	95	13 (13.75)*	3 (3.2%)[†]	1 (1.1%)[‡]	8 (8.4%)**

[a] Data from southeast health area, Santiago, Chile, 1974–1977.
[b] χ^2 between A and B   * = 15.768 $p < .005$, [†] = 3.824 $p < .100$, [‡] = 10.861 $p < .005$, ** = 0.015 n.s.

necessary. Evaluation of nutritional intervention programs for pregnant women has usually been based on their effects on the newborn, using indicators such as weight, maturity, intrauterine growth, postnatal growth, and development. This seems adequate since the fundamental objective is prevention of fetal undernutrition. However, since fetal undernutrition may be caused by many factors and the relative importance of nutrition among them has not yet been defined, it appears useful to evaluate changes in the nutritional status of pregnant women before and after pregnancy. These changes constitute the fundamental nutritional variable and represent an excellent parameter to evaluate the effectiveness of supplementation. Even more so when the concept is that accumulation of reserves during pregnancy is one of the phenomena inherent to optimal conditions for gestation and might also be associated to quality and duration of breast feeding. To reach the biological objectives of food supplementation, it is essential that there is a real increase in nutrient intake of the selected group with the supplement and not a replacement of the daily food usually ingested.

SUPPLEMENTATION DURING LACTATION

We have intentionally left for the end our comments on programs of nutritional intervention aimed at nursing mothers. The information available is scarce, contradictory, and/or of doubtful significance (15). The objectives of a nutrition intervention program for nursing mothers are to protect her nutritional status and to obtain adequate duration and quality of breast feeding. Undoubtedly, breast feeding has a nutritional cost that is reflected in increased nutritional requirements by nursing women. Information regarding the impact of this increase on the nutritional status of nursing mothers of different socioeconomic levels does not agree with estimates of a progressive deterioration of nutritional status of women ingesting diets calculated to be inadequate (16–18). Although within the same socioeconomic level there are individual differences, there is on overall tendency toward more marked nutritional deterioration in groups with lower levels of food intake.

The controversy is even greater when evaluating feeding and nutritional status of nursing mothers related to the length of lactation, as well as to quantity and quality of milk (19).

There is fundamental evidence of changes of fat, fat-soluble vitamins, and water-soluble vitamins levels in the milk of malnourished women. These changes can be corrected by means of caloric and vitamin supplementation. There is inadequate information, however, regarding the significance of these changes for the growth and development of the infant and/or as to their influence on the infant's micronutrient status. In view of this, we consider that nutritional intervention programs for the nursing mother, at present, are mainly based on theoretical considerations and that their evaluation is extremely difficult.

REFERENCES

1. Iygenar, L. Effects of dietary supplements late in pregnancy on the expectant mother and her newborn. *Indian J. Med. Res.* **55**, 85 (1967).
2. Lechtig, A., Delgado, H., Klein, R. E., Yarbrough, C., and Martorell, R. Effect of food supplementation during pregnancy on birthweight. *Pediatrics* **56**, 508 (1975).
3. Osofsky, H. J. Relationships between prenatal medical and nutritional measures, pregnancy outcome, and early infant development in an urban poverty setting. I. Role of nutritional intake. *Am. J. Obstet. Gynecol.* **123**, 682 (1975).
4. Edozien, J. C., Switzer, B. R., and Bryan, R. B. "Medical Evaluation of the Special Supplemental Food Program for Women, Infant and Children," Report. Dept. Nutr. School of Public Health, University of North Carolina, Chapel Hill, 1976.
5. Higgins, A. C., Crampton, E. W., and Mosley, J. E. Nutrition and the outcome of pregnancy *In* "Endocrinology" (R. O. Scow, ed.), p. 1071. Excerpta Medica/Am. Elsevier, Amsterdam, 1973.
6. Workshop on Maternal Nutrition and Infant Health. *Arch. Latinoam. Nutr.* **29**, Suppl. 1 (1979).
7. U.S. Dept. of Health, Education and Welfare. "Nutrition Evaluation of the Population of Central America and Panama 1965–1967, No. 72-8120." USDHEW, Washington, D.C., 1972.
8. U.S. Dept. of Health, Education and Welfare. "Ten State Nutrition Survey 1968–1970," Publ. No. 72-8131. USDHEW, Washington, D.C., 1972.

9. Arteaga, A., Foradori, A., Lira, P., Grebe, G., Vela, P., Cubillos, A. M., Jofre, M. A., Polanco, E., Valenzuela, M., Godoy, S., and Acosta, A. M. Caracteristicas de la alimentacion y estado nutritivo de una poblacion de embarazadas del Area Sur Oriente de Santiago-Chile. *Rev. Med. Chile* **105**, 873 (1977).
10. Thomson, A. M., and Billewicz, W. Z. Clinical significance of weight gain during pregnancy. *Br. Med. J.* **1**, 243 (1957).
11. Eastman, N. J., and Jackson, E. Weight relationships in pregnancy. I. The bearing of maternal weight gain and pre-pregnancy weight on birth weight in full term pregnancies. *Obstet. Gynecol. Surv.* **23**, 1002 (1968).
12. Rosso, P. Effect of maternal dietary restriction during pregnancy on fetal growth and maternal-fetal exchange in the mammalian species. *In* "Nutritional Impacts on Women" (K. Moghissi and T. Evans, eds.), p. 49. Harper & Row, New York, 1978.
13. Johnstone, F. D., MacGillwray, I., and Dennis, K. J. Nitrogen retention in pregnancy. *J. Obstet. Gynaecol Br. Commonw.* **79**, 777 (1972).
14. Smith, C. A. Effect of maternal undernutrition upon the newborn infant in Holland (1944–1945). *J. Pediatr.* **30**, 229 (1947).
15. Thomson, A. M. and Black, A. E. Nutritional aspects of human lactation. *Bull. W.H.O.* **52**, 163 (1965).
16. Shutz, Y., Lechtig, A., and Bradfield, R. B. Energy intakes, energy expenditures, and weight changes of chronically malnourished lactating women in Guatemala. Summary. *Nutr. Transition Proc., West. Hemisphere Nutr. Congr., 5th, 1977* p. 48 (1978).
17. Geisler, C., Calloway, D. H., and Margens, S. Lactation and pregnancy in Iran. *Am. J. Clin. Nutr.* **31**, 341 (1978).
18. Gopalan, C., and Belavady, T. Nutrition and lactation. *Fed. Proc., Fed. Am. Soc. Exp. Biol.* **20**, (1), Part III, Suppl. 7 (1961).
19. Jelliffe, B. D. World trends in infant feeding. *Am. J. Clin. Nutr.* **29**, 1227 (1976).

12 Effectiveness of Supplementary Feeding Programs in Chile

NICOLAS GONZALEZ, ANTONIO INFANTE,
CARLOS SCHLESSINGER, AND FERNANDO
MONCKEBERG

During the last two decades, there has been a significant improvement in the health and nutritional conditions of the infant population in Chile. This is substantiated by both direct and indirect indicators. Twenty years ago, infantile mortality (taken as 100%) decreased in 1980 to 31%. Over the same period, the mortality rate of preschool children (1 to 4 years old) decreased from 7 to 1.2% (Fig. 1). Also during the same period of time, death caused by diarrhea and bronchopneumonia in infants 1 year of age diminished considerably (Fig 2). Today malaria, tetanus neonatorum, and poliomyelitis have virtually been eradicated.

The direct evaluation of nutritional conditions determined by anthropometric measurement confirms that an important decrease in child malnutrition has occurred in Chile. Current weight information from 85% of the children in the country (0–6 years of age) indicates that this percentage has decreased to 11%, which 1.5% was in the category of moderate and severe malnutrition (Table I).

The remarkable progress shown by health indicators during the last two decades has not been paralleled by an equivalent improvement in the socioeconomic development of the country. From 1960 to 1976, the annual economic growth per capita was only 1.3%. Obviously, progress in health and nutrition has surpassed progress achieved in economic development. It should be pointed out though that in the last 3 years the

NUTRITION INTERVENTION STRATEGIES IN NATIONAL DEVELOPMENT

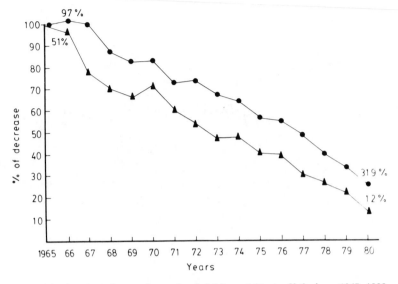

Fig. 1. Decline in infant and preschool child mortality in Chile from 1965–1980.

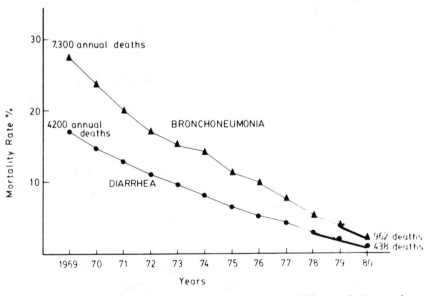

Fig. 2. Deaths due to diarrhea and bronchoneumonias in children under 1 year of age in Chile from 1969–1980.

TABLE I

Percentage of Children under 6 Years of Age with Some Degree of Weight Deficit in Chile (1975–1980)

	1975	1980
Percentage of children with mild under-nutrition	12.1	10.0
Percentage of children with moderate under-nutrition	2.7	1.4
Percentage of children with severe under-nutrition	0.7	0.1
Total	15.5	11.5

economic growth has shown a greater rate of increase. This suggests that the changes observed are due to the nutrition and health intervention programs.

DESCRIPTION OF INTERVENTION PROGRAMS WITH NUTRITIONAL IMPACT

Up to 1951, health interventions programs in Chile were limited, disorganized, and had little coverage. Since that date, and mandated by state law, all the country's health services were merged into the "Servicio Nacional de Salud" (National Health Service), thus initiating a social health system. Since then, and with an adequate financial plan, health and intervention programs were extended to all social strata. Presently, more than 85% of the population is covered by this health system. It is composed of more than 4200 physicians, 2500 registered nurses, 1850 midwives, 750 nutritionists, and a total of 59,274 employees distributed throughout the country (1). The health system has 250 hospitals with a total of 33,400 beds (3.1 bed per 1000 inhabitants) and 1520 Primary Care Centers. Since 1951, the educational system has also improved. Presently there are 7200 primary schools. Illiteracy has decreased to 6%.

Several nutritional and health protection programs have been designed to be implemented through health and educational infrastructures. Collectively, these programs can fully explain the progress achieved.

1. Since 1952, a distribution program through Health Centers was initiated providing powdered milk and/or food enriched with proteins, vitamins, and minerals to all children under 6 years (Table II). Figure 3 shows the amount annually distributed during the last 20 years.

The food is distributed through Primary Care Centers together with promotional and health care programs. These programs, which have improved with time, include growth and development monitoring, nutrition education in healthy feeding, early psychosensorial stimulation, immunization, pregnancy control, etc.

In 1980, 30,700 tons of food were distributed, covering 86% of the country's children under 6 months old (131,000 children), 91% of children between 6 and 23 months (340,000 children), and 79% of children between 2 and 5 years old (780,000 children). Figure 4 shows a close relationship between amounts of food distributed and the number of primary medical care visits. Attendance to Primary Health Centers is noticeably related to the amount of food distributed, which means that both programs are interrelated and complementary.

Obviously, food donation is an important factor leading to the increased coverage in medical care and mother–infant protection programs. Recent evaluations suggest that, depending on the population's social economic level, the medical care coverage increases inversely to the rate that the socioeconomic level decreases (2).

2. Since 1974, another selective food program has been developed through Primary Health Centers that distributes rice, wheat flour, and oil to families with one or more children with or at risk of malnutrition.

TABLE II

Monthly Amount of Food Distributed by the National Health Service to Children at Different Ages

		Composition per 100 gm	
Target group	Type of product and amount	Calories	Proteins (gm)
0–5 months	Milk, 26% fat, 3 kg/month	496	27
6–23 months	Milk, 26% fat, 2 kg/month	496	27
2–5 years	Weaning food, 1½ kg/month	420	20
Pregnant women	Milk, 12% fat, 2 kg/month	410	31.6
Nursing mothers	Milk, 26% fat, 3 kg/month	496	27

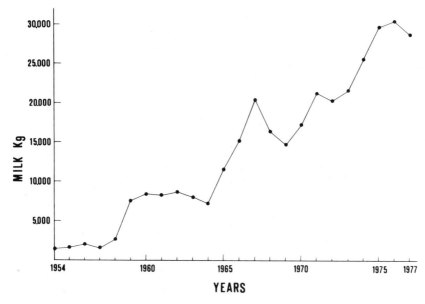

Fig. 3. Amount of powdered milk distributed by the National Health Service to children under 6 years of age.

The amount of food provided surpasses the child's needs. The objective of this program is not only to help the child, but also the family living in poverty-stricken conditions and to improve its nourishment. Families with children suffering from malnutrition are chosen according to the following criteria: (a) children born with low weight (less than 2.5 kg), (b) a deficient weight increase for two consecutive months, (c) children born to a mother under 20 years old, (d) parity of 5 or more, (e) family group with social economic problems. This program utilizes the child with malnutrition as an indicator of a family of greater risk. The amount of food distributed annually through this program has reached 6000 tons.

3. A food distribution program through the Primary Health Centers has been developed to provide powdered milk to pregnant women and nursing mothers. Each pregnant mother receives 2 kg of powdered milk monthly, whereas the nursing mothers receive 3 kg. At present, 70% of the pregnant women in the country are participants (290 thousands women). Figure 5 shows, as in previous programs, a parallel increase in prenatal visits with the amount of milk distributed.

4. Through the health system's structure, the percentage of births in hospitals have gradually increased to 92%. In addition, during the last 5

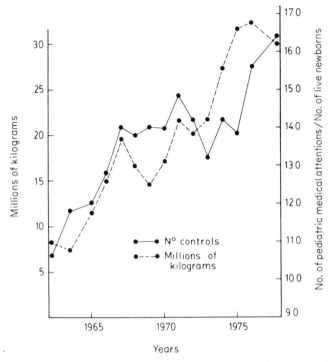

Fig. 4. Children attended by the National Health Service and amounts of milk distributed. As milk distribution increases, there is also an increased utilization of medical services.

years, another program called "Home of the Pregnant Women," has been developed. This program provides for pregnant women living in rural areas far away from hospitals. These women are admitted to such homes 10 to 15 days before delivery and return periodically afterward. The purpose is to assure a normal birth and to provide educational programs. Presently, there are 42 of these homes near maternal hospitals providing for the rural population (20% of the population is rural).

5. During the last 15 years a family planning program has been developed through the health structure. Mothers are advised regarding parental responsibility and methods of spacing births. They are free to choose pills or contraceptive devices and receive them free of charge. The significant decrease in population growth that has occurred indicates the success of this program.

In 1965, the growth rate was 2.8% per year, decreasing in 1979 to 1.6% a year. This occurred in parallel to diminishing malnutrition in the first year of life and to decreasing infantile mortality rates.

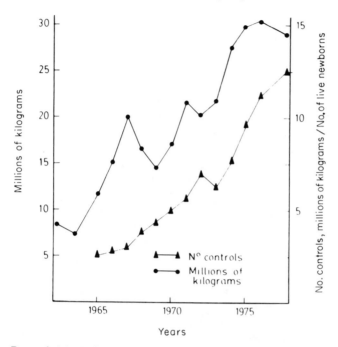

Fig. 5. Prenatal visits and amount of food distributed. As food distribution increases, so does the number of controls of pregnant women.

6. During the last 5 years, another program that treats the child with advanced malnutrition has been started to aid the recovery of children under 2 years of age who have advanced malnutrition. Severe malnutrition beyond infancy has practically disappeared, as malnutrition prevention programs have improved. Today children with protein malnutrition (Kwashiorkor) are seldom seen. Serious malnutrition, however, is seen in children under 1 year old, although the prevalence has declined. In children under 2 years ten thousand cases of serious marasmus, which required hospitalization when complicated by bronchopneumonia or diarrhea, were found in 1970. This condition produced a serious health problem. In 1973, 73% of the infant beds or pediatric hospitals were occupied with children with severe malnutrition. Thirty five percent died in the hospitals. Practically none of them recovered. Readmittance to the hospital was usual or the children died at home. Further studies indicated that a 6 month old with severe malnutrition had only a 15% chance of surviving the first year of life. In the few survivors, the physical and psychological development was seriously impaired (3). With this background data in hand, a treatment

and recovery program for children with severe malnutrition, mostly (90%) under 1 year of age, was started. A private organization was formed (Corporacion para la Nutricion Infantil—CONIN) which, with funds obtained from the organized community, equipped 1500 beds in small hospitals for the exclusive use of the recovery of infants with severe malnutrition. In 1980, this Foundation built, equipped, and started 34 small hospitals, each having 40 to 60 beds. Up to the present, 9200 children have been treated; a mortality rate is now under 2%. This program has made an important contribution toward decreasing the infantile mortality rate. Program costs are covered in part by the Ministry of Health and in part by the CONIN Foundation, which obtains funds from the community. The cost for the recovery of a child are approximately 1000 dollars. The average treatment time is 140 days, which includes both nutritional rehabilitation and affective psychomotor stimulation.

7. During the last 7 years, an educational and psychomotor stimulation program for preschool children in poor areas was started through the Ministry of Education. The objective was to directly help preschool children (2 to 6 years old), who were living in poverty-stricken areas, by changing the negative environment and, in this way, preventing malnutrition. Kindergartens have been built in poor sections of the cities, each accommodating approximately 200 children per day (8 AM–5 PM). There they receive three meals which satisfy the daily nutritional requirements and an educational and psychomotor stimulation program, managed by a specially trained nursery teacher. At present, this program covers 80,000 children and plans are in progress to expand it to 120,000 in the future.

8. The Ministry of Education provides all public schools in the community with a food allowance for children between the ages of 7 to 15 years old. Through this program, 900,000 breakfasts (400 calories) and 250,000 lunches (850 calories) are distributed daily.

GENERAL COMMENTS

Results obtained by all the programs that utilize the existing broad-based health and educational system to obtain a large coverage demonstrate its usefulness in the prevention and treatment of malnutrition in the vulnerable groups. It is important to point out that this success is not only due to the programs of food supplementation, but also to the simultaneous programs of health, nutritional education, and family planning. All of them contribute to the progress achieved in reducing mortality rates and undernutrition.

REFERENCES

1. Monckeberg, F., and Valiente, S. "Antecedentes y acciones para una Política Nacional de Alimentación y Nutrición en Chile. Consejo Nacional para la Alimentación y Nutrición (CONPAN). Gabriela Mistral, Santiago, Chile, 1976.
2. González, N., and Infante A. Programas de alimentación complementaria del sector Salud en Chile. *Bol. Of. Sanito Panam.* **8,** 563 (1980).
3. Monckeberg, F. Malnutrition and mental capacity. *Sci. Publ.—Pan Am. Health Organ.* **251,** 48–54 (1972).

13 Comments on the Supplementary Feeding Programs in Chile

At the onset, it is important to point out the positive aspects of the Suplementary Feeding Programs presently being carried out in Chile. Comments on those aspects that may cause some doubts to arise or require a clarification will be discussed later in this chapter. Some changes aimed at improvements will also be suggested.

One of the most interesting aspects of these programs is the conceptual framework. They operate not as isolated projects but within the context of the food and nutrition policies established by the Chilean National Food and Nutrition Council [Consejo Nacional para la Alimentación y la Nutrición (CONPAN)]. It is not unusual to observe in developing countries that implementation of this type of program, even those with wide population coverage, is not preceded by adequate planning within the context of national development. Planning in this latter context would certainly allow better adjustment to the requirements of the problems, to the target population, and to the institutional, financial, technical, and administrative resources available. Improvisation has also been frequently stimulated by agencies donating food, which, despite their best intentions, initiate distribution programs through connections with public or private entities not always linked to government planning. As a result, they follow policies and regulations of their own, which frequently do not adjust to those of the recipient country.

CONPAN has planned its programs adequately. This process has included identification of food and nutrition problems and of the nutritional implications of current policies, formulation of well-defined food

NUTRITION INTERVENTION STRATEGIES IN NATIONAL DEVELOPMENT
Copyright © 1983 by Academic Press, Inc.
All rights of reproduction in any form reserved.
ISBN 012-709080-0

and nutrition policies, identification of weak points and bottlenecks in the existing plans, identification of the most vulnerable population groups, and establishment of specific objectives, quantifiable goals, and multisectorial information systems. Adequate follow-up and evaluation of these programs has been thus ensured. Specific food and nutrition projects formulated by CONPAN have been incorporated into the plans for national development and are already being implemented. They aim at introducing favorable modifications in the production, marketing, consumption, and biological utilization of food. The target of these nutritional intervention programs are the population groups with highest risks.

The supplementary food programs in Chile appear, therefore, as one of several coordinated interventions directed to ensure the health, nutrition, and welfare status of the population, particularly for those groups with higher risk because of socioeconomic, biological, or environmental conditions. Furthermore, these programs are closely linked to the expansion and improvement of the national mother–child health program, which included medical care, inmunization, health education, and environmental sanitation. These are important to ensure optimal utilization of nutrients.

Another positive aspect worth emphasizing is the critical analyses and reorientation of the supplementary feeding programs being carried out. Throughout many years of operation obstacles for the attainment of the objectives have been identified in these programs. One of these is the utilization of half skimmed milk, which has proved inadequate to cover the caloric requirements of infants while it exceeds their protein needs. Other problems such as lactose intolerance in a high percentage of children, inadequate packing of the milk, inefficient distribution systems, and intrafamilial dilution of the food intended for mothers and infants have been identified and practical measures taken to solve them. This has resulted in significant modifications of the programs, including distribution of milk with higher fat content, improvement of containers and product presentation, acidification of milk to increases its reaching the target children, fortification with iron, distribution of rations that do not require elaboration, etc. It is worthy of mention that those individuals responsible for these programs have not routinized their approach and techniques. On the contrary, they have shown dynamism and resolution to modify actions that proved to lack efficiency and to actively search for the best solutions.

One aspect that is considered important is the identification of vulnerable population groups, for which different specific strategies have been created and put into operation, ensuring greater efficacy for each group. Six nutritional interventions programs aimed at these groups of population have been implemented:

1. Supplementary Feeding Programs developed by the National Health Service.
2. Preschool child day care centers in areas of extreme poverty.
3. Nutritional, psychomotor, and social rehabilitation of infants with severe malnutrition in Closed Nutritional Recovery Centers.
4. Rehabilitation of children with advanced malnutrition in their home environment.
5. School feeding programs.
6. Food supplementation to beneficiaries of the Minimum Employment Program.

Among these interventions are two particularly preventive approaches oriented at providing nutritional protection to specific population groups with high risk: (1) the preschool child day-care centers in areas of extreme poverty, in which children not only received food but also psychological and social stimulation, affection, and health care, which they would not receive in their home environment because of adverse socioeconomic conditions of their family; (2) the supplementation program for beneficiaries of the Minimum Employment Program, through which a minimal salary adjusted to the increases in the cost of living, as well as food, are provided to the unemployed while he seeks employment. The aim is to avoid deterioration of the nutritional status of the family during periods of unemployment.

There is another interesting and positive aspect of the Chilean supplementary feeding programs which should be discussed. This is the active coordinated participation which public and private institutions from Chile, foreign agencies (CARITAS, CARE, OFASA), and international organization such as PIA/PNAN (Interagency Program for National Food and Nutritional Policies) PAHO, AID, and others have had in the planning, implementation, and reorientation of these policies. Indeed this is a valuable characteristic of these programs, which ensures their orientation and progress through the coordinated participation of CON-PAN, the University of Chile, the Catholic University of Valparaiso, the Institute of Nutrition and Food Technology (INTA), the Institute for the Promotion of Fishing of CORFO [Corporación de Fomento de la Producción (Corporation for the Promotion of Production)], the National Health Service, the Ministry of Education, the Women's Secretariat, CONIN [Corporación para la Nutrición Infantil (Chilean Nutrition Foundation)], the mother centers, and private food industries. Through coordination with the latter, the programs have become an effective stimulus for the development of the country's economy, and this is a positive element within the Food and Nutrition Systems.

There are, however, some controversial aspects of these programs. For example, it appears that the community has not sufficient active participation in the development of the Supplementary Feeding Programs. The community receives food and the input of educational actions but participates very little, if at all, in specific program actions. There are various aspects of the Chilean programs in which the community could be a valuable resource for program development and even for decreasing program costs. Among these aspects can be mentioned the transportation of food from warehouses to the communities (especially in far way places), storage repackaging and final distribution of rations, control of their receipt prior to meal preparation, cleaning and maintenance of utensils and facilities, care of children, etc. All this can be accomplished through community voluntary "nutrition groups." Small periodic contributions of money or goods by members of the community may be low when considering individually but represents, when considered in total, valuable local resources for the programs.

In countries where there is active and organized participation of the community in the implementation of programs, the following objectives have been proposed:

1. Elimination of paternalism. Despite its limited contributions to defray the cost of the program, the community should feel that the program is theirs, that it is not a gift or something being forced from the outside.

2. Establishment of efficient control of the program at the local level. Because the participating community considers the program as its own, it is more watchful of development, of failures or omissions, and makes important contributions to the orientation and supervision of its activities.

3. Creation of a spirit of cooperation. Because the community participates with local health and educational services there is established a greater receptivity toward similar programs.

4. Establishment of modest operation funds administered by the health services or the community, which are utilized to improve the infrastructure of the program and to pay for some inputs or even salaries of the auxiliary personnel.

Positive results have already been observed when the community participates in the development of nutrition programs, results which are accepted, supported, and defended with great enthusiasm. The developmental potential represented by the community is enormous. It is a resource which must always be utilized to a maximum, because of the beneficial collateral effects that it triggers. In supplementary feeding programs of this type in Colombia, covering nearly 2 million mothers and children, approximately 35,000 community volunteers have cooperated, supported, and defended their programs. A cost evaluation carried out some years ago revealed that 30% of the national funding of the program came from small contributions from the communities.

Another problem of the Chilean supplementary feeding program is the actual utilization of the foodstuffs provided. This type of program has two main drawbacks which may interfere with its objective of narrowing the food consumption gap in the target population. One of these drawbacks is dilution, i.e., the consumption by other members of the family of foodstuffs intended for mothers and children; there are several studies on program modifications that make it possible to counteract dilution problems. The other problem is substitution, i.e., the decrease in the family budget of expenditures for food being received from a supplementation program. This is one of the most serious obstacles to the adequate coverage of the nutritional needs of intended beneficiaries. However, this effect seems to have been the subject of very little consideration. It is important, therefore, to determine the percentage of substitution in families covered by the program and the relationship to income levels in order to establish the true efficiency of the program and provide guidance in the application of corrective measures.

Furthermore, more detailed knowledge is needed of the specific objectives and aims of each one of the six types of programs, the methodology employed to evaluate their effects, and their cost/benefit ratio. This information would allow for comparative evaluations of the various programs and their systematic and periodic reorientation.

Still another aspect which deserves comment is the unfavorable effect which the Supplementary Feeding Programs have had on breast feeding. The decline in breast feeding in Chile has been and presently is a matter of serious concern for the country's pediatricians and nutritionists. Therefore, it would be useful to learn what the actual situation is, whether the tendency toward early weaning has continued, and what measures have been taken to counteract it. This is important because of the detrimental effect of early weaning on the physical and psychological development of the infant, particularly, in those population groups of low socioeconomic level.

After referring to the favorable and unfavorable aspects of the programs a comment on their costs is warranted. We have no information on the exact figures but we understand that costs are very high. One of the greatest criticisms to these types of programs is the exceptionally heavy financial burden they represent for the country. However, we assume that this enormous effort is adequately planned, and implemented and that it accomplishes its objectives of improving the nutritional status of the target population, then the costs have a clear social justification. This is not always recognized by the economic planners who have generally been more interested in so-called "productive projects."

Economic and social planners need to be aware that the impact of the supplementary feeding programs, especially those directed to mothers and children, is not only reflected in the complete development of the genetic potential for physical growth and mental development but also generate socioeconomic progress in other important areas:

1. In the health sector, through a decrease in mortality and morbidity, especially among younger children and, therefore, a concomitant reduction of medical care costs.

2. In the educational sector by improvement of school attendance and learning capacity of children, thus making possible the attainment of higher educational levels. This, is turn, increases the efficiency of Government investments in this area. At present, a significant percentage of these expenditures is lost because of school desertion, decreased learning capacity, etc., due to malnutrition.

3. In the agricultural and industrial sectors, through adequate nutrition of the workers, which is reflected in increased productivity.

Although it has not been easy to determine the magnitude of the final affects of the food and nutrition programs in the general economy of countries, it may be assumed that improved nutrition and health of the population increase the possibilities of higher family incomes, which thereby stimulates the national economy. Furthermore, it has been widely recognized that balanced diet and good nutrition are fundamental human rights and a component of the "quality of life." The high priority assigned to Supplementary Feeding Programs in the National Development Plan in Chile is certainly a demonstration of the technical capabilities, foresight, and breadth of scope of the Chilean planners in the solution of the problems of underdevelopment.

14 Case Study of a National Supplementary Feeding Program: The WIC Program in the United States*

JOHANNA DWYER

INTRODUCTION

The Women, Infants, and Children (WIC) program is one of the most politically successful nutritional intervention programs in the history of the United States. This special supplemental food program for women, infants, and children authorizes payment of cash grants from the federal government's Department of Agriculture to state health departments and approved local health clinics. The purpose is to provide special nutritious food supplements to low income pregnant or lactating women, to infants, and to children who have not reached their fifth birthday and who are considered to be in danger of malnutrition.

In order to qualify for the program, several criteria must be met. First, individuals must be pregnant women, lactating, or up to 6 months postpartum or infants and children in low income groups. Second, they must be certified to need food supplements because of poor nutritional status or related characteristics that are thought to predispose them to malnutrition. Third, in some states, they must reside in an approved WIC project area. Finally, they must be eligible for free or reduced cost medical treatment by the approved agency (77).

The WIC program provides certain foods (or vouchers which can be

*With the assistance of Nan Allison and Christine Larsen.

NUTRITION INTERVENTION STRATEGIES IN NATIONAL DEVELOPMENT
Copyright © 1983 by Academic Press, Inc.

redeemed for specific foods) on a monthly basis. Those foods are to be used as supplements to the diet of participating individuals. In addition, participants receive nutrition education and referral for diagnosis, surveillance, or treatment of health related problems. Table I presents a list of foods that are currently provided and selected nutrients contained as a percentage of the recommended dietary allowances.

In this chapter, WIC's history will be presented and the major strengths and weaknesses as revealed by various evaluation efforts will be discussed. In addition, possible object lessons that may be drawn from this case study for planning nutrition-related interventions will be highlighted.

HISTORY

If government programs were people, a biography of WIC would make a fine fairy tale. Conceived in poverty during a period of great civil unrest in the late 1960s, the program was frequently at risk of induced abortion. Born at last in 1972 in an undernourished state, WIC was subjected to extensive periods of failure to thrive in infancy. Her childhood nutritional status was poor, growing up as an unwelcome Cinderella in a house increasingly divided against itself. But just as she was about to wilt away, Prince Charming in the form of an ex-presidental candidate rescued WIC and showered her with riches. Emerging as a favored program supported by Congress, nutritionists, public health professionals, and formula companies, WIC experienced a precocious puberty full of exuberance. Now an older and wiser young woman, WIC exhibits increasing wisdom in her decisions, with only an occasional lapse into braggadocio and overspending of operating budgets. WIC appeared to be fondly regarded and seemed assured of a secure place in the American community of food and health programs until 1981, when with a change of administration in the federal government, the need for the program again began to be questioned. Surely, such a saga is the stuff of which soap operas are made (50).

Background

By government definition, an individual or a family is declared to be poor if total cash income falls below the so-called "poverty line." The poverty line is calculated by computing the cost of a minimally adequate diet as formulated in the economy food plans issued periodically by the

TABLE I

Percentage of Recommended Dietary Allowances (1980) for Selected Nutrients Provided per Day from Sample WIC Food Packages[a]

	Children						Women					
	0–3 Months		4–12 Months		1–5 Years		Pregnant		Breast-feeding		Postpartum	
Nutrient	Amount	%	Amount	%	Amount	%	Amount	%	Amount	%	Amount	%
Energy (calories)	533	77	660	72	898	64	980	41	930	36	753	36
Protein (g)	12	92	15	88	39	156	45	60	43	65	34	74
Total fat (g)	28	—	29	—	40	—	52	—	38	—	32	—
Saturated fat (g)	0	—	0	—	17	—	25	—	21	—	17	—
Unsaturated fat (g)	0	—	0	—	1	—	14	—	13	—	11	—
Cholesterol (mg)	8	—	8	—	324	—	351	—	344	—	324	—
Carbohydrate (g)	57	—	84	—	100	—	88	—	108	—	86	—
Sugar (g)	0	—	0	—	2	—	3	—	2	—	2	—
Fiber (g)	0	—	0	—	0	—	0	—	0	—	0	—
Ash (g)	0	—	0.8	—	6.	—	7	—	6	—	5	—
Vitamin A (IU)	1959	139	2147	107	3221	161	3529	71	3420	57	3032	76
Vitamin C (mg)	43	123	81	232	131	290	128	160	131	131	93	155
Vitamin D (IU)	315	79	315	79	363	91	257	43	377	63	363	91
Vitamin E (IU)	13	296	13	231	0	0	0	0	0	0	0	0
Niacin (mg)	6	92	14	179	10	99	10	61	8	41	7	51
Thiamine (mg)	0.5	170	1.2	248	1.0	123	0.9	61	1	69	0.9	82
Riboflavin (mg)	0.8	196	1.4	242	2.0	229	1.8	110	2.0	115	1.9	145
Folacin (mg)	78.	262	85	198	78	61	75	9	101	20	64	16

(continued)

TABLE I *Continued*

Nutrient	Children						Women					
	0–3 Months		4–12 Months		1–5 Years		Pregnant		Breast-feeding		Postpartum	
	Amount	%	Amount	%	Amount	%	Amount	%	Amount	%	Amount	%
Vitamin B$_6$ (mg)	0.32	105	0.40	71	0.96	96	0.90	35	0.99	40	0.9	48
Vitamin B$_{12}$ (µg)	1.18	235	1.175	86	5.13	256	4.71	118	5.38	135	5.14	171
Iron (mg)	9.4	94	26.5	184	12.2	87	12.5	70	13.0	72	11.6	64
Calcium (mg)	400	111	587	113	1000	125	1120	70	1157	72	982	82
Phosphorus (mg)	306	127	421	122	950	119	1016	64	1060	66	869	72
Magnesium (mg)	32	65	58	86	114	71	98	22	123	27	114	38
Zinc (mg)	3.9	131	4.6	98	4.3	44	5.3	26	4.5	18	3.9	26
Copper (mg)	0.5	66–94	0.6	60–84	0.1	3–4	0.1	1–2	0.1	1–2	0.05	1–2
Potassium (mg)	610	66–174	886	72–213	1889	104–312	1558	34–102	1995	44–131	1597	35–105
Sodium (mg)	194	55–168	206	30–89	889	83–250	1133	42–126	913	34–101	802	30–89
Iodine (µg)	83	207	83	170	0	0	0	0	0	0	0	0

[a] Sample food items upon which intakes were calculated for infants 0–3 months were Similac with iron, 403 fl oz per month. For infants 4–12 months, the same formula, 24 oz dry barley cereal and 92 fl oz orange juice, used in calculations. Children 1–5 years of age were assumed to consume 24 qt whole milk, 36 oz corn cereal, 276 fl oz orange juice, 2 dozen eggs, and 18 oz peanut butter with their WIC supplement. For pregnant women, the supplement assumed consisted of 16 qt whole milk, 64 oz cheddar cheese, 36 oz corn cereal, 276 oz orange juice, 2 doz eggs, and 18 oz peanut butter. For breast-feeding women, similar foods were consumed with 16 oz pinto beans being substituted for peanut butter. For postpartum women, the supplement was assumed to contain 24 qt milk, 36 oz corn cereal, 184 oz orange juice, and 2 doz eggs.

United States Department of Agriculture (74). The costs of food are then multiplied 3 times* to allow for other basic expenses and further adjustments are made for family size and other factors. Those whose cash incomes fall below this figure are considered to be poor.

During the Great Depression of the 1930s, as many as one-half of the citizens of the United States were poor as judged by today's standards. By the 1940s the figure had fallen to perhaps 25%, and by the late 1950s it had decreased to approximately 20% (17). With the advent of the "Great Society" and the War on Poverty of the mid-1960s, the notion of eliminating poverty altogether became popular.

During the spate of legislation enacted early in the Johnson administration, government spending on public welfare measures of direct benefit to families and individuals increased dramatically. Legislation was enacted which increased public welfare benefits for the middle class by Social Security, pensions to retired government workers, medical care for the elderly, educational benefits, unemployment insurance, veterans' benefits, hospital construction, and other medical programs. At the same time other large government spending programs were also directed toward the poor. Public spending for the poor increased the most in in-kind benefits and subsidies rather than in direct cash income transfers. These in-kind transfers included surplus food commodities, Medicaid, and social services, to mention only a few.

Impetus to Public Policy

Food and feeding programs for children first become popular when, during World Wars I and II, the poor physical status secondary to poor nutrition of some recruits was attributed to poor nutrition (47). From the early 1960s onward, national attention focused increasingly on the relatively unfavorable ranking of the nation in comparison to many other highly industrialized countries with respect to the outcomes of pregnancy and infant mortality (9). At the same time the realities of poverty-related malnutrition and ill health permeated the national consciousness (23, 40). Of special concern were poor minority groups living in big cities and rural areas in the South and Southwest.

In the late 1960s several large scale surveys of nutritional status had been launched. Preliminary results indicated that a significant proportion of infants and children were smaller than expected and that size, growth, and development of preschool children were positively associ-

---

*In earlier years the USDA determined that a family of three persons or more spent approximately one-third of its income on food; hence the multiplier of 3.

ated with indices of socioeconomic status (28, 57, 83). Inadequate iron intakes were common, and risk of iron deficiency anemia was found to be especially high among children 1 to 2 years of age. Dietary data suggested that undernutrition was the result of decreased food intakes and not solely due to inappropriate food choices. It was unclear whether these mild and moderate forms of undernutrition affected subsequent intellectual development of infants and children, but some experts were concerned that the effects might be adverse (34, 62). The surveys also identified very poor pregnant women and children, migrant workers, and Native Americans as especially vulnerable groups from the standpoint of nutritional status (67, 75, 76, 82, 83).

Other studies indicated that nutritional factors, especially those influencing the weight status of the pregnant woman, were associated with the incidence of low birth weight (53, 55). Socioeconomic characteristics, prenatal care and the prevalence of health problems were also found to be correlated with pregnancy outcomes (10, 38). The elimination of preventable problems in the preconceptional and prenatal periods was thought to have the potential for significantly reducing low birth weight and other poor outcomes of pregnancy (46).

Events that focused public attention on malnutrition and hunger among the poor included the 1967 investigative hearings of the Senate Committee on Employment, Manpower, and Poverty in Jackson, Mississippi, chaired by Senators Robert Kennedy and Joseph Clark, a popular book by Michael Harrington entitled *The Other America* on the plight of the poor, CBS television's documentary on "Hunger in America," a report by a special Citizens' Board of Inquiry entitled "Hunger, USA," and a critical study of the school lunch program by a consortium of women's voluntary groups entitled "Their Daily Bread."

By the end of the 1960s sentiment for acting to remedy these problems was widespread. Frequent meetings between officials in the USDA, the department responsible for surplus food distribution programs, and officials in HEW, the department responsible for most of the other health, social services, and welfare programs, were devoted to discussions of possible government actions which might be taken, but progress slowed after the 1968 presidential election. One possible measure was a supplementary food and health program.

On the international level there were a number of precedents for a food supplementation program for poor pregnant women and young children which were delivered in a health setting and linked closely to health and educational services. Perhaps the best known of these to American policymakers was the program at the Royal Victoria Hospital in Toronto, which had operated with considerable success for several decades (31, 65).

Programs to improve the nutritional status of pregnant women, infants, and children were also in existence in the private and voluntary sectors before the turn of the century in the United States. Some of these early efforts combined the provision of health care and food supplements. Public sector programs involving nutrition interventions were not linked in this manner, however. They were more categorical in nature, providing income assistance, surplus commodities, health services, or the like, usually with differing eligibility requirements for each benefit. The notion of a combination of food supplements and nutrition education delivered along with health services in the health care system appealed to cabinet level officials in both agencies, and plans were laid for launching demonstrations of the concept in 1968. However, these plans received a setback in the shift from Democratic to Republican control of the executive branch of government, while both houses of Congress remained in Democratic hands.

The White House Conference on Food, Nutrition, and Health of 1969 (78) further focused national attention on the plight of the poor and other nutritionally vulnerable groups and called for action to better their status. The Senate Select Committee on Nutrition and Human Needs became increasingly active with a membership that included some of the most distinguished Democrats and Republicans in the Senate. It continued to hold hearings and to issue news bulletins on the topic.

With the Vietnam War expanding inexorably and the advent of the Republican Nixon administration in 1969, the public welfare policies of the previous Democratic administrations were called into question. Because there was a great deal of public pressure to expand benefits in nutritional and health areas, these issues were subjected to particular scrutiny. The major debates centered on the number of poor people in the country, who among them were malnourished, and appropriate government actions to achieve greater equity and an adequate standard of living for all while assuring program efficiency and incentives for self-help.

By 1969 about 24.1 million persons or approximately 12.1% of the population of the United States were living in poverty using a definition of poverty which included real income plus direct cash income transfers.* However, the contention that in order to assure all citizens a minimally adequate standard of living, the "income deficit" of the poor (e.g., the difference between the income needed to exceed the poverty line and actual cash income) had to be made up by additional income

---

*By 1979 25.2 million or 11.6% of the population were living in poverty. Rates vary greatly by race, sex, and family size, being highest in families headed by a woman and among blacks.

transfers was challenged on definitional as well as philosophical grounds. The definitional criticism centered on whether, in addition to cash income, subsidies and payments of in-kind services, such as Medicaid or commodity foods, should also be counted in estimating the size of the gap between what poor people needed in contrast to what they actually received. The government's calculation of the poverty line included only the cash income of the poor from work or from direct government cash subsidy. In 1969 in-kind transfers accounted for approximately 16% of the government's expenditures on the poor. By 1975 these had risen to about 30% of all expenditures. If in-kind as well as cash payments were counted, the calculated income deficit of the average poor person in 1969 would have fallen by nearly one-sixth, and in 1975 it would have fallen by nearly one-third (17). Using both in-kind and cash payments as the criterion, the number of persons in poverty would have declined from approximately 24.1 million persons to a smaller but indeterminate number.

The definition of malnutrition was also widely debated. Some inferred that all of the poor who fell below the "poverty line" were suffering from malnutrition, whereas others claimed that only a small proportion were affected. This definitional problem was the subject of much acrimonious discussion. Different, more specific criteria were proposed by some experts as being better and more conservative indices for estimating the extent of malnutrition among the poor. Table II summarizes estimates of the prevalence of malnutrition, which varied by 10-fold depending upon the index that was used.

Another issue, which was widely debated in the late 1960s, involved how differences between the states in welfare benefits could be reduced. The various states differ in the extent to which they make welfare benefits available. In high welfare benefit states, such as New York and California, the poor receive more income assistance than they do in low welfare benefit states, such as most of those in the South. When in-kind assistance was added to cash welfare payments provided by some high welfare benefit states, some of those in poverty often fared better than persons immediately above the poverty line who were ineligible for both types of benefits. Such a situation was thought to act as a disincentive to the poor to better their state.

The Nixon administration's response to these problems was to study large-scale welfare reform measures which established minimum guaranteed income payments on a national basis for the poor and eliminated in-kind programs.

By 1970 the administration and the Congress were increasingly preoccupied with growing civil unrest at home, the demands of the Vietnam

TABLE II

Estimated Extent of Malnutrition Using Various Indices in the United States Poverty Population 1969[a]

Indicator of malnutrition	Estimate of poor persons affected (%)	Number of persons (millions)
Below poverty line	100	24.3 (or approximately 12% of the entire population)
Clinical signs[b]	Fewer than 4	Fewer than 1
Biochemically at risk[c]	38	9
With "poor" diets[d]	36	9
Unable to meet food needs without spending 50% or more of income on food[e]	44	11

[a] Adapted from Wilson (79, p. 130).

[b] Based on preliminary findings of the Ten State Nutrition Survey in the low income population of four states with respect to certain physical signs associated with primary or secondary malnutrition.

[c] Based on preliminary data from the Ten State Nutrition Survey in Texas. Indicates the number of poor with two or more biochemical values unacceptable.

[d] Based on US Department of Agriculture data.

[e] Food needs are defined as the cost of the USDAs economy food plan.

war abroad, and rising deficits in the federal budget. Bold proposals by the new administration for wholesale welfare reform based on an income maintenance program, which would eliminate in-kind and categorical forms of public assistance, were foundering. Federal officials took a jaundiced view toward the expansion of in-kind transfer programs in specific and more generally to any new programs which might increase federal expenditures in the poverty field until reform was achieved. Yet public pressure to doing something about the nutritional status of the poor continued to mount, to which the administration responded by considering the possibility of demonstration projects.

The Rocky Road to Implementation

A history of legislation and significant political events from the planning stages of WIC in the late 1960s until today is provided in Table III and has also been described elsewhere (49, 60). Briefly described, the road to implementation involved a classical struggle between a loose coalition of liberal Democrats and Republicans in Congress led by Sena-

TABLE III

History of Legislation, Regulatory Decisions, and Politics Involving the Women, Infants, and Children's Supplemental Food Program (WIC)

Date	Stage	Significant legislation, regulations, and political events
Mid- to late 1960s	Notion of special food supplements for pregnant and lactating women and infants proposed	• Senate Select Committee on Nutrition and Human Needs established and begins hearings. • Widespread public concern about poverty-related malnutrition in the United States and the country's relatively poor standing with respect to infant mortality in comparison to other wealthy countries. • 1969. Pilot Commodity Supplemental Food Program launched for pregnant women and young infants by USDA. Since the program was not mandated by direct legislative action, USDA exerted complete control over program regulations, levels of funding, and the commodities which were supplied. • The program made certain surplus agricultural commodities available to those certified to be in nutritional need in these groups. Commodities varied, but all were high in nutritional value and appropriate for supplementing the diets of mothers and infants in energy, protein, and certain vitamins. The value of the surplus commodities was approximately $120 per capita per year. Storage costs and administrative costs of distributing the food were not provided by the program. Frequently, distribution costs were financed by the Emergency Food and Medical Services Program of the Office of Economic Opportunity (OEO) in the Executive Office of the President.
1970, 1971	Experiments and administrative delays in implementation of pilot programs	• Surveys of the nutritional status and health of the poor revealed that malnutrition problems were more common among them than had previously been expected. • Racial and ethnic minorities appeared to be particularly vulnerable nutritionally. • 1970. Pilot Food Certificate Program (PFCP) for milk to pregnant women and baby formula and cereals to young infants begins. Script or vouchers which could be redeemed for specified foods rather than the foods themselves were distributed. • Program is tested in five sites and simultaneously evaluated. • 1971. Evaluation indicates that recipients and providers are enthusiastic about PFCP. However, food supplements provided were found to be substituted for foods normally purchased, and consumption of desired foods was not greatly increased. These findings were taken to indicate that the program was of dubious value to the target groups. Program expenses were also claimed to be high. On these grounds, the PFCP program was discontinued. • 1971. Commodity Supplemental Food Program funds frozen at current levels, supplies of surplus commodities dwindle, and funds for distributing foods formerly available from OEO are curtailed. Other regulations restrict program only to counties which do not receive food stamps.

1972	Congress steps in	•Senate Select Committee on Nutrition and Human Needs continues to hold hearings on malnutrition, especially among low income pregnant women and children in the South. •Senator Hubert Humphrey introduces amendment to pending school lunch legislation to provide nutritious food to low income pregnant and lactating women and children up to age 4 on the basis of reports of malnutrition among these groups. This becomes the basis for the WIC program. •Amendment passes Senate and is agreed to in conference with the House of Representatives, even though the House has not considered the issue.
1972	Congress steps in	•1972. Pilot women, infants, and children's supplemental food program for pregnant and lactating women and infants authorized by PL92-433 (National School Lunch Act and Child Nutrition Act of 1966 Amendments). Two years were funded at $20 million per year. Pregnant or lactating women or infants who were determined by competent professionals to be nutritional risks were eligible in pilot program sites. Evaluation components were also mandated. 10% of total program costs were permitted for administrative purposes. Direct provision of food supplements in clinics, home delivery of supplements and vouchers for supplements were all to be tested. USDA and the General Accounting Office were required to submit evaluations within 2 years of both the medical and administrative aspects of the program.
1972	USDA attempts to transfer and later to delay the program	•USDA attempts to transfer pilot program to HEW because of inadequate staffing for medical evaluation. HEW refuses to accept transfer because of difficulties involved in administering food program component which would remain under USDA's authority. •USDA proposes to complete evaluation studies before spending monies for demonstration projects not involved in the medical or administrative evaluation studies. Advocacy and public interest groups bring lawsuit against USDA to force the agency to spend all funds, which eventually was successful.
1973	Congress and advocacy groups insist upon implementation	•USDA retains responsibility for WIC and delays allocation of funds. Task force on program development convened by USDA in early 1973. USDA delays issuing regulations and processing grant applications. •Law suits initiated by public interest and advocacy groups force USDA to carry over unspent funds from 1973 into 1974. Further legal actions by the same groups finally force USDA to announce all 255 program grants before January 1, 1974. However, only 6 months now remained before funds authorized for 1973 and 1974 fiscal year were due to expire. •In order to comply with the court order, USDA officials rush to fund 143 programs. •Only one-half of the programs were actually operating by the end of the 2-year pilot phase.
1974		•In January, 1974 the first WIC recipients actually received food.

(continued)

TABLE III *Continued*

Date	Stage	Significant legislation, regulations, and political events
1974	Rapid expansion forced by Congress	•Congress doubles yearly funding for 1975, extends dates for evaluations through rapid expansion legislation (PL93-150). Indian tribes permitted to administer program at the local level. USDA approves large number of programs. Case loads escalate.
		•Congress increases funding levels for 1975 to $100 million in order to avoid cuts in caseloads through passage of PL93-326.
		•USDA continues conservative program management, issuing regulations insisting that the program only be administered by health clinics and refusing to certify welfare agencies, maintaining existing eligibility and cut-off requirements, and refusing to reimburse agencies for nutrition education expenses.
		•Advocates of program continued to press Congress to be more specific in legislation to prevent USDA from overly narrow interpretations of legislative intent in regulations.
		•Congress enacts legislation which forces the executive branch to spend funds for programs which have been authorized unless Congressional consent is obtained for impoundment.
1975	Evaluations of pilot WIC programs completed with ambiguous results	•Two evaluations of the pilot program dealing with medical and administrative aspects of WIC were completed. Results were positive, but most programs were still in the start up phase.
		•President Nixon resigns.
1975	Congress becomes specific and provides clear directives to USDA	•Additional legislation passed by Congress over President Ford's veto, appropriations to $250 million per year. Twenty percent of total program costs were permitted to be used for administrative costs, and three months of start-up costs were paid by USDA for new programs. Nutrition education services were mandated, to be paid for out of administrative costs. Eligibility extended to children up to five years of age and postpartum women who were not breast feeding until 6 months.
1975		•WIC program stated as being supplementary to other food programs, and directed toward the family rather than in lieu of other food programs. USDA was required to insure that program was extended to those most in need.
		•WIC advisory committees established: an expert committee to successfully evaluate the health benefits of the supplemental feeding program in economical fashion, and an expert committee to continue studies of WIC and other diet supplementation programs. Annual reports of advisory committees required by Congress.
		•Lawsuit by public interest groups over delays and failures of USDA to appropriate funds results in an order for the agency to report to the court quarterly on progress in WIC implementation and monies spent.

1976	Continued battles over WIC implementation between Congress and USDA	•USDA forced to spend left over funds from 1975 and 1976 fiscal years and to make greater efforts to serve those most in need (Durham vs. Butz, Civil Action 76-358). •President Jimmy Carter elected. •WIC advocates appointed to high office within USDA.
1977	USDA adopts a supportive posture but concerns about costs continued	•First results of WIC child health surveillance program of the Center for Disease Control, US Public Health Service, released. •USDA issues regulations specifying that existing state agency income criteria for eligibility in health programs could apply to WIC. Both poverty and nutritional risk were required for eligibility. Nutritional need determinations gave priority to those whose anthropometric indices or biochemical tests were indicative of malnutrition, with lower priority for those who exhibited only inadequate dietary intakes. Only if approved caseload registers had available places could the latter groups be accepted. •States were permitted to choose between three WIC distribution systems (direct food package distribution, home delivery of foods, or vouchers for retail purchase, but all programs within a state were required to use the same system). States were further required to develop plans using income and health criteria, for areas most in need of new programs. Priorities were set favoring health clinics as local agencies.
1978	WIC expands further and targets efforts toward the most vulnerable	•Office of Management and Budget objects to costs of program and further expansion. •WIC is authorized for 4 additional years at $550 million for 1979, $800 million guaranteed for 1980, $900 million for 1982 budgeted with passage of PL95-627. •Monies set aside for evaluation of program performance and health. •Administrative costs funded at 20% of program funds, with reimbursements on a sliding scale depending upon the number of agencies and recipients participating. Permissable costs included start-up expenses, costs of certification, processing of forms, outreach, nutrition education, monitoring and general administration.
1978	Consolidation	•Some substitutions permitted in food packages in recognition of special cultural and medical needs, with proviso that substitutes are nutritionally equivalent to original foods. •Eligibility restricted to those at nutritional risk who were below 195% of the poverty line. •Priority given to pregnant women and infants over children, and those with bio-chemical or anthropometric indicators of risk over those who only gave evidence of inadequate dietary intakes. •Criteria for terminating participation in the program remain obscure. •Studies documenting WIC effectiveness from the health standpoint are published. •HEW proposes takeover of WIC and food stamp programs to Office of Management and Budget. USDA successfully struggles to maintain the programs.

(continued)

129

TABLE III *Continued*

Date	Stage	Significant legislation, regulations, and political events
1979	Further consolidation with carefully planned expansion	•Evaluation of program effectiveness remains unresolved. •Shifts in eligibility criteria continue toward those exhibiting overt problems, emphasizing remediation and rehabilitation over prevention. •USDA specifies nationwide income eligibility requirements for WIC program, rather than permitting local standards to apply. •Criteria for nutritional risk further specified to include abnormal anthropometric indices, suboptimal biochemical indices, clinical signs of excess or deficiency, poor dietary habits and conditions often associated with poor dietary intakes such as chronic infections, drug or alcohol abuse, adolescent pregnancy, prematurity or smallness for dates in newborns, previous history of low birth weight in the mother, short (e.g., less than 16 months) birth intervals, current multiple pregnancy, mental retardation in the infant or other offspring of mothers who were at nutritional risk during pregnancy.
1980	Further efforts to serve those most in need	•Inflation and food prices soar. Congress adjusts WIC funding levels. •Regulations favor participation of states with the largest numbers of poor children and highest infant mortality rates. Regulations also provide additional monies for programs with high administrative costs, such as those with many participating agencies, those serving rural populations, and those in states with high costs of living. •States are required to encourage needy localities to implement or expand program operations. However, they are not required to reallocate existing funds to the programs in needy areas or to earmark funds for new programs. •Regulations continue to give priority to health agencies for WIC operations.

tors Hubert Humphrey and George McGovern (the Democratic candidates for President in 1968 and 1972) and a reluctant Republican administration. The problem of implementation was also within the USDA. Regulations were issued late. Authorized funds were not allocated, and other roadblocks (some at the agency level) were frequent. As Congressional power waxed and Presidential power waned in the mid-1970s, WIC expanded, and with the advent of a Democratic administration in 1977, further rapid growth occurred. With the return of a Republican administration and a newly conservative Congress in the 1980 election, the program again returned to the "endangered species" list where it remains today. Although funding levels have not yet been cut, great infusions of dollars will be needed to reach those potentially eligible persons who are not currently participating in the program. More ominous are proposals to merge WIC with other food or health programs that emerged late in 1981.

What accounted for WIC's spectacular growth in a time when other social programs were withering on the vine? Was it merit, connections, or just plain luck which led to its success? In retrospect, it seems clear that WIC's political support and its unique nature as the first program which included social welfare, health, food, nutritional, and educational benefits targeted to high risk groups played the major role in determining its success. But the continuous process of evaluation which was built into the legislation establishing the program played a greater role than has usually been the case in this country. Indeed, these evaluations may help the program to survive the budget cuts of the 1980s.

The WIC evaluations are of interest from several standpoints. First, their wide scope and number exemplify the new and different roles that evaluations and policy research are playing in the politics which shape public policy today. Second, they point to the broader criteria than alterations in nutrition-related indices alone upon which the effectiveness of such interventions are now being evaluated. For WIC these have included not only controlled large-scale observational and experimental studies of health impacts, but analysis of its impact as a social welfare program and management studies of the efficiency, effectiveness, and costs of alternative arrangements for food delivery. Third, the evaluations demonstrate the inability of science to provide definitive answers to researchable questions within a time frame dictated by the political agenda of the day. Fourth, they illustrate that even the imperfect evaluation methods which are available today can play a constructive role in facilitating program modifications to increase effectiveness and efficiency. Finally, they illustrate that legislative goals are difficult to evaluate because of their lack of measurability.

WHAT WIC DOES

Health Impacts

The WIC program is one of the most extensively evaluated nutrition intervention programs in the United States today. Therefore, it is somewhat surprising that definitive answers to the question of what the program's health benefits are still cannot be given. Among the difficulties which have been encountered in attempting to provide evidence on this question are the following:

1. *Health impact studies are few in number.* Basic studies on hypothesized health effects and impact studies of supplemental food programs of various types directed toward mothers, infants, and children, especially those living in developing countries are plentiful (32). They suggest that the combination of supplemental food, nutrition education, and adjunctive health care inputs may potentially have effects upon mortality, morbidity, and psychomotor and intellectual development during the perinatal period, infancy, and childhood. The various hypotheses that are relevant and a summary of findings are summarized in Table IV and discussed in detail elsewhere (18, 32, 60).

In contrast, evaluations specifically involving populations with characteristics similar to those of WIC populations are fewer in number. Studies which examine the characteristics of the WIC population served, delivery of services, and other issues involving program quality and effectiveness are available, however. In brief, they suggest that neither the nutritional nor the health status of the WIC population in the United States are analogous to that seen among the very poor in developing countries. Therefore, the effects of nutrition interventions may differ from those reported in the literature, and thus there is a need to evaluate the WIC program impact rather than relying on theoretical effects. The major evaluations of the health and nutrition outcomes of the WIC program number less than 6. These are summarized in Table V.

2. *Studies which do exist have shortcomings.* The health impact studies of WIC which do exist have a number of problems. The major ones are summarized below.

a. Programs Were Sometimes Evaluated Prematurely before All Intervention Components Were Operating. Most of the early evaluations were weakened by the presence of three common problems which often arise in attempts to identify and measure the effects of an intervention in new programs (3).

i. Social policy was packaged as a program, without careful specification of interventions which would achieve objectives. In most of the

TABLE IV

Evaluation of Evidence for Various Hypotheses Relevant to the WIC Program

Hypotheses	Extent to which current knowledge confirms hypotheses
Nutrition Status and Pregnancy Outcomes	
1. Energy intake throughout pregnancy is positively related to maternal weight gain.	Caloric intake does affect pregnancy weight gain and fetal growth throughout gestation, but especially in the third trimester.
2. Weight gain in pregnancy is positively related to birthweight and gestational age. However, weight gain is also affected by pregravid maternal weight and the presence of complications. Women having the lowest pregravid weights will demonstrate the most effects of weight gain on birthweight.	Gestational duration is affected by maternal nutritional status, among other factors. Pregravid maternal weight also influences the effect of caloric intake on weight gain, and the influence of weight gain on birth weight and gestational age. When pregravid maternal weight is low, all of these effects are more marked. Women with more adequate pregravid weights show lesser effects of energy intakes on fetal weight.
3. Maternal weight gain is negatively related to perinatal mortality, when pregravid weight, birth weight, gestational age, and other factors influencing them are controlled for.	Maternal weight gain shows the most striking effects on birth weights and perinatal mortality among women who are undernourished. Perinatal mortality is relatively insensitive to alterations in nutritional status during pregnancy.
4. If dietary intakes of iron or folic acid are increased during pregnancy, measures of body stores of these nutrients will also increase.	Data is inconclusive. There is little evidence of any effect on body stores from raising folic acid levels. Increased storage levels of iron may result, but active transplacental transfer to the fetus may be so great that gains are small.

(continued)

TABLE IV *Continued*

Hypotheses	Extent to which current knowledge confirms hypotheses
Nutritional Status in Infancy or Childhood with Health and Developmental Outcomes:	
1. Energy intake is positively related to growth in length and weight.	These effects are most striking when infants or children are greatly undernourished. Since significant growth retardation is rare in the American infant and child population, effects are not likely to be pronounced. The effects of energy intake increase on the prevalence of obesity in children of this age are not well documented.
2. Iron intake is positively related to nutritional status for iron.	Iron intake is associated with improved iron status as measured by hematologic indices and iron stores. Supplemental feeding can improve hemoglobin and hematocrit values.
3. Iron intake and iron status are negatively related to morbidity from infectious diseases.	Iron intake and consequent improved iron status are negatively related to morbidity from acute infections.
4. Iron intake and iron status are positively associated with attention span, concentration, and emotional stability. In older children they are negatively related to the prevalence of pica.	Iron intake and consequently improved iron status are positively related to behavioral and emotional indices. Data with respect to pica are not definitive.
5. In the presence of severe undernutrition, energy intake is positively related to psychomotor and intellectual development. It is negatively related to morbidity and mortality from infection.	These effects are demonstrable only when undernutrition is prevalent and severe. Such conditions are not common in the young child population in the United States. Other variables, such as marital instability, low parental education, unemployment, and other socioeconomic factors also are involved.

Effects of WIC Program Variables (Supplemental Food, Nutrition Education, and Linkages in Health Services) on Nutritional Status Outcomes

1. Supplemental food exerts a positive influence on weight gain in pregnancy, birth weight, and duration of gestation. The effect is especially apparent among women with low pregravid weights.	Evidence is good for weight gain in pregnancy and birthweight and less definitive for effects on gestational age.
2. Supplemental food has a positive effect on growth of groups of infants and young children.	Evidence is good when children are undernourished.
3. Supplemental food has a positive influence on iron status, health and developmental outcomes in infancy and early childhood.	Evidence is good for iron status. Other indices appear to be most affected when children are quite undernourished prior to reception of the supplement.
4. Comprehensive prenatal and postnatal health care enhance the positive effects of supplemental food.	Evidence is strongest from supplemental food programs in developing countries.
5. Nutrition education integrated into services provided enhances the positive effects of supplemental food.	Evidence is weak.
6. The positive effects of food supplements, health services and nutrition education are easiest to demonstrate when WIC programs cover all eligible members of the population.	Evidence is good. As program interventions reach a greater proportion of the eligible population, it becomes easier to demonstrate population effects.

TABLE V
Major Health Evaluations of the WIC Program

Title and date	Hypothesis	Population studied	Design	Comparison groups	Indices assessed	Findings	Problems and threats to validity
Langham (43)	WIC program participation and length of exposure positively affect general health status.	6202 children and 84 women surveyed in region for EPSDT screening and 1465 WIC child participants who had also been screened for EPSDT in Louisiana and 148 WIC women.	Nonequivalent control group.	Poverty group children in the region who had been screened for the early periodic screening diagnosis and treatment program (EPSDT) in Louisiana were resurveyed after the introduction of WIC program. Children who had received EPSDT living in areas not served by WIC were compared to those living in areas which were served by the program. Comparisons were also made between WIC participants and WIC dropouts. Trends in the indicators were followed quarterly for a year.	Weight and height of infants and children. Biochemical indicators of iron nutriture (hemoglobin, hematocrit). Birth weight. Demographic data. WIC participation information. Program administrative information.	At screening 20% of the infants and preschool children examined were below the 5th percentile of height and weight reference standards; some 15% more than would normally be expected. About 20% of the population were also found to have low hemoglobin and hematocrit values. Low values were especially common in blacks. Participation in WIC was associated with increased height, weight, hemoglobins and hematocrits. Children who dropped out of WIC had more signs at screening of poor nutritional status than did those continuing in the program.	Poor data collection methods used at the clinical level. Poor quality control of data. Variation in instruments between WIC sites. Variation in training of persons collecting data. Use of secondary data. Hematological standards used were inappropriate (i.e., the same standard was used for black and for white children).
Edozien et al. (20)	Participation in the WIC program will improve the nutri-	Initial visits: 41330 WIC infants and children.	Pretest, posttest with cohort analysis.	Measurements made on WIC participants after varying	Dietary intakes. Weight gain during pregnancy.	Weight gain during the third trimester of pregnancy.	Large attrition rate from those evaluated at entry to

136

| Edozien et al. (20) | Participation in the WIC program will tion and health status of participants. | Initial visits: 41330 WIC infants 9867 WIC women. Revisits: at 6 months: 11,390 infants and children. At 11 months: 6256 children 5417 women. Note: at 6 months 72% of infants and children had been lost to follow-up, and at 12 months 84% attrition was noted. Dropout rates for pregnant and postpartum women were somewhat lower, but still reached 45%. | Pretest, posttest with cohort | Measurements made on WIC participants in the program were compared to results of similar measurements made at entry to the program. | Dietary intakes. Weight gain during pregnancy. Biochemical indicators of iron nutriture. Weight and height of infants and children. Medical complications of pregnancy. Birth weight of infants. | Weight gain during the third trimester weight gain in pregnancy and birth weight were increased among pregnant participants and the prevalence of anemia was decreased. Dietary intakes of pregnant women increased in protein, calcium, phosphorus, iron, vitamin A, B_1, and niacin. Postpartum women's intakes of vitamins B_1 and C increased. Dietary intakes of 6–12 month infants increased in iron, vitamins A, B_1, and C, but were reduced in protein, calcium, phosphorus, and vitamin B_{12}. Children's intakes were increased for most nutrients. Incidence of anemia was reduced for all age groups. The accelerations in height and weight and reductions in the prevalence of anemia were greatest in | Large attrition rate from those evaluation those followed up. Understandardized data collection methods used at the clinical level. Poor quality control of data resulting in missing data. Participants studied were not representative. Initial survey population was 92% urban and consisted of those already receiving health care at clinics. Rural populations were underrepresented, especially those residing in medically underserved areas. Dropouts were extensive. Strength and integrity of interventions were weak, especially for health services and nutrition education. Programs were structurally incomplete when they were evaluated. Designs for evaluation used nonspecific nutritional status indicators. inadequate |

(continued)

TABLE V *Continued*

Title and date	Hypothesis	Population studied	Design	Comparison groups	Indices assessed	Findings	Problems and threats to validity
						the first 6 months of WIC participation.	controls. Regression toward the means posed a problem.
Center for Disease Control (8)	Participation in the WIC program will decrease the incidence of anemia among infants and children, and weights for length and other anthropometric indices will become more like the general population.	Baseline measurements for reference population norms involved 115,249 children WIC participants. Follow-ups at two subsequent WIC visits, 6 months apart were reported for 6000 children.	Posttest only with comparison groups.	WIC children's indices are compared with standards based on reference population.	Biochemical indices of iron nutriture. Length and weight for length by age. Overweight and underweight by age.	Children entering WIC had a high prevalence of anemia, but after a year of WIC participation rates fell. A large number of children were short for their age at their initial visits; 22% of those surveyed were overweight using a definition of weight for height over the 90th percentile. The percentage of children under the 10th percentile using the same criteria were within usual limits. After 6 months in the program, children who were overweight or underweight at entry tended to normalize their weights. However, some	Data are of uncertain quality owing to large number of participating clinics and varying training of observers. Cut-off points to measure "anemia" are arbitrary.

138

Reference/Hypothesis	Sample	Design	Measure	Variable	Results	Comments
Participation in WIC will decrease the incidence of low birth weight infants.	1580 WIC participants while pregnant.	Posttest only with comparison group.	Rate of low birth weight in WIC population is compared to national and regional standard rates.	Birth weight.	who entered at normal weights became overweight. Rates of low birth-weight among WIC participants were no higher than those of the general population. Since poverty populations at risk of undernutrition usually exhibit higher rates of low birthweight than the general population, this was taken as evidence of a program benefit. However, it is possible that diet was not the limiting factor among them.	Reference standard for low birth weight rates is not specified. WIC populations may be self-selected. Not all states are represented and, therefore, population is probably not representative of entire WIC population in the US. Measurements may not be standardized, and data was of variable quality. Inadequate controls; so that an appropriate comparison group for birth-weights is unavailable.
Carabello et al. (7) Participation in WIC will decrease the incidence of low birth weight infants.	WIC infants born in Connecticut: 1776 infants, 15 deaths. Non-WIC infants in same locality 2415 infants, 56 deaths.	Posttest with a comparison group.	WIC participation in the prenatal period was compared retrospectively with a non-WIC population.	Infant mortality.	Decreases were noted.	Non-WIC comparison group was not matched for income, nutritional status or other eligibility criteria. In and out-migrations were not measured. As a result, mortality rates were probably underestimated.

(continued)

TABLE V *Continued*

Title and date	Hypothesis	Population studied	Design	Comparison groups	Indices assessed	Findings	Problems and threats to validity
	Participation in WIC improves general infant health status with respect to growth, regardless of breast or bottlefeeding status.	61 infants, participating in WIC, 65 infants not participating.	Posttest with a comparison group.	Infants were randomly selected from WIC and non-WIC populations. Anthropometric measurements were compared at birth, 6 months and 1 year of age using hospital and health center records.	Weight, length, head circumference, hematocrit.	WIC children were at an advantage in all of these characteristics.	Non-WIC comparison group was not matched for income, nutritional status, or other eligibility criteria and, therefore, had different socioeconomic characteristics. Sample size was small.
	Participation in WIC improves size of children in kindergarten.	102 WIC children; 91 non-WIC children within a specified census tract in Connecticut and 139 non-WIC children outside of this tract.	Posttest with a comparison group.	Anthropometric "score" was devised. Mean scores for WIC participants were compared to both groups of non-WIC participants.	Weight, height, nutritional problems. Immunizations.	WIC children exhibited improvements in of these respects.	Both populations were chosen from a hospital population and may not be representative of WIC and non-WIC groups. Population surveyed was not representative of larger WIC or non-WIC populations. Data sets were incomplete.

Author	Hypothesis	Design	Sample	Procedure	Measures	Findings	Limitations
Kennedy et al. (37)	Participation in WIC during the prenatal period decreases the incidence of low birth weight infants.	Posttest only with comparison group.	918 WIC participants and 410 women from a WIC and non-WIC agency who were not participants in the Massachusetts program.	Mean birth weights of WIC and non-WIC women's infants were compared. Birth weights were also compared for WIC sites which provided health services and those that did not. Pre-pregnancy weight, previous low birth weight deliveries and age of mother were controlled.	Birth weight.	Mean birth weights and percentage of low birth weight infants among WIC women in centers with WIC programs were higher than those of the offspring of women in these centers who did not participate in WIC. WIC participation was associated with a lower incidence of prematurity. Benefit-cost ratios were favorable for WIC.	Population studies represented only WIC and non-WIC participants in clinics in Massachusetts, and therefore, may be unrepresentative. Differences between these groups and the eligible WIC population could not be assessed. Intervening variables could not be controlled completely, possibly leading to overattribution of effects on birth weights to the program, and underestimates of the differences between WIC and non-WIC participants which also affect birth weights.
Kennedy and Gershoff (36)	WIC participation has a positive effect on hemaglobins and hematocrits of prenatal patients.	Nonequivalent control groups.	148 WIC participants and 84 non-WIC participants.	WIC and non-WIC participants' hemaglobins and hematocrits were compared at the first prenatal visit and during the third trimester of pregnancy.	Hemoglobin. Hematocrit.	WIC participants had higher hemoglobins and hematocrits.	Possible unrepresentativeness because populations studied represented only WIC and non-WIC participants in Massachusetts.

(continued)

141

TABLE V *Continued*

Title and date	Hypothesis	Population studied	Design	Comparison groups	Indices assessed	Findings	Problems and threats to validity
Kotelchuk *et al.* (39)	WIC participants will show better outcomes with respect to the outcomes of pregnancy (e.g., birth weight, length of gestation, 1 and 5 minute Apgar scores, complications, malformations, neonatal deaths, and other indices (prenatal health care visits, month health visits began) than controls not in WIC.	WIC participants matched with nonparticipants by age, race, parity, marital status, education and town of residence. Birth certificates of offspring compared.	Compare outcomes of WIC and non-WIC groups in state and differences by race, age, redemption rates of WIC vouchers, length of WIC participation.	Nonparticipants matched to WIC participants on age, race, parity, marital status, education, town of residence.	Offspring's birth-weight, length of gestation, 1 and 5 minute Apgar scores, complications, malformations. Also prenatal health visits of mother, month health visits began.	WIC participants were less likely to have inadequate prenatal care, they had slightly more prenatal visits and prenatal care began slightly earlier. WIC offspring were born slightly later, were slightly less likely to be low birth weight, had better 5 minute Apgar scores, and lower neonatal mortalities. Birth weights of offspring were positively correlated to the length of the mother's participation in WIC. Duration of participation in WIC also was positively associated with birth weight, gestational age, adequacy of prenatal care, number of prenatal visits, and negatively associated with neonatal death.	Random assignment was not possible.

early studies of WIC operational features of the program other than the provision of food were only vaguely specified. The program as it actually existed in the field was not necessarily that implied by the legislation or hoped for by federal officials. For example, at some sites the program consisted in its early days of little more than passing out food. Nutrition assessment and educational methods were poorly developed, and liaison to health services was virtually nonexistent. Thus translation of the plan into action was extremely variable.

ii. Only a few program elements were established when programs were evaluated. Until 1975, WIC program effectiveness was limited by lack of funding and start-up problems. In the next few years, the frequent turnabouts in regulations, legislative changes, and legal actions against administrators further disrupted smooth program functioning. Thus early evaluations of program effects were carried out on programs which were constantly undergoing major changes. The links to health services, viable nutrition education components, and eligibility requirements, which focused on groups that might be expected to be at greatest risk from the poverty and nutritional status standpoint, were not realities until the late 1970s.

Only in the past few years has policy of the program plan in WIC-related health care and nutrition education been specified precisely enough to ensure some homogeneity in the translation of legislation into action. Therefore the early studies of program impact were hardly conclusive tests of policy (58, 59, 69). They often became political issues and were criticized in this context (4, 12) as a result.

iii. Incomplete delivery: reception of the program at the individual level was not assessed. Delivery of health services and nutrition education was poor at some project sites. Often in a new program exhortation and encouragement are necessary to encourage adherence to new treatments. This was apparently not done routinely except for encouraging pregnant and lactating women to eat their supplements and to provide the babies with their special foods.

b. Designs for Evaluation and Inadequacies. The early evaluations of the WIC also fell short in other methodologic respects. The major problems were these:

i. Nonspecificity of nutritional status indicators. Height, weight, weight gain, head circumferences, measures of iron nutriture, and clinical signs indicative of deficiencies, imbalances, or nutritional excess are affected not only by inadequate diet but by myriad other factors which were not controlled for. Expert opinion was also divided on levels of these parameters which should be taken as indicative of risk. Only recently have reference standards for nutritional status in pregnancy become available (27), and similar standards for infancy are also now more refined, but they were not available when the evaluations were mounted.

ii. Inadequate controls. Random assignment to treatment groups was not possible in the WIC medical evaluation. Quasi-experimental designs have been relied upon, with resulting inadequacies which made for difficulties in interpretation (6, 16, 29, 80).

The first problem in the quasi-experimental designs employed was that, because comparison groups also differed in other significant ways, it could not be unambiguously stated that findings were attributable only to WIC. Participants differed from nonparticipants, and WIC counties differed from non-WIC counties.

A second problem afflicting the medical evaluation involved the statistical phenomenon of regression toward the mean. When repeated measures are made upon individuals who have been selected for attention at a specific point in time because of their extreme values (e.g., low weights, low hemoglobins or hematocrits, poor dietary intakes, or the like), a certain amount of regression toward more normal values can be expected even in the absence of program effects. However, if only two measurements are taken in a pre- and posttreatment design, posttreatment results involve both the program effect and an unknown, but probably large, tendency for values to regress toward the mean. Thus even in the absence of treatment effects, positive benefits might be wrongly attributed to the program. More sophisticated designs, which employ several baseline measurements prior to program initiation, permit the size of the effect of regression toward the mean to be measured. The use of a simultaneous nontreatment control group during the treatment period further safeguards against this error. Unfortunately neither of these measures was available in the WIC medical evaluation.

iii. Evaluators were unable to separate out impacts of other programs or effects of specific intervention components within the WIC itself. WIC recipients were usually eligible for a variety of other food programs, health and social services, which may have had effects on nutritional status. Even in the studies in which simultaneous non-WIC controls were employed, it was not possible to control for differences in participation in other programs among the two groups.

Impact evaluation involves estimating, in the least equivocal and biased way possible, the relative effect of a program on a target group (3). It focuses on overall effects rather than on individual attributes. In such studies, it is difficult to parcel out each component from the whole. Few of the WIC evaluations had unambiguous measures which would permit them to evaluate the effects of each intervention component separately.

It is of great interest for program planners to know what it is in the program intervention mix that is key to achieving satisfactory outcomes and the extent to which different intervention components (e.g., food supplements, nutrition education, and health services) interact with one another. Once the WIC enabling legislation was passed, experiments which tested different program mixes were not possible, because all programs furnished supplements, available health services, and (as time went on) nutrition education. There is no doubt that programs varied with respect to the mode of food delivery (vouchers, home delivery of direct distribution), as well as in the extent and adequacy of the nutrition education and health services they provided to clients. However, it was impossible to find programs that were completely devoid in one or more of these program elements because all were specified in the enabling legislation. Only recently have evaluations compared programs on the basis of the strengths or weaknesses of the latter two components, although such information is vital for improving program planning (2, 36, 37, 39).

iv. Participants were unrepresentative of the larger population. Frequently the health impact studies were carried out in patients in a specific clinic or location. Their characteristics were not such that they could be generalized to the overall population.

3. *Other nutrition related considerations have not been addressed.* a. Effect on Breast-Feeding. Breast-feeding has undergone a remarkable renaissance in the United States over the past decade (48). Although the greatest increases have been apparent in upper socioeconomic groups not served by WIC, low income populations have shown some increases as well. Some nutritionists have expressed concern that, because the WIC provides free infant formula for up to 1 year of age, it may act as a disincentive to breast feeding. One possible disincentive is the fact that until recently the nutrition education component of WIC was poorly developed, and thus the pros and cons of various infant feeding regimens (such as breast versus bottle) were often not discussed. Second, the breast-feeding woman receives the same amount of supplemental foods as her non-breast-feeding counterpart, whereas her infant receives no food supplement. The bottle-fed infant, however, receives an additional supplement of its own. Thus more food is provided to bottle as opposed to breast feeders. Finally, economic incentives to breast-feeding are removed because fortified infant formula is provided at no cost. It is to be hoped that in the future, more extensive nutrition education efforts to prepare new mothers to make the choice of how they will feed their infants will become a part of the WIC program.

b. More Inclusive Indices of Nutritional Status Are Needed. The evaluations have not focused on biochemical indices of folic acid nutrition or blood lead levels (68), which may be influenced by the WIC program services.

c. Effect on the Types of Food Fed to Infants. In the late 1960s, few infants in poverty groups were fed commercial infant formula fortified with iron; home prepared formulas based on evaporated milk with early introduction of whole cow's milk and solids were common (26, 64). In the past few years, a trend toward use of iron-fortified infant formula for a longer period and later introduction of solids has been noted in all income groups (48). Commercial formulas are somewhat more expensive than home-prepared formulas, and their increased use among the poor is probably due in part to the WIC program, which provides them free (42). It is possible that the benefits of longer continued feeding of iron-fortified formula from the health standpoint, such as the lesser prevalence of iron deficiency anemia, the lowered risk of intolerances, and decreased probability of feeding dilute or overconcentrated formulas of whole milk, offset these increases in the costs of feeding.

d. Nutrients Supplied. The WIC program food package emphasizes the contributions of nutrients such as protein, ascorbic acid, calcium, iron, vitamin A, and energy-producing substances, which are assumed to be low in the diets of the target groups. The evidence is fairly convincing that some low income women, infants, and children do in fact receive less energy-producing substances, iron, and folic acid than is recommended and that increases in intakes are associated with alterations in biochemical indices of nutriture for these nutrients. Whether increased intakes of calcium, vitamins A, C, or folic acid increase maternal or infant stores is more problematic (32, 56, 57). The evidence that low income women, infants, or children are deficient in protein or that increased protein intakes are associated with better outcomes is less convincing. In a carefully controlled randomized clinical trial in low-income pregnant women, provision of a high protein supplement as opposed to a more balanced supplement lower in protein indicated that differences in the birthweights of infants delivered to women who had received high as opposed to lower protein supplements did not reach statistical significance except among heavy smokers (66). The major effect upon birth weight appears to be through energy intakes in populations such as those represented in WIC (52). Similar findings have been reported in other populations in developing countries (44, 45). These findings are not directly applicable to WIC since a variety of foods rich in a number of nutrients rather than solely in protein are provided instead of a single supplement, and health outcomes other than those upon birth weight are desired. However, they do point to the need for stressing energy and micronutrient intakes rather than solely protein intakes in the nutrition counseling of WIC participants.

e. Foods Provided. Ever since the inception of WIC, the contents of the WIC food package have been the source of a good deal of controversy. Among the criticisms which were directed at earlier packages was that they provided solids and juices earlier than current professional recommendations for pediatric populations, that the iron fortification levels for the womens' and childrens' packages were so high that some low-cost whole grain cereals were excluded, whereas some high-priced iron-fortified sugared cereals were allowed. Also previous WIC regulations did not permit modifications to deal with the special foods required to feed infants with inborn errors of metabolism, allergies, or intolerances, nor were there modifications of the foods provided permitted for cultural or personal reasons. The single exception allowed was the use of soy instead of regular formula for infants with allergies to milk protein. WIC administrators argued that funds were available through other government programs for supplying special dietary products to treat some of these disorders, but not all infants were referred to these other programs. Revised regulations issued late in 1980 overcame many of these objections (22).

Presently six food packages are available, one for infants from birth through 3 months (providing formula) and a second package for infants 4–12 months providing iron-fortified cereals, formula and fruit juices. A third package is for children and women with special dietary needs, and language in the regulation permits some substitutions based upon documentation of need and approval by the Food and Nutrition Service. The fourth package is for children 1 to 5 years. A fifth package is tailored for pregnant and breast-feeding women, and the last package is for postpartum women who are not breast feeding. The packages for women and older children contain milk, eggs, cheese, iron fortified cereals, legumes, and juices.

Although some shortcomings still do exist, under current regulations it is possible to alter the amounts of foods provided to better "tailor" the food package to the size and growth of infants. In practice the maximum allowable quantities of foods under the program guidelines are usually prescribed, even though for some very young infants the amounts of food provided may be in excess of their needs for energy, protein, iron, calcium, ascorbic acid, thiamine, riboflavin, and niacin. Although greater tailoring might be preferable from the medical standpoint and to avoid waste, it is unpopular with providers in programs because of the greater time it requires and the more cumbersome reporting procedures involved, and also with parents.

f. Sharing of WIC Foods. There is little doubt that some of the WIC foods are shared with others in the family who are not WIC participants (73). The issue is whether this is so severe that it compromises program effectiveness. Since infant growth and nutritional status do appear to have improved, this seems unlikely. The few studies on sharing which do exist indicate that it is least in early infancy (when formula and infant cereals make up the bulk of the infant's diet) and greater in older groups of children who receive food supplements which appeal more to other family members. Data are lacking on the question of whether or not participation in other food programs (which presumably would increase food availability and food consumption of other family members) decreases the extent of WIC food sharing.

4. *Screening indices need further refinement.* The importance of appropriate indices for screening mothers for food supplementation during pregnancy and the inadequacy of the measures which have usually been employed have been well reviewed by Habicht and Yarborough (30). None of the evaluations of the WIC program has furnished the data necessary to develop efficient screening indices for such intervention programs. Until studies are available that permit the development of screening devices on the basis of appropriate responses to supplementation, benefits of public health importance will be difficult to document.

5. *Nutritional surveillance also needs more attention.* The difficulties encountered in trying to assess the WIC and other nutrition related programs have pointed to the need for more sophisticated and integrated nutritional surveillance systems (14).

Social Welfare Impact

The major studies addressing the social welfare implications of WIC are summarized in Table VI. In general these reports and broader evaluations of the food programs (11, 33, 54, 61) indicate that many goals of this nature have been achieved. Additional comments which address specific social welfare criteria are summarized below. The basic question which remains is what is the best program mix to achieve these ends.

Assets Distributed

WIC distributes in-kind assets rather than cash. Some social welfare theorists believe that freedom of choice would be increased if less categorical forms of support were provided instead or if a different mix of services were provided. There is neither scientific nor social consensus on this issue. However, there is some evidence that alterations in categorical food programs without the addition of other measures is associated with a deterioration in the nutritional status of the target groups (81).

TABLE VI

Social Welfare Related Evaluations of the Special Supplemental Food Program for Women, Infants, and Children

Title and date	Population studied or subject	Findings
Senate Select Committee on Nutrition and Human Needs (71)	Examines Federal food programs by counties in the United States contrasting coverage in 1969 to that in 1973.	Poverty was defined as a yearly family income less than 3 times the cost of a minimal adequate diet as formulated by USDA, adjusted for differences in cost of living by region of the country. Using these indices, the incidence of poverty (and by extension, malnutrition) was found to have increased threefold since 1969, food assistance still reaching only half of the poor. However, great progress was made in the interval in the South. The report was useful in that it documented where poverty existed and trends.
Senate Select Committee on Nutrition and Human Needs (72)	Survey of 34 states Puerto Rico and the Virgin Islands on progress of WIC program.	63 WIC project applications were underfunded. Estimates of total eligible participants were 4,000,000, which would necessitate a budget of $876 million if all were served. Most states used retail vouchers for the WIC food package, smaller numbers used direct distribution or home delivery of food. About a third of the states had no nutrition education because of inadequate administrative funds. Only a quarter of the states were pleased with the package; most states wanted more flexibility in the choice of cereals.
Fleming (24)	Report and summary by a private advocacy group for children on need for WIC issues related to its implementation and the merits and problems of grantee agencies. Anecdotal information is used rather than a formal study.	The legislative intent of WIC is reviewed and administrative realities at the federal and state level summarized. In 1975, USDA was judged to be an unwilling administrative agency. States were found to vary from enthusiasm to apathy in implementing programs. The progress and difficulties of local agencies are discussed. Recommendations are made for continuation of the program but for increased funding, extended eligibility and clear regulations.
Urban Institute (73)	Sample drawn to represent various types of delivery systems geographic locations, and ethnic groups. 96 WIC clinics in 30 states, 71 food retailers, 3600 participants and 141 nonparticipants interviewed.	Most WIC participants (66%) had incomes below poverty threshold. Most participants (94%) were satisfied with WIC foods but some sharing of foods in families (81%) occurred. Participants reported greater use of health care facilities as a result of the program. Delivery systems evaluation showed direct food package distribution at clinics was least costly and was best for controlling contents of food package, but most inconvenient for clients. Home delivery of foods was most expensive but more convenient. Vouchers for retail distribution struck the middle ground. The retail voucher system was judged the most satisfactory. Findings on nutrition counseling were also discussed.

(continued)

TABLE VI *Continued*

Title and date	Population studied or subject	Findings
Burke (5)	Survey of 58 income security programs at the federal level benefiting persons of limited income, including the various fund programs.	The funding formulas for benefits, eligibility requirements and benefits of each program were discussed. 1975 and 1976 expenditures were also documented. Funding formulas and eligibility criteria vary widely, as do state matching requirements. Cost and numbers of recipients rose for nearly all programs over the period studied.
Fleming *et al.* (25)	Report of national conference on WIC convened by Children's Foundation, a nonprofit, antihunger foundation.	The program was assessed and recommendations for improvements were made, but views toward it were generally favorable. Recommendations included different foods in the food package, more attention to breast feeding and nutrition education within WIC programs, more integration of WIC with health care programs, improvements in administrative procedures, especially reallocation of unspent funds, more flexibility in delivery systems, more emphasis on nutritional/medical risk as well as income for determining eligibility and on preventive aspects of the program. States were seen as needing to establish better communications between both WIC regional offices and local programs. More technical assistance to local programs was desired especially on nutrition education. Special administrative problems such as lack of referrals for other programs of WIC participants in urban areas, lack of health care in rural areas, and the special needs of Indian populations and migrants were discussed. Evaluations at both the national and local level were called for; including behavioral studies of the effects of nutrition education. WIC program expansion was urged.
Comptroller General of the United States (13)	The benefit overlaps, gaps, eligibility differences, administrative inconsistencies, and coordination problems of 13 major programs providing food or food-related assistance to Americans are surveyed.	Overall effectiveness of the programs is limited by piecemeal authorization, rapid expansion over the past decade, and lack of nationwide data on program benefits and nutritional impacts. Proposal for comprehensive welfare reform must be based on such reviews. Steps should be taken to determine extent of overlaps, gaps, and eligibility differences. Also recommended were making measurements of nutritional status to determine the effectiveness of nutrition programs, development of consistent eligibility criteria, and exploration of alternatives to WIC delivery systems.

TABLE VI *Continued*

Title and date	Population studied or subject	Findings
Comptroller General of the United States (14)	Reviews a proposal of USDA and HEW for a comprehensive nutritional status monitoring system.	The proposal would create a comprehensive nutritional status monitoring system to determine nutritional and dietary status of Americans, nutritional quality of food, dietary practices and knowledge and impacts of nutrition interviews. However, the role of the system in program evaluation remains vague, as do other issues requiring collaboration.
Development Associates, Inc. (19)	Demonstration project involving 13 states in the midwest experiencing seasonal influxes of migrant workers to determine if issuing a WIC certification card entitling participant to WIC benefits at any program site would be helpful.	WIC certification cards do help to ensure continuity in delivery of WIC benefits even if the participant moves from one program to another. However, some locations lack WIC programs and others place migrants on waiting lists.
Comptroller General of the United States (15)	Review of legislation and regulations governing the WIC programs authorizations and operations. Policies, practices, and procedures of 20 local health clinics in four states, one Indian reservation, and four regional WIC offices were reviewed. Attempts were made to obtain medical information on the health status of 25 participants at each clinic site.	Some local WIC programs do not provide health services as adjuncts to the WIC program. Other problems sometimes present which need attention are professional assessments of WIC applicants' nutritional status, use of uniform criteria for determining nutritional risk and eligibility for the program, more tailoring of the food package to individual need; more nutrition education and program evaluation components, and revision of provisions in program regulations which inhibit effective evaluation.
Kotz (41)	Reports the finding of a group of physicians which had toured depressed communities in the United States in 1967 when they returned in 1977.	Improvements were found in most of the communities upon resurvey in the proportion of malnourished infants and children. Their findings were attributed to feeding as well as health programs.
Harvey (302)	Report of the second national conference on WIC convened by the Children's Foundation, a nonprofit, antihunger foundation.	Recommendations for improvements included that some items be introduced earlier, a wider variety of infants formulas be made available, guidelines be developed to encourage the proper use of food supplements, priority be given to adolescent females who are pregnant, and that a special food package for Indians be developed.

Adequacy

The question here is whether the entire benefits package is sufficient to provide a reasonably adequate overall diet, assuming that the WIC acts as a supplement. In view of the fact that inflation has been rampant in the past few years and benefits have not increased accordingly, it is doubtful that previous concerns about excesses in food provided by the sum and total of food programs provided to the WIC populations are warranted.

Efficiency

At issue here is whether distributive efforts such as WIC are warranted for the poor. This question was answered affirmatively by studies in the late 1960s and early 1970s and has only again arisen in 1981. The question now is whether the present program mix is the best means of achieving the goal or whether other mixtures of in kind or cash benefits might be more appropriate.

Horizontal Equity

Since WIC is not an entitlement program, the law does not require that all eligible persons in a given category receive its benefits. However, it is desirable from the standpoint of equity that within the program all persons in like circumstances are treated equally. Current regulations are such that priority on the basis of poverty and vulnerability to malnutrition determine how quickly one is likely to be accepted for the program. However, those enrolled in the program are not necessarily discharged simply because more needy individuals are on the waiting lists, although there is a trend in this direction. Also, because criteria for eligibility and the number of WIC programs may vary from one part of the country to another, those who reside in some areas are more likely to be eligible than those who live in other areas. Finally, those who live in areas which do not have suitable health services or which have not applied for the program may lack WIC services, even if they are at very high risk.

Vertical Equity

This social welfare measure attempts to determine if differences are preserved although gaps are narrowed between those who are eligible for the program and those who are not. Although data are lacking on the issue, it is likely that this occurs today because of tightened eligibility requirements which insist on indices other than income to determine program eligibility.

Incentives

It is desirable that programs provide assistance in such a manner that includes incentives to adequately nourish participants and their children. Anecdotal reports of parents fasting their children prior to WIC recertification visits to ensure continued eligibility abound, but firm evidence that this occurs is lacking. It is important not to make criteria for nutritional risk synonymous with outright malnutrition to avoid encouraging such behavior. Also, incentives to maintain adequate nutritional levels once they are achieved are necessary. These difficulties are especially vexing since the program is presently being operated *de facto* if not *de jure* as a rehabilitation program concentrating upon those at risk or already in a poor nutritional state.

Efficiency

The measure assesses the extent to which fraud, error, other abuses and inefficiencies are present. The major investigations of these questions have indicated that few participants do not in fact qualify for the program and that although some sharing with other family members occurs, it is not of great magnitude. The efficiency and effectiveness of the links to health services have been found to be lacking in several investigations. However, WIC recipients are more likely to receive health services than their non-WIC counterparts in poverty groups, which may confer some advantage nonetheless.

Impacts of the Evaluations on the WIC Program

WIC is an excellent example of the increasing role that program evaluations are playing not only in providing technical information for shaping program policy but in the political process. Signs of the growing influence of evaluations are evident in all areas of government. Legislation in most government program areas now specifically mandates that a fixed percentage of allocations be set aside for evaluations. Also, the Office of Management and Budget and offices in the domestic agencies within the executive branch of government are expanding their role of carrying out evaluations. Within Congress, the General Accounting Office, the Office of Technology Assessment, the Congressional Budget Office, and the Congressional Research Section are doing likewise (63).

The WIC evaluations are interesting because they are illustrative of the growing tendency of Congress to use findings for broader political purposes than their more traditional use of helping to solve specific technical issues. These other uses to which the WIC evaluations were put included the role they played in identifying problems as a step toward putting them on the political agenda, in mobilizing government action, and in confronting and settling dilemmas and trade-offs (63). The WIC evaluations were also used for other political purposes, such as strengthening the position of various Congressional committees, agencies, professional and industry groups, containing problems and oversight of government operations. Finally the evaluations represent a new type of scientific information which does not reach the peer-reviewed scientific literature until months or years after program and policy decisions based upon them have been made and implemented.

The WIC evaluations have by no means been overwhelmingly positive nor have they always been free of methodological shortcomings or political bias. Nevertheless, each evaluation has served as the basis for program modifications. These have gradually increased the program's effectiveness as a nutrition and health intervention effort and have permitted the program to successfully counter its critics. Among the specific positive effects which evaluations have had in program improvement, the following stand out.

1. *Encouraging greater precision with respect to specification of target groups and program components.* The evaluations have been helpful in speeding up the process of defining eligibility requirements, priorities with respect to target groups and in spelling out precisely what it is that the program components should consist of. These objectives could have been achieved in other ways, but the evaluations did furnish legislators and civil servants alike with timely information on program realities.

2. *Providing documentation of progress useful for accountability purposes and for justifying program continuation.* Evidence of accomplishment is an important factor which often determines whether nutrition intervention programs succeed or fail. The ability of the WIC program to demonstrate positive (although small) effects was helpful in sustaining Congressional support when many other social programs were foundering.

3. *Identifying barriers to program participation.* Studies such as Popkin's (60) review of previous evaluations and the Urban Institute Study (73) have been helpful in pointing out barriers to program participation and altering program regulations and delivery systems to lessen them.

4. *Highlighting disparities in eligibility and benefits in social welfare programs.* The rapid growth and expansion of many of the food programs in

the 1970s occurred later than that of health and social welfare programs, which had their period of most rapid growth in the 1960s. WIC and the other food programs are administered by the Food and Nutrition Service of USDA with different legislative objectives and requirements for participation than those of the health and welfare programs as well as each other. The most pressing question in this regard has to do with eligibility for health care, the criteria for which vary not only from one federal program to another but by income in various parts of the country; income differences being much greater than simply those due to cost of living. Uniform nationwide standards for eligibility with respect to income adjusted for regional variations in cost of living might eliminate some of these problems. Additionally, if WIC and health services eligibility were always synonymous, confusion would also be lessened.

WIC IN THE FUTURE —EXPANSION, STABILIZATION, OR EXTINCTION?

The Future

WIC enters its second decade in a healthy state, having received increases in appropriations when many other social programs have been pruned. Whether WIC will expand, stabilize, or disappear in the coming years will depend upon larger questions having to do with social welfare policies.

The disposition of six broad issues which Congress has debated with increasing frequency in the past few years is likely to have major repercussions on the WIC program in the 1980s (1). These include the following:

1. *Federal accountability versus state autonomy.* Increasing pressure is being exerted at the federal level to improve accountability for federal monies being spent across the country. At the same time states are demanding greater freedom from federal direction and regulation, claiming that centralization stifles innovation. One possible solution to this dilemma would be to make requirements more consistent across programs, to reduce reporting requirements, and to make the broad demonstration, experimentation and waiver authorities more accessible in the WIC program.

2. *Entitlements versus limitations.* There is growing pressure to limit previously open-ended reimbursement programs and to avoid the establishment of new programs which entitle all of those in a particular

category to obtain services or to obtain reimbursements for services on an open-ended basis. This trend does not augur well for WIC advocates who wish to see the program expanded to all eligible children. Present (1980) WIC appropriations and authorizations are $900 million, whereas calculations of program costs based on a total eligible population of 3.1 million children indicate that at least $2.8 billion would be necessary to reach them all. A recent report found that in all, 9.1 million women, infants, and children were financially eligible for WIC benefits, but only 2.1 million are now served by the program (70). Less than 30% of the eligible population can presently be served. It is unlikely that, given the state of the economy in the near future, appropriations will expand sufficiently to guarantee that all eligible individuals will be served unless the state of the economy greatly improves.

3. *Limiting program eligibility.* At both state and federal levels, there is a growing tendency to limit either eligibility for benefits or the scope of benefits and services provided. Health and welfare programs have been especially hard hit, with ambulatory services suffering the most. In the past few years eligibility for WIC has become increasingly restrictive both with respect to income requirements and the type of evidence of nutritional risk which is considered to be acceptable. Indeed, some have criticized present regulations as being so stringent that they have converted a program of prevention into one of remediation (50). But it is likely that this trend will continue.

4. *Limiting legislation and increasing oversight.* Congress has increasingly pulled back from enacting new legislation, choosing instead to exercise better oversight over existing authorizations. These trends have long been evident in the WIC program, which owed its very existence in its early years to Congressional oversight. This trend is likely to continue in the 1980s.

5. *Coordinating service delivery programs without undue federal control.* Intergovernmental operations to improve the delivery of in-kind services are also receiving a great deal of attention. The dilemma is how this can be accomplished without undue federal interference with state and local government activities. Most observers agree that so many programs exist at the federal level that it will take several years to coordinate them. The field of maternal and child health is a good example of the potential for doing this, inasmuch as a number of programs already exist which are often uncoordinated (21, 84).

One major source of funding for maternal and child health services is Title V of the Social Security Act, which provides grants to states and territorial health agencies to reduce maternal and infant mortality, mental retardation, and handicapping conditions and to promote the health of mothers and children. Prior to the mid-1970s nutritionists funded from these grants furnished the major sources of professional nutritional advice, counseling, and advocacy for pregnant women and children living in low income areas. Although the regulations under Title V provided for nutrition services and supplemental minerals and vitamins in projects, they prohibited the provision of food supplements. In the late 1960s low income families were often unable to purchase the foods nutritionists recommended even if they used food stamps or commodities distributed by USDA to low income families. Nutritionists employed by Title V programs were vigorous supporters of the WIC program, which they believed would fill this gap in the services they provided. However, in recent years funding under Title V has not expanded rapidly, and thus the development of Maternal and Infant Care Projects has not kept pace with that of the WIC program, so that the availability of health services rather than of the WIC program is often the limiting variable in achieving the goal of comprehensive nutrition services.

Another source of funding for child health services is the Early Periodic Screening Diagnosis and Treatment Program, which is a component of a 1967 amendment to Title XIX of the Social Security Act. All states administering a Medicaid program (a health care program for low income groups) are required to offer a range of preventive and treatment services to all Medicaid eligible children under age 21. The states must provide periodic screening diagnosis and treatment for eligible children and reimburse for health services provided. States have moved slowly to implement this program, and the treatment services which are paid for vary greatly across the country. In 1977 10 million or more children were eligible, but only 2,250,000 were being served. The inertia in implementation has a number of causes, chief among them the desires on the part of the States to limit costs by limiting program scope and implementation. The lack of a comprehensive system for delivering health services in the volume required by EPSDT, unfamiliarity with large-scale screening programs, the virtual lack of any health care system in other areas, and the lack of incentives for developing a new network of health providers also contributed to slow implementation of the program. Since 1977, efforts have been made to expand and improve EPSDT by adoption of the Child Health Assessment Program (CHAP) which would provide federal assistance for certain needed services, but as yet such a bill has not been passed by Congress.

Ultimately expansion of these programs may be such that it keeps up with the growth of WIC, but presently WIC programs are being established at a faster rate than any of these health services, especially in rural areas. The primary care capacity building initiative program of the Department of Health and Human Services has been suggested to alleviate this situation. This program is designed to develop the capacity of communities to deliver primary health or ambulatory care services to medically underserved rural and urban populations. Greater coordination between the USDA and the DHHS in launching new WIC and health programs in the same areas would also be helpful.

6. *Consolidation of existing programs versus maintenance of categorical programs.* Broader questions of whether child welfare and health problems are best solved by a combination of categorical programs or by direct cash transfer payments remain unanswered. It is clear that categorical programs frequently overlap. Presently a patchwork of child health, education, and other social welfare services exist in addition to WIC, most of which are administered by the Department of Health and Human Services. Plans for integrating services into one comprehensive and large scale child health program have been proposed and widely discussed over the past decade, but have never been successful in Congress (51). During the Nixon and Ford administrations, the proposals were coupled with an approach for bloc grants to states. In the past year Congress has appeared more receptive to the proponents of an approach which would consolidate existing programs and retain federal control, although no legislation has been enacted.

There is growing sentiment that many of the current difficulties in administering child health and welfare programs could be decreased by consolidating all programs related to a particular problem or population together, eliminating much red tape and many of the coordination problems which now exist (15). It is assumed that the task of achieving accountability would be easier if this were done. Duplication and overlap are real problems. However, consolidation may not be the answer either; there is no guarantee that it automatically increases efficiency or effectiveness, and it is likely to meet resistance in Congress, where committee jurisdictions are along more categorical lines.

a. Integration of WIC with the Maternal and Child Health Services System. Recent surveys indicate that the extent to which WIC is integrated with the larger health services system for mothers and children is extremely variable and needs improvement (15).

b. Decrease in Non-WIC Nutrition Services. WIC has grown and expanded during a period when other maternal and child targeted programs with public health nutrition components were decreasing in size. This is particularly evident in the amount of nutrition services provided under funding from Title V of the Social Security act. Faced with the pressures of inflation, states have increasingly used these funds for the provision of other services, transferring public health nutritionists previously funded by them to the WIC program. The major problem this creates is that WIC regulations have stricter age, income, and nutritional risk criteria for services eligibility than do Title V funds. As a result, services are lacking for children older than 5 years of age or for those from slightly more affluent families. In 1978, 583 nutritionists at the local level were supported by WIC funds, 246 by Title V funds, and 375 by city or country health departments (35). WIC funds cannot cover the costs of continuing health supervision nor do they necessarily cover the full costs of services such as certification, counseling, and the like which are required for program participation. Thus some children cannot be served.

The major roadblock is lack of money. Including food costs, WIC budgets exceed all of the federal monies available for maternal and child health services by the federal government, and increases in funding of the health services component do not appear to be likely. A substantial number of federally sponsored health services in the prenatal, postnatal and child health fields do not contain a WIC component. Planning for expansion of health and WIC program services has traditionally been done separately by USDA and DHHS. Only lately have efforts at integrated planning begun. In spite of greater coordination, the two agencies have not yet been able to reach an accomodation which would permit expansion of both WIC and more comprehensive health services in the same areas. Nor have reporting requirements for programs which have both a WIC and other federally sponsored services been simplified.

CONCLUSION

Although the practice of providing supplemental foods through the health rather than through the welfare system is by no means new, it represented a breakthrough in American social welfare policy in the 1970s. Theoretically, it permitted greater specificity in the determination of nutritonal risk than that provided by income alone or other demographic criteria employed in the programs administered through the social welfare system at the time. However, it took over a decade before this concept was finally put into operation at the program level. Concepts of screening, prevention, outreach, and linkages between services have also received greater attention as a result of the program. As time has gone on more attention has been paid to the need for comprehensive health services, including nutrition education and food, for mothers, infants, and children.

A good deal of progress has been made in identifying desirable health and nutrition benefits of WIC. The extent to which these benefits can be attributed to the WIC program varies, but at least some of the positive effects are due to the program. However, little information is available on the characteristics and components of the WIC and other categorical programs with similar purposes that are responsible for these benefits. Neither have the effects of alternative "mixes" of programs or direct income transfers been studied. WIC program costs are high—more than the total per capita health care budget of most developing countries. The United States is in a less favorable economic position today than it was a decade ago, and all federal expenditures are being closely examined for their effectiveness. Only time will tell if the program will survive as a separate, categorical service during the inevitable retrenchment of the 1980s. It is to be hoped that when and if a consolidation occurs, the end result will not simply be greater economies in the delivery of services, but that more comprehensive and individualized attention to the health and nutrition of mothers, infants, and children of the poor is achieved as well.

REFERENCES

1. Amidei, W. Select Panel on Child Health, Institute of Medicine, National Academy of Sciences, 1980 (personal communication to J. Butler).
2. Berkenfield, J., and Schwartz, J. B. Nutrition intervention in the Community: The WIC Program, *N. Engl. J. Med.* **302,** 579–581 (1980).
3. Boruch, R. F., and Gomez, H. Sensitivity bias and theory in impact evaluation. *In* "Evaluation Studies Review Annual" (L. Sechrest, S. G. West, M. A. Phillips, R. Redner, and W. Yeaton, eds.), Vol. 4, Chapter 6, pp. 127–147. Sage Publications, Berkeley, California, 1979.
4. Brickell, H. M. The influence of external political factors on the role and methodology of evaluation. *In* "Evaluation Studies Review Annual" (T. D. Cook, M. L. DelRosario, K. M. Hennigsen, M. M. Mark, and W. Trochin, eds.), Vol. 3, pp. 94–99. Sage Publications, Berkeley, California, 1978.
5. Burke, V. "Income Security for Persons with Limited Income: Program Summaries, Recipient and Expenditure Data. Congressional Research Service, Library of Congress, 1976.
6. Campbell, D. T., and Boruch, R. F. Making the case for randomized experiments: Six ways in which quasi-experimental evaluations in compensatory education tend to underestimate effects. *In* "Evaluation and Measurement" (A. Lamsdaine and C. Bennett, eds.). Academic Press, New York, 1975.
7. Carabello, D. *et al.* "An Evaluation of a Supplementary Feeding Program for Women, Infants and Children" (Waterbury Study). Yale University School of Medicine, New Haven, Connecticut, 1978 (unpublished).

8. Center for Disease Control, Public Health Service, CDC Analysis of Nutrition Indices for WIC Participants. "Nutrition Surveillance." U.S. Dept. of Health, Education and Welfare, Washington, D.C., 1977.

9. Chase, H. C. "International Comparison of Perinatal and Infant Mortality: U.S. and 6 Western European Countries," PHS Publ. 1000, Ser. 3, U.S. Govt. Printing Office, Washington, D.C., 1967.

10. Chase, H. C. A study of risks, medical care and infant mortality. *Am. J. Public Health* **63**, Suppl. (1973).

11. Clarkson, K. W. "Food Stamps and Nutrition," Eval. Stud. No. 18. American Enterprise Institute for Public Policy Research, Washington, D.C., 1975.

12. Comptroller General of the United States. "Observations on the Evaluation of the Special Supplemental Food Program, Food and Nutrition Service," Report to Congress, RED 75-310. U.S. General Accounting Office, Washington, D.C., 1975.

13. Comptroller General of the United States. "Federal Domestic Food Assistance Programs: A Time for Assessment and Change." U.S. General Accounting Office, Washington, D.C., 1978.

14. Comptroller General of the United States. "Summary of a Report: Joint Proposal for a Nutrition Surveillance System." U.S. General Accounting Office, Washington, D.C., 1978.

15. Comptroller General of the United States. "The Special Supplemental Food Program for Women, Infants, and Children: How Can It Work Better?" CED 79-55. U.S. General Accounting Office, Washington, D.C., 1979.

16. Cook, T. D., and Campbell, D. T. "The Design and Analysis of Quasi-Experiment for Field Settings." Rand McNally, Chicago, Illinois, 1979.

17. Davenport, J. A. The Welfare State vs the Public Welfare. *Fortune* June, pp. 132–135, 198–206 (1976).

18. Delgado, H. L., Lechtig, A., Yarborough, C., Martorell, R., Klein, R. E., and Irwin, M. Maternal nutrition—Its effects on infant growth and development and births. "Nutritional Impacts on Women: Throughout Life With Emphasis on Reproduction" (K. S. Moghissi and T. N. Evans, eds.), Chapter 11, pp. 133–150. Harper & Row, Hagerstown, Maryland, 1977.

19. Development Associates, Inc. "Evaluation of the WIC Migrant Demonstration Project." Development Associates, Inc., Arlington, Virginia, 1979.

20. Edozien, J. C., Switzer, B. R., and Bryan, R. B. Medical evaluation of the special supplemental food program for women, infants and children. *Am. J. Clin. Nutr.* **32**, 677–692 (1979).

21. Egan, M. C. Federal nutrition support programs for children. *Pediatr. Clin. North Am.* **24**(1), 229–239 (1977).

22. Federal Register. *Fed. Regist.* Nov. 12, 74874–74877 (1980).

23. Field Foundation. "Hunger USA." Beacon Press, Boston, Massachusetts, 1968.

24. Fleming, V. "Women and Children—First or Last?" Report on the special supplemental food program for women, infants and children. Children's Foundation, Washington, D.C., 1975.

25. Fleming, V., Harvey, S., and Keefer, J. "Overcoming Malnutrition: Putting Federal Programs to Work." Children's Foundation, Washington, D.C., 1977.

26. Fomon, S. J., and Anderson, T. A., eds. "Practices of Low Income Families in Feeding Infants and Small Children." DHEW Publ. No. (HSA) 75-5605, U.S. Dept. of Health Education and Welfare, Rockville, Maryland, 1975.

27. Food and Nutrition Board. National Research Council "Laboratory Indices of Nutritional Status in Pregnancy." Natl. Acad. Sci., Washington, D.C., 1977.

28. Garn, S. M., and Clark, D. C. Nutrition, growth, development and maturation. Findings from the Ten State Survey of 1968–70. *Pediatrics* **56**, 306–319 (1975).
29. Habicht, J. P., and Butz, W. P. Measurement of health and nutrition effects of large scale nutrition intervention projects. In "Evaluating the Impact of Nutrition and Health Programs" (R. E. Klein, M. S. Read, H. Riecken, J. A. Brown, A. Pradilla, and C. H. Oaza, eds.), pp. 133–170. 1979.
30. Habicht, J. P., and Yarborough, C. Efficiency in selecting pregnant women for food supplementation during pregnancy. In "Maternal Nutrition During Pregnancy and Lactation" pp. 314–336. Nestle Foundation Publication Series, Huber, Zurich, 1980.
30a. Harvey, S., ed. "Second National WIC Symposium." Children's Foundation, Washington, D.C., 1981.
31. Higgins, A. C., Crampton, E. W., and Mosley, J. E. Nutrition and the outcome of pregnancy. In "Endocrinology" (R. W. Scow, ed.), pp. 1071–1077. Am. Elsevier, New York, 1974.
32. Iseley, R. B., Mulinare, J., Cuatrecasas, C., Schiller, E. L., Frazas-Castro, E., Katona Apte, J., Hollonbeck, D., and Crawford, J. N. "Evaluation of the Impact of Supplemental Food Programs for Women, Infants and Children: Evidence from the Literature," Task Report, FNS Contract No. 53-3198-9-87. Center for Health Studies, Research Triangle Institute and Department of Nutrition and Food Sciences, University of North Carolina at Greensboro prepared for Family Programs Branch, Program Evaluation Division, Food and Nutrition Service, U.S. Department of Agriculture Washington, D.C., 1980 (unpublished).
33. Kafatos, A. G., and Zee, P. Nutritional benefits from federal food assistance. *Am. J. Dis. Child.* **131**, 265–269 (1977).
34. Kallen, D. J. Nutrition and society. *J. Am. Med. Assoc.* **215**, 94–100 (1971).
35. Kaufman, M. Prepared for the Select Panel on Child Health Institute of Medicine, National Academy of Sciences, Washington, D.C. 1980 (unpublished manuscript).
36. Kennedy, E., and Gershoff, S. Effect of WIC Supplemental Feeding Hemoglobin and Hematocrit of Prenatal Patients." *J. Am. Dietet. Assoc.* **80**, 227–230 (1980).
37. Kennedy, E., Gershoff, S., and Reed, R. Effect of supplemental feeding on birth weight. *J. Am. Dietet. Assoc.* **80**, 220–226 (1982).
38. Kessner, D. "Infant Death: An Analysis by Maternal Risk and Health Care." Nat. Acad. Sci., Washington, D.C., 1973.
39. Kotelchuck, M., Schwartz, J. B., Anderka, M., and Finison, K. "1980 Massachusetts Special Supplement Food Project for Women, Infants and Children." Division of Family Health Services, Community Health Services, Massachusetts Department of Public Health, Boston, Massachusetts, 1981 (unpublished manuscript).
40. Kotz, N. "Let Them Eat Promises: The Politics of Hunger in America." Prentice-Hall, Englewood Cliffs, 1967.
41. Kotz, N. "Hunger in America: The Federal Response." Field Foundation, New York, 1979.
42. Lamm, L., Delaney, J., and Dwyer, J. T. Economy and efficiency in infant feeding. *Pediatr. Clin. North Am.* **24**, 71 (1976).
43. Langham, R. A. A state health department assesses undernutrition. *J. Am. Diet. Assoc.* **65**, 18–23 (1974).
44. Lechtig, A., Habicht, J. P., Delgado, H., Klein, R. E., Yarborough, C., and Martorell, R. Effect of food supplementation in pregnancy on birthweight. *Pediatrics* **56**, 508 (1975).
45. Lechtig, A., Yarborough, C., Delgado, H., Habicht, J. P., Martorell, R., and Klein, R. E. Influence of maternal nutrition on birth weight. *Am. J. Clin. Nutr.* **28**, 1223 (1975).

46. Lesser, A. J. The federal government in health care. *Pediatr. Clin. North Am.* **16,** 891–900 (1969).

47. Martin, J. School nutrition program perspective. *J. Am. Diet. Assoc.* **73,** 389 (1978).

48. Martinez, G. A., and Nalezienski, J. P. The recent trend in breast feeding. *Pediatrics* **64,** 686–692 (1979).

49. Mauer, A. M. The WIC program: Tying supplemental foods to nutritional need. *J. Fla. Med. Assoc.* **66**(4), 453–456 (1979).

50. Mauer, A. M. The WIC program, or the perils of Pauline. *Am. J. Dis. Child.* **133,** 478–480 (1979).

51. Message from the President of the United States Urging Enactment of the Proposed Child Nutrition Reform Act of 1976. 94th Congress, 2nd Session, House Document 94–42. U.S. Govt. Printing Office, Washington, D.C., 1976.

52. Naeye, R. L. Weight gain and the outcome of pregnancy. *Am. J. Obstet. Gynecol.* **135,** 3–9 (1979).

53. National Academy of Sciences, Committee on Maternal Nutrition. "Maternal Nutrition and the Course of Pregnancy." Natl. Acad. Sci., Washington, D.C., 1970.

54. National Council of Organizations for Children and Youth. "America's Children: A Bicentennial Assessment." National Council of Organizations for Children and Youth, Washington, D.C. 1976.

55. Niswander, K. R., and Gordon, M., with Berendes, H. *et al.* "The Collaborative Study: The Women and Their Pregnancies." Saunders, Philadelphia, Pennsylvania, 1972.

56. Owen, G. M., and Lippman, G. Nutritional status of infants and young children, USA. *Pediatr. Clin. North Am.* **24,** 211–288 (1977).

57. Owen, G. M., Kram, K. M., Garry, P. J. *et al.* A study of nutritional status of preschool children in the United States, 1968–70. *Pediatrics* **53,** 597–646 (1974).

58. Patton, M. Q. "Utilization-focused Evaluation." Sage Publications, Beverly Hills, California, 1978.

59. Patton, M. Q. Evaluation of program implementation. *In* "Evaluation Studies Review Annual" (L. Sechrest, S. G. West, M. A. Phillips, R. Redner and W. Yeaton, eds.), Vol. 4, Chapter 16, pp. 318–346. Sage Publishers, Berkeley, California, 1979.

60. Popkin, B. M., Akin, J., Kaufman, M. S. *et al.* Nutritional program options for maternal and child health. *In* "Better Health for Our Children," Vol. IV, Background Papers, pp. 87–126. USDHHS Pub. No. 79-55071 Washington, D.C., 1981.

61. Price, D. W., West, D. A., Scheier, G. C., and Price, D. A. Food delivery programs and other factors affecting nutrient intake of children. *Am. J. Agric. Econ.* **60**(1), 609–618 (1978).

62. Reed, M. S. Malnutrition, hunger and behavior. *J. Am. Diet. Assoc.* **63,** 379–391 (1973).

63. Rein, M., and White, S. Can policy research help policy? *In* "Evaluation Studies Review Annual" (T. Cook, M. DelRosario, K. Hennigan, M. Mark, and W. Trochin, eds.), Vol. 3, Chapter 1, pp. 24–47, Sage Publications, Berkeley, California, 1978.

64. Rivera, J. The frequency and use of various kinds of milk during infancy in middle and lower income families. *Am. J. Public Health* **61,** 277 (1971).

65. Rush, D., Higgins, A. G., Sudow, M. D., and Margolis, S. "Dietary Services During Pregnancy and Birthweight: A Retrospective Matched Pair Analysis." Division of Epidemiology and Department of Pediatrics, Columbia University, New York, 1976.

66. Rush, D., Stein, Z., and Susser, M. A randomized controlled trial of prenatal nutritional supplementation in New York City. *Pediatrics* **65,** 685 (1980).

67. Schaefer, A. E. Nutrition needs of special populations at risk. *Ann. N. Y. Acad. Sci.* **300**, 419–427 (1977).
68. Scheffler, W. Preventing lead poisoning: WIC clinics help reach children at risk. *Food Nutr. (FAO)* **10**(3), 4–7 (1980).
69. Sechrest, L., West, S. G., Phillips, M. A., Redner, R., and Yeaton, W. Introduction. *In* "Evaluation Studies Review Annual" (L. Sechrest, S. G. West, M. A. Phillips, R. Redner, and W. Yeaton, eds.), Vol. 4, pp. 15–35. Sage Publishers, Berkeley, California, 1974.
70. Select Panel for the Promotion of Child Health. "Better Health for Our Children: A National Strategy," Report of the Select Panel for the Promotion of Child Health to the United States Congress and the Secretary of Health and Human Services, Vol. II, p. 61, No. 79-55071. U.S. Dept. of Health and Human Services, Washington, D.C., 1981.
71. Senate Select Committee on Nutrition and Human Needs. "Hunger 1973 and Press Reaction," Committee Print, No. 73-S582-6. U.S. Govt. Printing Office, Washington, D.C., 1973.
72. Senate Select Committee on Nutrition and Human Needs. "WIC Program Survey, 1975." Committee Print Select Committee on Nutrition and Human Needs, U.S. Senate, U.S. Govt. Printing Office, Washington, D.C., 1975.
73. Urban Institute. "Special Supplemental Food Program for Women, Infants and Children." Delivery Systems Evaluation, Urban Institute, Washington, D.C., 1975.
74. U.S. Department of Commerce, Bureau of Census. "Consumer Income: Characteristics of the Population Below the Poverty Level: 1978," Curr. Popul. Rep., Ser. P-60, No. 124, p. 205. USDC, Washington, D.C., 1980.
75. Van Duzen, J., Carter, J. P., Second, J., and Federspiel, C. Protein and calorie malnutrition among preschool Navajo Indian children. *Am. J. Clin. Nutr.* **22**, 1362–1378 (1969).
76. Van Duzen, J., Carter, J. P., and Van Der Swagg, R. Protein-calorie malnutrition among preschool Navajo Indian children: A follow-up. *Am. J. Clin. Nutr.* **29**, 657–662 (1976).
77. Watts, M., Gregory, T., and Jensen, C. T. WIC: The special supplemental food program for women, infants and children. *Food Nutr. (FAO)* **7**(1), 2–7 (1977).
78. "White House Conference on Food, Nutrition and Health." U.S. Govt. Printing Office, Washington, D.C., 1970.
79. Wilson, D. The economic analysis of malnutrition. *In* "Nutrition National Development and Planning" (A. Berg, N. S. Scrimshaw, and D. L. Call, eds.), Chapter 13, pp. 127–144. Massachusetts Institute of Technology, Cambridge, 1973.
80. Wortman, C. B., and Rabinowitz, V. C. Random assignment: The fairest of them all. *In* "Evaluation Studies Review Annual" (L. Sechrest, S. G. West, M. Phillips, R. Redner, and W. Yeaton, Vol. 4, Chapter 9, pp. 177–184. Sage Publishers, Berkeley, California, 1979.
81. Zee, P. Three steps forward and one step backward. *In* "Stokeley Van Camp Annual Symposium Food in Contemporary Society: Public Policy and Preventive Nutrition," pp. 169–172. University of Tennessee, Knoxville, 1979.
82. Zee, P., and Kafatos, H. G. Nutrition and federal food assistance programs: A survey of impoverished preschool blacks in Memphis, Tennessee. *Fed. Proc., Fed. Am. Soc. Exp. Biol.* **32**, 3 (1973).
83. Zee, P., Walters, T., and Mitchell, C. Nutrition and poverty in preschool children. *JAMA, J. Am. Med. Assoc.* **213**, 739–741 (1970).
84. Zigler, E. The unmet needs of America's children. *Child. Today* May-June, pp. 39–42 (1976).

15 School Feeding Programs in the Philippines

RODOLFO F. FLORENTINO

INTRODUCTION

Nutrition survey data collected from 1958 to 1968 by the Food and Nutrition Research Center (FNRC) of the National Science Development Board showed that diets of Filipinos were both inadequate in quantity and quality. Moreover, it was shown that among subjects classified as having poor general appearance, the highest incidence was in the 7 to 12 years age group (1).

The poor state of nutrition among school children was confirmed by subsequent studies of the Department (now Ministry) of Education and Culture.

In 1974, the Department of Education and Culture described the nutritional status of Filipino elementary school children based on Iowa standards. Results showed that out of the 31,000 randomly selected children 6 to 14 years old from Grades I–VI in forty-five selected pilot feeding schools assisted by CARE, 94.0% were underweight, 5.4% normal, and 0.6% overweight. Using the recommended weight for Filipino children in 1977, the nutritional status of 37,000 public elementary school children also 6 to 14 years old from Grades I–IV in eighty-five schools randomly selected school divisions with CARE and CRS supplementary feeding showed that 2.1% were severely underweight, 28% moderately underweight, 48.5% mildly underweight, 20% normal weight, and 1.3% overweight (2).

A recent study conducted by the Ministry of Education and Culture (MEC) for the school year 1979–1980 showed that most of the school children were underweight. Of the 20,808 school children ages 7–14

NUTRITION INTERVENTION STRATEGIES IN NATIONAL DEVELOPMENT

randomly selected from 31 of the 125 school divisions in the country, 75.5% were underweight and 20.8% underheight according to the recommended height and weight standards for Filipino children. The underweight children were further classified into severely malnourished, 2.7%, moderately malnourished, 25.6%, and mildly malnourished, 47.2% (3).

With the recognition of the malnutrition problem among school children, school feeding programs were launched as early as 1958 using Food for Peace commodities by CARE. The programs supplied skim milk to over 3 million elementary school children (4). Since then, other food supplements have been used according to the amount and type of commodities available.

In 1964, supplementary feeding to school children of the Applied Nutrition Program was implemented. Snacks or hot lunches were provided to school children. The feeding programs in schools were classified into assisted programs, which made use of donated food commodities from CRS and CARE, self-help programs, which made use of local foods, and other special types of feeding programs, such as the subsidized lunch feeding program.

To help solve malnutrition among school children, the Nutribun was formulated in 1970 containing 500 calories and 17 g protein based on a study that diets of Filipino children between 4 to 9 years are deficient by 69% of the calories and 30 to 39% of the protein recommended for daily consumption (5). Thus CARE and CRS assisted school feeding programs used the Nutribun as a snack food to school children.

The Catholic Relief Services (CRS) started supplying school children with a variety of food commodities like flour, cornmeal, soybean oil, rolled oats, drymilk, beans, and butter cooked into native delicacies in 1963 (6). However, in 1968 due to limited food resources, this feeding was made available only to underweight school children. Because of further restrictions in the food assistance program in 1975, the Nutribun recipients were limited to underweight children in the kindergarten and the primary level only (Grades I–IV). Likewise the size of the Nutribun was reduced to provide only 300 calories and 11 grams protein.

The Nutribun formulation currently being used supplies 250 calories and 8.4 g protein, the bulk of which comes from United States donated soy fortified wheat flour. Schools put in an additional 50 calories per bun, through fillings, soups, and fruit juices boosting the total supplementation to 300 calories.

The World Food Program-assisted Elementary Feeding in Mindanao was made possible through a government request for WFP assistance to an elementary school feeding. After an appraisal was made by an interagency mission, the project was approved in 1977. Project operation began in January, 1979.

The World Food Program-assisted Project like the CRS and CARE, provides school children with soy fortified wheat flour baked into Nutribuns. In addition is the corn soy milk used as a hot lunch supplement in the form of porridge, soups, viands, and desserts.

This chapter describes in more detail the various school feeding programs that have been in operation in the Philippines.

APPLIED NUTRITION PROGRAM (ANP)

To support the Philippine Nutrition Program, the Ministry of Education and Culture launched the Applied Nutrition Program in 1963 with the help of cooperating American voluntary agencies. The objective of the program is to eliminate undernourishment in children between the ages 7 to 14 years. To achieve this, activities such as nutrition training, food production, supplementary feeding, and nutrition education are being undertaken.

Self-help supplementary feeding to public elementary school children is in the form of snacks and hot vegetable soup. This is available 2 to 3 times a week. As a counterpart contribution, children pay P0.15 (US $0.02) per feeding. There are 2200 participants of the program at present. Indigenous foods produced in school, home, and community gardens are utilized, whereas other items are bought locally or supplied by the community. Recipes served are legume–cereal and root crop–legume based. Other food items such as tripe, dried shrimps, anchovies, or other fish with green leafy vegetables are added to soups, whereas boiled root crops are served with grated coconut and sugar. The foods are prepared in school kitchens and distributed from a central point.

Changes in the nutritional status of children are determined by taking their weights 3 times a year, and height 2 times a year. Supervisory visits by the Applied Nutrition Project regional and division personnel are also conducted in the local schools implementing the program.

Program results observed and recorded among school children were improved weights and general physical condition; more active responses and participation in class, play, and work activities; less school absences and improved health habits (7).

Another activity of the ANP is food production, the long-range goal of which is to attain self-sufficiency in food for supplementary feeding. This is to ensure continuous supply of foodstuffs. There were improvements in the kind of food crops grown in the gardens such as a balanced proportion of legumes to other crops. It was also observed that school lunches brought by children improved in quality.

In implementing the program, one major difficulty is inadequate funds for the operation of the project. This accounted for lack of garden tools and water supply in some schools (reducing food production for the school feeding project) and lack of food preparation and serving utensils. Other problems are lack of teachers and other personnel to take charge and strengthen various activities at the school level and poor interpretation of the integrated approach of the nutrition program.

COOPERATIVE FOR AMERICAN RELIEF EVERYWHERE (CARE)

One cooperating American voluntary agency that has been supplementing the diets of school children is the Cooperative for American Relief Everywhere (CARE). The CARE-assisted school feeding program is assisting a national effort to eradicate malnutrition among children in the primary grades.

CARE's target beneficiaries for 1979 are 3.6 million school children in Regions I–VIII and X in the country. However, only 1.5 million school children were reached for the school year 1979–1980.

As of 1971, CARE provided school children with the Nutribun made of the Blend K-flour or the soy fortified wheat flour (SFWF) instead of the original skim milk flour mixture. A bun provides 250 calories and 8.4 g protein with additional 50 calories from the filling, hot vegetable soup, or vegetable side dish provided by the schools from school gardens or local source to supply a total of 300 calories per day for each child.

CARE provides food commodities for the nutribun, whereas the Ministry of Education and Culture provides in-country transportation costs, facilities, sites, personnel, and funds for project operation. Nutribuns are prepared by commercial bakeries contracted by local school authorities or school bakeries. These are given free to children, who cannot afford to pay the ₱0.10 ($0.014) counterpart contribution to cover baking cost. The total cost to CARE in administering the program for the school year 1979–1980 was US $280,259.17 (8).

To monitor the nutritional status of beneficiaries in the program, they are weighed at the start of the school year against the weight for age standard for Filipino children. Children are weighed every 3 months thereafter.

In 1971–1972, a study in eight elementary public schools participating in the Nutribun program of MEC and CARE in one province (Bulacan) of the country was conducted to assess the progress of the program.

Children were weighed at the start of the feeding period and at quarterly intervals thereafter. The nutritional status of a child was determined by using the Student Nutrition chart, devised by the Food for Peace Division of the USAID, based on the Iowa Growth Norms. The feeding period averaged 17 weeks for all schools.

The result showed that before the feeding program, an average of 35.6 per cent of the children were malnourished; after the feeding program, this average was reduced to 29.1%. The mean increase in weight percentage of standard ranged from 0.7 to 3.3% with an overall average of 1.6%. It was noted that the school with the highest percentage of malnourished children made the best showing in improving the nutritional status of its school children (9).

An assessment of the MEC-CARE School Nutrition Program has been conducted for the school year 1978–1979 to collect accurate and reliable data on feeding program. A systematic random sample of 219 schools was selected out of all the schools participating in the program with a minimum of one school per division being included in the selection. The sample size was 5% of the total schools in the program. The CARE field

TABLE I

Nutritional Status of the Children When They Entered Grade I as Compared to Present Status in Grade II[a]

	Original nutritional[b] status (no. of children)					
	1	2	3	4	5	6
Third degree, 189	37%	2%	—	—	—	—
Second degree, 1611	—	28%	1%	—	—	0.6%
First degree, 3018	—	—	17%	—	3%	—
Normal, 1074	—	—	—	9%	—	—

[a] One major difficulty in administering the MEC-CARE Assisted Feeding Program is delayed distribution of food commodities to recipient schools. This limited the target feeding days. On the average 75% of the feeding days had been met; of the lost days, 48% were lost due to lack of stock. Other problems are monitoring the nutritional status of the school children, financial accounts on the sale of Nutribuns, and utilization of profits from Nutribun sales, and submission of monthly reports to the District/Division on time. 174 second grade classes out of 323 classes in 153 random schools where data was available were sampled.

[b] 1, Improved to second degree; 2, improved to first degree; 3, improved to normal; 4, regressed to first degree; 5, regressed to second degree; 6, regressed to third degree.

officers visited the schools and collected the data. The study showed that only 153 of the 219 sample schools maintained the required weight for age information for each child. From this data, 87% of schools have average attendance of not less than 97% of enrollment.

From 174 second grade classes out of 323 classes in 153 random sample schools, 89% of school children improved their nutritional status at various levels while some regressed. This is shown in Table I (10). It was noted that schools with the most malnourished children showed better nutritional improvement.

CATHOLIC RELIEF SERVICES (CRS)

The Catholic Relief Services (CRS) of the United States Catholic Conference (USCC) is another integral component of the Applied Nutrition Program through its Targetted School Feeding Program. The Ministry of Education and Culture administers and implements the program, and CRS provides food resources and technical assistance. Supplementary food is given to underweight school children in the kindergarten and primary level of public schools in the country to improve their nutritional health.

For the school year 1980–1981, the CRS-TSFP target beneficiaries were 200,000 underweight primary school children in four cities of the National Capital Region (Metro Manila); Iligan City, and Lanao del Norte of Region XII; Culion, Palawan of Region IV; Olongapo City, Region III, and other areas specified by the Ministry of Education and Culture not covered by CARE and WFP.

Like CARE, the supplementary food given to school children is in the form of Nutribun made of the Blend K or soy-fortified wheat flour, providing 250 calories and 8.4 g protein. Schools provide 50 calories in the form of fillings, soups, and fruit juices, which increase the total calories to 300 for each child per day.

CRS contracts commercial bakeries to bake and deliver the nutribun requirements of the participating schools which in turn make these available to school children at a cost of ₱0.15 (US$.02) per bun. Nutribun is provided free to indigent malnourished school children. As projected by the CRS, the direct program cost for the school year 1980–1981 is $1,071,012.92, excluding the value of school inputs such as facilities and services of school personnel (11).

The nutritional status of the children is determined through an initial height–weight survey taken at the start of the school year. Subsequent weighing and height measurements are done every 3 months thereafter.

The nutritional progress of each participant is determined by comparing the report of the initial weighing with that of the final one.

In addition, other aspects such as interest and attitudes of the program cooperators, the participants and their parents towards the program are also monitored.

In 1973, an evaluation of the weight response of elementary school children to the feeding of the Nutribun was conducted among 1119 children from Grades I–VI in five Manila schools. The experimental feeding period lasted for an average of 22 weeks or 5.5 months. Weights of the children were taken at the beginning and end of the feeding period using clinical scales and classified according to the Gomez standard. Weight response was measured as the change in percentage of standard weight for age. Result showed an increase in percentage standard weight by an average of 1.35%. The average initial weight was 66.6% of standard weight for age; the final weight was 67.9% (5).

Another study was conducted in Metro Manila schools among 1820 Grade I pupils in eleven randomly selected public elementary schools. Weights and heights of children were taken at the start and end of the school year by school teachers and home economics supervisors/nutrition coordinators. Nutritional levels were determined using the height and weight charts based on Philippine standards. Actual number of feeding days ranged from 80 to 125. It was shown from the study that 909 or 92.3% of the children who started the school year suffering from

TABLE II

Distribution of Children by Nutritional Status before and after Feeding[a]

Nutritional level	Before feeding		After feeding		Percent change
	Number	%	Number	%	
Weight					
Overweight	21	1.2	32	1.8	52.4
Normal	345	19	462	25.4	33.9
Mild	979	53.8	941	51.7	3.9
Moderate	446	24.5	375	20.6	15.9
Severe	29	1.6	10	.5	65.5
Height					
Normal	1286	70.7	1332	73.2	3.6
Underheight	534	29.3	488	26.8	8.6
Total	1820	100/0	1820	100.0	

[a] Mean height gain was 1.2 cm. and 0.6 cm. for males and females, respectively, whereas mean weight gain was 0.7 kg. for both sexes.

mild undernutrition were either maintained or improved by one nutritional level or more; some 75 children or 7.7% regressed to moderate level at school year's end (12). Table II shows the weight and height changes of children before and after the feeding period.

A study on the attitudes of program participants and implementors was also conducted by CRS during the latter part of the school year 1979–80 in 25 Metro Manila schools and 8 Iligan schools among 112 teachers, 257 children, and 31 mothers. Results showed that Nutribun is well accepted by all respondents and that they have a very good concept of it, as a factor in the improvement of nutritional status. Teachers and parents claimed that health and physical condition of the children improved. Teachers also observed an improvement in class attendance and class participation of children (13).

The same study also showed that the feeding program has generated much interest among school administrators. Several schools were able to establish their own baking units, thus supplying their Nutribun requirement and at the same time providing vocational skills to older children. Funds generated enabled most schools to improve the program and to include such benefits as financial subsidy for indigent children, provision of additional calories and protein, and integration of nutrition-related projects including school gardens, raising rabbit, poultry, pigs, and fish culture.

Some difficulties encountered by MEC and CRS in administering the program are inability of qualified participants to buy the Nutribun and in the instrument used in assessing the nutritional status of school children. For instance, most schools have only bathroom scales, instead of clinical scales for weighing.

WORLD FOOD PROGRAM ASSISTED PROJECT

Another school feeding program is the World Food Program-Assisted Elementary School Feeding in Mindanao (WFP-ESFP). This 3-year (1979–1981) food assistance project aims to strengthen and support the Philippine Nutrition Program by improving the nutritional status of public elementary school children in four regions (IX, X, XI, XII) of the country except those assisted by CARE and CRS.

The project's recipients are 1 million school children in 2856 public elementary schools, Grades I–VI. Participating schools are mostly located in depressed areas.

WFP supplies two food commodities in the form of soy-fortified wheat flour (SFWF) and corn soy milk (CSM). Like CARE and CRS, the SFWF is baked into Nutribuns. However, a piece of Nutribun provides 380 calories; 15 g protein, 6 g fat, and 882 I.U. of vitamin A, as compared to the 250 calorie and 8.4 g Nutribun used by CARE and CRS. This is served daily to 500,000 school children. The Nutribun is accompanied with a filling, a fresh fruit juice or a vegetable soup twice a week to provide variety and increase its nutritive value. Recipients pay ₱0.10 to ₱0.30 (US $0.0135 to $0.04) as counterpart contribution to defray cost of local foods and expenses in the preparation of the bread and accompanying foods.

The corn soy milk is used to prepare snacks or hot lunch supplements in the form of porridge, soups, desserts, and/or beverages. Vegetables from school, home, and community gardens as well as other local foods are cooked with CSM for each child per day provides 370 calories, 13 g protein, 6 g fat, and 1700 I.U. of vitamin A. This is served 2 to 3 times daily since one serving cannot be consumed by a child at one sitting. The target beneficiaries are another 500,000 school children.

Nutribun is baked in school or commercial bakeries whereas CSM is prepared in school kitchens and served to school children in a center. Both rations are served 5 days a week for the first year, 4 days a week for the second year, and 3 days a week for the third year.

For the 3-year project, WFP has committed a total cost of $16.2 million. The Ministry of Education and Culture on the other hand has a budget allocation of ₱34,123,540 (US $4,630,059.7) for 4 calendar years (14).

The impact of the feeding program on the health and nutritional status of the beneficiaries is determined by comparing the results of height and weight surveys taken at the start and end of the feeding period. This is measured by the decrease in the number of underweight children and by increase in the number of children of normal weights for given ages. A 3-year longitudinal study on the effects of deworming implemented in conjunction with supplementary feeding, health education, and improvement of environmental sanitation has also been started in one region.

After 1 year of operation, MEC and WFP observed a significant increase in enrollments in schools participating in the feeding program, the number of dropouts has appreciably decreased in these schools, and the attendance (both in regularity and punctuality) has substantially improved. According to teachers' reports, the number of normal weight children has increased and the number of children in underweight categories has consequently decreased. The active participation also of mothers and other adult women in the community in activities of the project is an evidence that women realize the importance of the project to the health of the children (14).

The feeding program, besides augmenting the diets of school children, served as a vehicle for the introduction of other nutrients found in other foods prepared and served with the donated food commodities. Another aspect of the program is that it benefits parents and communities as well. This is through nutrition and health knowledge, which parents acquire in their participation in project activities, opportunity for the participants and possibly other family members to avail of health services offered by the school, projects which the participants are expected to bring to their homes and the community, and jobs for out-of-school youths in school bakeries.

Though the project has reached its target beneficiaries, difficulties have been encountered in its implementation. For instance, the absence of satisfactory and safe storage of the food commodities at destination prevented the shipment of commodities, thus limiting the target of 160 feeding days to 80 for the first school year. There was also loss of commodities from torn bags due to rough handling during loading and unloading.

The selection of beneficiary schools has not followed the concept of the project as designed in that the more needy, deserving, and disadvantaged schools have not been reached for lack of accessibility.

Difficulties in supplementary feeding operation included lack of food preparation and distribution utensils, as well as feeding paraphernalia, inability of parents to give their counterpart contribution, and losses in food production in some schools due partly to inadequate water supply.

Evaluation of the nutritional status of children using the height and weight survey was not conducted in many participating schools for lack of weighing scales. Also the use by some schools of inaccurate bathroom scales for measuring changes in body weight and use of ruler for measuring height against calibration on a wall limited the usefulness of the height and weight data collected in these schools.

FUTURE PLANS AND CONCLUSIONS

Of the four school feeding programs being implemented in the country by the Ministry of Education and Culture, only the Applied Nutrition Program operates on a self-help basis. The other programs—CARE, CRS and WFP-Assisted—although using their resources, also believe in people's ability to help themselves. CARE, for example, plans for an expanded Nutribun distribution but with gradual reduction of donated commodities through substitution with local foods.

The CRS, in preparation for the eventual phase-out of the donated food commodities, plans to cooperate with the Ministry of Education and Culture in stimulating local involvement and participation among schools. It shall encourage and assist in the implementation of the project toward the development of alternative feeding schemes geared towards the promotion and utilization of nutritious, inexpensive indigenous snack foods for a more self-reliant school feeding program. The World Food Program is phasing out its food commodities after the planned 3-year project. These commodities will be replaced by local foods provided and financed by the communities.

All voluntary agencies are for school feeding on self-help basis. This is in line with the Philippine Nutrition Program's (PNP) plan for programs directed to school children. As envisioned by the then Applied Nutrition Project of the Department of Education and Culture in 1960, supplementary feeding to school children should consist of locally available foods which form part of their normal diet.

As a component of an intervention program supporting the PNP, the School Feeding Program has shown some beneficial effects. This is shown in a recent study conducted by the Ministry of Education and Culture. There was a general improvement in the nutritional status of school children as compared with the previous years. This is also attributed to other aspects that come along in the implementation of the program like the development of desirable food habits among school children, food production, deworming in some schools, and awareness of parents and people in the community of the objectives of the program.

On the other hand, the Philippine Nutrition Program of which the School Feeding Program is a part places primary emphasis on preschool children for nutritional rehabilitation. Through teaching of nutrition in schools, thorough integration of the subject in the curriculum will have to remain as the mainstay of the School Nutrition Program in order to achieve its long-term objectives in line with the objectives of the Philippine Nutrition Program.

REFERENCES

1. Summary results of the eight regional nutrition surveys conducted in the Philippines by the Food and Nutrition Research Center, NIST-NSDB. *Philipp. J. Nutr.* **22,** 61–101 (1969).
2. Department of Education and Culture. "A Study of the Nutritional Status of Filipino Elementary School Children." Manila (mimeographed).

176 Rodolfo F. Florentino

3. Ministry of Education and Culture—School Health and Nutrition Center. "A Study of the Nutritional Status of Filipino Public Elementary School Children Ages 7–14 Years School Year 1979–80." Summary Report. Manila, 1981.
4. CARE-Philippines. A Profile of CARE in the Philippines. Manila, 1978 (mimeographed).
5. Wolgemuth, J. C. "An Evaluation of the Weight Response of Elementary School Age Children to the Feeding of the Nutribun," unpublished USAID Report. Manila, 1973.
6. Ministry of Education and Culture–Catholic Relief Services. USCC Targeted School Feeding Program Guidelines, School Year 1980–81 (mimeographed).
7. The Philippine Applied Nutrition Program, 1975 (mimeographed).
8. Ministry of Education and Culture. Summary Report on the Projects of the School Health and Nutrition Center. Manila, 1980 (typewritten).
9. Caedo, M. M. "Integrated Nutrition—Family Planning Program: Province of Bulacan, 1971–72." USAID Food Nutr. Prop. Attachment 6, pp. 10–12. Manila, 1963.
10. Ministry of Education and Culture and CARE. "An Assessment of the MEC-CARE School Nutrition Program, 1978–79" (mimeographed).
11. Ministry of Education and Culture—Catholic Relief Services. USCC Targetted School Feeding Program Description, School Year 1980–81 (mimeographed).
12. Catholic Relief Services. "An Evaluation of the Nutritional Impact of Nutribun Feeding Among Grade I Pupils in Eleven Public Elementary Schools in Metro Manila." Manila, 1978 (mimeographed).
13. Catholic Relief Services. "A Study on the Attitudes of Participants and Cooperators on the Targeted School Feeding Program." Manila, 1980 (mimeographed).
14. The World Food Program Assisted Project. Manila, 1980 (typewritten).

IV Strategies for Treatment of Protein Energy Malnutrition

16 Rehabilitation of Protein Energy Malnutrition in Young Infants: Hospital and Community Based Programs in Chiang Mai, Thailand

OUSA THANANGKUL, DAMRI
DAMRONGSAK, VICHARN VITHAYASAI,
TASANAWAN VANIYAPONG, AND JURAI
CHAMNAN

There is still a controversy over the best place in which to rehabilitate a child suffering from severe protein energy malnutrition (PEM). Bengoa in 1966 (1) stated that severe PEM is an indication for immediate admission to a hospital. Behar in 1968 (2) also commented that children with advanced forms of PEM, or with complications, must be considered as emergency cases and immediately hospitalized. However, Sadre and Donoso in 1969 (3) felt that under the present circumstances, the admission of malnourished children to hospitals is not effective. Cook (4), in his review in 1971, expressed the view that there is very little that can be done for the child in a hospital that cannot be done as safely, cheaply, and effectively outside a hospital.

Reports from several places record that large numbers of malnourished children died after discharge from the hospital and that many survivors relapsed. For example, McLaren in 1964 (5) reported that 15 to 30% of the children they treated died after discharge from the hospital and that hardly any of the survivors were thriving. MacWilliam and Dean in 1965 (6) reported that 18% of children with PEM who were

NUTRITION INTERVENTION STRATEGIES IN NATIONAL DEVELOPMENT
Copyright © 1983 by Academic Press, Inc.
All rights of reproduction in any form reserved.
ISBN 012-709080-0

treated in an Infant Malnutrition Research Unit died at home after discharge, 70% of them within 12 months. Ifekwunigwe (7) also felt that not all malnourished children should be admitted to the hospital and that the results of treatment of PEM outside the hospital were equally good or even better.

On the other hand, there are several centers that report successful experience in the rehabilitation of children in a hospital or research unit. Garrow and Pike (8) achieved almost complete survival among their malnourished children while in the hospital and among those followed-up after discharge. Whitman *et al.* (9) followed 130 cases of kwashiorkor for more than 5 years and found good recovery; even though these children remained in their unfavorable environment, their growth was comparable with that of their siblings. Graham (10) followed 60 infants and children for a period of 2–5 years and from his experience found that children with severe PEM, unless accompanied by prolonged and severe calorie restrictions, are not likely to have permanent growth defects.

EXPERIENCE WITH HOSPITAL REHABILITATION OF SEVERE PEM AT CHIANG MAI

The results in Chiang Mai of treatment of severe protein energy malnutrition in hospital have been good. The mortality rate in our unit is 5–7% and follow-up after discharge has shown that 70% of the patients remained well with continuing catch-up growth (11). The readmission rate of our severe PEM children is only 1%.

A cardinal aim of research centers in different parts of the world should be a careful investigation of the local variations in disease patterns. The findings should result in developing guidelines for management of the problem as well as for preventive actions adapted to prevailing local conditions.

The term "severe protein–calorie malnutrition" as used in our unit should first be clarified. Gomez in 1955 (12) suggested the use of the deficit of percentage of body weight for age when compared with the reference standard as an indicator to evaluate the severity of severe protein calorie malnutrition. This classification with the Harvard reference standard (13) has been widely accepted all over the world. In 1970, as the result of the Wellcome Trust-sponsored meeting in Jamaica (14), the recommendation was to use the presence of edema, coupled with the deficit of body weight for age, as a yardstick to classify subgroups of PEM. However, the average growth curve of children in North Thailand is equivalent only to the tenth percentile of the Harvard reference standard. (Fig. 1). Therefore, when determining the deficit in percentage of weight for age by this method, several of our children fall into the severe marasmus category even though there is not severe wasting. Waterlow in 1974 (15–17) proposed the use of the percentage of the weight for height as an index to evaluate the state of nutrition. We find this index more useful and more definitive than other methods both for diagnosis of severe marasmus defined when the body weight for height is below 75% and for following the improvement of children. To illustrate this, we evaluated children with severe marasmus in two ways: one group by using the weight for age and the other by using weight for height (Fig. 2). At the end of the study, when all the children were well nourished,

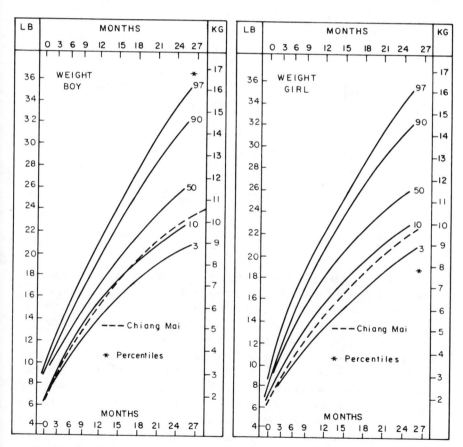

Fig. 1. Growth pattern of northern Thai children compared with Harvard growth curve.

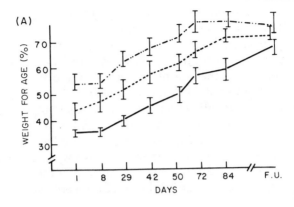

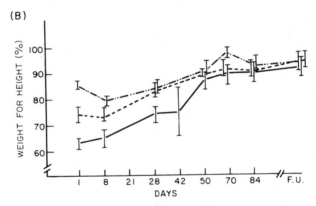

Fig. 2. Weight changes (%) for age (A) and height (B) in Marasmus.

some of them still had a body weight of less than 60% of normal according to the Harvard reference, which by the Gomez's classification would be defined as third-degree malnutrition. However, when weight for height as a percentage of reference was used, all children had improved to 90%, regardless of their deficit on admission.

Recently Habicht *et al.* (18) demonstrated that there is little difference in the genetic potential for growth in different races. It is therefore appropriate that an international reference for growth be adopted and that most widely used internationally has been the Harvard reference standard. Van Wieringen (19) showed that the weight at any given height is independent of age. In our experience the weight for a given height is linear when the height is between 50 and 95 cm, regardless of whether the Harvard reference or the local Chiang Mai reference is used. The equation to calculate the expected weight for a given height is:

(For boys) weight = 0.24 × height − 8.13 (r = 0.995)
(For girls) weight = 0.24 × height − 8.28 (r = 0.997)

For other subclasses of severe PEM, we use our own scoring system. This is a combination of the percentage of weight for height, the clinical findings, and the laboratory findings (Table I).

Even though the purpose of the RIHES classification is for use in hospitals or research units, it can be applied even in small rehabilitation centers. One can determine total serum protein by using the $CuSO_4$ method or by using the urinometer to measure the total serum solids (TSS) and serum albumin (TSP). We compared serum protein values determined by the biuret procedure and albumin levels by electrophoresis, with the TSS and TSP determined by the urinometer. We have found that in kwashiorkor and marasmic–kwashiorkor cases, the two values are similar. Even though the TSS is slightly higher in marasmus cases than the total protein (Table II), the values are sufficiently

TABLE I

Scoring for PEM as Used at RIHES CHIANG MAI

Indicators	Score
Weight/height > 80% with edema	5
Weight/height between 70–80% with edema	4
Weight/height below 70% with edema	3
Weight/height between 70–80% without edema	2
Weight/height below 70% without edema	1
Weight/height > 80% without edema	0
Dermatosis	3

Serum albumin	Total protein	Score
<1.00	<3.25	5
1.00–1.49	3.25–3.99	4
1.50–1.99	4.00–4.74	3
2.00–2.49	4.75–5.49	2
2.50–2.99	5.50–6.24	1
3.00	6.25	0

	Score
Score for marasmus	1–3
Score for Marasmic–Kwashiorkor	4–7
Score for kwashiorkor	≥8

TABLE II

Evaluation of Serum Protein Levels by Different Methods ($\bar{X} \pm$ SE)[a]

Types of patient	TP (g/dl)	TSS (g/dl)	Alb. (g/dl)	TSP (g/dl)
Marasmus	5.9	6.8	2.9	4.3
(30)	±0.2	±0.2	±0.1	±0.2
Marasmic–kwashiorkor	4.7	4.7	2.1	3.2
(30)	±0.2	±0.8	±0.1	±0.6
Kwashiorkor	4.0	4.0	1.6	2.7
(30)	±0.1	±0.5	±0.1	±0.4

[a] TP, Total protein by biuret procedure; TSS, total serum solids; Alb., albumin determined by electrophoresis; TSP, total serum protein.

close to allow the use of the TSS procedure to estimate the level of serum protein.

We feel that our classification is a qualitative one and relates to the morbidity and mortality of children with severe protein energy malnutrition. The mortality from different types of malnutrition is shown in Table III. In our experience, mortality from marasmus is less than other forms of PEM. The mortality among children with kwashiorkor is highest. The therapeutic plan we use for treatment of PEM consists of (1) therapy for fluid and electrolyte imbalance, (2) therapy for infection, (3) dietary therapy, and (4) vitamins therapy.

FLUID AND ELECTROLYTE IMBALANCE THERAPY

Children admitted to our metabolic unit frequently present with low or normal sodium, low potassium, and often low magnesium levels (Table IV). Low serum potassium is a common finding among kwashiorkor cases, especially when diarrhea is present. The supplement

TABLE III

Mortality Rate in PCM at RIHES[a]

Diagnosis	No.	Mortality (%)
Marasmus	51	5.9
Marasmic–kwashiorkor	60	8.3
Kwashiorkor	56	12.5

[a] 167 cases.

TABLE IV

Serum Electrolyte Values in Kwashiorkor at RIHES

	Days					
Electrolyte	1	2	8	29	50	71
Sodium	132.10	132.60	133.70	135.10	133.50	135.00
Potassium	2.74	3.95	4.38	4.42	4.38	3.60
Calcium	3.67	3.54	3.60	3.89	4.65	4.70
Magnesium	1.56	1.61	1.65	1.61	1.83	2.00

of potassium given should be about 7–8 mEq/kg/day initially and 5 mEq/kg/day thereafter. High sodium therapy is not used. Our maintenance dose of sodium is about 2.7 mEq/kg, which is the same as the amount of full milk formula at intakes of 5–6 oz/kg/day. With this level of sodium intake, cardiac failure during the initial course of treatment does not emerge as a problem. Fluid and electrolytes can be given either orally or intravenously. Intravenous fluid is used when the patient is vomiting or in cases of suspected septicemia. We found that the gastric passage time is slow among these children; therefore oral feeding, when used, should be given in frequent small amounts to prevent vomiting. Tube feeding is needed among those who cannot take adequate food orally.

THERAPY FOR INFECTION

Prophylactic antibiotics are not needed for the treatment of infection. The type and dosage of antibiotics depends on the site of the infection, its severity, and availability of the antibiotic. The prevalence of infection among children is shown in Table V. In cases of septicemia, gram-negative bacteria (including pathogenic *E. coli* and *Pseudomonas*) are more common than gram-positive bacteria. Staphylococcal septicemia when it occurs is mainly associated with infected dermatosis. Gram-negative bacteria are also commonly associated with genitourinary tract infection. Septicemia is very serious when associated with severe PEM. One should suspect septicemia if the patient has hypothermia, or hypotension, if petechia develop after applying pressure to the skin, and if hyponatremia with serum sodium level below 125 mEq/liter are noted. When septicemia is suspected, an adequate amount of antibiotics, especially to treat *Pseudomonas* and other gram-negative bacilli, should be given; anti-staphylococcus antibiotic should be added for individuals who have infected skin lesions.

Ousa Thanangkul et al.

TABLE V

Infections in PEM at RIHES[a]

Types	M (%)	MK (%)	K (%)
Pneumonia	54.41	45.00	29.27
Gastrourinary infection	29.41	45.95	24.39
Otitis media	22.06	31.60	23.17
Stool pathogen	26.47	38.00	45.12
Skin infection	10.29	10.00	31.71
Sepsis	5.88	14.00	28.05

[a] M, marasmus; MK, marasmic–kwashiorkor; K, kwashiorkor.

DIETARY THERAPY

Dietary therapy is one of the keys for the recovery of these children. Most of our severe PEM cases arrive with a history of diarrhea. An electrolyte mixture or clear liquids is given during the first 24 hours followed by dilute milk formula providing about 1 g protein and 25–30 kcal/kg/day. This is gradually increased to 100 kcal/kg/day by the end of the first week. To start the children on a full diet is less effective in reducing diarrhea than the gradual approach just described. Lactose-free formula is not needed with our regimen of treatment.

We have studied the effect of different protein and calorie levels upon the recovery of children, as judged by anthropometric measurements and by the regeneration of serum albumin levels. Our results showed that the protein requirement for recovery from severe PEM is approximately 3 g/kg/day. At this level of protein intake, the growth rate is proportional to calorie intake in the range of 120–250 kcal/kg/day. Our experience indicates that 175 kcal/kg/day is sufficient to promote adequate gorwth.

At RIHES patients generally are treated in the metabolic ward for 2 or 3 months. As our understanding increased of how the pathogenesis of severe PEM affects protein and calorie requirements and needs for minerals, vitamins, and antibiotics, it was possible to reduce the mortality among our patients from 30% in 1968 to its present level of 7%. As already noted, the children are thriving on discharge, and their body weight for height is about 90% of reference.

We routinely followed patients 1 month after discharge and yearly thereafter. We have followed 70% of our total admissions. Among them, eight children, 6% of those followed, died from other diseases, and none directly from malnutrition. The causes of death included encephalitis, fever of unknown origin, and food poisoning. Our teams who follow these children in their homes also provide health and nutrition education. Most of the children remain well and show continuing catch-up growth. Only 1% had a recurrence of malnutrition.

Although we get very good results from our regimen of treatment and follow-up, we realize that in developing countries bed space may be scarce and that it is not practicable to keep PEM children hospitalized for long periods. It is suggested that convalescent homes be utilized for patients who have passed the serious stage of PEM. The mothers should be encouraged to stay with their children at these homes, where they can receive health and nutrition education.

In concluding this section on hospital-based treatment of severe PEM, I would like to elaborate on follow-up of PEM children after discharge from our unit. We have followed the children at yearly intervals for the past 10 years, and have provided in their homes education in nutrition and health, as well as health services. As mentioned, most children have shown definite progress in catch-up growth, and only 1% had a relapse of malnutrition.

ACKNOWLEDGMENT

The work on which this paper is based was supported by the National Institutes of Health of the U.S.A. (Grant AM 11044) and by the Royal Thai Government.

REFERENCES

1. Bengoa, J. M. *Proc.—West. Hemisphere Nutr. Congr. [1st]*, 1965 36 (1966).
2. Behar, M. *J. Trop. Pediatr.* **14**, 233 (1968).
3. Sadre, M., and Donoso, G. *Lancet* **2**, 112 (1969).
4. Cook, R. *J. Trop. Pediatr.* **17**, 15 (1971).
5. McLaren, D. S., Ammoun, C., and Houri, J. *Leban. Med. J.* **17**, 85 (1964).
6. MacWilliam, K. M., and Dean, R. F. A. *East Afr. Med. J.* **42**, 297 (1965).
7. Ifekwunigwe, A. E. *In* "Protein Calorie Malnutrition" (R. E. Olson, ed.), p. 389. Academic Press, New York, 1974.
8. Garrow, J. S., and Pike, M. C. *Lancet* **1**, 1 (1967).
9. Whitman, W., Moodie, A. D., and Hansen, J. D. L. *S. Afr. Med. J.* **39**, 414 (1967).
10. Graham, C. G. *In* "Calorie Deficiencies and Protein Deficiencies" (R. A. McCance and E. M. Widdowson, eds.), p. 301. Churchill, London, 1967.
11. Suskind, R. *In* "Protein Calorie Malnutrition" (R. E. Olson, ed.), p. 403. Academic Press, New York, 1974.
12. Gomez, F., and Frank, S. *Adv. Pediatr.* **7**, 131 (1955).

13. Stewart, H. C., and Stephenson, S. S. *In* "Text Book of Pediatrics" (W. Nelson, ed.), p. 12. Saunders, Philadelphia, Pennsylvania,1959.
14. Classification of infantile malnutrition. *Lancet* **2,** 302 (1970).
15. Waterlow, J. C. *Br. Med. J.* **2,** 566 (1972).
16. Waterlow, J. G. *Lancet* **2,** 87 (1973).
17. Waterlow, J. C. *Br. Med. J.* **4,** 88 (1974).
18. Habicht, J. P., Martorell, R., Yarbrough, C., Malina, R. M., and Klein, R. E. *Lancet* **2,** 611–615 (1974).
19. Van Wieringen, J. C. "Secular Changes of Growth." Netherland Institute for Preventive Medicine, T.N.O., Leiden, 1972.

17 Nutrition Recovery Centers: The Chilean Experience

FERNANDO MONCKEBERG AND JOSE
RIUMALLO

GENERAL BACKGROUND

During the last decades, a positive change in health and nutritional conditions of the infant population has become evident in Chile. This has been confirmed by direct and indirect indicators. Mortality rates during the first years of life have been accepted internationally as an indirect indicator. If rates are high, there is also a high prevalence of malnutrition. Different studies have pointed out that malnutrition is the first cause of early mortality in underdeveloped countries.

Fifteen years ago, infant mortality (0–1 year) in Chile was 97‰. Since then, a steady decline has been observed, reaching 31‰ in 1980. There have been similar observations with preschool mortality (1–4 years). In 1965 this was 5‰; in 1978 it decreased to 1.2‰. During this period, a very significant diminution in death due to diarrheas, bronchoneumonia, and infectious diseases has been observed, a fact that also indicates that nutritional conditions have improved, since there is a close association between malnutrition and severity of infectious diseases.

Anthropometry, a direct indicator, also confirms a decline in the prevalence of infant malnutrition. In 1968, in the central zone of the country, a high percentage of children under 6 years old presented mild, moderate or severe malnutrition (65%) (1). At present, this percentage, in this same zone, is 12%, the average for the country being 11%.

This important reduction in malnutrition cannot be attributed solely to improvement of socioeconomical conditions of the country, because

189

NUTRITION INTERVENTION STRATEGIES IN NATIONAL DEVELOPMENT
Copyright © 1983 by Academic Press, Inc.
All rights of reproduction in any form reserved.
ISBN 012-709080-0

during this period, the economical growth per inhabitant was only 1.5% per year. Thus, this observation can be explained by an increase and improvement in health and nutritional programs. Indeed, during the last 20 years, the National Health Service has improved remarkably, covering more than 80% of the population. At the same time, extensive nutritional programs, especially for children between 0–5 years of age, pregnant women, and nursing mothers, have been implemented. Apart from this, the growth rate of the population has decreased notably— 2.8% per year in 1965 to 1.5% per year in 1979.

All of these actions seem to have had more favorable effects on children older than 1 year of age. In children less than 1 year old, the progress has been much slower. For example, when analyzing the mortality rates of both groups, it can be observed that the greater decrease is shown by the first group. In 1940 (Table I), the relationship between mortality from 0–1 year old and mortality from 1–4 years old was 6.6. In 1980, this relationship was 26. It can be concluded that, although it is true that both mortality rates have diminished, a greater proportional reduction has occurred in preschool children.

This was confirmed when studying the frequency of severe cases of malnutrition in relation to age that required hospitalization. An investigation of this aspect in five pediatric hospitals during the years 1940, 1967, and 1977 showed that a marked variation could be observed in regard to age of admission of children with severe undernutrition (period between 1940–1977). In 1940, 25% of the children hospitalized for severe undernutrition were under 1 year of age. In 1977, 88% were under 1 year of age; in this same year, 76% were under 6 months old (2). The important fact is not only the earlier age of acquiring undernutrition but that the clinical type has also changed. In 1940, protein malnutrition (kwashiorkor) was more frequent. At present, kwasiorkor has been almost completely replaced by the marasmus (severe undernutrition in the first year of life).

These observations demonstrate that there has been a relative dis-

TABLE I

Mortality Rates in Children from 0–4 Years of Age in the Years 1940, 1967, and 1977 in Chile

Mortality	1940	1967	1977
0–1 year of age (%)	130	106	47
1–4 years of age (%)	18.0	5.1	1.8
Ratio (0–1 years of age)/(1–4 years of age)	7.2	20.8	26.1

placement of moderate and severe undernutrition toward the first years of life. This can be exlained by the higher vulnerability of the smaller infant, together with demographic phenomena which have occurred during the last few decades. Amoung poor families the youngest or last born children are always more severely affected by malnutrition (1). During this time, there has also been a massive migration from rural areas toward urban centers that were not prepared to receive the increased population. Slum areas have formed in the big cities, and with them, inadequate living conditions: crowding, poor sanitation, precarious housing, and unemployment. This consistutes a high risk, particularly affecting the younger infant. In addition, the practice of breast-feeding has diminished, thus leaving the infant without protection in a very adverse environment (2).

THE NEED FOR A STRATEGY OF DIRECT PROTECTION TO THE INFANT

As was pointed out, it can be seen that to progress in the fight against undernutrition, it is absolutely necessary to concentrate efforts on the first and second years of life. During the last 6 years, there has been an increase in the distribution of foods (whole milk with 26% fat), and health actions by the National Health Service, which cover almost 90% of the children under 2 years old. A revival of interest in breast-feeding, along with improvements in nutritional education and child care, has done much to improve conditions. In spite of this, it has not been possible to eliminate malnutrition during the first year of life. Infant mortality, although reduced, is still high when compared to rates in developed countries.

Severe malnutrition acquired during the first year of life is very difficult to treat, even in very sophisticated hospital centers. This can be easily explained by the physiological changes that malnutrition produces during this vulnerable age:

1. The cellular immunity is altered, raising the susceptibility to and severity of infection, thus creating a vicious circle between malnutrition and infection (3).

2. The mechanism of acid–base balance is altered, which is particularly precarious during the first months of life. This increases susceptibility to severe dehydration, thus increasing the risk of death (4).

3. Finally, severe malnutrition during the first months of life produces a series of metabolic disturbances that do not allow or retard the absorption and/or utilization of different nutrients (5,6).

Follow-up studies of children with severe malnutrition under 1-year of age demonstrate that the risk of dying is 65%, whereas a child between the ages of 1 and 2 years suffering from severe undernutrition has a 35% risk (6).

Although it is true that all efforts should be focused on the prevention of early undernutrition because of its poor prognosis, there is still a high percentage of children that become severely malnourished. In spite of all the preventive actions, the realities of adverse sociocultural and poor sanitary conditions persist. These require long-term solutions. Thus, there is a need to develop a strategy to treat these children efficiently.

In practice, it is very difficult for an infant with severe undernutrition to recover in his own home. Clinically such infants are extraordinarily fragile and belong to extremely poor families. The extreme poverty presents very high environmental risks. The income of the family group is low, illiteracy is high, the housing conditions are very bad, and there is crowding and insalubrity. The severity of the clinical picture is such that hospitalization, with intensive and specialized care, is required since the majority of these infants are under 1 year old. Treatment in conventional hospitals is excessively expensive, particularly if the program must be extended to the national level in order to obtain broader coverage. Moreover, besides cost, the treatment in pediatric hospitals is very difficult for other reasons:

1. The high susceptibility of these infants to infections implies very prolonged hospitalization. Experience indicates that continuous reinfection (7) impedes recovery.

2. During the last few years, there has been great emphasis given to the necessity of psychoaffective stimulation, which increases the chances of recovery of these infants. This is very difficult to achieve in a conventional hospital, whose facilities are geared to other pathologies.

3. It is also necessary to educate the mother in the treatment and care of her infant. The conventional hospital is not equipped to deal extensively with this problem.

This explains, to some degree, the failure of treatment in hospitals and the repeated rehospitalizations that occur. In a study done in different hospitals in Santiago, Chile in 1974, it was observed that, on the average, the severely undernourished child under 1 year of age required 2.8 hospitalizations per year, with an average of 120 days in hospital per year and a 28% mortality rate. The pressure of new admissions forces early discharge, which leads to recurrence of the condition. In 1974, of beds occupied by infants, 58% were occupied by severely undernourished children, thereby limiting the care and treatment of other pathologies. This experience pointed to the need for finding alternative solutions that would permit the lowering of costs and increase the efficiency of treatment, thus reducing the chance of relapse. This could only be done in specialized centers with a highly motivated, professional staff and by integrating the family in the recovery process.

CREATION OF THE CHILEAN NUTRITION FOUNDATION (CONIN)

All the reasons noted have led to the creation of the Chilean Nutrition Foundation (CONIN), a nonprofit private foundation whose main objective is the recovery of severely undernourished children. This corporation is sponsored by the Health Ministry which, by agreement provides the funds to operate this system. CONIN is responsible for organizing the community in order to obtain the necessary resources to build and habilitate its Recovery Centers.

During the years 1975–1980, 33 Centers were put into operation with a total of 1360 beds. The total investment was approximately 8 million dollars. The centers were responsible for the recovery of more than 8000 children under 2 years of age. In all of them, a special program was developed in order to obtain an integral recovery of the child and at the same time to modify the family environment so as to prevent relapses.

Each center is under the direction of a pediatrician (part time) who acts as director of a multiprofessional team, including a nurse, a nutritionist, a specialized preschool teacher, and social worker, all of whom work full time. Each center has approximately 36 auxiliary nurses (shifts of 8 hours) and volunteers (between 30 and 180 in each center).

A central technical professional team outlines the description of roles and curricula. They suggest the treatment that must be followed inside the center and in follow-up and determine the activities to be developed within the families. The same group is also in charge of the permanent evaluation of the program, thus incorporating new technologies in the diagnosis and treatment of these children.

The activities of these Recovery Centers include the following:

1. Adequate feeding based on cow's milk and other foods prepared under the stringent supervision of a nutritionist.
2. Early psychosensorial stimulation, based on the concepts of Piaget, supervised by a specialized teacher.
3. Physiotherapy.

4. Affective stimulation performed by the auxiliary nurses as well as volunteers.
5. Incorporation of the mother into the care and stimulation of her child.

The results obtained to date in the treatment inside the centers and during the follow-up in the home have been extremely positive, exceeding all expectations. The advantages are summarized below.

1. Nutritional recovery in a much shorter period than is found by conventional treatment in a pediatric hospital (7) (Figs. 1 and 2).

2. Very low risk during treatment. The mortality rate in the center was less than 2% whereas the mortality rate of infants with severe undernutrition in pediatric hospitals (7) was 28%. This difference can be explained by the high suceptibility to infection and the severity with which they occur in undernourished infants. The involvement of the pediatric hospital in the treatment of a great variety of infectious diseases presents a high risk of contamination (bronchopneumonias, diarrheas, piodermitis, etc.) to undernourished children.

3. The recovery of the undernourished child has a positive effect on the economical and social development of the family.

Base on accumulated experience, it can be inferred that the nutritional status of the infant is an excellent indicator of impoverished families, a fact that is very important when developing and implementing programs directed to this portion of the population. The undernourished child is the result of a very adverse environment. As a general rule, a family with severely undernourished children belongs to the lowest socioeconomical group.

During the process of recovery of the malnourished child obvious changes occur which can be used to interest and integrate the parents

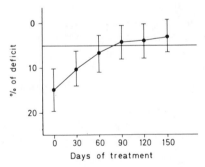

Fig. 1. Weight/height deficit in 7000 marasmic infants during recovery in centers of CONIN.

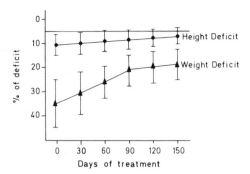

Fig. 2. Weight/height deficit in 7000 marasmic infants during recovery in centers of CONIN.

into the recovery process. In this way it is possible to influence their habits and modify their attitudes toward their child. In extremely impoverished families, there is frequently a natural distrust of anyone who tries to interfere in their environment. The integration of the family in the child's recovery is a way of gaining the families confidence, a fact that is absolutely necessary in obtaining real participation in the recovery process.

Families living under conditions of extreme poverty generally adapt to this condition, and are not entirely aware of the abnormality of their situation. This constitutes an obstacle for the success of any program intended to improve their standard of living. For them, the undernourished child is not the consequence of poverty. When asked about the condition of the child, they find explanation factors inherent to the child and not the environment (the child is weak, or ill). The recovery of the child provides evidence of the abnormality of the situation, which facilitates participation in other programs intended to improve the quality of life.

Finally, the recovered child is a positive demonstration to the family, alleviates hopelessness, and making it easier to implement preventative actions.

4. A follow-up study of 7400 recovered children revealed that only 4% did not continue to grow normally after return to the families. Moreover, only 1% required rehospitalization. The education of the mother in the care of the child and the need for psycho-affective stimulation has allowed continued recovery from the physical and psychomotor retardation. After 2 years following the initial recovery (as an average), the child attains normal psychomotor development (Table II).

5. The treatment of severely undernourished children in these centers

TABLE II

Follow-up Studies after Discharge from Nutritional Recovery Centers[a]

Months	0	1	6	12	24
Percentage ideal weight for age	80.3 ± 8.0	84.2 ± 9.2	85.8 ± 10.9	85.9 ± 10	85.6 ± 10.1
Percentage ideal height for age	89.6 ± 3.5	90.0 ± 3.5	90.8 ± 4.3	91.6 ± 4.1	91.4 ± 4.1
Percentage weight/ height	95.8 ± 10.9	95.5 ± 11.0	92.8 ± 11.5	90.0 ± 10.9	95.8 ± 11.3
Developmental quotient (D.Q.)	79.1 ± 12	88.6 ± 14.0	89.6 ± 11.0	95.3 ± 12	98.5 ± 6.0

[a] Results are expressed as average ± S.D.

has a lower cost than conventional hospitalization ($8 per day in the center versus $42 per day in a pediatric hospital).

6. The implementation of Recovery Centers has permitted better functioning of the Hospital system. These Centers have resulted in fewer hospital admissions, thus making beds available for patients suffering from other diseases.

7. The program has stimulated the solidarity of the community, providing the resources to build and operate the Recovery Centers.

The effect of these centers has been, from every viewpoint, a very positive one, contributing to improved health indexes and especially to lower mortality rates. However, we do not believe that this program, as such, could be reproduced in every underdeveloped country. It is justified in Chile, where undernutrition has decreased notably, and where there exists an efficient infrastructure of health with which to coordinate the described programs. Although the cost is less than that of a conventional hospital, it is still high. For example, 120 days of treatment in a center has an approximate cost of $1000. In countries where the rate of infant malnutrition is very high this investment would be prohibitive and limited to only small numbers of children.

RECOVERY OF THE IMPOVERISHED FAMILY

A program of recovery would make no sense, if it were aimed only at the recovery of the child. Since he is the product of poverty and misery, his return to that environment would cause a relapse. Therefore, it is also necessary to make changes in the family. This is not an easy task. These families suffer from sociogenic-biological damage because of their condition of chronic marginality (9), sometimes persisting for generations. They are detached from the economic and social structures of the country and are groups that historically have never participated in the obligations or the advantages of society. In this group, 54% of the mothers are illiterate as compared to the average for the country, which is under 4% (Table III). Parents are often unemployed, and if they work they do so only occasionally. Incomes tend to be very low. Their housing conditions are always unhealthy and are absolutely inadequate.

To obtain significant results any new strategy must be designed to include the reality of these conditions. At the same time, it is absolutely necessary to achieve participation of the affected group. The interventions must consider, simultaneously, the educational aspects, health, labor capability, and housing. It is necessary to create new expectations and provide the tools with which to reach them. It is necessary also to reawaken human dignity and stimulate a sense of self-esteem. A program must be implemented which provides for the following:

1. Education of the mother including care of the child, nutrition, psychoaffective stimulation, and housekeeping techniques.
2. A program of family planning.
3. Legalization of the family, when possible.
4. Treatment of alcoholism.
5. Training of the father and/or mother to improve labor capability.
6. Improvement of the sanitary conditions, providing technical help as needed.
7. Improvement of housing, providing technical assistance when necessary.
8. Stimulation of family minifarms.

TABLE III

Conditions of the Families of Undernourished Children Attended by CONIN

A. Frequency of illiteracy of the mother	54%
B. Father's work:	
1. Full-time work	8%
2. Part-time work, self-employment, unemployment	92%
C. Legal situation of the parents:	
1. Married	35%
2. Unmarried	65%
D. Mother's age:	
1. Over 18 years	62%
2. Under 18 years	38%
E. Housing conditions:	
1. Adequate	8%
2. Inadequate	92%

9. Food supplementation to children under 6 years old.
10. Education in the use of the legal, health, and educational structures of the country.

While developing these interventions, it is necessary to eliminate any factor that could be misconstrued as charity, paternalism, or missionary. The important thing is to stimulate self-esteem and effect active participation in the program.

Despite the objectives, the system often fails. Frequently (10%) children cannot be returned to their parents after recovery for a number of reasons. Lack of acceptance of the child by the mother could be due to mental retardation, alcoholism, or simply because of child abandonment. In these cases, children are placed for adoption either temporarily or permanently or they remain in state institutions.

The results obtained to date indicate that it is possible to recover these marginal groups provided there are adequate resources and structures capable of reaching established goals effectively and integrally.

SUMMARY

Malnutrition is the final result of poverty. Any strategy which attempts to eliminate malnutrition must include the causes and effects associated with poverty. It is possible to counter undernutrition even before poverty has disappeared, if adequate interventions are designed. In Chile, the recovery from severe undernutrition not only satisfies humanitarian objectives but also complements the national nutrition policy potentiating its effects.

REFERENCES

1. Monckeberg, F., Donoso, G., Valiente, S., Maccioni, A., Merchak, N., Arteaga, A., Oxman, S., and Lacassie, Y. Condiciones de vida, medio familiar y examen clínico y bioquímico de lactantes y pre-escolares de la provincia de Curicó. *Rev. Chil. Pediatr.* **38,** 499 (1967).
2. Monckeberg, F. "Artificial Feeding in Infants; High Risk in Underdeveloped Countries," pp. 57–63. Supreme Council for Population and Family Planning, Egipto, El Cairo, 1979.
3. Schlesinger, L., and Stekel, A. Desnutrición e inmunidad. *Rev. Chil. Pediatr.* **44,** 455 (1973).
4. Monckeberg, F., Perretta, M., Beas, F., Rubio, S., Aguiló, C., Maccioni, A., and Rosselot, J. Algunos aspectos de la deshidratación aguda del lactante. *Gac. Sanit.* **20,** 1 (1965).

5. Monckeberg, F. Adaptation to chronic calorie and protein restriction in infants. *In* "Calorie Deficiencies and Protein Deficiencies" (R. A. McCance and M. Widdowson, eds.), pp. 91–108. Churchill, London, 1968.
6. Monckeberg, F. Treatment of severe infant malnutrition. *Symp. Swed. Nutr. Found.* **9**, 74–83 (1971).
7. Monckeberg, F., and Riumalló, J. "Treatment of Severe Malnutrition." National Insitute of Health, Washington, D.C., 1977.
8. Pollit, E., and Thompson, C. Protein-calorie malnutrition and behaviour: A view from psychology. *In* "Nutrition and the Brain" (R. Wurtman and J. Wurtman, eds.), Vol. 2, pp. 261–306. Raven Press, New York, 1977.
9. Monckeberg, F. "Daño sociogénico-biológico producido por la miseria: Nutrición, Educación y Salud," pp. 9–16. Santiago CONPAN, 1976.

18 Comments on Nutrition Rehabilitation Center Programs

NEVIN S. SCRIMSHAW

In a country where the cases of severe malnutrition in children have been reduced to a relatively small number, and especially where they are accessible because of a predominantly urban population, as is the case in Chile, closed nutritional rehabilitation centers appear to represent the most effective direct way of dealing with the residual problem. They are certainly less costly and more effective than the hospital system. It has been demonstrated that, in other specific situations, open rehabilitation centers can have a dramatic effect. One such example is in the Des Chapelles Valley in Haiti, where, from its inception, the hospital had a ward that was overcrowded with cases of severe malnutrition, largely of the kwashiorkor type. The pressure for admissions was such that children rarely stayed for more than 2 to 3 weeks and were discharged once the edema had diminished, although recovery was not complete. There was no follow-up when they went back to their villages, and the subsequent mortality was undoubtedly high. The cost was high and the treatment ineffective. A system of rehabilitation centers was set up in the villages in Des Chapelles Valley, whereby homes were canvassed for children with second- and third-degree malnutrition, and these were brought in to receive local foods. As a result, admissions to the hospital ward for treatment of malnutrition decreased dramatically, to the point that the children coming were almost entirely from outside of the districts (1).

Clearly, it is an important step to go from hospitalization to the recuperation center, but the really crucial step is to move from rehabilita-

NUTRITION INTERVENTION STRATEGIES IN NATIONAL DEVELOPMENT

tion to primary prevention. Rehabilitation is obviously not prevention, and in the Chile situation, as in other countries with rehabilitation centers, children generally arrive too late for complete recovery either physically or in psychomotor performance, despite the best efforts. Even with an effective program of prevention, or with a relatively affluent population, there will be residual cases for which a country must provide. A good example of this is the fact that in Cambridge, Massachusetts, Ernesto Pollitt was able to identify a significant number of failure-to-thrive children who were clearly malnourished and whose psychomotor indices were severely affected. The problem, however, invariably went back to social disruption within the home (2). In some cases, mothers were well educated and had good jobs, but simply had no one competent with whom to leave the child. In that situation, the existing health delivery system and social services were not effective.

In a country such as Chile, with remarkably extensive health services and food distribution programs targeted to vulnerable groups, the persistence of a need for recuperation centers is a social challenge more than a health challenge. The simultaneous existence in Chile of an impressive program for keeping children healthy and of a group of children still in need of rehabilitation centers is clear evidence of that challenge.

I will not comment further on the nutrition program in Chile, which is appropriate, clearly successful, and evolving. It is worth noting, however, how different it is from Bengoa's original concept of open rehabilitation centers and from the conditions that gave rise to the original concept (3). Bengoa was concerned with the fact that for children among the lower socioeconomic groups of developing countries, once breast-feeding was no longer sufficient, or weaning was under way or had occurred, the weaning foods were grossly inadequate, child growth faltered, infections became frequent, and the vicious circle of malnutrition–infection–malnutrition followed. His was also a concept of centers where the mother would bring the child during the day to receive meals and where the mothers would be educated by participation in preparing food for their children. The intent was that these mothers would then have the information to prevent malnutrition when their child returned home and to avoid it in subsequent siblings. There was the hope that the mothers would somehow transfer this information and thereby influence the level of knowledge of the community.

Centers based on these concepts have been most extensively developed in Guatemala, Haiti, and Colombia. They have had modest success, but have encountered many problems (4). One of the problems repeatedly referred to is the danger of oversimplified or erroneous criteria for the diagnosis of undernutrition. If one uses the criterion of weight-for-age for children under 1 year of age the problem is not encountered to a significant degree. If the criterion of weight-for-age is applied in the second year of life, it is still reasonably effective. But if it is applied to 3-, 4-, and 5-year-olds, it means children are often selected who are of adequate weight-for-height. The nutrition rehabilitation center is not likely to benefit such children significantly, and when discharged with the same retardation in weight-for-age at which they entered, they may be considered treatment failures unless the criteria are looked at more carefully. Second, the mothers who have malnourished children tend to be the least competent in the community, frequently the least intelligent, and certainly the least likely to have an influence on other mothers. Accordingly, the idea of using them as vehicles for educating the rest of the community has been somewhat unsuccessful.

Another problem has been that where the predominant cause of malnutrition is ignorance of the appropriate feeding practices, the centers have been reasonably successful. However, in situations where economic factors have become the major limiting ones or at least equally limiting, as in the case of Haiti some years after the original centers were established, there is then very little that a center based on this kind of concept can do to prevent subsequent malnutrition in the individual or in the siblings. There has also been the difficulty in using local personnel of relatively limited education, of maintaining either adequate control of sanitation to prevent an increase in infections, or of conveying the importance of stimuli. Thus, rehabilitation centers may be conceptually sound but operationally difficult to implement. Most importantly, the effects on primary prevention remains uncertain.

It is clear, however, that in any situation the material and social cost of hospitalization of cases of severe malnutrition is relatively high, is relatively ineffective, and the influence on prevention of future cases minimal. Moving from hospitalization management to rehabilitation center management is a real improvement. In the latter, the costs are moderate compared to hospitalization costs. Moreover, effectiveness is, in general, greater, and there is a better chance of influence on future prevention. But clearly the next step should be a system that prevents the children from arriving at the point where they need to go to rehabilitation centers.

It is increasingly recognized that the programs to meet this need require some kind of preventive home visits. Programs of this sort have the lowest cost and have frequently been demonstrated on a pilot scale to be effective and need now to be demonstrated on a regional and national scale. The cost would be lowest and the program apparently more effective if tied to community participation, to community volunteers, and to periodic weighing of the children. It need not be dependent on someone from a health center going into the community to do this periodically. In fact, the latter simply has not worked in most cases where it has been planned.

An early example of this approach was the program in Candelaria (near Cali, Colombia) that started with a conventional rehabilitation center following the Bengoa concept. It was quite effective in reducing the frequency of severe malnutrition in the community and the number of admissions for severe PEM at the local hospital, but the cost was relatively high. Shortly thereafter, dried skimmed milk was provided on an ambulatory basis along with an education program for the whole community, and the rehabilitation center was closed without any rise in frequency of severe malnutrition (Joe D. Wray, personal communication, 1974). But these two programs then evolved into a system in which volunteers visited the homes, and at still lower cost, the frequency of severe PEM was greatly reduced and largely prevented (5).

In Cebu, in the Philippines, Florentino Solon established a system of community participation, community weighing, and home visits that proved highly effective. He was then asked to replicate it on a national scale and is attempting to do so despite complications inevitable in such an effort (6). In Yogyakarta, Indonesia, Jon Rohde and a local health group have shown that illiterate women in rural Indonesian communities can interpret growth charts and be motivated by such charts to prevent the deviation of their children from normal growth standards. Moreover, the interaction among the mothers discussing the deviation of their children and the measures to prevent it and the participation of the community with its own resources to help mothers with children who are persistently deviating was shown to be a very effective process (7). In both North Vietnam and China, weekly visits by individuals who are responsible to the community prevent children from reaching the degree of malnutrition that requires rehabilitation.

There is a limit to the extent to which any system of recuperation or stimulation can achieve the goals that we would like in normal psychomotor and psychosocial development. There is much to learn in this regard from the study by McKay *et al.* in Cali, Colombia (8). They brought children from urban slums in Cali into a day care center for 5 days a week, had them there for approximately 8 hours, gave them essentially five meals a day, and provided cognitive stimulation as well as good nutrition. The first group exprienced this regimen for 4 years, the second for 3 years, the third for 2 years, and the fourth for 1 year. Throughout, these children were compared in their psychomotor performance with a group of age-matched individuals from middle and upper income homes in Cali. The study showed that the earlier the children entered the program and the longer they participated in it, the less was the deficit in psychomotor performance. However, at the end of 4 years of good nutrition and physical and cognitive stimulation, they still remained considerably behind well-nourished children in the normal conditions of upper class homes. This indicates the distance that we need to go in bringing the performance of children from lower socioeconomic groups up to genetic potential. Solution of these long-term problems requires social changes beyond those of such direct intervention programs as we have discussed.

REFERENCES

1. Berggren, W. L. Evaluation of the effectiveness of education and rehabilitation centers. *Proc.—West. Hemisphere Nutr. Congr., 3rd, 1971* p. 84 (1972).
2. Pollitt, E., and Paradise, E. Social antecedents and correlates of preschool malnutrition in Cambridge, Massachusetts. *Adv. Behav. Biol.* **14,** 127–142 (1974).
3. Bengoa, J. M. Nutritional rehabilitation programs. *J. Trop. Pediatr.* **10,** 63–68 (1964).
4. Beghin, I. D., and Viteri, F. E. Nutritional rehabilitation centres: An evaluation of their performance. *J. Trop. Pediatr. Environ. Child. Health* **19,** 404–416 (1973).
5. Drake, W., and Fajardo, L. "Evaluación de Promotoras de Salud en Candelaria" (mimeo.). Universidad del Valle, Cali, Colombia, 1975.
6. Solon, F. "The Philippine Nutrition Program." Nutrition Centre of the Philippines, Manila, 1976.
7. Rohde, J., Ismail, D., and Sutrisno, R. Mothers as weight watchers: The road to child health in the village. *J. Trop. Pediatr. Environ. Child Health* **21,** 295–297 (1975).
8. McKay, H., McKay, A., and Sinisterra, L. Intellectual development of malnourished preschool children in programs of stimulation and nutritional supplementation. *In* "Early Malnutrition and Mental Development" (J. Cravioto, L. Hambraeus, and B. Vahlquist, eds.), pp. 226–232. Almqvist & Wiksell, Stockholm, 1974.

V Nutrition–Infection Cycle as Related to Intervention Techniques

19 Importance of Infection and Immunity in Nutrition Intervention Programs and Priorities for Interventions

NEVIN S. SCRIMSHAW

INTRODUCTION

The interrelationship between malnutrition and infection is a major determinant of health in developing countries. Infections worsen nutritional status (a) by the depression of appetite and hence food intake; (b) by the associated tendency to provide a diet that is less nutritious to individuals with infection, (c) by a decrease in intestinal absorption of nutrients whenever the gastrointestinal tract is affected, (d) by an increase in the excretion of nitrogen, vitamin A, vitamin C, zinc, and some other nutrients through the stress response to infection, and (e) by an internal diversion of nutrients, particularly amino acids, for the synthesis of acute-phase reactants.

The metabolic consequences have been best characterized by Beisel (1). A cumulative loss of nitrogen occurs with any infectious episode, even one that is mild or subclinical (2). Part of this loss is due to the spontaneous decrease in food intake, and part is due to an increase in nitrogen excretion associated with the stress response. This is illustrated in Fig. 1 for an individual with subclinical Q fever (3). Following immunization with yellow fever vaccine, nitrogen retention in eight of nine Guatemalan children decreased significantly for several days, although the children remained asymptomatic (4). In the well-nourished young adult, the effect of this agent on urinary nitrogen excretion was not

NUTRITION INTERVENTION STRATEGIES IN NATIONAL DEVELOPMENT

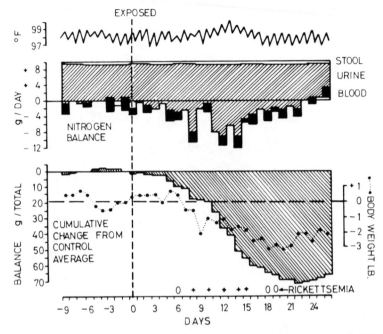

Fig. 1. Nitrogen balance data in a subject who remained asymptomatic despite sub-clinical Q fever (3). This individual showed neither an elevation of rectal temperature above 100°F nor a diminution of dietary intake, despite the presence of *Coxiella burnetii* in the blood over an 8-day period.

detectable, but in subjects on a low-protein intake, the increased urinary nitrogen excretion following immunization was also apparent (5).

Measles has a particularly severe effect on poorly nourished children. Figure 2 illustrates the decrease in serum albumin associated with an episode of measles (6). Unpublished INCAP studies by Viteri of children after an epidemic of measles in a rural highland village showed that, as judged by the creatinine-height index (CHI) (7), those who had experienced measles had a significant loss of lean body mass compared with well-nourished children of the same height. Of course, it was not as marked as the loss seen in kwashiorkor (minus 30–40%) or marasmus (40–60%), but the loss was still quite substantial (minus 20–30%). Frequent or prolonged infectious episodes also had a profound effect on the growth of children whose diet was borderline or deficient.

Figure 3 shows the consequences of a single episode of whooping cough on the growth of a child in a Guatelmalan highland village. Although growing poorly compared with well-nourished children, the child was following village growth norms until an episode of whooping

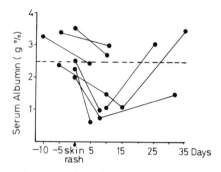

Fig. 2.   Effect of measles on nutritional status measured by serum albumin concentration. In all patients, a significant drop in albumin level occurred. In those with low-normal levels before the infection, a more pronounced fall in serum albumin concentration, often associated with the appearance of dependent edema, was observed. Recovery occurred several weeks following medical nutritional management (6).

cough at 42 weeks of age. Not until 59 weeks of age did the child begin to resume growth at a rate normal for the village, and the child was 78 weeks old before it reached its pre-whooping cough weight. Poorly nourished children in these highland Guatemalan villages take a long time to recover from whooping cough. For 44 children studied by Mata in Guatemala, recovery was not complete until 25 weeks or longer in 25% of the cases (8, p. 290).

There is a direct relationship between the number of days of illness with diarrhea and the growth increment during a 6-month period. The more days of illness, the poorer the growth (9,10). Mata *et al.* (11) also found that those children in the tercile with the highest frequency of viral infection during the first 6 months of life, as determined by bi-weekly fecal cultures, grow more slowly than those with a lesser frequency of viral infections.

Figure 4 is one of the many now famous illustrations of Mata's findings on this same Guatemalan village, showing the relationship between growth failure and the frequency of disease episodes (8). Case histories of this kind are common in almost all developing countries, and some are far worse, ending in death from marasmus, kwashiorkor, or infection. Figure 5 shows the growth of a child in a study by Adolfo Chavez in Mexico (unpublished data). This child began life with a low birth weight and experienced multiple episodes of diarrhea, broncho-pneumonia, bronchitis, and other infections. The child's weight at 2 years of age was only that of a normal newborn, an example of severe marasmus.

The practical consequences of repeated infections are impaired

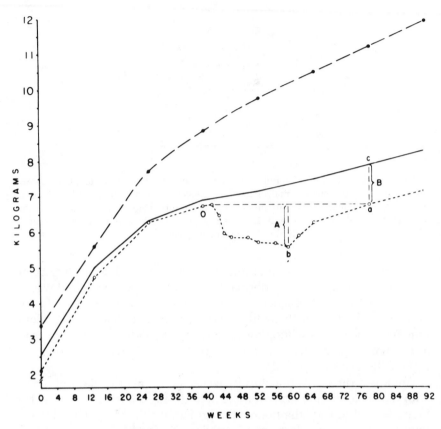

Fig. 3. Weight change in a child with whooping cough. The weight change with time in a child experiencing an episode of whooping cough is compared with the average for children in the same Guatemalan highland Mayan Indian village and with the INCAP standard for well-nourished children in the region (8). (●) Average standard weight; (——) average village weight; (- - -) weight of child; (0) onset; (A) weight loss; (B) expected weight loss.

growth, possibly with actual loss of weight and lean body mass, and, importantly, the frequent precipitation of nutritional disease in individuals already on a borderline diet. It is doubtful whether there would be much overt nutritional disease in developing countries were it not for the precipitating effects of infections. Their effects are cumulative when there is not enough time for full recovery from one infectious episode before the next comes along. The individual may then be progressively depleted to the point where an illness seemingly no worse than many of the preceding ones is sufficient to precipitate clinical signs of malnutrition.

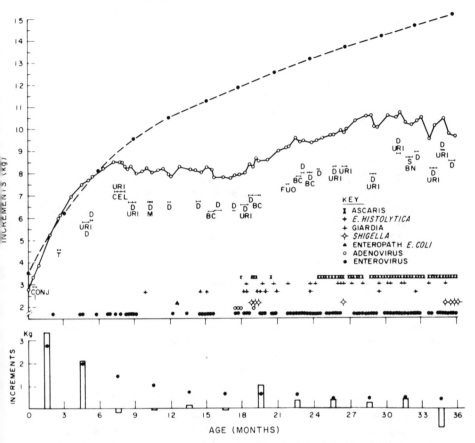

Fig. 4. Weight, infections, and infectious diseases in male child. Top, solid line represents weight of child; broken line is median of the standard. Length of each horizontal line indicates duration of infectious disease. Each mark shows 1 week positive for the particular infectious agent. Bottom, observed weight increments (vertical bars) and expected median increments of the standard (8). (BC) Bronchitis; (BN) bronchopneumonia; (CEL) cellulitis; (CONJ) conjunctivitis; (D) diarrhea, (FUO) fever of unknown origin; (I) impetigo; (M) measles; (S) stomatitis; (T) oral thrush; (URI) upper respiratory infection.

The effects are reciprocal, because not only does infection worsen the nutritional status, but the poorer nutritional status also results in increased frequency and severity of infection. Malnutrition and infections are synergistic in the sense that the effects of infection and malnutrition on morbidity and mortality in the same individual are greater than would be predicted from studying the two disease processes separately. The remainder of this discussion will concentrate on the effects of malnutrition on infection and the mechanisms by which these effects are mediated.

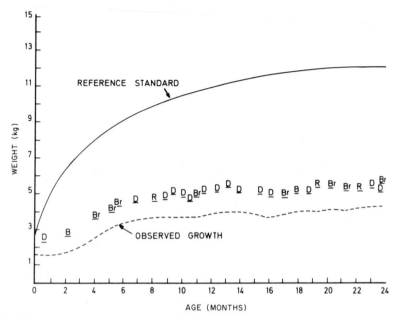

Fig. 5. Illnesses and growth of a boy in Tezonteapan. (D) diarrhea; (B) broncho-pneumonia; (Br) bronchitis; (C) conjunctivitis; (E) erysipelas; (R) "grippe." From a study by A. Chavez and P. Martinez, INN, Mexico, 1971 (unpublished data).

There are a number of nonspecific mechanisms. Table I lists some of the changes that nutritional deficiencies cause in tissue integrity and in epithelial barriers. There may also be a decrease in inflammatory response and in febrile response, as noted, for example, in kwashiorkor. A decrease in lysozyme activity of body secretions has also been reported. For example, Chandra et al. (12) showed an average plasma lysozyme activity of 8.29 μg/ml in an infected, well-nourished child as compared with only 3.18 μg/ml in malnourished children with infection.

There are also endocrine changes. The anterior pituitary secretes additional growth hormone, ACTH, and thyrotropin. The adrenal cortex responds by releasing greater than normal amounts of both glucocorticoid and mineralocorticoid hormones, while the medulla, depending on the type of infection, pours out catecholamines. Pancreatic insulin and glucagon secretion are higher in acute infection, and susceptibility to new infection is enhanced.

In addition to the metabolic responses to infection already mentioned, iron is sequestered, which may be a protective mechanism that deprives the invading microorganism of the iron it needs for replication (13).

TABLE I

Examples of Epithelial Changes in Nutrient Deficiencies That Could Influence Resistance to Infection[a]

Deficiency	Epithelial changes
Protein	Hyper- and parakeratosis, ulceration
Vitamin A	Metaplasia, keratinization
Riboflavin	Maceration, seborrheic dermatitis, glossitis and mucosal ulceration
Pyridoxine	Seborrheic dermatitis
Folic acid	Glossitis, mucosal changes

[a] From Scrimshaw *et al.* (16).

Alteration of the gastrointestinal flora may be an important mechanism, and in kwashiorkor, for example, the upper gastrointestinal tract becomes colonized (14). There are alterations in other nonspecific factors, e.g., properdin and interferon, which Schlesinger and co-workers (15) found significantly reduced in children with marasmus.

Until recently, the most important mechanism of resistance to infection was considered to be humoral immunity. As shown in Table II, almost *any* severe, specific deficiency has been shown in experimental studies to interfere with antibody formation (16), but generally the malnutrition employed in these experimental studies is more nutrient-specific and more severe than occurs in human populations. There are, of course, the clinical observations of decreased antibody formation in kwashiorkor, as demonstrated with diphtheria toxin (17) and with typhoid and paratyphoid antigens (18,19). Whenever investigators have failed to find an interference with antibody formation in kwashiokor, it

TABLE II

Number of Experimental Studies in Which Moderate and Severe Deficiencies of Specific Nutrients Have Been Shown to Interfere with Antibody Formation[a]

Nutrient	Number	Nutrient	Number
Vitamin A	15	Vitamin B_{12}	8
B vitamins	7	Folic acid	4
Thiamine	15	Biotin	6
Riboflavin	15	Vitamin C	9
Niacin	6	Vitamin D	7
Pyridoxine	18	Protein or amino acids	52
Pantothenic acid	25	Niacin–tryptophan	6

[a] From Scrimshaw *et al.* (16).

has been because they have delayed the study until therapy had been initiated. Once therapy began and amino acids were supplied by the diet, antibody synthesis returned to a normal level.

Adult men consuming an experimental diet, which was deficient only in panthothenic acid, exhibited improved antibody production to tetanus antigen (20). Experimental pyridoxine deficiency slightly improved antibody response to both tetanus and typhoid antigens (21). Scrimshaw et al. (16, pp. 154–55) reviewed several studies that reported reduced antibody formation during severe protein deficiency in human subjects.

Field observations have been equivocal. Studies in Africa indicated that retarded growth had no effect on the antibody response to live measles vaccine (R. E. Brown, personal communication, 1965). This was also true in India (22) for small pox and polio immunizations. Presumably, viruses can replicate within the body until the quantity of antigenic material is able to overcome any disadvantage that might be associated with mild to moderate malnutrition. However, eight children with kwashiorkor did not show any antibody response to yellow fever vaccine (23).

Edsall (24) cites evidence that considerable immunity can be induced by a single dose of potent tetanus toxoid and that a second dose 1 year later induces high levels of immunity, even in malnourished children showing retardation in physical growth and development. Kielmann (22), in India, also was unable to find an impaired response to DPT (diphtheria, pertussis, and tetanus) antigens in malnourished children. There have been some evaluations before and after feeding poorly nourished children. For example, Mathews in New Guinea used a rather peculiar antigen from flagella (25). He reported a somewhat improved serum antibody response in school children following supplementary feeding.

Although there are abundant data to indicate that severe protein–calorie malnutrition suppresses antibody formation in animals and man, there is no convincing evidence that the kind of mild-to-moderate PEM is associated with growth failure and no other clinical signs sufficiently affects humoral antibodies to account for increased morbidity from infection and the reduced morbidity with subsequent nutrient administration or feeding. The same conclusion applies to phagocytosis. Severe deficiencies of any of the nutrients listed in Table III (16) have an adverse effect on leukocytic response and function. Again, this is easy to demonstrate with severe, specific deficiencies in experimental animals, but phagocytosis per se is not reduced in the mild-to-moderate malnutrition that is associated, under field conditions, with an increase in infection.

TABLE III

Number of Experimental Studies in Which Moderate and Severe Deficiencies of Specific Nutrients Have Been Shown to Interfere with Leukocyte Response or Function[a]

Nutrient	Number	Nutrient	Number
Protein	14	Riboflavin	6
Vitamin A	5	Pyridoxine	1
Ascorbic acid	4	Folic acid	5
B vitamins	3	Vitamin B_{12}	1
Thiamine	2	Inanition	6
Iron	2		

[a] From Scrimshaw et al. (16). There have been many similar articles published since this compilation.

Phagocytes, however, must not only engulf, but must also kill microorganisms. In rats, iron (26,27) and protein deficiency (28) have been demonstrated in experimental studies at MIT to increase morbidity and mortality from *Salmonella* in direct proportion to the reduction in myeloperoxidase-staining granulocytes in the intestinal wall. A reduction in bacterial killing power of leukocytes has been demonstrated in children with severe protein–calorie malnutrition in India (29,30) and Guatemala (31).

There is no doubt that constant phagocytic activity is a prerequisite for survival and that lymphocyte-mediated immune systems are critical. Other macrophage products that could be influenced by nutrition are lysozymes, collagenase, plasminogen activator, endogenous pyrogens, interferon, and properdin.

Studies of Eskimo children in Alaska indicated that anemia is associated with increased case fatality from meningitis (32), diarrheal disease, and otitis media (33). In these cases, the mechanism was unknown, but it could be reduced cell-mediated immunity (CMI), as reported from the studies in rats. Many investigators have shown that children with kwashiorkor have a decrease in circulating lymphocyte concentration and in lymphocyte response, as well as various enzyme defects in these cells. Findings of this kind have been reported from Egypt (34), Guatemala (35,36), India (37), Mexico (38), Thailand (39), and Rhodesia (40). However, the functional significance of these enzyme changes is really not known, and it is not clear whether they are relevant to the increased susceptibility to infection in children with mild-to-moderate protein–calorie malnutrition.

The most plausible and current explanation for the decreased resistance to infection—in mild-to-moderate malnutrition under field conditions when iron deficiency and some other nutrient deficiencies are present in a population—is cell-mediated immunity (CMI). Good (41) summarized the experimental evidence by saying that "We can show almost every conceivable alteration of the T-cell population and its functions and of the B-cell population and its functions through nutritional manipulation" in laboratory animals.

The epidemiological evidence for the role of CMI is still relatively limited. Studies of delayed cutaneous hypersensitivity to tuberculin in Chile (15), India (42–44), Nepal (45), Nigeria (46), and Tunisia (47) have shown reduced or absent responses in malnourished children. A decrease in delayed cutaneous hypersensitivity and an increase in morbidity from diarrheal and respiratory disease were found to be proportionate to a decreased weight-for-age in preschool children (Cholera Research Laboratory, Dacca, Bangladesh, unpublished data), but which of these factors is primary is not as yet known. Chandra and Newberne (48, pp. 80–85) summarized extensive evidence that cutaneous delayed hypersensitivity is impaired with iron deficiency as well as moderate-to-severe forms of protein–energy malnutrition.

Deficits in the complement system are also associated with increased susceptibility to bacterial infections (48, pp. 104–110). One of the ways in which complement appears to function is through a peptide generated when the C-3 complement fraction is acted upon, and this peptide serves as a chemical attractant to phagocytic cells. It enhances antigen binding to B lymphocytes, and without C-3 bound to the microorganism, phagocytosis is less effective *in vitro*. Genetically C-3-deficient individuals have a tendency to severe pyogenic infections. Finally, C-3 reacts with mast cells to release the chemical mediators of immediate sensitivity.

There is considerable evidence for C-3 impairment in severe protein–calorie malnutrition from work in Ghana (49), South Africa (50), Thailand (51,52), and India (42,53). There is good evidence for recovery of C-3 function with the treatment of kwashiorkor. For example, Neumann *et al.* (49) described a return to normal in the first 2 weeks of treatment of kwashiorkor. However, the relevance of all of this to increased susceptibility to infection in mild-to-moderate PEM is unknown. Properdin is an alternate system to activate C-3 that has been too little studied in malnutrition to warrant comment at this time.

In summary, there is no doubt of the importance of decreased resistance to infection with mild-to-moderate as well as severe malnutrition in human subjects, but the precise mechanisms are still uncertain. Of the several possible mechanisms, CMI and associated lymphocyte function appear to be the most sensitive to malnutrition. Morbidity and mortality in poorly nourished populations are due to a synergism of malnutrition and infection, each exacerbated by the other. Whether the predominant disease manifestation at a given time is that of infection or of malnutrition is really not important from a public health point of view. It is the synergistic interaction of the two that is responsible for the health consequences. Programs of intervention must be directed against both malnutrition and infection to achieve satisfactory effectiveness, particularly in correcting impaired growth and development, whether physical or mental.

PRIORITIES FOR INTERVENTIONS ON THE NUTRITION–INFECTION COMPLEX IN DEVELOPING COUNTRIES

Some studies demonstrated the relative success of interventions that address the issue of nutrition and health, separately or in concert. The Candelaria study in Columbia, for example, in the early phase gave food to take home to mothers of young children who were suffering from second- or third-degree malnutrition; some children with third-degree malnutrition were admitted to a rehabilitation center within the clinic. In both cases, there was some rather general instruction given about sanitation, but it was probably not very effective. There was some decrease in morbidity from diarrheal disease with this specific intervention. During the next period, when dried skim milk was distributed generally to preschool children, and mothers were given additional nutrition and health education, this decrease in morbidity from diarrhea was maintained, but not improved (54).

At about the same time, a 5-year study was initiated in three Guatemala highland villages (55). In one village, there was supplementary feeding and advice on nutrition, but no other intervention. The people in this village continued to have access to the government health services, although they were available to only a limited degree. A second village was provided with regular medical treatment and improved sanitary conditions, and everything possible was done to decrease the frequency of infection. A third village served as the control, where the same baseline data were gathered on death rate, nutritional status, and disease, but no intervention was introduced.

This was originally designed as a four-village study, to include one with both nutrition and the other with health interventions. The National Institutes of Health Study Section refused to grant enough money to support study of the fourth village because it felt it was obvious that health care, improved sanitary conditions, and supplementary feeding would improve nutritional status. We knew that the issue was much more complex than that, but we could not convince the Study Section.

The supplement given in the "feeding" village included Incaparina made with dried skim milk, which, when served with a banana, supplied about 450 calories and 15 g of protein. In the "treatment" village, a clinic was staffed by a full-time physician in attendance 5 days a week, a graduate nurse who was there 6 to 7 days a week, and a sanitary inspector was there much of the time to assist individuals to build latrines. At the start of the study, there had been only two or three latrines for the entire village. After 2 years, all of the houses had latrines and the sanitary inspector instructed the people in their use. In addition, the quality of the water supply, most of which came by way of a fountain in the center of this village of about 140 families, was improved, although there was no increase in the total amount of water available or in its total distribution.

To be brief, in the feeding village, there was a decrease in morbidity from both diarrheal and respiratory diseases, even though participation in the program was irregular. In the treatment village, there was no decrease in overall morbidity, and there was an actual increase in the prevalence of diarrhea, perhaps associated with the increase in the number of people coming into and going out of the community. There was essentially no change in mortality in the control village. A small reduction in mortality rate occurred in the treatment village because of fewer early deaths. There was a distinct decrease in postneonatal infant mortality in the feeding village, although neonatal mortality was not affected. As breast milk gradually became inadequate after the first few months as the sole source of food, the supplementary feeding program began to save the lives of infants who would have otherwise died of complications from measles, diarrhea, and other infections.

When deaths were analyzed for the period from 6 to 18 months of life, when breast feeding would still be important, and also from 18 to 36 months, when it was less so, there were fewer deaths in the feeding village compared to the number in the control village in both categories.

In summary, supplementary feeding alone did have some effect on morbidity; it had a more pronounced effect on mortality, but had essentially no effect on the severe degree of growth impairment of these children. More important and difficult to accept was the finding that medical treatment, which went far beyond anything that the national health service could afford to supply in rural villages, plus the construction of latrines, improvement in the quality of water, and an immunization program that provided small pox, DPT, and polio vaccines (measles vaccine was not available at that time) had no perceptible effect on either infectious disease morbidity or nutritional status, as judged by growth measurements.

The feeding results were significant but inadequate and unsatisfactory, and the treatment results were largely negative. What would have happened if the two interventions had been combined? Given the limiting factors in the villages and the need for increased quantity of water for environmental sanitation, the combined program might not have been a great deal more effective. Our failure to find conspicuous benefits from this costly and elaborate medical care and environmental sanitation program has made quite a few people disbelieving or even angry. Some say, "There must be some benefit from a preventive and curative medical program; you just did not do enough." The point is that the treatment program provided more services than the Government will be able to furnish for many years, yet they alone were not effective in reducing morbidity and mortality in preschool children.

In Narangwal in northern India, Taylor, Kielmann, and their co-workers attempted to repeat the design of the Guatemala study, but added a fourth village in which medical attention, immunizations, and supplementary feeding were combined (56). The result was a decrease in mortality, some decrease in morbidity, and some slight improvement in growth, but again, the improvements were disappointingly small, and there was no dramatic return to health. The conclusion from both of these studies is that we are dealing with such high morbidity from both infection and malnutrition interacting synergistically and with so many other etiological factors that a successful program requires an effective multifactorial approach.

One cannot, however, neglect partial approaches. There are a number of individual actions that might not in themselves produce very significant results but that are part of the preconditions that must be established for the improvement of nutritional and health status. If one can start some of these and then add others, the cumulative effects should become apparent.

There are also some circumstances when a single intervention might have quite an appreciable effect. In a study in Indonesia, where 100 mg of iron were given daily for 60 days to rubber plantation workers who were anemic, a comparison of the morbidity for four weeks before the study and for the four weeks of the intervention showed a decided decrease in cases of influenza, enteritis, overall morbidity, and in absenteeism (57). Morbidity and attendance could be checked every day because the men were paid every day. It was also possible to go to the homes when they did not report for work to determine whether they were sick or absent for some other reason. There is no question that this intervention not only increased their take-home pay and their productivity, but also decreased their morbidity from infectious disease.

To bring about improved nutritional status under conditions of high rates of infectious disease morbidity and much malnutrition, one intervention that would be likely to have some effect is a good immunization program, particularly if it includes vaccines against measles as well as whooping cough. These two diseases are in themselves responsible for a considerable amount of growth failure, serious malnutrition, and death. Programs that tend to result in improved personal hygiene and environmental sanitation should also have a high priority. It is a mistake, however, to emphasize environmental sanitation without realizing that this is of relatively little meaning unless accompanied by improved personal hygiene. Neither diarrheal disease nor respiratory infections are spread by contaminated water except in rare instances. Diarrheal disease is largely spread by contact. This, in turn, is due largely to a lack of water for washing.

The important question is how to achieve these three elements—immunization, better personal hygiene, and nutritional improvement—in view of the existing social, economic, and political contraints. Some would add to this program early rehydration of children with diarrhea, which certainly would save many lives, but I do not give this the same priority because obviously it would be unnecessary if public health measures largely eliminated either diarrhea, malnutrition, or both.

Although there is sometimes a tacit assumption that it does, improved nutritional status does not necessarily require food distribution programs. Frequent visits of health workers to homes are the key to the virtual elimination of clinical malnutrition in young children in North Vietnam (58) and China. There are also examples of programs in Colombia, Indonesia, India, and elsewhere showing that frequent home visits of village workers to detect early malnutrition in infants and young children, combined with advice to mothers and involvement of the health delivery system where indicated, have improved the nutritional status of these children without resort to subsidized food supplements.

In particular, careful periodic monitoring of infant weights utilizing growth charts kept in the home by mothers who learn their interpretation and the role of proper feeding can prevent most early malnutrition, as can alerting the health services of individuals at risk.

REFERENCES

1. Beisel, W. R. Magnitude of the host nutritional responses to infection. *Am. J. Clin. Nutr.* **30,** 1236 (1977).
2. Powanda, M. C. Changes in body balances of nitrogen and other key nutrients: Description and underlying mechanisms. *Am. J. Clin. Nutr.* **30,** 1254 (1977).
3. Beisel, W. R., Sawyer, W. D., Ryll, E. D., and Crozier, D. Metabolic effects of intracellular infections in man. *Ann. Intern. Med.* **67,** 744 (1967).
4. Gandra, Y. R., and Scrimshaw, N. S. Infection and nutritional status. II. Effect of mild virus infection induced by 17-D yellow fever vaccine on nitrogen metabolism in children. *Am. J. Clin. Nutr.* **9,** 159 (1961).
5. Scrimshaw, N. S. Environmental factors in the interrelationships of nutrition and infection. *In* "Proceedings of the First Asian Congress of Nutrition, 1971" (P. G. Tulpule and K. S. Jaya Rao, eds.) p. 571. Nutrition Society of India, Hyderabad, 1972.
6. Dossetor, J. F. B., and Whittle, H. Protein-losing enteropathy and malabsorption in acute measles enteritis. *Br. Med. J.* **2,** 592 (1975); cited in Chandra, R. K., and Newberne, P. M., "Nutrition, Immunity, and Infection," p. 48. Plenum, New York, 1977.
7. Viteri, F. E., and Alvarado, J. The creatinine height index: Its use in the estimation of the degree of protein depletion and repletion in protein-calorie malnourished children. *Pediatrics* **46,** 696 (1970).
8. Mata, L. J. "The Children of Santa Maria Cauqué: A Prospective Field Study of Health and Growth." MIT Press, Cambridge, Massachusetts, 1978.
9. Martorell, R., Habicht, J. P., Yarbrough, C., Lechtig, A., Klein, R. E., and Western, K. A. Acute morbidity and physical growth in rural Guatemalan children. *Am. J. Dis. Child.* **129,** 1296 (1975).
10. Mata, L. J., Urrutia, J. J., Albertazzi, C., Pellecer, O., and Arellano, E. Influence of recurrent infections on nutrition and growth of children in Guatemala. *Am. J. Clin. Nutr.* **25,** 1267 (1972).
11. Mata, L. J., Urrutia, J. J., and Lechtig, A. Infection and nutrition of a low socioeconomic rural community. *Am. J. Clin. Nutr.* **24,** 249 (1971).
12. Chandra, R. K., Khalil, N., Howse, D., Chandra, S., and Kutty, K. M. Lysozyme (Muramidase) activity in plasma, neutrophils, and urine in malnutrition and infection. *In* "Malnutrition and the Immune Response" (R. M. Suskind, ed.), p. 408. Raven Press, New York, 1977.
13. McFarlane, H., Reddy, S., Adcock, K. J., Adeshin, H., Cooke, A. R., and Akene, J. Immunity, transferrin, and survival in kwashiorkor. *Br. Med. J.* **4,** 268 (1970).
14. Schneider, R. E., and Viteri, F. E. Luminal events of lipid absorption in protein-calorie malnourished children; relationship with nutritional recovery and diarrhea. II. Alterations in bile acid content of duodenal aspirates. *Am. J. Clin. Nutr.* **27,** 788 (1974).
15. Schlesinger, L., Ohlbaum, A., Grez, L., and Stekel, A. Cell-mediated immune studies in marasmic children from Chile: Delayed hypersensitivity, lymphocyte transformation, and interferon production. *In* "Malnutrition and the Immune Response" (R. M. Suskind, ed.), pp. 91–98. Raven Press, New York, 1977.
16. Scrimshaw, N. S., Taylor, C. E., and Gordon, J. E. "Interactions of Nutrition and Infection" W.H.O. Monogr. Ser. No. 57. World Health Organ., Geneva, 1968.
17. Olarte, J., Cravioto, J., and Campos, B. Immunidad en el niño desnutrido. I. Pro-

ducción de antitoxina diftérica. *Bol. Med. Hosp. Infant. Mex. (Span. Ed.)* **13,** 467 (1956).

18. Budiansky, E., and Da Silva, N. N. Formaçao de anticorpos na distrofía pluricarcencial hidropigenica. *Hospital (Rio de Janeiro)* **52,** 251 (1957).

19. Reddy, V., and Srikantia, S. G. Antibody response in kwashiorkor. *Indian J. Med. Res.* **52,** 1154 (1964).

20. Hodges, R. E., Bean, W. B., Ohlson, M. A., and Bleiler, R. E. Factors affecting human antibody response. III. Immunologic responses of men deficient in pantothenic acid. *Am. J. Clin. Nutr.* **11,** 85 (1962).

21. Hodges, R. E., Bean, W. B., Ohlson, M. A., and Bleiler, R. E. Factors affecting human antibody response. IV. Combined deficiencies of pantothenic acid and pyridoxine. *Am. J. Clin. Nutr.* **11,** 187 (1962).

22. Kielmann, A. A. Nutritional and immune responses of subclinically malnourished Indian children. *In* "Malnutrition and the Immune Response" (R. M. Suskind, ed.), pp. 429–440. Raven Press, New York, 1977.

23. Brown, R. E., and Katz, M. Failur of antibody production to yellow fever vaccine in children with kwashiorkor. *Trop. Geogr. Med.* **18,** 125 (1966).

24. Edsall, G. Malnutrition and simplified immunization. *In* "Malnutrition and the Immune Response" (R. M. Suskind, ed.), pp. 445–448. Raven Press, New York, 1977.

25. Mathews, J. D., Mackay, I. R., Whittingham, S., and Malcolm, L. A. Protein supplementation and enhanced antibody-producing capacity in New Guinean school children. *Lancet* **2,** 675 (1972).

26. Baggs, R. B., and Miller, S. A. Nutritional iron deficiency as a determinant of host resistance in the rat. *J. Nutr.* **103,** 1554 (1973).

27. Baggs, R. B., and Miller, S. A. Defect in resistance to *Salmonella typhimurium* in iron deficient rats. *J. Infect. Dis.* **130,** 409 (1974).

28. Nelson, D. P., and Newberne, P. M. Protein deficiency and mucosal granulocytes. *Nature (London), New Biol.* **236,** 28 (1972).

29. Selvaraj, R. J., and Bhat, K. S. Metabolic and bactericidal activities of leukocytes in protein-calorie malnutrition. *Am. J. Clin. Nutr.* **25,** 166 (1972).

30. Seth, V., and.Chandra, R. K. Opsonic activity, phagocytosis and intracellular bactericidal capacity of polymorphs in undernutrition. *Arch. Dis. Child.* **47,** 282 (1972).

31. Keusch, G. T., Urrutia, J. J., Guerrero, O., Castenada, G., and Douglas, S. D. Rosette-forming lymphocytes in Guatemalan children with protein-calorie malnutrition. *In* "Malnutrition and the Immune Response" (R. M. Suskind, ed.), pp. 117–122. Raven Press, New York, 1977.

32. Fortuine, R. Acute purulent meningitis in Alaska natives: Epidemiology, diagnosis and prognosis. *Can. Med. Assoc. J.* **94,** 19 (1966).

33. Brown, C. V., Brown, G. W., and Bonehill, B. Relationship of anemia to infectious illnesses on Kodiak Island. *Alaska Med.* **9,** 93 (1967).

34. Shousha, S., and Kamel, K. Nitro blue tetrazolium test in children with kwashiorkor with a comment on the use of latex particles in the test. *J. Clin. Pathol.* **25,** 494 (1972).

35. Béhar, M., Arroyave, G., Tejada, C., Viteri, F., and Scrimshaw, N. S. Desnutrición Severa en la Infancia. *Rev. Col. Med. Guatem.* **7,** 221 (1956).

36. Tejada, C., Argueta, V., Sanchez, M., and Albertazzi, C. Phagocytic and alkaline phosphatase activity of leukocytes in kwashiorkor. *J. Pediatr.* **64,** 753 (1964).

37. Selvaraj, R. J., and Bhat, K. S. Phagocytosis and leukocyte enzymes in protein-calorie malnutrition. *Biochem. J.* **127,** 255 (1972).

38. Yoshida, T., Metcoff, J., and Frenk, S. Reduced pyruvic kinase activity, altered growth patterns of ATP in leukocytes and protein-calorie malnutrition. *Am. J. Clin. Nutr.* **21,** 162 (1968).
39. Kulapongs, P., Edelman, R., Suskind, R., and Olson, R. E. Defective local leukcocyte mobilization in children with kwashiorkor. *Am. J. Clin. Nutr.* **30,** 367 (1977).
40. Kendall, A. C., and Nolan, R. Polymorphonuclear leukocyte activity in malnourished children. *Cent. Afr. J. Med.* **18,** 73 (1972).
41. Good, R. A. Biology of the cell-mediated immune response. A review. *In* "Malnutrition and the Immune Response" (R. M. Suskind, ed.), pp. 29–46. Raven Press, New York, 1977.
42. Chandra, R. K. Immunocompetence in undernutrition. *J. Pediatr.* **81,** 1184 (1972).
43. Manerikar, S., Malaviya, A. N., Singh, M. B., Rajgopalan, P., and Kumar, R. Immune status and BCG vaccination in newborns with intra-uterine growth retardation. *Clin. Exp. Immunol.* **26,** 173 (1976).
44. Kielmann, A., Uberoi, I. S., Chandra, R. K., and Mehra, V. L. The effect of nutritional status on immune capacity and immune responses in preschool children in a rural community in India. *Bull. W.H.O.* **54,** 477 (1976).
45. Ziegler, H. D., and Ziegler, P. B. Depression of tuberculin reaction in mild and moderate protein-calorie malnourished children following BCG vaccination. *Johns Hopkins Med. J.* **137,** 59 (1975).
46. Harrison, B. D. W., Tugwell, P., and Fawcett, I. W. Tuberculin reaction in adult Nigerians with sputum-positive pulmonary tuberculosis. *Lancet* **1,** 421 (1975).
47. Smith, N. J., Khadroui, S., Lopez, V., and Hamza, B. Cellular immune response in Tunisian children with severe infantile malnutrition. *In* "Malnutrition and the Immune Response" (R. M. Suskind, ed.), pp. 105–109. Raven Press, New York, 1977.
48. Chandra, R. K., and Newberne, P. M. "Nutrition, Immunity, and Infection." Plenum, New York, 1977.
49. Neumann, C. G., Stiehm, E. R., and Swenseid, M. Complement levels in Ghanaian children with protein-calorie malnutrition. *In* "Malnutrition and the Immune Response" (R. M. Suskind, ed.), pp. 333–336. Raven Press, New York, 1977.
50. Smythe, P. M., Brereton-Stiles, G. G., Grace, H. J., Mafoyane, A. Schonland, M., Coovadia, H. M., Loening, W. E. K., Parent, M. A., and Vos, G. H. Thymolymphatic deficiency and depression of cell-mediated immunity in protein-calorie malnutrition. *Lancet* **2,** 939 (1971).
51. Sirisinha, S., Suskind, R., Edelman, R., Charupatana, C., and Olson, R. E. Complement and C3-proactivator levels in children with protein-calorie malnutrition and effect of dietary treatment. *Lancet* **1,** 1016 (1973).
52. Suskind, R., Edelman, R., Kulapongs, P., Pariyananda, A., and Sirisinha, S. Complement activity in children with protein-calorie malnutrition. *Am. J. Clin. Nutr.* **29,** 1089 (1976).
53. Chandra, R. K. Serum complement and immunoconglutinin in malnutrition. *Arch. Dis. Child.* **50,** 225 (1975).
54. Wray, J. D. Direct nutrition intervention and the control of diarrheal diseases in preschool children. *Am. J. CLin. Nutr.* **31,** 2073 (1978).
55. Scrimshaw, N. S., Béhar, M., Guzmán, M. A., and Gordon, J. E. Nutrition and infection field study in Guatemalan villages, 1959–1964. IX. An evaluation of medical, social, and public health benefits, with suggestions for future field study. *Arch. Environ. Health* **18,** 51 (1969).
56. Taylor, C. E. Comment. *In* "Nutrition and Agricultural Development—Significance and Potential for the Tropics" (N. S. Scrimshaw and M. Behar, eds.), pp. 60–62. Plenum, New York, 1976.

57. Basta, S., Soekirman, Karyadi, D., and Scrimshaw, N. S. Iron deficiency anemia and the productivity of adult males in Indonesia. *Am. J. Clin. Nutr.* **32**, 916 (1979).

58. A Study Mission Report: "Relief and Rehabilitation of War Victims in Indochina: One Year after the Ceasefire," Prepared for the Subcommittee to Investigate Problems Connected with Refugees and Escapees of the Committee on the Judiciary, United States Senate, Ninety-Third Congress, Second Session, January 27, 1974. U.S. Govt. Printing Office, Washington, D.C., 1974.

20 Evaluating the Health Benefits of Improved Water Supply Through Assessment of Nutritional Status in Developing Countries

LINCOLN C. CHEN

INTRODUCTION

The provision of adequate water supplies to the millions of rural people in low-income countries presents an enormous challenge. Conservative estimates indicate that over 1 billion people in Asia, Africa, and Latin America do not have access to safe and reliable drinking water (1). In rural areas, over four-fifths of low-income populations may lack adequate water facilities, and the proportion of similarly disadvantaged may approximate one-third among urban dwellers. In recognition of these enormous human needs, 1981–1990 has been declared "The International Drinking Water Supply and Sanitation Decade." Substantial infrastructural investments, internally and externally financed, are therefore anticipated in a massive effort to bring modern water and sanitation facilities to thousands of villages of many developing countries.

There are several reasons why improved nutritional status of a community, as an explicit goal of the water programs, should not be a neglected factor in the water improvement efforts. First, although man can survive for weeks without food, deprivation of water results in death within days. Adequate water to support basic biological processes

NUTRITION INTERVENTION STRATEGIES IN NATIONAL DEVELOPMENT
Copyright © 1983 by Academic Press, Inc.
ISBN 012-709080-0

(for human metabolic waste disposal, replacement of insensible losses, and heat control) is fundamental to human survival. As such, water can be considered as the most fundamental of the various *nutrients*.

Second, there is increasing evidence that the "malnutrition problem" is not simply due to insufficient food availability. The heavy burden of infections and infestations, especially among children, has been shown to retard growth and physical development and, under some circumstances, may precipitate or exacerbate frank clinical malnutrition (2). Since the quality and quantity of water is associated with the incidence of infections and infestations, efforts aimed at improving water supply may be an important approach to the reduction of infection and the consequent improvement of nutritional status.

Third, anticipated health benefits is one of the major rationale and purposes of investments in water supply. As such, there is a need to develop evaluation methodologies for assessing the specific outcomes and benefits obtained with the provision of clean and sufficient drinking water (3). Of particular interest are morbidity, nutritional, and mortality indicators, all reflective of the health status of a community. Although several methods are available to obtain reliable mortality data, comparison of death rates between two populations (one served with water and another without) requires large sample sizes. More commonly employed therefore have been morbidity data, a far more frequent event, such as the incidence or prevalence of the diarrheal diseases. Where attempts have been made, it has been difficult to document reduced diarrheal attack rates due to water interventions (4–9). This is not surprising given the well-known problems of defining and confirming field diarrheas and the probably multiple pathways of diarrheal disease transmission, only some of which may be related to water. Another measure, not commonly used, is nutritional status. Nutritional status may be estimated, by objective and simple field techniques and thus may be an indicator of potential usefulness (10).

Unfortunately, published literature relating improved water supply to measurable improvements of nutritional status is scant. Moreover, improved nutritional status per se, in contrast to reduction of infection, has been usually an implicit rather than explicit aim of water interventions. The conceptual base of possible mechanisms through which improved water supplies might operate to affect nutritional status has heretofore not been articulated.

The purpose of this chapter is to address some of these deficiencies. More specifically, this chapter reviews briefly concepts related to water improvement and health benefits; non-health benefits are also examined because of their often under-appreciated role in determining nutritional status. Then, an integrated framework identifying the major determinants of nutritional status is presented. Within this framework, the various mechanisms through which improved water supply might operate to affect nutritional status are postulated. Finally, empirical field data from rural Bangladesh on the relationship between the installation of tubewells and cholera attack rates are reviewed with the aim of illustrating some of the problems associated with evaluating the health impact of water interventions.

WATER SUPPLY AND HEALTH BENEFITS

The single most important conceptual advance in understanding the mechanism through which water supply improvement might operate to affect health is the framework developed by Bradley (11–13), which classifies water-associated diseases according to their relationship to water (Table I). *Waterborne* diseases, such as cholera and infectious hepatitis, are contracted through the drinking of water, which acts as the passive carrier of pathogenic organisms. These diseases are combatted through improvements of water quality and the prevention of casual use of other unimproved sources. *Water-washed* diseases, such as shigellosis and scabies, may be reduced following improvements in domestic and personal hygiene. When increased quantities of water become available,

TABLE I

Mechanisms of Water-Related Disease Transmission and Control Strategies[a]

Mechanisms	Illustrative diseases	Control strategies
I. Water-borne	Cholera	Improve water quality
	Typhoid	Prevent casual use of other unimproved sources.
	Hepatitis	
II. Water-washed	Shigellosis	Improve water quantity
	Scabies	Improve water accessibility
	Ascariasis	Improve personal hygiene
III. Water-based	Schistosomiasis	Decrease need for water contact
	Guinea worm	Control population of aquatic host
		Improve quality
IV. Water-related	Malaria	Improve surface water management
	Onchoceriasis	Destroy breeding sites
	Sleeping sickness	Decrease need to visit breeding sites

[a] Adapted from Bradley (12) and Feacham (14).

irrespective of quality, the incidence of these diseases may decrease presumably because of increased water use for household and personal hygiene. *Water-based* diseases, such as schistosomiasis and guinea worm, are ones in which the pathogen spends part of its life cycle in an intermediate aquatic host. The preventive strategy is to decrease human–water contact, control the population of the aquatic host, and improve the water quality. Diseases such as malaria are transmitted by *water-related* insect vectors, which either breed or bite near water. Control strategies include improved surface water management, destruction of breeding sites, and decreased need to visit breeding sites.

A limitation of this framework is the restrictive definition of health. Health is equated simply to infectious and parasitic diseases, rather than to human well-being. The latter may be measured by other possible indicators, one of which is nutritional status. To gain systematic insight on how water improvement might affect nutritional status requires an examination of postulated non-health, as well as health, benefits. Table II shows a series of possible aims and benefits of water supply development programs in low-income communities in developing countries by Feacham (14). Table II lists three stages of potential benefits. They are organized chronologically; stage I benefits are likely to be realized earlier than stage II, which, in turn, would precede stage III benefits. The more distant the benefit, the more dependent is the benefit related to additional complementary socioeconomic development inputs, such as rural development, agricultural services, and basic health programs.

If realized, stage II and III benefits could have substantial nutritional effects. Crop production and improvements in animal husbandry could result in improved quality and quantity of family diets. So too, obviously, would higher family cash incomes. Stage I benefits relate to

TABLE II

Aims and Potential Benefits of Water Supply Improvements[a]

Immediate aims	Stage I benefits	Stage II benefits	Stage III benefits
Improved water quality, quantity, availability, reliability	Save time Save energy Improve health	Release labor Crop innovation Crop improvement Animal husbandry innovation Animal husbandry improvement	Higher cash income Increased and more reliable subsistence Improved health Increased leisure

[a] From Feacham (14)

direct health benefits (reduction of disease) and to changes in time and energy expenditure for water collection. Reducing energy expenditure for water collection, usually a task performed by nutritionally vulnerable women and children, could have significant nutritional implications. In some communities, the preexisting water supply situation may be convenient and proximal, and thus water improvements may not yield substantial time and energy savings. In other communities, such as parts of Subsaharan Africa, some families may live up to 13 km from permanent water sources. Extensive surveys in East Africa have documented that some individuals spend up to 5 hours daily in collecting water during dry seasons, with a mean collection time of 46 minutes (11). These surveys also showed that an average of 104 to 240 calories were expended daily for water collection. In several families, as many as 2,000 calories were expended. These energy expenditure approximated 12% of daily daytime energy availability, with some communities averaging 27%.

WATER AND NUTRITION RELATIONSHIPS

The health and nonhealth benefits of improved water supply may be related to the nutritional status of an individual woman or child by linking them to the basic factors that determine nutritional well-being (Fig. 1). Energy balance in an individual is basically determined by the balance of energy intake and energy expenditure (or loss). In order for energy to reach an individual, it must first be available to a family. Household *food availability* reflects the economic capacity of a family to procure food of adequate quality and quantity. Household food, in turn, is stored, processed, cooked, and distributed to individual members. Household *food efficiency and distribution* reflects the efficiency of households to optimize available food, and intrafamily food distribution determines how much food an individual receives. In addition to basic metabolic requirements, *energy expenditure* for work, leisure, personal maintenance, and other activities is the major form of energy utilization. Another pathway of energy loss is *nutrient wastage* due to infection and infestation. It has been well established that infections, such as diarrhea, causes unnecessary wastage of nutrients by reducing food intake, causing malabsorption of ingested nutrients, and promoting catabolic losses (2).

As shown in Fig. 1, the first two mechanisms may be seen to primarily regulate the inflow of nutrients to an individual, whereas the last two pathways determine the outflow of nutrients from an individual. As

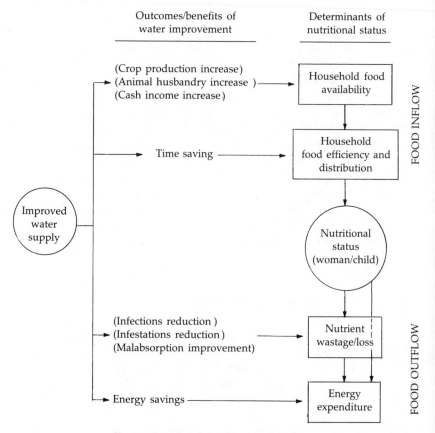

Fig. 1. Water and nutrition relationships.

such, interventions that increase household food availability or improve household food efficiency and distribution would be expected to result in improved nutritional status. Similarly, actions that reduce energy expenditure (for performing the same task) or reduce the burden of infections and infestations would also be expected to improve nutritional well-being.

Figure 1 shows that improvement of water supplies could theoretically affect nutrition through all four mechanisms. Increases of crop production, animal husbandry, or cash income could result in increased household food availability. Time savings generated from more proximal water sources could conceivably free up hard-pressed women's time to be used more effectively for child care, household food storage, processing, and cooking. Improved water supply could reduce the energy expended by women and children in water collection. And, the reduction of chronic and acute infections and infestations due to water improvement could lessen nutrient loss caused by these diseases.

Several features of this relationship deserve comment. First, as suggested by Fig. 1, the magnitude of the nutritional effects may vary significantly depending upon geography, characteristics of the community, nature of the water improvement, and preexisting nutritional problems in the community. Second, it is clear that any water improvement endeavor is likely to exert effects in multiple directions. In terms of nutritional impact, it seems likely that all four mechanisms affecting food inflow into and outflow from an individual may be influenced by water supply improvement. Finally, these features suggest that previous evaluation efforts, which examined only the reduction of disease, may be excessively restrictive, limiting the evaluation of program impact to only one of several possible health benefits.

TUBEWELL WATER AND CHOLERA IN RURAL BANGLADESH

To illustrate the difficulty of evaluating the impact of a water improvement program on health, empirical evidence from rural Bangladesh on the relationship between tubewell drinking water and cholera attack rates is reviewed. In this example, only one water intervention, hand tubewells, is examined for its effect on a single water-borne infectious disease—cholera. Figure 1 shows that the relationship under scrutiny is illustrative only of the effect of water improvement on infection, only one of the many potential effects of water interventions.

In 1972 the Bangladesh government, with the financial and technical assistance of UNICEF and WHO, initiated a massive $40 million project aimed at improving rural drinking water supplied through the installation of new shallow tubewells, new deep wells, and the rehabilitation of old choked up wells (15). By 1976, initial physical targets had been achieved, and a second phase was launched to provide essentially all rural households in Bangladesh with access to tubewell drinking water. An explicit goal of this program was to control cholera, water-borne diarrheal, and other infectious diseases by increasing the availability of clean drinking water through tubewell installation.

One of the areas covered by this program was Matlab Thana, Comilla District. Matlab, fortunately, is the field research site of the International

Centre for Diarrheal Disease Research, Bangladesh, (ICDDRB, formerly Cholera Research Laboratory). Since 1963, the ICDDRB had been operating diarrheal treatment services and demographic/epidemiologic surveillance systems among a 1978 study population of 177,000 (16). As a consequence, a unique opportunity presented itself for the study of the possible health (diarrheal) effects of the tubewell program.

ICDDRB published at least seven field studies on the risk of cholera and other diarrheal diseases in relationship to water use (17–23). The study by Curlin and his colleagues (17) was selected for review here because tubewell drinking water in households was confirmed by field workers and because diarrheal incidence data were obtained by longitudinal surveillance. About 20,000 residents of 12 randomly selected villages were prospectively followed during the calendar year 1975. Field workers visited each family weekly to enquire about diarrhea over the past week, and basic data regarding the source of water use for domestic purposes was recorded on 1 day in each month. In a systematic 5% sample of households, the validity of responses on tubewell water use was confirmed by measuring the electrical conductivity of water in household containers; tubewell water, because of high iron content, was confirmed to demonstrate consistently high conductivity.

The results of the study, contrary to expectations, showed that field diarrheal attack rates were similar between households that used bacteriologically inferior surface water for drinking in comparison to users of clean tubewell water (Table III). This lack of differential between tubewell and surface drinking water was noted also in the cholera- and shigella-positive cases presented to the Matlab diarrhea treatment unit.

These surprising findings are consistent with the results reported in other Matlab studies. What then is the explanation for the negative effect of tubewell water in reducing cholera risk? Briscoe (24) attempted to identify the factors responsible by offering the following explanations:

TABLE III

Diarrhea Attack Rates Per 1000 Population (Field and Hospital) According to Drinking Water Source in Matlab 1975[a]

	Field observations	Hospital observations	
Drinking water source	diarrhea	Cholera	Shigella
Tubewell	789	4.3	0.9
Other sources	757	1.0	1.5

[a] From Curlin *et al.* (17)

1. Cholera, contrary to evidence, is not a water-borne disease; the provision of clean drinking water would therefore not be expected to protect individuals against cholera.
2. In families who use tubewell water, some members, particularly children, may consume water from other sources instead of or in addition to tubewell water.
3. The small amount of protection afforded by drinking tubewell water is overwhelmed by repeated exposure to polluted surface water through bathing, food preparation, washing, cooking, and cleaning of dishes and utensils.

In addition to these explanations, another possibility exists:

4. There was a genuine reduction of water-borne diarrheal diseases, but the measurement of field diarrheas and hospital cholera and shigella cases may have failed to detect an impact.

The first explanation (1) was recently refuted by Mosley (19), who in a review of cholera epidemiology reaffirmed the importance of polluted water in cholera transmission, and Briscoe himself in subsequent field observations (24) discarded the second explanation (2). The third possibility (3) is consistent with a recent environmental bacteriological study by Spira and colleagues (23). Careful cultures from environmental samples of water sources within and outside of homes of cholera index cases and matched controls were examined to determine secondary attack rates of cholera. The study noted that the risk of cholera was tenfold higher among families where any water source within a household (drinking, washing, food preparation, cooking) was contaminated in comparison to noncontaminated households (Table IV). Contamination of water outside of the house, although related to household contamination, was not as strongly associated with cholera attack rates. While

TABLE IV

Cholera Infection Rate according to Exposure to Contaminated Household Water in Matlab[a]

Household water jars	Total no. of persons	No. with cholera infection	Cholera infection rate (%)
Cholera contaminated	306	33	10.8
Uncontaminated	296	3	1.0
All	602	36	5.6

[a] From Spira et al. (23).

possibly important, clean drinking water alone would appear to exert little influence on cholera attack rates.

Although this third possibility (3) seems plausable given Spira's study, it is also possible that there was a genuine reduction of cholera and field diarrheal rates but that methodological limitations prevented a detection of this effect. This last explanation (4) cannot be excluded, because reported field diarrheas and hospital-treated cholera and shigella cases were selected as the health variables of interest. Field diarrheas are notoriously difficult to record reliably and accurately, because personal recall alone determined reporting accuracy. Moreover, subclinical infections were not included. Even bacteriologically confirmed hospital cases were subject to problems because of an unquantifiable bias associated with the types of people who utilized hospital facilities. For example, if tubewell users in comparision to nonusers were more likely to use hospital facilities, a genuine reduction of cholera attack rates may have been counterbalanced by utilization patterns.

DISCUSSION

In summarizing empirical data relating health benefits to water improvement programs, Bradley (3) concluded that "several attempts to measure the impact on rural health of interventions such as water supplies have proved very inconclusive." The reasons for such lack of success are not difficult to identify. Water improvement affects disease incidence by changing water quality, water availability and patterns of use, of human contact with water bodies containing intermediate hosts, and the number of habitats for insect vector breeding. Modern water technology in isolation does not appear to be sufficient to achieve significant changes. For technology to be effective, a host of administrative, financial, communication, extension, and maintenance services must be provided. Moreover, water use and behavioral patterns among beneficiaries must change in response to the provision of modern facilities.

Thus, it was indeed discouraging to find that field and hospital observations of cholera incidence, did not differ between tubewell users and nonusers. Subsequent environmental and microbiological studies suggested that pollution of secondary household water (washing, cleaning, food preparation, cooking) may have overwhelmed the protective effect of clean drinking water.

Another explanation, however, could not be excluded: a genuine reduction was achieved, but not measured, because of methodological constraints. A common difficulty in health studies is the selection of an appropriate health indicator. In the Bangladesh example, both field (di-arrhea) and hospital (cholera and shigella) observations were employed, i.e., morbidity data were obtained from field enquiries, hospital records, or clinical and laboratory tests. But clinical examination and laboratory tests are time-consuming and require skilled and expensive manpower and sophisticated and expensive equipment. Hospital records, because their primary purpose are not research oriented, may be incomplete and inadequate or may reflect biased patterns of health service utilization. Field enquiries of diarrhea morbidity depended upon client recall, a notoriously unreliable method, especially if definitions are imprecise, and recall intervals are infrequently spaced. The time interval between interviews is especially critical because the symptoms being measured occurred with high frequency and the clients could easily forget. An optimal health indicator should possess the following characteristics: simplicity, reliability, minimal time and financial requirements, and per-formed by briefly trained nonprofessionals; they should have the capaci-ty to measure several dimensions simultaneously (3).

The contention advanced in this paper is that the assessment of the *nutritional status* of women and children may qualify as a health indicator of potential usefulness. Nutritional status can be measured by several techniques: food balance sheets, dietary surveys, clinical or biochemical examinations, or field anthropometry (10). Field measurement of body weight, height, and arm circumference can be conducted quickly and precisely with simple equipment by unsophisticated workers.

Another significant contribution that nutritional assessment might add is its lack of dependence on a single effect. Nutritional status re-flects, as shown in Fig. 1, the *net* influence of multiple pathways through which water improvement might affect health. The absence of a single impact, as demonstrated in the rural Bangladesh case study, does not necessarily imply that no health impact was attained. It is possible that single water improvement effects may not be detected by methodologi-cal limitations, may change in intensity over time, may be overwhelmed by other factors (such as other contaminated household water), or may exert its ultimate effect through multiple indirect mechanisms not easily quantified. The selection of a dependent health variable that reflects multiple effects of water improvement therefore may be more re-warding.

Another advantage of employing nutritional status is the special role of women and children. In most societies, women and children are responsible for domestic water collection; thus the time and energy sav-ings most directly affect these population subgroups. These same sub-groups, in most low-income countries, are the ones most susceptible to poor health and malnutrition. As such, the impact of water improvement should be most readily detected amongst these groups. Finally, nutritional status facilitates an assessment of distributional patterns. Undernutrition is more common among the economically disadvantaged. Water improvement programs that fail to reach the disadvantaged, therefore, cannot be expected to improve the nutritional status of most of the malnutrition in a given community. Thus, in addition to direct health assessment, the measurement of nutritional status among representative individuals of a community could shed light on the distributional impact, indicating whether the poorest and most disadvantaged in a community have received the newly introduced facilities.

In conclusion, this chapter contends that the nutritional status of women and children in the community is a health indicator of potential usefulness in the evaluation of the impact of water interventions. Several limitations of morbidity data were noted, and the advantages of nutritional assessment by field anthropometry were reviewed. It should be noted that although field anthropometry may be superior to certain morbidity measures, it also possesses limitations, the major one of which is the dependence of anthropometry on variables beyond those affected by water improvement, i.e., age, sex, season, demography, socioeconomic status, diet, and activity. Lack of comparability between populations or non-water-related changes over time in one population are likely to limit the interpretation of such field investigations. The potentials of anthropometry, however, are sufficiently promising as to deserve empirical field validity testing.

REFERENCES

1. Feacham, R., McGarry, M., and Mara, D. eds. "Water, Wastes, and Health in Hot Climates." Wiley, New York, 1977.
2. Scrimshaw, N. S. Synergism of malnutrition and infection: Evidence from field studies in Guatemala. *JAMA, J. Am. Med. Assoc.* **212,** 1685–1692 (1970).
3. Caincross, S., Carruthers, I., Curtis, D., Feacham, R., Bradley, D., and Baldwin, G. "Evaluation for Village Water Supply Planning." Wiley, New York, 1980.
4. Feacham, R., Burns, E., Caincross, S., Cronin, A., Cross, P., Curtis, D., Khan, M. K., Lamb, D., and Southall, A. "Water, Health and Development: An Interdisciplinary Evaluation" Tri-med Books, London, 1978.
5. Hollister, A. C. *et al.* Influence of water availability on shigella prevalence in children of farm labor families. *Am. J. Public Health* **45,** 354–362 (1955).
6. Moore, A. A. *et al.* Diarrheal disease studies in Costa Rica: 'IV. The influence of sanitation upon the prevalence of intestinal infection and diarrheal disease. *Am. J. Epidemiol.* **82,** 162–184 (1966).

7. Watt, J. Diarrheal diseases in Fresno County, California. *Am. J. Public Health* **43**, 728–741 (1953).
8. Strudwick, R. H. The Zaina environmental sanitation project. *East Afr. Med. J.* **39**, 311–331 (1962).
9. Schliessmann, D. J. *et al.* Relation of environmental factors to the occurrence of enteric diseases in areas of Eastern Kentucky. *U.S., Public Health Serv., Public Health Monogr.* **54** (1958).
10. Jelliffe, D. B. "The Assessment of the Nutritional Status of the Community," W.H.O. Monogr. No. 53. World Health Monogr., Geneva, 1966.
11. White, G. F., Bradley, D. J., and White, A. V. "Drawers of Water: Domestic Water Use in East Africa." Univ. of Chicago Press, Chicago, Illinois, 1972.
12. Bradley, D. J. Water supplies: The consequences of change. *Ciba Found. Symp.* **23** (new ser.), 81–98 (1974).
13. Bradley, D. J., and Emurwon, P. Predicting the epidemiological effect of changing water sources. *East Afr. Med. J.* **45**, 284–291 (1968).
14. Feacham, R. Water supplies for low-income communities in developing countries. *J. Environ. Eng. Div. (Am. Soc. Civ. Eng.)*, 687–702 (1975).
15. Government of Bangladesh. Department of Publich Health Engineering: Plan of Operations for the Second Rural Water Supply Construction Project in Bangladesh, Dacca, 1975.
16. Chen, L. C., Ahmed, S., Gesche, M. C., and Mosley, W. H. A prospective study of birth interval dynamics in rural Bangladesh. *Popul. Stud.* **28**, 277–297 (1974).
17. Curlin, G. T., Aziz, K. M. A., and Khan, M. R. The influence of drinking tubewell water on diarrhea rates in Matlab Thana, Bangladesh. Paper presented at a meeting of the U.S.-Japan Cholera Panel, Sapporo, 1976.
18. Sommer, A., and Woodward, W. E. The influence of protected water supplies on the spread of Classical Inaba and El Tor Ogawa cholera in rural East Bengal. *Lancet* **2**, 985–987 (1972).
19. Mosley, W. H., and Khan, M. U. "Cholera Epidemiology: Some Environmental Aspects" (unpublished mimeo.) Cholera Research Laboratory, Dacca, 1978.
20. Khan, M. U., Mosley, W. H., Chakravorty, J., Sarder, A. M., and Khan, M. R. "Water Source and the Incidence of Cholera in Rural Bangladesh," Sci. Rep. No. 16. Cholera Research Laboratory, Dacca, 1978.
21. Hughes, J. M., Boyce, J. M., Levine, R. J., Khan, M. U., and Curlin, G. T. "Water and the Transmission of El Tor Cholera in Rural Bangladesh," Work. Pap. No. 2. International Centre for Diarrheal Disease Research, Bangladesh, Dacca, 1977.
22. Khan, M. U., and Mosley, W. H. Contrasting epidemiologic patterns of diarrhea and cholera in semi-urban community. *J. Pak. Med. Assoc.* **19**, 380–385 (1969).
23. Spira, W. M., Saeed, Y. A., Khan, M. U., and Satter, M. A. Microbiological surveillance of intra-neighborhood. El Tor cholera transmission in Rural Bangladesh. *Bull. W.H.O.* (1980).
24. Briscoe, J. "The Role of Water Supply in Improving Health in Poor Countries," Sci. Rep. No. 6. Cholera Research Laboratory, Dacca, 1977.

21 Environmental Sanitation: A Nutrition Intervention

LIANA SCHLESINGER, JORGE WEINBERGER,
GUILLERMO FIGUEROA, M. TERESA SEGURE,
NICOLÁS GONZÁLEZ, AND FERNANDO
MONCKEBERG

INTRODUCTION

Overcrowding and deficient environmental sanitation are conditions common to all Latin American countries. This situation has become worse during the past decades as a result of the explosive growth of the population and increased migration to the cities. At present, almost 64% of the population has become urban and over 40% lives in the so-called "extreme poverty belts" with practically no environmental sanitation (1). All these factors negatively affect the nutritional status of the infant population and favor the occurrence of gastrointestinal and other infectious disease. The decline of breast-feeding and its substitution by bottle-feeding among other factors has been a consequence of this migration (2). The use of diluted, contaminated formulas is one of the main contributors to the shift in the incidence of malnutrition to the early months of life, and this, in turn, is associated with high risk of death (3).

In the light of these circumstances, carefully planned and implemented pilot interventions on environmental sanitation and the quantitation of their impact upon nutritional status become especially important as tools to optimize cost benefits and to enable comparisons with other types of intervention.

A report in "World Health Statistics" includes the following statement: "Diarrheas and enteric diseases caused by polluted water supplies and insanitary disposal of excreta are, as a group, a major cause of

NUTRITION INTERVENTION STRATEGIES IN NATIONAL DEVELOPMENT
Copyright © 1983 by Academic Press, Inc.

illness and death, particularly among children in developing countries"
(4). However obvious this statement may appear, it has not been always
feasible to compare the impact of environmental sanitation upon diarrhea and infant malnutrition with that of other forms of intervention.
Recent reports on these types of intervention programs fail to show
clearcut effects on the incidence of diarrhea and even less repercussion
on the prevention of malnutrition (5, 6). This is probably explained by
the multifactorial origin of the problem, defective sanitation being just
another causative factor. To achieve actual sanitation of the environment
is neither easy nor inexpensive. It requires, for example, provision and
the use of large volumes of running water per person. It is therefore

Fig. 1. Latrine.

possible that partial improvements of the system will not induce significant effects, and this explains why conclusive results are frequently not obtained.

In the project reported herein, efforts were made to eliminate other factors contributing to malnutrition. At the same time, important improvements of environmental sanitation were planned by providing both adequate volumes of drinking water and means for the sanitary disposal of excreta. This experimental design was also used in order to analyze the effects of housing improvement on the personal attitudes of the family and on their expectations for better standards of life.

EXPERIMENTAL DESIGN

A slum in the periphery of greater Santiago, Chile, whose socioeconomic level was among the lowest in the city, was chosen for this study. The slum was built in 1965 in a well-delimited area. The Ministry of Housing provided plots of 8 by 19 m to 570 families. Drinking water was supplied by a tap installed within each site and the possibility of connections to the city's sewage system were available because the underground ducts had been built earlier. Families built provisional dwellings in the back of the plots as best they could, using pieces of scavenged timber, plastic, cardboard, and other materials. However, they did not have money to connect their houses either to the city's sewage and/or the water supply system. As a consequence, they dug unsanitary latrines for the disposal of excreta (Fig. 1). Tap water had to be hand carried into the houses in containers.

Most groups had migrated from rural areas, and the great majority of the heads of household had no permanent jobs. Health care was provided by the National Health Service. A Health Center located about 1 km from the slum provided health care, immunizations, medical treatment, advise on family planning, and supplementary food under the National Food Supplementation Program* to pregnant women and to children under 6 years of age (7).

As far as can be discerned, practically no changes took place in either the socioeconomic level or the living patterns (family structure, attitudes, habits, concepts of human dignity, etc.) of the population from 1965 to 1977.

---

*Distribution of (a) 3 kg/month of powdered milk (26% fat) for children under 2 years of age; (b) 2 kg/month of powdered food enriched with 22% protein (NPU similar to casein) for children 2 to 6 years of age, and (c) powdered milk, 1 kg/month for pregnant and nursing women.

Fig. 2. Sanitary unit (exterior view). On the left, kitchen door. On the right, bathroom door.

The program for improvement of sanitary conditions in the slum included building a brick-and-timber "sanitary unit" in each plot (Fig. 2). The unit had a kitchen and a bathroom and an outdoor sink to wash clothes. The kitchen was equipped with shelves and sink; the bathroom had a lavatory, flush toilet, and shower (Fig. 3). Hot water was supplied for the whole unit by a geyser. The unit covered an area of 6 square meters and was built in the front area of the plot, near the street. This location was chosen so that the family could build their "definitive" house as an extension of this unit.

The program was implemented in two successive stages. During the first stage, 270 sanitary units were built. In a second stage (20 months after the first one was started), units were provided for the remaining families. This made it possible to consider two groups of families for study purposes: group A, which received a sanitary unit, and group B (control), which remained without them during the 20 months covered by the study. Units were delivered to the families in group A in July, 1977. Their construction was funded by a loan from USAID to the Chilean National Council for Food and Nutrition (CONPAN).

Informed consent for family participation in the evaluation projects was requested. Out of the 270 families of group A, 78 families agreed to

Fig. 3.   Bathroom of the sanitary unit.

participate. Of the 300 families in group B, 60 families participated. Group A included 120 and group B included 89 children under 4 years of age.

The socioeconomic level of the families was assessed prior to the beginning of the study by a modification of the Graffar scale (8), which was especially adapted to evaluate differences in the lower strata. The participating families were shown to belong to the low stratus. No illiterates were found among the household heads. However, 70% of them had not completed 8 years of elementary education, and 5% had completed their high school training.

Families to whom sanitary units were provided were selected at random. However, in some cases, the extreme poverty of a few families mandated that units be allocated to them without further waiting. Because of this, it turned out that group A included, on the average, families who were worse off than the control group.

Adequate utilization of the units was controlled by weekly interviews by trained registered nurses. Water consumption was measured monthly by reading the meters installed in each plot. Table I shows that the average water consumption during summer and winter was significantly higher in group A, i.e., the group having sanitary units.

EVALUATION OF BACTERIAL CONTAMINATION OF FEEDING BOTTLES

The contamination of bottles prepared with powdered milk was determined monthly. An unscheduled visit was made each month by the nurse, and samples were taken from the contents of bottles ready to be fed to infants. The samples were processed with conventional techniques (9) at the microbiological laboratories of INTA (Instituto de Nutrición y Tecnología de los Alimentos, Universidad de Chile). The percentage of bottles contaminated with fecal *Escherichia coli* or with more than 10^4 mesophilic bacteria per milliliter was determined in two consecutive summers (summer weather in Santiago, October through March, is dry and warm with an average of 30°C and maximum of about 34°C).

Results of this study are summarized in Table II and III. Similarly high levels of contamination with fecal *E. coli* were detected in the first summer period of the study in both groups. During the second summer, i.e., about 1 year after the sanitary units had been made available, a signifi-

TABLE I

Average Drinking Water Consumption (m³/Inhabitant/Month) in Groups A and B[a]

Group[b]	Families (number)	Winter (1977)	Summer (1977–1978)	Winter (1978)	Summer (1978–1979)
A	76	2.09 ± 1.28	3.43 ± 2.12	3.18 ± 2.39	3.71 ± 2.68
B	58	1.48 ± 1.60	2.46 ± 1.60	1.92 ± 1.17	2.50 ± 1.42
p[c]		< .01	< .01	< .001	< .001

[a] Values expressed as mean ± SD.
[b] Group A, with sanitary unit; group B, without sanitary unit.
[c] p per Student's t test.

TABLE II

Average Percentage of Bottles Contaminated with Fecal *E. coli* in Two Consecutive Summers[a]

	First summer		Second summer		
Group[b]	No. of bottles	Contaminated (%)	No. of bottles	Contaminated (%)	p[c]
A	197	72.6 ± 3.2	168	37.5 ± 3.7	< .001
B	179	66.7 ± 3.5	76	37.2 ± 5.4	< .001
p[c]		N.S.		N.S.	

[a] Values expressed as mean ± SD.
[b] Group A, with sanitary unit; group B, without sanitary unit.
[c] p per Z test.

cant, comparable decrease of fecal *E. coli* contamination was found in both groups (Table II).

Table III shows the percentage of bottles contaminated with mesophilic bacteria. Results demonstrate that during the first summer period there was a high percentage of positive samples in children from both groups of population, with no differences between them. However, during the second summer contamination declined significantly in group A (with sanitary units), whereas there was not any significant change in group B.

These results suggest that installation of the "sanitary unit" decreased bacterial contamination. This was also evident in the control group and may be explained by the fact that families with and without units lived

TABLE III

Average Percentage of Bottles Showing Mesophilic Bacteria Contamination in Two Consecutive Summers[a]

	First summer		Second summer		
Group[b]	No. of bottles	Contaminated (%)	No. of bottles	Contaminated (%)	p[c]
A	197	74.1 ± 3.1	168	43.5 ± 3.8	< .01
B	179	65.4 ± 3.6	76	52.6 ± 5.7	N.S.
p[c]		N.S.		N.S.	

[a] Counts in dilution of more than 1×10^4. Values expressed as mean ± SD.
[b] Group A, with sanitary unit; group B, without sanitary unit.
[c] p per Z test.

close to each other and that improvement in living conditions in one group is somehow reflected on the other.

EVALUATION OF SEASONAL DIARRHEA EPISODES

At the same time that bacterial contamination of bottles was evaluated, the frequency of diarrheal episodes was studied in the children under 4 years of age in both groups. Diarrhea was detected by specially trained registered nurses who visited the families every week and recorded the frequency of diarrheal episodes in ad hoc questionaires. Diarrhea was defined as the passage of two or more liquid stools per day. A preceding interval of at least 7 days of normal stools defined a new episode. The average number of diarrheal episodes in relation to the number of weekly surveys for the two summer periods is shown in Table IV. Our data reveal a significant high incidence of diarrheal disease during the first summer period in group A. This may be explained by taking into account that some of the families selected to receive sanitary units were among those with the lowest socioeconomic level. In the second warm season, the number of diarrheal episodes significantly decreased in group A, whereas no changes were observed in group B. These results suggest a beneficial effect of the use of sanitary units.

EVALUATION OF NUTRITIONAL STATUS

One of the objectives of this study was the assessment of the impact of environmental sanitation on the nutritional status of the 209 children of 0 to 4 years of age. To this effect, all children were weighed every month throughout the whole study period.

TABLE IV

Average Percentage of Diarrheal Episodes during Two Consecutive Summers[a]

Group	First summer episodes (%)	Second summer episodes (%)	p^c
A	28.4 ± 1.96	16.6 ± 1.46	< .01
B	14.8 ± 1.91	17.7 ± 1.75	N.S.
p^c	< .001	N.S.	

[a] The percentage of diarrhea was considered as the number of episodes /no. of interviews × 100. Values expressed as mean ± SD.

[b] Group A, with sanitary unit; group B, without sanitary unit.

[c] p per Student's t test.

The weight:age ratio was used as the index of nutritional status. Children were defined as low weight when their deficit for age was 10% or more below the 50th percentile of the NCHS tables (10). At the beginning of the study, almost all the low-weight children in both groups had deficits of between 10 to 25%. The deficit exceeded 25% in only four children, and in none of these did this deficit amount to more than 40%. The initial percentage of low-weight children was 31% in group A and 23% in group B. Twenty months later, the percentage of low-weight children increased to 33% among families belonging to the control group (B) and decreased to 25% in group A (Table V). Differences were significant for group B according to McNemar's test (11), which studies the comparative behavior of each group at the beginning and at the end of the study period. No differences were seen in group A.

The increment in the percentage of low-weight children in the control group was indeed foreseeable, since the effects of the factors conditioning chronic malnutrition are cummulative (12). Therefore, as time goes by, more and more children tend to enter the low-weight category. This increase of low-weight children not only failed to materialize in group A, but on the contrary, it experienced a notable reduction. The improvement of nutritional status in children of group A supports the basic hypothesis of our study—that within the causative context of malnutrition, environmental sanitation plays an important role.

CHANGES OF ATTITUDES, HABITS, AND QUALITY OF LIFE

As already noted, prior to installation of the sanitary units the population lived in deplorable environmental conditions. Their houses were built with pieces of discarded materials, little or no furniture, dirt floors, and no sewage disposal. We intended to analyze the impact that ownership of a bathroom with hot and cold running water, an adequate kitch-

TABLE V

Percentage of Low Weight Children at the Beginning and by the End of the Study

		Low Weight Children (%)		
Group[a]	No. of children	At start of study	20 Months later	p[b]
A	113	31.0	25.6	N.S.
B	84	22.6	33.3	< .05

[a] Group A, with sanitary unit; group B, without sanitary unit.
[b] p per McNemar's nonparametric test.

en, abundant drinking water, and facilities for washing may have on the behavior of the families, on their expectations for improvement, and on their efforts to fulfill these. As already mentioned, the sanitary units were designed to serve as the basis for the construction of definitive houses. This objective was extensively discussed with all families in the community and blueprints of several types of houses were provided. This facilitated the opportunity for them to built their new houses as extensions of the sanitary units.

Twenty months after the installation of the sanitary units an evaluation of the actions taken by the families themselves toward improving their housing conditions was carried out. This evaluation revealed some interesting facts. Without having been provided with money or building materials, a high percentage of the families had started or completed the construction of their new houses using conventional building materials (timber, brick and mortar) (Table VI). Though the quality of the construction varied widely, on the average it was quite satisfactory (Fig. 4). These results were observed both among the families that received sanitary units, as well as among those promised to receive one at the end of the study.

The impact was even more spectacular when the changes in household furnishings were analyzed. Four "large" household appliances were used as indicators: (1) sewing machine; (2) washing machine; (3) refrigerator; (4) TV set. The percentage of families owning these items before and 20 months after installation of the sanitary units was determined (radio sets were not taken into consideration because close to 100% of the families had at least one before this study was started). By the end of the 20-month period, the number of household appliances had increased significantly in both groups (Table VII). This reflects an improvement of living standards. In group A, the percentage of families that did not have any of the "large" household items decreased from 42

TABLE VI

Percentage of Families That Had Begun or Completed Self-Construction of Their Houses at 20 Months of Initiation of the Program

Group[a]	No. of families	Self construction (%)
Group A	74	60
Group B	56	35
p^b		< .01

[a] Group A, with sanitary unit; group B, without sanitary unit.
[b] p per χ^2 test.

Fig. 4.   New house (on the left) built as an extension of the sanitary unit.

to 8%. In group B the decrease was from 41 down to 7%. These changes may be interpreted as a result of the desire to live under better conditions, motivated perhaps by the stimulus of improved personal hygiene, cleaner food and clothing, adequate disposal of excreta, etc. However, general economic factors may also have influences these changes. During 1975–1978, prices of household appliances decreased significantly as

TABLE VII

Percentage of Families That Had One or More Household Appliances before and after 20 Months of the Installation of the Sanitary Unit[a]

| | | Had 1 or more appliances | | |
| | | --- | --- | |
Group[b]	No. of families	Before (%)	After (%)	p[c]
A	74	58.1	91.9	< .01
B	56	58.9	92.9	< .01

[a] TV set, washing machine, sewing machine, and refrigerator.
[b] Group A, with sanitary unit; group B, without sanitary unit.
[c] p per Sign nonparametric test.

a consequence of reductions of duties for imported goods from 300 to 10%.

Other changes of attitudes, revealing an increment of solidarity in the community, were also observed. Thus, without programing or external influences, the population spontaneously organized and successfully operated a social center, an administrative committee, and a sports club. The appearance of the area improved: green areas were established, most of the families developed and tended gardens, and trees were planted on the sidewalks. At present the population looks cleaner, more pleasant and beautiful than 4 years before.

FINAL COMMENTS

It is possible that the availability of sanitary units exerted a significant impact on the whole population. This impact is evidenced by the decrease of bacterial contamination and diarrhea, improvement of the nutritional status of the population, changes in attitudes, and raised expectations for better living standards. These indices improved not only in the households belonging to group A (with sanitary units), but spilled over into group B (without sanitary units). This latter phenomenon may be due to "cultural contamination" and emulation, favored by the fact that the groups were geographically close and, consequently, communicated freely. Probably this would not have happened if the two groups of families had been living in separate areas.

The data in this study are not enough to fully assess the value of intervention on environmental sanitation in terms of cost–benefit compared to other types of intervention. We think, however, that it is a useful experience because it demonstrates a significant impact of environmental sanitation on nutritional status and on the quality of life.

Perhaps the most meaningful and interesting results are the striking change in the attitudes of the families. The pessimistic and fatalistic approach to life, the hopelessness and acceptance of a miserable life prevailing in the community before the sanitary units were installed, changed into a sincere and deeply felt desire for improvement of their physical and spiritual living conditions. This led spontaneously to cooperation among the families and to increased individuals efforts to meet the challenge of improving the quality of their lives and attaining human dignity. The end result was a significant rise of living standards.

It seems to us that this psychosocial impact, that stands out so clearly in the case of our environmental sanitation project, is a factor that may be of importance for the success of other types of nutritional intervention. It should be taken into consideration in the design of interventions, specially when the targets are groups in the lowest levels of extreme poverty and marginality. These groups are usually the most difficult to be reached, and from this originates the assumed irreversibility of their status.

REFERENCES

1. Terra, J. P. Situación de la infancia en América Latina y el Caribe. Reunion Especial de Unicef solere la Infancia en America Latina y el Caribe Ciudad de Mexico, May 16–18, 1979.
2. Monckeberg, F. Factors conditioning malnutrition in Latin America, with special reference to Chile. Advices for a volunteers action. *In* "Malnutrition Is a Problem of Ecology" (P. György and O. L. Kline, eds.), pp. 23–63. Karger, Switzerland, 1970.
3. Monckeberg, F. Artificial feeding in infants, high risk in underdeveloped countries *In* "At Risk Factors and the Health and Nutrition of Young Children," (M. Gahbr, ed.), pp. 57–63. Supreme Council for Population and Family Planing, Egypt, 1979.
4. World Health Statistic Report (Special Issue). Community water supply and excreta disposal in developing countries. Review of progress. *World Health Organ.* **20,** 544 (1976).
5. White, G. F., Bradley, D. J., and White, A. V. "Drawers of Water. Domestic Water Use in East Africa." Univ. of Chicago Press, Chicago, Illinois, 1972.
6. Saunders, R. J., and Warford, J. J. "Village Water Supply: Economics and Policy in the Developing World." Johns Hopkins Univ. Press, Baltimore, Maryland, 1976.
7. Monckeberg, F. "Crear para Compartir." Editorial Andrés Bello, Santiago, Chile, 1980.
8. Graffar, M. "Cinq Cents Familles d'un Commune de l'agglomeration Bruxelloise." Institut de Sociologie, Solvay, Bruxelles, 1957.
9. Thatcher, F. S., and Clark, D. S. "Microorganisms in Food." Univ. of Toronto Press, Toronto, 1968 (reprinted, 1973).
10. Hamill, P. V., Drizd, T. A., Johnson, C. L., Reed, R. B., Roche, A. F., and Moore, W. M. Physical growth: National center for health statistics percentiles. *Am. J. Clin. Nutr.* **32,** 607 (1979).
11. Sokal, R. R., and Rohlf, F. J. "Biometry." Freeman, San Francisco, California, 1969.
12. Monckeberg, F., Donoso, G., Valiente, S., Maccioni, A., Merchak, N., Arteaga, A., Oxman, S., and Lacassie, Y. Condiciones de vida, medio familiar y examen clínico y bioquímico de lactantes y preescolares de la provincia de Curicó. *Rev. Chil. Pediatr.* **38,** 499 (1967).

VI Nutrient-Specific Interventions

22 Iron Deficiency: Methods To Measure Prevalence and Evaluate Interventions

JAMES D. COOK

Nutritional anemia is a health problem of increasing concern both in lesser developed countries and in highly industrialized nations. Because the lack of iron is the major cause of this anemia, laboratory methods for assessing iron status are needed for determining the prevalence of iron deficiency and for monitoring the effectiveness of intervention strategies. The capability of evaluating iron status in prevalence surveys has been greatly facilitated in recent years by the development of newer techniques and the continuing refinement of long established methods.

Of the variety of laboratory methods that have been proposed to assess iron nutrition, there are four that have now assumed major importance in population studies. These are listed together with levels that signify iron deficiency in Table I. The advantages and limitations of these four parameters will be reviewed in the order in which they became available for use in prevalence studies.

The earliest and most widely used parameter of iron status is the hemoglobin (Hb) level, in large part because the objective in most nutritional surveys has been to define the prevalence of anemia rather than iron deficiency per se. However, there are serious drawbacks with Hb measurements, particularly when more specific measures of iron status are not performed simultaneously. The major limitation with Hb determinations is the large overlap of values between normal and anemic individuals. This was first demonstrated in a study by Garby et al. (1), who administered iron orally to a population of adult women; he defined as anemic those who showed a significant increase in Hb. It was

NUTRITION INTERVENTION STRATEGIES IN NATIONAL DEVELOPMENT

TABLE I

Laboratory Parameters of Iron Status

	Critical value
Serum ferritin (SF)	< 12 μg/liter
Transferrin saturation (TS)	< 16%
Free erythrocyte protoporphyrin (FEP)	> 100 μg/dl RBC
Hemoglobin concentration (Hb)	
Men	< 13 gm/dl
Women	< 12 gm/dl

observed that 21% of normal women (who did not respond to iron) were incorrectly classified as anemic on the basis of the initial Hb level, whereas 17% of the anemic women (who responded to iron) had been incorrectly classified as normal. A similar result was observed in a collaborative survey of nutritional anemia in seven Latin American countries (2). A computer simultation of the frequency distribution curves of Hb in pregnant women indicated that about 30% of the anemic population were incorrectly classified as normal and that the number of normal women misclassified as anemic actually exceeded the number of truly anemic women. Clearly, the Hb when used alone is not sufficiently sensitive to accurately gauge the iron status of a population.

The serum iron and total iron-binding capacity (TIBC) are more specific measures of iron status and have been used extensively in prevalence surveys during the past two decades. Because the serum iron decreases and the TIBC increases with iron deficiency, the most sensitive expression is the serum iron:TIBC ratio or transferrin saturation (TS). When the level falls below 16%, hemoglobin production in the developing red cell becomes impaired, a condition referred to as iron-deficient erythropoiesis (3). Although the TS has been extensively used in prevalence studies, there are significant disadvantages with these measurements. Iron contamination often plagues serum iron measurements especially with time-consuming manual methods. This problem can often be circumvented by employing automated techniques, although there is still no widely accepted automated method for measurement of TIBC. From a physiologic standpoint, the serum iron is subject to wide diurnal variations in normal subjects, which reduce its sensitivity. A fall in TS is not specific for true iron deficiency because the level is also reduced with chronic infection or inflammation. Moreover, although the TS is useful for identifying iron-deficient erythropoiesis, the level can fall abruptly with even mild infections and, therefore, gives no indication of the duration or severity of iron-deficient erythropoiesis.

Another parameter, which gives very similar information to the TS, is the free erythrocyte protoporphyrin (FEP). When iron supply to the developing red cell becomes restricted, the FEP in circulating red cells rises long before the onset of identifiable anemia. FEP measurements have been available for a number of years, and their value for detecting iron deficiency is well documented (4). However, earlier laboratory methods for measuring FEP are far too cumbersome for survey work. Renewed interest in FEP for population studies resulted from the development of abbreviated techniques (5) and, more recently, from fluorometric assays, which are exceedingly rapid and simple to perform (6). The level of FEP diagnostic of iron deficiency depends on the method employed, and normal ranges must be established in each laboratory. In a recent survey in adult subjects, a level of 100 µg/ml packed RBC was found to indicate iron deficiency (7). In a recent pediatric study, the FEP:Hb ratio appeared to enhance the sensitivity of FEP for detecting and monitoring iron-deficiency anemia (8). One disadvantage of the FEP in children as compared with other parameters of iron status is that the level increases with lead poisoning. Apart from this, an important advantage of FEP as compared with TS is greater stability. Elevations in FEP occur only after several weeks of erythroid iron deprivation, and following treatment of iron deficiency, the FEP returns slowly to normal over a period of many weeks. A comparison of FEP and TS measurements for detecting iron deficiency was made recently in a study performed in 20 anemic and 20 normal infants under the age of 2 years (8). The FEP:Hb ratio gave the sharpest separation between the two groups and showed the most consistent and uniform change in response to iron therapy. However, the FEP or FEP:Hb ratio may be more useful in children with severe iron deficiency anemia than in adults with less severe degrees of iron lack.

The most recent and apparently most sensitive parameter of iron status described to date is the serum ferritin (SF). Ferritin has long been known to function as the major form of storage iron within cells, but it is only recently that it is possible to detect and quantify the minute amounts that are invariably present in human serum (9,10). The SF is measured by sensitive immunoradiometric assays similar to those used for the detection of hepatitis B antigen or various circulating hormones. In normal men and women, the SF averages 90 and 3 µg/liter, respectively, a difference that accurately reflects the known threefold sex difference in iron stores. In adults, values below 12 µg/liter are diagnostic of iron deficiency (11). An excellent correlation has been demonstrated between SF and body iron stores as measured either directly by quantitative phlebotomy (12) or indirectly by iron absorption measurements

(11). The close correlation that has been demonstrated in various clinical disorders between the SF and marrow iron stores assessed histologically (13) suggests that the reticuloendothelial cell is the immediate precursor compartment for the SF.

An important feature of SF measurements is the ability to distinguish between true iron deficiency and the anemia of chronic infection. In contrast with FEP and TS levels, which are similarily affected in these two disorders, the TS falls with iron deficiency but increases with inflammation (13). The diagnostic value of including SF measurements in prevalence surveys was demonstrated recently in a study on the effect of three months of iron supplementation in Eskimo children (14). Following iron supplementation, the number of children with an abnormal SF fell from 41 to 6%, although there was little or no change in frequency of anemia as measured by Hb or of iron-deficient erythropoiesis as monitored by TS levels. It was concluded that infection was a major cause of anemia and that SF reflected an improvement in iron nutrition that was not apparent by other measurements. A similar finding was reported in patients with juvenile rheumatoid arthritis where anemia may occur due to chronic disease, iron deficiency, or both (15). A pretreatment SF below 25 μg/liter was useful for predicting the response to iron therapy in anemic children, whereas the Hb, FEP, and TS were not. Therefore, although the level of SF, which signifies iron deficiency, may be altered in the presence of chronic disease, it still remains a useful measure of iron status.

Other measurements of iron status are less suitable for prevalence studies than the above parameters. An important consequence of continued undersupply of iron to the developing erythron is hypochromia and microcytosis as detected by changes in the red cell indices. The latter were not particularly useful in earlier surveys because of the unreliability of manual methods and particularly the red cell count. However, there has been renewed interest in the mean corpuscular volume (MCV) because of the improved accuracy of electronic counters (16, 17). In children, the MCV serves as a reliable index of iron-deficient erythropoiesis, although it does not distinguish between microcytosis due to true iron deficiency, thalassemia minor, or chronic disease. The lower cutoff levels for MCV are distinctly different in infants and children than in adults. The diagnostic level is below 70 fl in children 6 months to 2 years of age, below 74 fl from 2 to 6 years of age, and below 76 fl from 6 to 12 years of age. The normal level in adult subjects is above 80 fl. Although the usefulness of the MCV has been clearly demonstrated in pediatric surveys, it may be less useful in adult subjects either because anemia is often less pronounced in adults or because micro-cytosis develops less consistently in the adult in response to iron-deficient erythropoiesis (18).

The definitive test of iron-deficiency anemia is the therapeutic iron trial. Failure of a reduced hemoglobin level to respond to full therapeutic doses of medicinal iron excludes true iron deficiency as a cause of the anemia. An important constraint with the therapeutic iron trial however, particularly in adult subjects, is the difficulty in ensuring that the prescribed iron is actually ingested. Certainly, failure of compliance remains the commonest cause of so-called "refractory" iron-deficiency anemia in the adult. Compliance is less often a problem in infants and children, particularly in supplementation programs in school age children where iron can be administered under direct supervision. With this exception, the therapeutic iron trial is not well suited to prevalence studies, particularly since more specific and less costly laboratory measurements have become widely available.

The four main survey parameters of iron status (Hb, TS, FEP, and SF) are useful not only in detecting iron deficiency but also for gauging its severity. Three stages of iron deficiency can be defined by performing these measurements simultaneously (Fig. 1). The initial stage is iron depletion, which is defined as a reduction in storage iron prior to en-

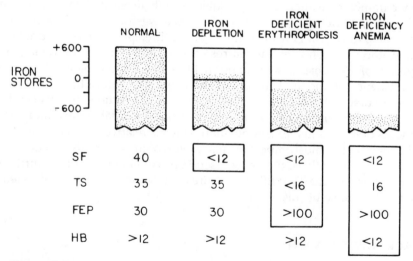

Fig. 1. Parameters of iron status in relationship to body iron stores. Negative iron stores indicate the amount of iron that must be replaced in circulating red cells before iron reserves can reaccumulate.

croachment on functional (hemoglobin) iron. This earliest stage of iron lack can be detected only by SF measurements, which can be used to assess iron status in iron-replete segments of the population. In the second stage of iron deficiency, iron stores are completely exhausted and in addition there is evidence of iron-deficient erythropoiesis based on a decrease in TS or increase in FEP or both. These parameters of intermediate iron deficiency are therefore useful in detecting iron lack before the development of frank anemia. In the final stage of iron-deficiency anemia, all four survey parameters are abnormal, and with continuing negative iron balance, the Hb level becomes directly proportional to residual body iron.

Iron deficiency anemia can be detected more precisely by performing SF, TS, and FEP simultaneously rather than Hb alone. Evidence for this was obtained in a recent nutritional survey in northwest United States (7). In a combined population of 1564 subjects, anemia as defined by World Health Organization criteria occurred in 8.3% of the entire population. When only one of the three parameters of iron status was abnormal, the prevalence of iron deficiency was 14.2% based on a decrease in TS, 17.5% based on an increase in FEP, and 13.5% as defined by a low SF. In the total group with at least one abnormal parameter, the abnormality occurred as an isolated finding in about one-half of the subjects. The most important finding concerned the relationship of iron deficiency parameters to anemia. In 313 subjects with an isolated abnormality in TS, FEP, or SF, the prevalence of anemia was only slightly increased from 8.3 to 10.9%. However, if two of the three parameters were abnormal, the prevalence of anemia rose to 28%, whereas in the remaining group of 68 subjects with abnormalities in all three parameters, the prevalence of anemia was 63%. It was concluded from this study that the accuracy of detecting iron deficiency in population surveys can be substantially improved by employing a battery of laboratory measurements of iron status. In a population which is relatively iron replete, the SF may be the most important parameter. With severe iron deficiency however, the Hb is the most useful measurement of iron nutrition providing that the TS, FEP, and SF are included to identify iron deficiency as the cause of this anemia.

ACKNOWLEDGMENT

This investigation was supported by USPHS Grant No. AM-19011 and Contract No. 223-76-2112, Food and Drug Administration.

REFERENCES

1. Garby, L., Irnell, L., and Werner, I. Iron deficiency in women of fertile age in a Swedish community. III. Estimation of prevalence based on response to iron supplementation. *Acta Med. Scand.* **185**, 113–117 (1969).
2. Cook, J. D., Alvarado, J., Gutnisky, A., Jamra, M., Labardini, J., Layrisse, M., Linares, J., Loria, A., Maspes, V., Restrepo, A., Reynafarje, C., Sanchez-Medal, L., Velez, J., and Viteri, F. Nutritional deficiency and anemia in Latin America: A collaborative study. *Blood* **38**, 591–603 (1971).
3. Bainton, D. F., and Finch, C. A. The diagnosis of iron deficiency anemia. *Am. J. Med.* **37**, 62–70 (1964).
4. Langer, E. E., Haining, R. G., Labbe, R. F., Jacobs, P., Crosby, E. F., and Finch, C. A. Erythrocyte protoporphyrin. *Blood* **40**, 112–128 (1972).
5. Heller, S. R., Labbe, R. F., and Nutter, J. A simplified assay for prophyrins in whole blood. *Clin. Chem. (Winston-Salem, N.C.)* **17**, 525 (1971).
6. Piomelli, S., Brickman, A., and Carlos, E. Rapid diagnosis of iron deficiency by measurement of free erythrocyte porphyrins and hemoglobin: The FEP/hemoglobin ratio. *Pediatrics* **57**, 136 (1976).
7. Cook, J. D., Finch, C. A., and Smith, N. Evaluation of the iron status of a population. *Blood* **48**, 449–455 (1976).
8. Thomas, W. J., Koenig, H. M., Lightsey, A. L., and Green, R. Free erythrocyte porphyrin: hemoglobin ratios, serum ferritin, and transferrin saturation levels during treatment of infants with iron deficiency anemia. *Blood* **49**, 455–462 (1977).
9. Jacobs, A., Miller, E., Worwood, M., Beamish, M. R., and Wardrop, C. A. Ferritin in the serum of normal subjects and patients with iron deficiency and iron overload. *Br. Med. J.* **4**, 206–208 (1972).
10. Jacobs, A., and Worwood, M. The biochemistry of ferritin and its clinical implications. *Prog. Hematol.* **9**, 1–24 (1975).
11. Cook, J. D., Lipschitz, D. A., Miles, L. E. M., and Finch, C. A. Serum ferritin as a measure of iron stores in normal subjects. *Am. J. Clin. Nutr.* **27**, 681–687 (1974).
12. Walters, G. O., Miller, F. M., and Worwood, M. Serum ferritin concentrations and iron stores in normal subjects. *J. Clin. Pathol.* **26**, 770–772 (1973).
13. Lipschitz, D. A., Cook, J. D., and Finch, C. A. A clinical evaluation of serum ferritin. *N. Engl. J. Med.* **290**, 1213–1216 (1974).
14. Burks, J. M., Siimes, M. A., Mentzer, W. C., and Dallman, P. R. Iron deficiency in an Eskimo village. *J. Pediatr.* **88**, 224–228 (1976).
15. Koerper, M. A., Stempel, D. A., and Dallman, P. R. Anemia in patients with juvenile rheumatoid arthritis. *J. Pediatr.* **92**, 930–933 (1978).
16. Koerper, M. A., Mentzer, W. C., Brecher, G., and Dallman, P. R. Development change in red blood cell volume: Implication in screening infants and children for iron deficiency and thalassemia trait. *J. Pediatr.* **89**, 580–583 (1976).
17. Dallman, P. R. New approaches to screening for iron deficiency. *J. Pediatr.* **90**, 678–680 (1977).
18. Kasper, C. K., Whissell, D. Y., and Wallerstein, R. O. Clinical aspects of iron deficiency. *J. Am. Med. Assoc.* **191**, 359–363 (1965).

23 Prevalence of Nutritional Anemias among Pregnant Women in Chile

PABLO LIRA

Several studies have demonstrated the high prevalence of nutritional anemia in women of child-bearing age, in pregnant women, and in children. Although this nutritional disturbance is found in every country of the world, its prevalence is higher in developing countries (1, 2).

Iron deficiency is the most frequent disorder and the most common cause of anemia; it is followed in frequency by folate deficiency. Lack of vitamin B_{12} and protein are less important causes of anemia.

PREVALENCE OF IRON DEFICIENCY

Previously we studied the frequency of anemia and iron deficiency in 94 men and 106 women 15 to 26 years of age, most of them university students of middle–high socioeconomic level. The frequency of anemia was 1.1% in men (Hb < 13 g/dl) and 2.8% in women (Hb < 12g/dl); the frequency of iron deficiency (transferrin saturation less than 15%) was 5.5 and 8.5%, respectively. Mean values of hemoglobin, hematocrit, mean corpuscular hemoglobin concentration, serum iron, and transferrin saturation were significantly higher in men (3). The average iron intake in these groups was 21.5 mg for men (15.9 mg of vegetable origin and 5.6 mg of animal origin) and 17.2 mg for women (12.1 mg of vegetable origin and 5.1 mg of animal origin). According to the WHO criteria (19 mg for women and 6 mg for men), the intake was below recommendations in 61% of women; men had adequate intakes (4).

NUTRITION INTERVENTION STRATEGIES IN NATIONAL DEVELOPMENT

Another study carried out in a group of university students showed only traces or absence of hemosiderin in the bone marrow of 11 out of 17 women, whereas each one of 8 men had moderate amounts of hemosiderin in their marrow (5).

The frequency of anemia in these studies was low. Nevertheless, it is worthwhile to note that in more than one-half of a small group of nulliparous young women deposits of iron were absent or minimal, i.e., they were in the initial stage of iron deficiency.

Our recent work concentrated on the study of iron deficiency in pregnant women (6,7). Three groups of pregnant women of lower socioeconomic condition from the southeast area of Santiago were examined. Group I consisted of 235 cases 6 to 20 weeks of pregnancy (average 13.4 weeks), group II of 215 cases from 21 to 38 weeks of pregnancy (average 25.3 weeks), and group III of 124 cases observed just prior to delivery (average 39 weeks). The frequency of anemia in these three groups of pregnant women is shown in Fig. 1. Compared with nonpregnant women and men, anemia occurred in 8.6% in group I, 18.7% in group II, and 18.5 in group III. Mean values of hemoglobin concentration were lower in groups II and III, as compared to group I.

The frequency of iron deficiency, estimated by measuring transferrin saturation, was higher than that of anemia: 9.9% in group I, 34.8% in group II, and 41.1% in group III. Thus, higher frequency of iron-deficient erythropoiesis was observed in more advanced stages of pregnancy (Fig. 2).

Iron depletion, defined by serum ferritin levels below 12 µg/liter occurred in 27% of pregnant women of group I, 50% of group II, and 62.5% of group III. Mean values of serum ferritin were 24 µg/liter, 13 µg/liter, and 6.7 µg/liter, respectively (Fig. 3). Bone marrow aspirations was carried out in 59 of 124 pregnant women before delivery to detect bone marrow hemosiderin in reticuloendothelial cells and to calculate sideroblasts. In 81.3% of the cases, there was no hemosiderin, 11.9% had traces, and only 6.8% had 1 to 2^+. Sideroblasts were absent in 86.4% of the cases; the remainder (13.6%) showed sideroblast values of 1 to 12%. Thus, a high prevalence of iron depletion existed in women before delivery, with very low or exhausted iron stores in nearly 80% of the subjects.

There were no significant differences in iron intake among the three groups of pregnant women (8); mean daily iron intake was 22.6 mg in group I, 18.4 mg in group II, and 21.1 mg in group III. No difference was observed between the groups in the proportion of animal iron sources ingested (18.3–19%). The iron intake of 46.9% of pregnant women of group I, 69.1% of group II, and 55.3% of group III was lower than 20 mg/

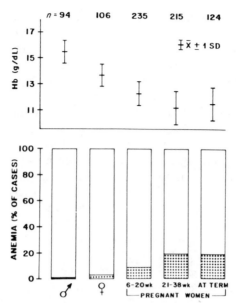

Fig. 1.   Frequency of anemia and hemoglobin concentration at three stages of pregnancy. Santiago, Chile (3, 6, 7).

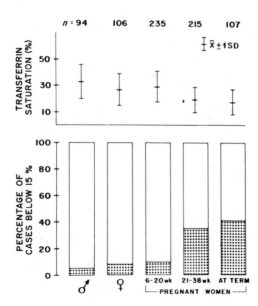

Fig. 2.   Frequency of iron deficient erythropoiesis and transferrin saturation at three stages of pregnancy, Santiago, Chile (3, 6, 7).

day, which is the minimum recommended by WHO for pregnant women receiving diets providing 10–25% calories of animal origin (9).

The data were also analyzed for each group to determine whether iron intake in those women with anemia or iron deficiency was different from those who did not show these disturbances; no significant differences in the amount of iron ingested were found. Mean hemoglobin concentration and transferrin saturation were very similar and no significant differences were observed in pregnant women with an iron intake above the recommended level, as compared to those having lower intakes (8). This finding indicates that although iron intake is insufficient in a significant number of pregnant women, this is not the main cause of the higher frequency of anemia, iron deficiency, or iron depletion in the later stages of pregnancy. An important consideration, however, is the amount of iron absorbed, which is affected by the composition of the diet, its content of heme and nonheme iron, and the presence of substances favoring or inhibiting absorption.

Another important factor in iron deficiency in pregnant women is the magnitude of iron deposits before pregnancy. Pregnant women without or with scarce deposits have a high probability of iron deficiency or anemia during pregnancy in spite of a satisfactory iron intake.

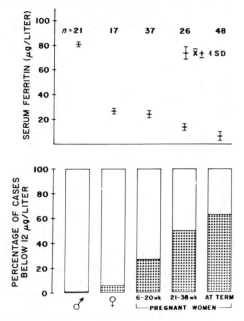

Fig. 3.   Iron depletion at three stages of pregnancy. Santiago, Chile (3, 6, 7).

Studies published by WHO, which were carried out in several countries, have shown the prevalence of anemia in pregnant women to vary from 21.8 to 80% (10); frequencies ranging from 20 to 50% have been reported in the United States (11, 12). An incidence of 55% has been reported in England (13). A cooperative study carried out in Latin America reported an actual frequency of anemia of 22% (14). Iron-deficient erythropoiesis and iron depletion are even more frequent in many countries.

The high prevalence of anemia and iron deficiency is justification enough for studies oriented toward its prevention through programs of iron supplementation during pregnancy or through fortification of foods (15). The latter would allow women to reach reproductive age with larger iron stores and to face the greater requirements of pregnancy, thereby decreasing the danger of anemia and maintaining adequate stores by the end of pregnancy.

PREVALENCE OF FOLIC ACID DEFICIENCY

Nutritional folate deficiency is mainly seen in cases of rapid cellular multiplication during periods of rapid growth in infants and during pregnancy. Negative folate balances result mostly from insufficient diet and from increased demands. Although iron deficiency is the most common cause of nutritional anemia, folate deficiency is prevalent in many poor countries and in certain population groups, such as pregnant women.

Our studies on a small number of young men and women from 15 to 25 years of age showed mean serum folate values of 10.4 ± 2.6 ng/ml and 10.3 ± 3.9 ng/ml, respectively. None of these subjects showed serum folate levels indicative of deficiency, i.e., below 3 ng/ml (Fig. 4).

Serum folate levels studied in the same groups of pregnant women in which the prevalence of iron deficiency was analyzed, showed the following mean values: 7.8 ng/ml for group I, 7 ng/ml for group II, and 8.7 ng/ml for group III. The frequency of deficiency (serum folate < 3 ng/ml) in these three groups was 7% in group I, 9.8% in group II, and 6.3% in group III (Fig. 4). Only 2 of the 59 pregnant women in whom prepartum bone marrow aspiration was performed showed slight megaloblastic changes, both cases having hemoglobin levels of 12 and 13 g/dl and serum folate levels between 3 and 6 ng/ml (7). The daily average folate intake was 123.7 μg in group I, 107.7 μg in group II, and 116.6 μg in group III. According to WHO standards, over 98% of the cases in the

Pablo Lira

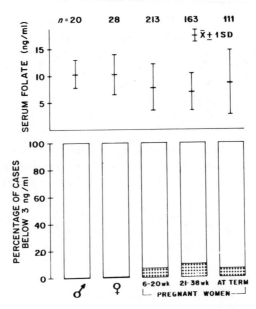

Fig. 4. Folate deficiency at three stages of pregnancy, Santiago, Chile (3, 6, 7).

three groups had an intake below that recommended (400 µg/day) (9). In spite of this, the prevalence of folate deficiency was low and no cases of megaloblastic anemia were seen; it is possible that folate stores were adequate to meet the higher requirements during pregnancy.

TABLE I

Prevalence of Iron and Folate Deficiency in Pregnant Women

	Group		
	I	II	III
Mean gestational age (weeks)	13.4	25.3	39.0
Anemia[a] (%)	8.6	18.7	18.5
Iron-deficient erythropoiesis[b] (%)	9.9	34.8	41.1
Iron depletion[c] (%)	27.0	50.0	62.5
Folate deficiency[d] (%)	7.0	9.8	6.3

[a] Hb < 11 g/dl (I) or < 10.5 g/dl (II–III).
[b] Transferrin saturation $< 15\%$.
[c] Serum ferritin < 12 µg/1.
[d] Serum folate < 3 ng/ml.

CONCLUSION

In Chilean women in advanced stages of pregnancy, there is a high prevalence of iron deficiency. About 20% are anemic and about 80% have depletion of iron deposits. Prevalence of folate deficiency is, however, low and without impact on erythropoiesis (Table I).

REFERENCES

1. Informe de un Grupo Cientifico de la OMS. Anemias nutricionales. *OMS Ser. Inf. Tec.* **405** (1968).
2. Informe de un Grupo de Expertos de la OMS. Anemias nutricionales. *OMS Ser. Inf. Tec.* **503** (1972).
3. Lira, P., Foradori, A., Grebe, G., and Legues, M. E. Valores hematológicos normales en una población de adultos jóvenes en Chile. *Rev. Med. Chile* **106**, 91 (1978).
4. Grebe, G., Lira, P., and Foradori, A. Carencia de hierro de origen nutricional. *Rev. Med. Chile* **104**, 954 (1976).
5. Foradori, A., Grebe, G., Lira, P., Legues, M. E., Muñoz, B., Gil, M., and Vergara, M. Estudio de la absorción y de los depositos de hierro en adultos jovenes. *Rev. Med. Chile* **104**, 893 (1976).
6. Lira, P., Foradori, A., Grebe, G., Legues, M. E., Muñoz, B., Arteaga, A. and Vela, P. Características hematológicas de una población de embarazados en Chile. *Rev. Med. Chile* **106**, 343 (1978).
7. Lira, P., Foradori, A., Grebe, G., Legues, M. E., Muñoz, B., Arteaga, A., and Vela, P. Iron and folate deficiency in pregnancy. *Abstr. Int. Congr. Nutr. 11th, 1978* No. 190.
8. Grebe, G., Lira, P., Arteaga, A., Valenzuela, M., Cubilles, A., and Foradori, A. Correlacion entre la Deficiencia de hierro y la ingesta dietetica de hierro en el embarazo. *Rev. Med. Chile* **107**, 989 (1979).
9. Arteaga, A., Foradori, A., Lira, P., Grebe, G., Cubillos, A. M., Jefré, M. A., Polanco, E., Valenzuela, M., Godoy, S., and Acost, A. M. Caracteríisticas de la alimentación y estado nutritivo de una población de embarazadas del Area Sur Oriente de Santiago. 1974–1975. *Rev. Med. Chile* **105**, 873 (1977).
10. Sanchez-Medal, L. Iron deficiency in pregnancy and infancy. *Sci. Publ.—Pan Am. Health Organ.* **184**, 65(1969).
11. Hunter, C. A. Iron deficiency anemia in pregnancy. *Surg., Gynecol. Obstet.* **110**, 210 (1960).
12. Lund, C. J. Studies on the iron deficiency anemia of pregnancy including plasma total hemoglobin, erythrocyte protoporphyrin in treated and untreated normal and anemic patients. *Am. J. Obstet. Gynecol.* **62**, 947 (1951).
13. Giles, C., and Burton H. Observation on prevention and diagnosis of anemia in pregnancy. *Br. Med. J.* **2**, 636 (1960).
14. Cook, J. D., Alvarado, J., Gutnisky, A., *et al.* Nutritional deficiency and anemia in Latin America. A collaborative study. *Blood* **38**, 591 (1971).
15. Informe de una Reunión Mixta ADI/OIHA/OMS. Lucha contra la anemia nutricional, especialmente contra la carencia de hierro. *W.H.O., Ser. Inf. Tec.* **580** (1975).

24 Evaluation of Iron Status and Prevalence of Iron Deficiency in Infants in Chile

ERNESTO RÍOS, MANUEL OLIVARES, MIRNA
AMAR, PATRICIA CHADUD, FERNANDO
PIZARRO, AND ABRAHAM STEKEL

Nutritional anemia is a highly prevalent disease. The main cause in developing countries is iron deficiency. It is generally accepted that negative iron biochemical balance has different stages of deficiency, which have been defined by laboratory parameters. Initially, there is a decrease in iron stores known as iron depletion, and it is diagnosed when the serum ferritin (SF) falls below 12 µg/liter (8). This is followed by iron-deficient erythropoiesis, which is defined as a transferrin saturation (TS) below 15% (1,4) or free erythrocyte protoporphyrins (FEP) over 70 µg/100 ml RBC (7). The last stage is iron-deficiency anemia with a decrease in hemoglobin (Hb) and hematocrit.

A representative sample of 4700 subjects of the Chilean population was studied in 1974 as part of a National Nutrition Survey. The figures in Table I show the magnitude of anemia and iron-deficient erythropoiesis in different segments of the population.

In the population studied, 28 and 65% of infants and children under 2 years of age had anemia and iron-deficient erythropoiesis, respectively. For some time, however, investigators have wondered about the high frequency of iron deficient erythropoiesis in the pediatric age group as defined by a transferrin saturation < 15%. This is the same cut-off as used for adults. Another interpretation could be that during infancy and early childhood lower values of plasma iron and transferrin saturation represent a physiological situation. If this is the case and adult values are

NUTRITION INTERVENTION STRATEGIES IN NATIONAL DEVELOPMENT

TABLE I

Prevalence of Iron Deficiency in Chile[a]

Group	N	Anemia[b] (%)	Transferrin saturation < 15% (%)
0–23 months	206	28.1	65.0
2–5 years	539	18.8	41.2
6–11 years	958	6.7	31.8
Males adolescent (12–17 years)	368	1.9	18.9
Females adolescent (12–17 years)	417	4.6	28.8
Males 18–44 years	532	1.1	12.3
Females 18–44 years	1006	8.4	33.3
Males over 45 years	392	2.8	21.2
Females over 45 years	485	4.5	28.0

[a] National Nutrition Survey, NHS-CONPAN, 1974–1975.
[b] As defined by WHO (10).

used for definition of normality, a much higher prevalence of iron deficiency will be obtained.

NORMAL HEMATOLOGICAL VALUES IN INFANTS

The results that follow were derived from different groups of infants studied over a period of several years. All of them were free of disease at the time of study and had a normal weight. All had received supplementary iron either by food fortification or by medication. Laboratory studies were done on venous blood.

Results in a group of 232 3-month-old infants, who received 150 mg of iron dextran i.m. in the newborn period, are shown in Fig. 1. It was assumed that infants receiving parenteral iron in the first 3 days of life do not have iron deficiency at 3 months of age. It can be seen that the mean Hb concentration was 11.3 g/dl and a lower limit of 2 SD of 9.4 g/dl. Hunter and Smith (5) in a group of 6- to 18-month-old infants, who had a TS > 15%, described the normal limit of Hb at this age as > 11 g/dl. Other studies have confirmed these results, but also report lower levels of Hb in the first trimester of life. Normal limits of Hb (2 SD below the mean) of 8.9 and 9.4 g/dl have been reported at 2 months of age by Matoth (9) and by Saarinen (12), respectively.

Since TS and FEP values do not follow a strict Gaussian distribution, the median and the limits of the 95% range were calculated according to

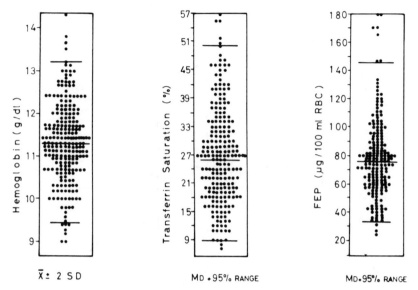

Fig. 1. Hematological values at 3 months of age in infants receiving 150 mg of iron dextran in the newborn period.

percentiles. As shown in Fig. 1, TS has a median of 26.1% and a lower limit of the 95% range of 9.2%. FEP has a median of 76 μg/100 ml RBC and a higher limit of 147 μg/100 ml RBC.

The distribution of serum iron, total iron-binding capacity (TIBC), and TS was studied in 114 9-month-, 99 15-month-, and 38 18-month-old children that had either received 150 mg of iron dextran in the newborn period or had been fed an iron-fortified formula since 3 months of age (15 mg/liter elemental iron as ferrous sulfate). The 18-month-old children had been given, in addition, 45 mg of medicinal iron as ferrous sulfate per day for 75 days before the study. Study infants and children met all of the following strict laboratory criteria of normal iron status: Hb ≥ 12 g/dl, FEP < 100 μg/100 ml RBC, and SF ≥ 15 μg/liter. Figure 2 shows results compared with those obtained in 60 normal adult men 20 to 40 years old. Results at 3 months are also shown for comparison. Median serum iron in infants fluctuated between 60 and 70 μg/dl with a low normal limit of about 30 μg/dl. After the lower values in the first trimester, median TIBC was 360–370 μg/dl with a high normal limit of 450 μg/dl. Median TS figures were 18–20% between 9 and 18 months with a lower limit of the 95% confidence range at 8–9%.

These results confirm that normal infants have lower serum iron and TS than adults and are in total agreement with results published by

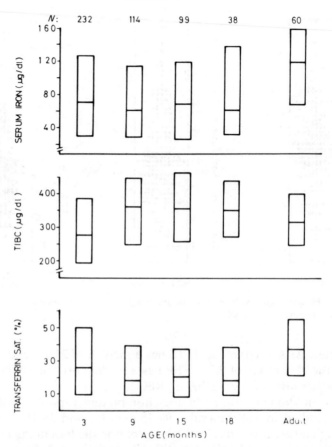

Fig. 2. Serum iron, TIBC, and transferrin saturation in infants and children with adequate iron nutrition. Bars represent median values and 95% confidence limits.

Koerper and Dallman (6) and also by Saarinen and Siimes (11) that show a lower normal limit of TS in infants in the 7–10% range.

The distribution of FEP values at 9, 15, and 18 months was studied in the same group of infants and children selecting those that had a Hb ≥ 12 g/dl, TS ≥ 15%, and SF ≥ 15 μg/liter. Figure 3 shows a progressive fall in the mean FEP values from 76 μg/100 ml RBC at 3 months to 52 μg/100 ml RBC at 18 months. The higher normal limit was from 147 μg/100 ml RBC at 3 months to 96 μg/100 ml RBC at 18 months of age. Table II summarized what appear to be normal laboratory parameters to evaluate iron deficiency in infants based on our studies.

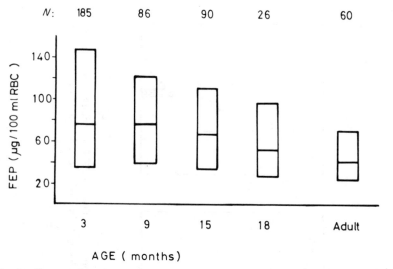

Fig. 3. Free erythrocyte protoporphyrins (FEP) in infants and young children with adequate iron nutrition. Bars represent median values and 95% confidence limits.

PREVALENCE OF IRON DEFICIENCY IN INFANTS

Application of different normal values in a population will obviously produce changes in the prevalence of iron deficiency. We know now that classical laboratory criteria of normality based on adult values artificially increase the prevalence of iron deficiency in infants.

Figures 4, 5, and 6 show the prevalence of different stages of iron deficiency at 3, 9, and 15 months of age in infants and children of

TABLE II

Normal Limits of Laboratory Parameters of Iron Status in Infants

Laboratory test	Age	Critical value
Hemoglobin	3 months	≥ 9.5 g/dl
	0.5 to 2 years	≥ 11 g/dl
Transferrin saturation	3 months to 2 years	$> 9\%$
Free erythrocyte proto-	First trimester	< 140 μg/100 ml RBC
porphyrins	First year	< 120 μg/100 ml RBC
	Second year	< 100 μg/100 ml RBC

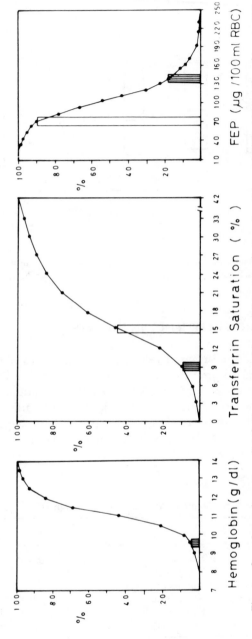

Fig. 4. Cumulative frequency distribution curves of hemoglobin, transferrin saturation, and FEP at 3 months of age in 372 infants of low socioeconomic conditions in Santiago. Bars represent the prevalence of iron deficiency calculated by classic criteria (bar) and by criteria derived from recent studies (hatched bar).

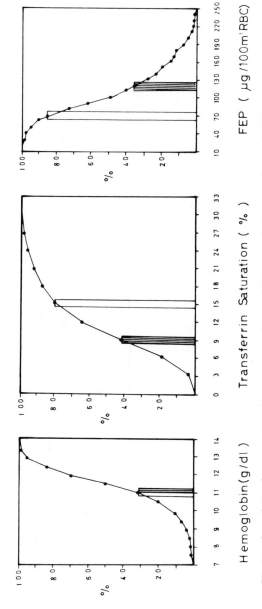

Fig. 5. Cumulative frequency distribution curves of hemoglobin, transferrin saturation, and FEP at 9 months of age in 313 infants of low socioeconomic condition in Santiago. Bars represent the prevalence of iron deficiency calculated by classic criteria (bar) and by criteria derived from recent studies (hatched bar).

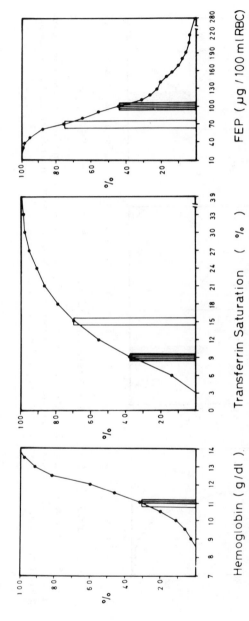

Fig. 6. Cumulative frequency distribution curves of hemoglobin, transferrin saturation, and FEP at 15 months of age in 233 children of low socioeconomic condition in Santiago. Bars represent the prevalence of iron deficiency calculated by classic criteria (bar) and by criteria derived from recent studies (hatched bar).

middle–low socioeconomical condition in Santiago, Chile. The subjects for these studies were randomly selected from infants attending National Health Service (NHS) well-baby clinics. In this population breast-feeding has a mean duration of about 3 months. Infants are weaned to nonfortified cow's milk distributed by the NHS, solid foods are introduced at 4 months, and iron supplements are rarely used. At the time of study, the infants were free of acute disease and most has a normal weight for age. Subjects with a low birth weight ($<$ 2500 g) were excluded.

The data are presented in cumulative frequency distribution curves, which help to visualize the percentage of patients that fall below a certain level defined as normal. It can be seen that at 3 months of age, latent iron deficiency is present in around 10% of the infants. At 9 and 15 months of age, there is anemia in 31% of the cases. There are enormous differences in the prevalence of iron deficient erythropoiesis depending on what limits of normality are employed. At 9 months of age, 43% of infants have a TS $<$ 9% and 36% had a FEP $>$ 120 μg/100 ml RBC, instead of the 80% with saturation $<$ 15% and 85% with FEP $>$ 70 μg/100 ml RBC using adult criteria. At 15 months of age, 38% of children have a TS $<$ 9% and 41% had an FEP $>$ 100 μg/100 ml RBC, instead of 70 and 74%, respectively, with the classic criteria.

IRON DEFICIENCY REDEFINED

Statistical criteria of normality are often not applicable to an individual subject (2). A different method for estimating the prevalence of iron deficiency anemia has been proposed (3). If a subject receives iron supplementation and his Hb increases significantly, he has anemia, independently of what the initial level was.

Forty-three 15-month-old infants received 45 mg of elemental iron daily, as ferrous sulfate, for 75 days. A significant increase in Hb was considered $\geq$ 1 g/dl between the initiation of study and the end of supplementation. Figure 7 shows the results. Twelve infants (28%) had anemia by the statistical criterion (Hb $<$ 11 g/dl), but 17 infants responded with increase in Hb $>$ 1 g/dl after supplementation (40% false negative). Thirteen infants considered nonanemic did not change (30% correctly classified) but one infant classified as anemic (Hb $<$ 11 g/dl) did not increase the Hb significantly (2% false positive). If this criterion of definition is used, a much higher level of iron deficiency anemia is found in this group: 65% instead of 28% by the statistical definition.

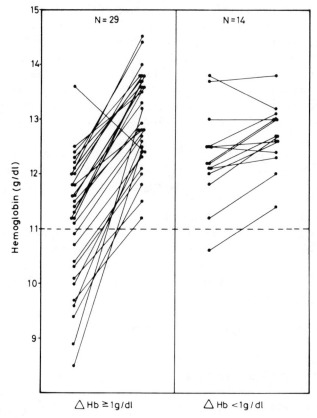

Fig. 7.   Change in hemoglobin concentration in 43 15-month-old children after receiving iron supplementation (Fe^{2+} 45 mg/day for 75 days).

CONCLUSION

Iron deficiency in infants has a high prevalence in Chile. However, prevalence figures can be overestimated by the use of criteria of normality derived from studies in adults. On the other hand, as has often been pointed out, the use of whatever reference standard for defining normal has its limitations. This method of using cut-off criteria tends to underestimate the prevalence of anemia because suboptimal individual levels of hemoglobin often fall within the normal range for the population.

ACKNOWLEDGMENTS

Supported by grants from Consejo Nacional para la Alimentación y Nutrición (CONPAN) and the United Nations University.

REFERENCES

1. Bainton, D. F., and Finch, C. A. The diagnosis of iron deficiency anemia. *Am. J. Med.* **37**, 62 (1964).
2. Dallman, P. R., and Siimes, M. A. Percentile curves for hemoglobin and red cell volume in infancy and childhood. *J. Pediatr.* **94**, 26 (1979).
3. Garby, L., Irnell, L., and Werner, I. Iron deficiency in women of fertile age in a Swedish community. *Acta Med. Scand.* **185**, 107 (1969).
4. Hillman, R. S., and Henderson, P. A. Control of marrow production by the level of iron supply. *J. Clin. Invest.* **48**, 454 (1969).
5. Hunter, R. E., and Smith, N. J. Hemoglobin and hematocrit values in iron deficiency in infancy. *J. Pediatr.* **81**, 710 (1972).
6. Koerper, M. A., and Dallman, P. R. Serum iron concentration and transferrin saturation in the diagnosis of iron deficiency in children: Normal developmental changes. *J. Pediatr.* **91**, 870 (1977).
7. Langer, E. E., Haining, R. G., Labbe, R. F., Jacobs, P., Crosby, E. F., and Finch, C. A. Erythrocyte protoporphyrin. *Blood* **40**, 112 (1972).
8. Lipschitz, D. A., Cook, J. D., and Finch, C. A. A clinical evaluation of serum ferritin as an index of iron stores. *N. Engl. J. Med.* **290**, 1213 (1974).
9. Matoth, Y., Zaizov, R., and Varsano, I. Postnatal changes in some red cell parameters. *Acta Paediatr. Scand.* **60**, 317 (1971).
10. Report of a WHO Group of Experts. Nutritional anaemias. *W. H. O. Tech. Rep. Ser.* **503** (1972).
11. Saarinen, U. M., and Siimes, M. A. Developmental changes in serum iron, total iron binding capacity and transferrin saturation in infancy. *J. Pediatr.* **91**, 875 (1977).
12. Saarinen, U. M., and Siimes, M. A. Developmental changes in red blood cell counts and indices of infants after exclusion of iron deficiency by laboratory criteria and continuous iron supplementation. *J. Pediatr.* **92**, 412 (1978).

25 Iron Fortification: What Must Be Considered?

JAMES D. COOK

The ultimate control of iron deficiency in an entire population requires some form of food fortification. The major advantage of food fortification is that the success does not require public participation, which is the major obstacle in iron supplementation programs. A well-designed fortification program has the lowest initial and maintenance cost and will reach the largest number of people.

A fortification strategy involves identification of a satisfactory iron compound and a suitable food vehicle. The most appropriate form of iron has been much debated, but there now appears to be a number of suitable compounds. Although there may be differences in availability when given alone, the majority of iron compounds exchange completely with native dietary iron and are, therefore, absorbed no better or worse than the common pool of food nonheme iron. A few iron sources such as ferric orthophosphate or sodium iron pyrophosphate are much less soluble and assimilable and should not be used in fortification programs. Recent studies suggest that NaFeEDTA (sodium iron ethylenediaminetetraacetate) may actually be better absorbed than dietary iron. The most important problem relating to the iron compound is that most available forms of inorganic iron produce various undesirable changes in food due to the inherent chemical properties of iron. Discoloration and rancidity may be major problems with certain vehicles; some of these difficulties might be circumvented by using NaFeEDTA as discussed by Dr. Viteri in Chapter 26.

A more difficult obstacle with fortification is the identification of a suitable *food vehicle*. The choice of the food is especially important, because it will determine the eventual distribution of iron in the popula-

NUTRITION INTERVENTION STRATEGIES IN NATIONAL DEVELOPMENT

tion. The chosen vehicle must be consumed in adequate amounts by the target group and yet should have no potential for heavy consumption in certain segments of the population. The vehicle should be prepared in only a few centers within the country and preferably under governmental control. The vehicle with its added iron should withstand prolonged storage under prevailing environmental conditions.

Unfortunately, there appears to be no one vehicle that is suitable for all countries. Processed cereal foods such as wheat flour have been popular in developed countries and, when available, fulfill most, if not all, of the requirements of a satisfactory vehicle. Other staple foods, such as rice, pose major technical problems. Common salt is frequently discussed as a possible vehicle, but the amount consumed places limits on the quantity of iron that can be supplied. In countries like Guatemala, where highly refined sugar is widely available to most segments of the population at low cost, sugar may be an optimal vehicle. However, in many developing countries the high cost and scarity of sugar is an important constraint. Since the effectiveness and safety of iron fortification depends in large part on the vehicle selected, we need to expand the number of options available for use in developing countries.

The most important limitation with fortification will probably be the inhibiting effect of many regional diets. Although there are promising preliminary data, the efficacy of any major fortification program has never been firmly established. It has been shown that the addition of more than 100 mg of iron to a regular diet increased absorption by only 1.5 mg per day in young iron-deficient subjects. An alternative to fortification may be to add a substance such as ascorbic acid to the diet to increase absorption of native food iron. Although a major limitation of this approach is cost, even small amounts of ascorbic acid may be effective, and this approach deserves further evaluation.

26 Prevention of Iron Deficiency by Means of Iron Fortification of Sugar

FERNANDO E. VITERI, E. ALVAREZ, OSCAR
PINEDA, AND BENJAMÍN TORÚN

INTRODUCTION

Available evidence indicates that iron deficiency is widespread in both developed and developing areas. Important characteristics of such deficiency differ from one area to the other. Affluent societies have a nutritionally better and more varied diet, which contains enhancers of iron absorption and a higher proportion of heme iron. Because of these circumstances, there is a higher availability of dietary iron. Iron deficiency, therefore, affects only the vulnerable groups—women of reproductive age, adolescents and small children, and individuals who suffer from secondary anemia due to chronic blood loss. In contrast, iron deficiency is more widespread in populations whose diets are monotonous, based on cereals and legumes, contain little heme iron, and often limited intakes of ascorbic acid (1). Moreover, in most developing tropical areas, chronic blood loss due to *N. americanus*, *A. duodenale*, and *T. trichura* infections accentuate the deficiency of iron in older children and adult males, who are, otherwise, not particularly at risk from severe iron deficit (2). Even in the absence of anemia, a condition aggravated by iron deficiency, iron deficiency still has a series of functional consequences that make its eradication desirable (3–6).

These circumstances have made the nutrition scientist more aware of the necessity to increase the iron intake by essentially all population groups. This situation led several decades ago to the introduction of iron

NUTRITION INTERVENTION STRATEGIES IN NATIONAL DEVELOPMENT
Copyright © 1983 by Academic Press, Inc.
All rights of reproduction in any form reserved.
ISBN 012-709080-0

fortified flour in developed countries. Later on, iron was added to baby cereals and to milk preparations designed for infants. A common flaw in this practice was the poor attention given to evaluating the results. Some studies suggested that cereal fortification has had very little effect in improving iron nutrition. These critical evaluations led to a reconsideration of the types of iron compounds used in the fortification of cereals. As a consequence, and based on new techniques that allow precise measurements of iron bioavailability, different forms of iron are being used in the fortification processes. These new forms of iron have been thoroughly studied and should be more effective than those previously used. However, to our knowledge, no evaluation of the effects of iron fortification on a broad population level has ever been carried out. In the pediatric population, positive effects have been clearly documented (7).

The design and implementation of a fortification program requires knowledge of a series of factors which, in the case of iron, are essential for the selection of the vehicle, the iron compounds to be used, and the amount that should produce the desired results. This knowledge ought to lead to fortification programs that are tailored to the necessities and the conditions of different population groups. In other words, a specific compound and/or vehicle may be adequate for populations that consume a certain diet and inadequate for others.

This chapter describes the ongoing experience in the design and evaluation of iron fortification of sugar in Central America.

BACKGROUND CHARACTERISTICS OF CENTRAL AMERICAN POPULATIONS

A complete epidemiological description of the population was performed to establish the status of erythropoietic nutrients and the prevalence of anemia. From this work, it became evident that close to 25% of the Central American population presents some degree of anemia and that the iron deficiency is primarily due to dietary origin, aggravated by hookwork infection in the lowlands (8–11). In fact, iron deficiency is present in nearly one-half the Central American population, being more prevalent in women of reproductive age and in children. There were biochemical indications of inadequate folate nutrition, but no correlation was found between folate deficits and anemia at the population level (10). Iron deficiency was primarily due to dietary factors, characterized by (1) poor bioavailability of dietary iron (12) and by (2) inadequate amounts of iron intake in about 40% of the families in the rural areas (8,10).

Supplementation trials with orally administered $FeSO_4$ as the only intervention in lowland populations resulted in significant improvement in hematological and iron status. A more homogeneous improvement in hematological and erythropoietic nutrient status was obtained by means of oral administration of $FeSO_4$ + folic acid (10,13). These positive effects took place in spite of an unaltered diet and parasite loads, which included hookworm and trichuris.

This background clearly indicated that nutritional anemia in the lowlands might be drastically reduced if iron intake and bioavailability were enhanced. Improvements in folate nutrition, however, would result only in a slightly better hematological response in about 10% of the responding cases. This confirmed that iron deficit was the main cause of nutritional anemias. With this diagnosis of the problem and its cause the prevention of iron deficiency could be undertaken. Two approaches, not mutually exclusive, were possible: (1) increase the bioavailability of dietary iron, and (2) increase the amount of iron intake.

INCAP explored the possibility of preventing iron deficiency through iron fortification of an appropriate food vehicle. Previous studies suggested that sugar would be an adequate vehicle for iron because it has been used successfully in vitamin A fortification programs in Central America (14), and sugar does not interfere with iron absorption (15). Alternately, cereals and flours could be used in countries where these foods are a basic part of the staple diet.

SELECTION OF THE IRON SALT

The problem was to select a form of iron that would have adequate bioavailability when consumed with the staple diets of the region. Several studies and preliminary trials led to the selection of a chelated form of iron NaFeEDTA (sodium iron ethylenediaminetetraacetate) as the most promising iron compound to use. The theory was that, somewhat like heme, the iron would be protected from inhibitors of absorption in the diet. This was a novel idea that required investigations, which yielded the following information:

1. NaFeEDTA is stable (its reactivity is low), soluble in water at physiological pH's, yellow in color, and produces very little metallic taste. The salt contains an average of 13% iron and no toxic substances; it is over 99.5% pure. Contaminants are mostly metals present in any iron compound, copper and zinc being the most important.
2. NaFeEDTA can be easily added to sugar with simple technology. It

sticks to the crystals when sugar has over 1% moisture; thus, segregation is not a problem. When added in a 1:1000 proportion, it contributes a barely detectable yellowish tinge to sugar, noticeable only when directly compared with unfortified sugar of similar quality. The taste is indistinguishable from sugar in the form normally consumed in Central America.

3. The salt does not interfere at all with vitamin A fortification of the sugar and vice versa. Tests have been done with regard to stability and bioavailability of both compounds, yielding excellent results (16).

4. The iron in NaFeEDTA ingested orally is bioavailable for hemoglobin synthesis. In fact, it is as effective in treating iron deficiency as many inorganic and organic iron salts of common therapeutic use, such as ferrous sulfate and ferrous fumarate (17, 18).

5. When NaFeEDTA is ingested with representative Central American diets, the iron is 1.5 to 2.5 times more available than food iron (19,20). Furthermore, NaFeEDTA mixes with the non-heme iron of the diet and makes it about 2 times more available (19,21). The presence of inhibitors to iron absorption is less important when NaFeEDTA is present, and iron absorption tends to remain proportionally constant even when the amounts of NaFeEDTA added to the diet vary tenfold (from 5 to 50 mg of iron) (19). These specific qualities have important implications in terms of the possible effectiveness of NaFeEDTA as a fortifying compound to cereal–legume-based diets. A simple example will make this clear.

An adult female of reproductive age requires about 2 mg of iron per day absorbed from the diet. The mean iron intake from representative diets is 27 mg/day, but its absorption is only 4%. Therefore, she absorbs about 1.1 mg of iron/day. The addition of NaFeEDTA to the sugar in a proportion of 13 mg of iron/100 g of sugar provides her with 5.2 mg of additional iron (mean sugar consumption for her age–sex group is 40 g/day), but what is more important, the 32 mg of iron she is ingesting are now absorbed in about 8%. The total absorbed iron becomes 2.5 mg, thus satisfying her iron requirements.

6. The greater the iron deficit, the greater the proportion of iron absorbed from NaFeEDTA and vice versa. (19).

Up to now, the iron compound NaFeEDTA appears to be the ideal one for fortification of the Central American diet. This salt is clearly superior to other iron salts now being used for food fortification in the cereal industry primarily in (1) stability, low reactivity, and essentially undetectable flavor; (2) the greater bioavailability that it also confers on dietary non-heme iron; and (3) the relative constancy of its proportional absorption within iron fortification levels ranging from 5 to 50 mg of iron.

NaFeEDTA potentially has certain disadvantages and possible undesirable characteristics, however, which are now under active research at INCAP. These include:

1. The higher cost relative to other possible iron fortification compounds. For example, NaFeEDTA is about 4 times as expensive as ferrous sulfate. However, its greater bioavailability (2 times) when consumed with Central American diets reduces its relative price to 2, and the greater bioavailability it confers to dietary food iron further reduces the price differential with $FeSO_4$. The approximate cost of fortifying 100 lb (46 kg) of sugar with 46 g of NaFeEDTA is about $0.16 (U.S. dollars). The price of 100 lb of sugar in Central America is close to $16.00. Thus the relative price increment is about 1%. In terms of costs per person per year, we have determined that the mean sugar consumption is 33 g per day. At present prices this represents $4.24 per year. One percent of the price of sugar, that is, $0.042, would be the cost of fortification per person per year. For 6 million inhabitants in Guatemala, this represents $254,400 per year. This cost seems reasonable, based on preliminary estimates of benefits from iron fortification.

2. The fact that NaFeEDTA has a strong chelating molecule (EDTA) could produce defects in absorption of other div.lent cations such as Zn, Cu, Mg, Ca, Mn, and Co. Various forms of EDTA (disodium, disodium–calcium, tetrasodium) in the proportions to be used in the iron fortification process do not interfere with the absorption of such cations. On the contrary, the literature indicates that EDTA enhances their absorption (22–24). We are currently studying these effects. Our results in rats showed a 1.6-fold enhancement of Zn absorption from corn–bean diets containing constant amounts of iron when either Na_2 EDTA or NaFeEDTA are added (25). Zinc turnover is accelerated as expected from its greater absorption, but no more than normal. In humans (26), NaFeEDTA at fortification levels does not alter the rise in serum Zn consequent to the intake of $ZnSO_4$.

3. Very few studies have been done on the absorption and metabolism of EDTA, and none using NaFeEDTA as absorptive substrate. Studies in this area are needed, because even though only a small proportion (about 5%) of EDTA seems to be absorbed, it appears in the urine most probably chelated with divalent cations. This could mean that a more rapid loss of cations from the body might occur. Studies concerning Zn presently in progress at INCAP indicate that the rate of loss from the body is not accelerated by consumption of a diet containing up to 4 times

as much NaFeEDTA as would be used in fortification programs (25). On the other hand, part of the NaFeEDTA ingested appears to be absorbed intact, and this iron is most likely excreted in the urine as intact NaFeED-TA. Still, a large proportion of the iron absorbed from NaFeEDTA and transported to the bone marrow is freed in the intestine and is bioavailable in amounts that are superior to those from the dietary iron alone (27).

4. Finally, the U.S. Food and Drug Administration recently published a document in which, as a consequence of long-term studies in rodents, asserts that EDTA is a *safe* food additive (28). The level of EDTA intake through iron fortification of sugar in Central America would probably reach, at most, similar levels of EDTA intake now being consumed in developed societies.

In brief, a series of studies have been performed or are at present in progress that strongly suggest that NaFeEDTA is ideally suited for the fortification of diets based on cereals and legumes. All available evidence at present point to it as being safe.

OTHER CONSIDERATIONS

Three other important aspects of iron fortification programs should also be considered:

1. *Cost-effectiveness of iron fortification.* Efforts are being made to obtain the necessary information to estimate accurately the costs the government and the private sector would incur yearly in the treatment of iron deficiency anemia. A preliminary and conservative estimate of costs yields a yearly figure of $800,000 for Guatemala, that is, an average cost of $0.13 per capita per year. If fortification is effective, these costs should be reduced by about 80%. This would mean a savings of $640,000 per year in medical treatment for iron deficiency. The cost of fortification and the treatment of residual cases of anemia of other than dietary origin would amount to $414,400 per year. Fortification would have a net saving of $385,600 per year ($0.064 per capita per year).

2. *The possibility of iron overload.* This will be only briefly discussed here. Suffice it to say that theoretical considerations make it extremely improbable that through fortification the situation in Central America will change from one of rampant iron deficiency to one of iron overload. On the other hand, subjects in the population who are genetically susceptible to iron overload will, no doubt, have more chances of expressing their genotype if available iron in the diet increases. This phe-

nomenon would also occur if these subjects were to consume western-type diets with high iron bioavailability.

3. *Surveillance and evaluation.* Any fortification program must have surveillance and evaluation as an integral part of it. Monitoring the compliance with fortification regulations and a periodic sampling of the population to evaluate iron reserves (e.g., serum ferritin levels) should be part of the surveillance. Also, fortification programs must be dynamic in that they must be amenable to modification as a consequence of the results of periodic evaluations.

Having considered these aspects of an iron fortification program in Central America, the following questions still remained: Is iron fortification of sugar with NaFeEDTA effective at a population level under tropical and temperate conditions? Is it feasible? Will it be accepted and tolerated by the population? Will there be any unpredictable, undesirable side effects when NaFeEDTA is chronically consumed?

OBJECTIVES OF THE FORTIFICATION STUDY

There were five primary objectives in conducting a field evaluation of sugar fortification with iron:

1. To evaluate the feasibility of fortifying sugar with iron and to monitor its long-term acceptance by population groups.

2. In population groups where iron deficiency anemia is endemic, to determine the long-term effectiveness of iron fortified sugar in (a) improving iron nutrition, thus preventing future cases of iron deficiency anemia, and (b) reducing the prevalence of anemia.

3. To define the relative importance of variables that are known to influence iron nutrition (diet, specific morbidity, parasite loads, physiological and specific nutritional status) in modifying the effects of iron fortification on iron nutrition and hematological condition of population groups.

4. To estimate costs of sugar fortification and compare them with the costs incurred at present by the population in treating its cases of iron-deficiency anemia. These cases usually relapse under present conditions.

5. To determine and identify any side effects secondary to the chronic intake of NaFeEDTA—fortified sugar—especially the effects on folate, Vitamin B_{12}, and trace mineral nutrition (emphasis on zinc, copper, and magnesium).

DESIGN OF THE STUDY

Four communities, two in the lowlands and two in the highlands, were studied. The populations range from 1200 to 1800 inhabitants. The original design was for one community in each location to receive fortified sugar and the other to serve as control. However, after the baseline data was obtained in the four communities that had been selected from 38 initially screened it was evident that one of each pair could not serve as adequate control for the other. The prevalence and severity of anemia and of iron deficiency was different in each community (Table I).

The severity of anemia in the lowland community 13 and in the highland community 15 was the most similar; the prevelance was intermediate. From the standpoint of iron deficiency, the two lowland communities were clearly more deficient than the two in the highlands. Community 14 was definitely very iron deficient and had the highest prevalence of hookworm infection. The two highland communities were very similar with respect to iron deficiency and hookworm prevalence.

Because of this situation, several alternatives to the original study design were considered. We decided to keep one community as control and to fortify the other three. Community 15 was chosen as the control

TABLE I

	Lowlands		Highlands	
Community	13	14	15	16
Percentage prevalence of				
Low PCV[a]	30.9	43.1	34.9	21.3
Low sat. TIBC	33.6	57.5	12.0	22.6
Low Ferritin	51.8	71.6	37.0	34.1
High FEP	49.6	71.8	23.7	29.3
Severity of Hb deficit and of iron deficiency among those deficient				
Mean deficit in Hb (g/dl)	3.1	4.6	2.9	0.9
Mean sat. TIBC (%)	9.3	6.8	11.5	11.2
Mean serum ferritin (ng/ml)	7.0	5.2	9.0	9.5
Mean FEP (µg/dl RBC)	183.5	234.2	145.7	138.8

[a] PCV, packed cell volume. Low values are indicative of anemia. Sat TIBC, saturation of total iron-binding capacity, indicative of iron transport. Ferritin, serum ferritin, indicative of iron reserves. High levels of free erythrocyte protoporphyrin (FEP) indicate iron deficit during red cell formation (see Chapters 22 and 25, this volume).

because of its similarity with community 13 in prevalence and severity of anemia and with community 16 in prevalence and severity of iron deficiency. The fact that we had other studies in lowland communities where blood samples had been obtained over a period of time (without interventions) also influenced our decision. These communities could serve with some reservations as lowland controls, showing the natural changes that occurred over time. The three "fortified" communities, two in the lowlands and one in the highlands, had been supplied with iron-fortified sugar since June, 1977. Community 15, the control village, had also been supplied with unfortified sugar. The fortified sugar was produced in large batches under our direct supervision in a single sugar mill. The iron compound added was iron-chelated NaFeEDTA, kindly supplied by Grace and Co., United States, and by BASF, Germany.

The target level of iron in fortified sugar was 13 mg/100 g. Repeated analyses for iron in samples of the sugar (over 100 samples) yielded a mean and SD of 12.05 ± 2.0 mg/100 g, with a range between 8.4 and 16.5 mg/100 g. This compound is added by hand as a fine yellow powder, when the sugar is dropped (with between 1.5 and 3% humidity) from centrifuges. Then it is mixed, dried, and packed in 100-lb bags. The sugar is then stored in warehouses under our close supervision and is sold to the store keepers in the fortified villages at a price slightly lower than the market price of sugar. The entire production and distribution process is closely monitored. The consumption level of fortified sugar in homes is also monitored and accomplished by a qualitatively rapid test for iron done 5 times per year in every household.

Throughout the year, dietary intake, including sugar consumption, is surveyed periodically in a subsample of nearly 1400 subjects in the four communities; in-depth studies of iron nutrition were performed on these 1400 subjects periodically. Periodically throughout the year, census updating and morbidity data were obtained at the home level. Constant free medical attention is provided to the study communities through a government health post in each village. We were in charge of these posts for many reasons, one being to keep a constant surveillance on cases and treatment of anemia. Once a year a hematological survey is done between January and March to avoid seasonal variations. Two quantitative parasitological surveys have been done.

Thus far, hematological and erythropoietic nutrients data has been obtained 4 times, the last time after 32 months of fortification in communities 13, 14, and 16. Data is available for the 1979 survey, performed after 20 months of fortification. All of the community members who volunteered to have a PCV done constitute the *sample*, which is to be followed throughout the study. A *subsample* was then selected to include the following three groups in each community:

Group I: All the severely anemics (PCV < 30% in the highland communities, and < 28% in the lowlands).

Group II: About 200 subjects whose PCV was greater than the above stated values but was below 1.5 SD from the mean for the normal population in each age–sex–altitude category (29).

Group III: About 150 subjects with PCV greater than 1.5 standard deviations below the normal mean for each age–sex–altitude category. These were considered normals.

All the subjects in the subsample had venous blood drawn to perform complete hematological determinations (PCV, Hb, RBC counts, and WBC counts) plus the following:

1. For evaluation of iron nutrition: serum iron, total iron-binding capacity (TIBC), transferrin saturation, free erythrocyte protoporphyrins (FEP), and serum ferritin.

2. For evaluation of folate nutrition: whole blood-folate level and RBC folate level.

3. For evaluation of Vitamin B_{12} nutrition: serum B_{12}.

4. For trace mineral nutrition: plasma, RBC, hair, and urinary Zn, Cu, and Mg.

After the baseline evaluation all subjects in Group I received $FeSO_4$ orally in amounts calculated to improve their PCV to that of subjects in Group II. From then on, any subject seeking medical care, whose PCV was below 30 or 28% in the highlands and lowlands, respectively, received the same treatment. Pregnant women attending the health post on a voluntary basis received 7.5 g $FeSO_4$ as tablets so that, assuming 20% absorption, it provides the equivalent of 300 mg of absorbed iron. This dose is administered during the second or third trimester of pregnancy following established practices of the Health Ministry of Guatemala.

RESULTS TO 20 MONTHS OF FORTIFICATION AND DISCUSSION

It must be realized that the results of the ongoing study here presented are only partial in terms of the areas covered and preliminary also because of the time at which the available hematological and biochemical information were collected. Results will be available shortly on the changes observed after 32 months of fortification; these data will be the final for the study.

Four data collection areas will be presented in some detail as indicative of the types of outcomes of the study: (1) fortified sugar intake; (2) dietary intake; (3) hematological changes, and (4) iron nutrition.

Fortified Sugar Intake

The means of six surveys covering a 2–7 year period are presented in Table II. Sugar intake is expressed as grams/person/day within household (the unit of observation is the family, in this case). It is evident that the means and standard deviations among the four populations are very similar over time. However, the variability of individual sugar intakes

TABLE II

Sugar Intake in the Study Communities in Six Surveys[a]

Survey		Communities			
		13	14	15	16
1	Mean	39	36	45	42
	SD	22	31	32	24
	No.[b]	246	360	204	338
2	Mean	32	34	33	34
	S.D.	22	24	15	16
	No.	248	372	213	346
3	Mean	30	33	30	36
	S.D.	21	27	13	14
	No.	263	401	235	375
4	Mean	31	32	30	31
	S.D.	23	24	19	17
	No.	267	392	238	388
5	Mean	33	34	29	29
	S.D.	23	27	16	17
	No.	270	410	236	391
6	Mean	31	30	30	30
	S.D.	16	22	16	16
	No.	271	412	239	400
All	Mean	33	33	33	34
	S.D.	21	26	20	18
	No.	1565	2347	1365	2238

[a] Data for 2 years, g/person/day.
[b] Number of families.

was high (coefficient of variation > 50% in over 80% of the surveys) and could be significant in terms of iron intake throughout time if families were consistently high or low consumers. The families were distributed in each community by terciles of sugar intake at each survey, in order to evaluate their stability in sugar intake. The limits of sugar intake between terciles ranged from 23 to 27 g/person/day and from 36 to 41 g/person/day for the lower and upper terciles, respectively, in the different surveys. The majority of families (between 50 and 63% of them) changed terciles during the 2-year period. Between 19 and 22% of families moved between the mid-upper or mid-lower terciles; only 2 and 5% of families consistently were either in the upper or lower terciles, respectively.

Sugar intake varied within households depending on the age of the family members. However, as shown in Table III, mean intakes are similar except for those for infants which were about one-half to three-fourth those of older age groups. Hence children will consume more iron from fortified sugar per kilogram body weight than adults.

The next important point in terms of fortified sugar intake is the compliance of the different families within the communities with the fortification program. Families were free to purchase their sugar at the regular price at the village stores. We provided the stores with fortified sugar. In the lowland communities there was filtration in of unfortified sugar from workers in nearby sugar mills who received a sugar quota

TABLE III

Sugar Intake (g/Person/Day) by Age Groups in the Study Communities in a Representative Survey

Communities		<1	1–4	5–8	9–12	13–16	17–20	21–49	50+
					Age groups (years)				
13	Mean	17	33	31	35	40	36	41	47
	SD	10	23	23	27	33	27	32	43
	No.	(15)	(126)	(115)	(98)	(83)	(57)	(271)	(131)
14	Mean	25	31	31	37	40	38	44	49
	SD	18	21	18	23	25	20	25	25
	No.	(26)	(239)	(214)	(158)	(145)	(95)	(482)	(183)
15	Mean	28	30	34	38	38	37	39	40
	SD	9	12	12	15	14	11	15	14
	No.	(10)	(127)	(148)	(145)	(97)	(55)	(257)	(130)
16	Mean	29	34	36	39	42	44	43	41
	SD	26	14	10	15	16	17	15	13
	No.	(23)	(175)	(165)	(167)	(139)	(89)	(439)	(185)

per day worked. In spite of all efforts to encourage the consumption of only fortified sugar in these communities (Nos. 13 and 14), compliance was less than optimal as shown in Fig. 1, which presents the cummulative plot of compliance per community. The highland fortified community (No. 16), for example, had an excellent compliance as judged by the number of times the test for iron in sugar was positive at the household level; more than 75% of families had over 80% positive tests. This percentage in the lowlands families was only 30%; however, 70% of lowland families complied with the program over 50% of the time.

These results stress the need of a close surveillance of pilot studies in free-living communities. It is obvious that the final analysis of the data will have to take into account each family's compliance record.

Dietary Intake

Nutrient intake by individuals has been obtained by repeated 24-hr recall surveys, with proper quality control. A summary of results of two surveys prior to the fortification program, contrasting the mean adequacy of nutrient intakes of nonanemic subjects with the anemic subjects is presented in Fig. 2. Differences between means are significant

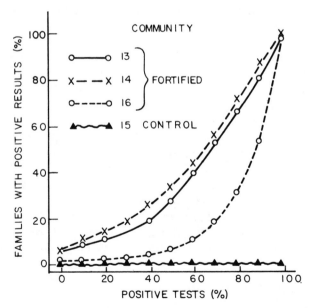

Fig. 1.   Cummulative plot of the detection of fortified sugar in the households in each of four communities. Data from 6 surveys per community.

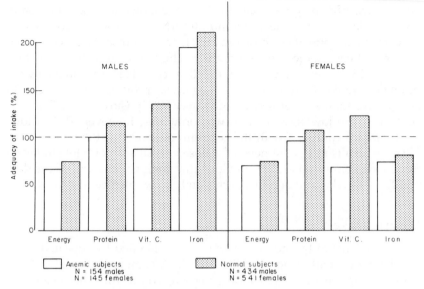

Fig. 2. Average adequacy of nutrient intake of subjects in each of the four communities studied.

except for energy intakes, and illustrate that energy intake is lower than desirable in both sexes and independent of hematological status. Without doubt the anemic female eats very poorly; mean adequacy is barely satisfactory only for total protein intakes. The most significant difference between anemic and normal subjects is vitamin C intake. This finding underscores the possible essential role of ascorbic acid intake on iron nutritional status at the population level where staple diets are predominantly cereal-pulse combinations. In the case of iron, an additional intake of 5 mg per person per day would bring adequacy to near 95%.

With regard to the types of iron ingested, the anemic subjects consumed less iron from animal sources than the nonanemic subjects. This was very evident in terms of heme iron: the range of mean intakes for anemic subjects was 2.7 and 3.6% of total iron intake, whereas for the normal population the range of mean intake was 3.8–5.7%.

These findings confirm the primary importance of the diet in determining the iron status of populations in developing countries.

Hematological Changes

First, the hemoglobin concentrations (Hb) in g/dl and the hematocrit (packed cell volume or PCV) in percentages and the changes in individuals in each community from initial to the 20 months evaluation are presented for children 5 to 12 years of age; for nonpregnant, nonlactating females older than 21 years of age and for males 21 years and over. These specific age and sex groups are analyzed separately because their expected changes in 20 months of observations are the least, compared to other age-sex groups (small children and adolescents) where age-sex related changes in Hb and PCV are predictably taking place. This first type of analysis ignores the initial hematological condition of the subjects, which has a definite influence on the degree of response expected from correction of iron deficits.

Second, the population as a whole in each community, independent of age and sex is divided into two groups, normal or low, based on cut-off points defined for Hb and PCV as 1.5 standard deviations from the Central American norms (29) below the normal mean value for each age–sex–altitude category. In each group the g Hb/dl and percentage PCV by which each individual differs from the normal mean for his/her corresponding age–sex–altitude category is expressed as Hb Units (HbU) or PCV Units (PCVU). Means and standard deviations are computed for HbU and PCVU initially and after 20 months evaluation, as well as for the individual changes which occurred in that lapse of time. This approach centers upon the differential responses obtained from normal and "anemic" individuals with Fe fortification.

Paired *t* tests of the individual changes between the two evaluations in the various categories described above were done to define whether the changes were significant within each community and category. This is designated t(a) in the tables. The mean changes in the various categories in each of the fortified communities (No. 13, 14, and 16) was then compared with the changes observed in the control community (No. 15) and is designated t(b) in the tables.

This type of statistical analysis is the simplest and provides only a baseline from which interpretation of the observed effects can be initiated. More complex analyses, including linear and nonlinear regressions, covariance analyses and multiple correlation analyses will be performed when the final data are available.

Results are presented in summary form in Tables IV to VII.

Hb increased in all communities and age-sex groups (Table IV), except for the adult males in the control community (No. 15). The increments in the fortified communities 13 and 16 are greater than those in the control, reaching significant *t* values in the child population. In community 14, the most anemic and iron-deficient one, children's Hb response was less relative to the control, suggesting the persistence of other factors which mask the response to iron fortification. A similar trend is observed in

TABLE IV

Mean Values in Hb by Age-Sex Groups and Communities and Changes between Baseline and 20 Months Evaluations

Group	13			14			15			16		
	N[a]	Basal[b]	20[b]	N	Basal	20[b]	N	Basal	20[b]	N	Basal	20[b]
Females > 21 years	33	13.1 ± 1.3	13.8 ± 1.8	36	11.1 ± 3.0	12.2 ± 1.7	58	13.3 ± 1.6	14.1 ± 1.2	54	13.7 ± 2.0	14.8 ± 1.5
Males > 21 years	25	14.7 ± 2.0	15.5 ± 1.2	30	12.5 ± 3.4	14.0 ± 2.3	28	15.5 ± 3.3	15.8 ± 1.5	29	16.1 ± 1.1	16.5 ± 1.5
Children 5–12 years	37	11.6 ± 1.4	13.8 ± 1.0	26	11.8 ± 1.7	12.2 ± 1.8	57	12.7 ± 1.3	14.2 ± 0.9	55	12.8 ± 1.7	14.9 ± 0.8

Group	Δ20-B[c] (13)	t(a)	Δ20-B (14)	t(a)	Δ20-B (15)	t(a)	Δ20-B (16)	t(a)
Females > 21 years	0.75 ± 1.86	2.32[d]	1.09 ± 2.42	2.70[d]	0.75 ± 1.55	3.69[d]	1.12 ± 2.10	3.92[d]
Males > 21 years	0.77 ± 1.41	2.73[d]	1.51 ± 2.70	3.06[d]	0.32 ± 2.79	N.S.	0.33 ± 0.91	N.S. (1.95[d] one tail)
Children 5–12 years	2.23 ± 1.65	8.22[d]	0.39 ± 1.55	N.S.	1.56 ± 1.24	9.50[d]	2.15 ± 1.53	10.42[d]

Group	t(b) 13 vs. 15	t(b) 14 vs. 15	t(b) 16 vs. 15
Females > 21 years	N.S.	N.S.	N.S.
Males > 21 years	N.S.	N.S.	N.S.
Children 5–12 years	2.11[d]	-3.39[d]	2.24[d]

[a] N, number of subjects.

[b] B, mean SD for baseline evaluation; 20 = mean ± SD for 20 months evaluation.

[c] Δ20-B, mean ± SD change between evaluations; t(a), t value for change within community; t(b), t value for comparison with community 15 (control).

[d] Statistically significant.

302

TABLE V

Mean Values and Changes in PCV by Age–Sex Groups and Communities and Change between Basal and 20 Months evaluations[a]

Group	13 N[a]	13 B[b]	13 20[b]	14 N	14 B	14 20	16 N	16 B	16 20	15 N	15 B	15 20
Female > 21 years	41	37.9 ± 4.6	37.8 ± 5.7	45	33.0 ± 7.5	34.2 ± 4.9	60	39.4 ± 4.8	41.0 ± 3.8	65	39.8 ± 4.1	39.1 ± 4.1
Male > 21 years	28	43.3 ± 5.6	42.1 ± 4.8	40	34.8 ± 9.6	37.5 ± 7.1	32	45.5 ± 4.0	45.8 ± 4.0	39	42.4 ± 6.1	44.5 ± 4.9
Children 5–12 years	117	35.6 ± 3.1	38.3 ± 2.8	221	34.8 ± 3.5	36.4 ± 4.1	242	38.6 ± 3.0	40.6 ± 2.3	192	37.6 ± 3.2	40.4 ± 2.8

Group	13 Δ20-B[c]	13 t(a)	14 Δ20-B	14 t(a)	16 Δ20-B	16 t(a)	15 Δ20-B	15 t(a)
Female > 21 years	-0.12 ± 6.00	N.S.	1.22 ± 7.03	N.S.	1.59 ± 4.84	2.54[d]	-0.65 ± 4.50	N.S.
Male > 21 years	-1.22 ± 1.75	-3.69[d]	2.69 ± 8.37	2.03[d]	0.28 ± 3.52	N.S.	2.00 ± 6.81	N.S.
Children 5–12 years	2.65 ± 3.86	7.43[d]	1.59 ± 4.72	5.01[d]	1.98 ± 3.29	9.36[d]	2.83 ± 3.44	11.40[d]

Group	13 vs. 15 t(b)	14 vs. 15 t(b)	16 vs. 15 t(b)
Female > 21 years	N.S.	N.S.	2.67[d]
Male > 21 years	-2.58[d]	N.S.	N.S.
Children 5–12 years	N.S.	-3.08[d]	-2.61[d]

[a] N, number of subjects.

[b] B, mean ± SD for baseline evaluation; 20, mean ± SD for 20 months evaluation.

[c] Δ20-B, mean ± SD change between evaluations; t(a), t value for change within community; t(b), t value for comparison with community 15 (control).

[d] Statistically significant.

303

TABLE 447

Mean Values and Changes in HbU by "Normality" Groups—Baseline and 20 Months Evaluations

	13 N^a	13 B^b	13 20^b	14 N	14 B^b	14 20	16 N	16 B^b	16 20	15 N	15 B^b	15 20
Normal	91	0.20 ± 0.87	0.51 ± 1.38	85	0.17 ± 1.06	-0.38 ± 1.34	137	0.08 ± 0.29	0.15 ± 0.53	146	0.12 ± 1.41	0.37 ± 1.04
Low	62	-3.13 ± 1.89	-0.01 ± 1.57	124	-4.56 ± 2.26	-1.84 ± 2.18	64	-0.90 ± 0.40	0.01 ± 0.33	75	-2.86 ± 1.38	-0.38 ± 1.54
Total	153	-1.15 ± 2.14	0.30 ± 1.47	209	-2.64 ± 2.98	-1.24 ± 2.02	201	-0.23 ± 0.56	0.10 ± 0.48	221	-0.89 ± 1.99	0.12 ± 1.28

	13 $\Delta20\text{-}B^c$	13 t(a)	14 $\Delta20\text{-}B^c$	14 t(a)	16 $\Delta20\text{-}B^c$	16 t(a)	15 $\Delta20\text{-}B^c$	15 t(a)
Normal	0.31 ± 1.38	2.29^d	-0.54 ± 1.46	-3.41^d	0.06 ± 0.50	N.S.	0.25 ± 1.45	2.08^d
Low	3.12 ± 2.07	11.87^d	2.72 ± 2.46	12.31^d	0.91 ± 0.50	14.56^d	2.48 ± 1.56	13.77^d
Total	1.45 ± 2.18	8.23^d	1.39 ± 2.65	7.58^d	0.33 ± 0.64	7.31^d	1.00 ± 1.82	8.17^d

	13 t(b) — 13 vs. 15	14 t(b) — 14 vs. 15	16 t(b) — 16 vs. 15
Normal	N.S.	-3.98^d	N.S.
Low	2.01^d	N.S.	-8.23^d
Total	2.10^d	N.S. (1.77^d one tail)	-5.13^d

^{a} N, number of subjects.

^{b} B, mean ± SD for baseline evaluation; 20, ± mean SD for 20 months evaluation.

^{c} 20Δ-B, mean ± SD change between evaluations; t(a), t value for change within community; t(b), t value for comparison with community 15 (control).

^{d} Statistically significant.

TABLE VII

Mean Values and Changes in PCVU by "Normality" Groups—Baseline and 20 Months Evaluations

	13			14			16			15		
	N^a	B^b	20^b	N	B^b	20^b	N	B^b	20^b	N	B^b	20^b
Normal	93	0.39 ± 2.49	-1.44 ± 4.26	62	0.42 ± 2.55	-3.51 ± 3.68	114	-0.02 ± 2.26	0.05 ± 3.40	113	-0.02 ± 2.48	-1.53 ± 3.88
Low	68	-7.01 ± 1.87	-2.51 ± 4.62	59	-7.52 ± 2.31	-5.09 ± 5.11	96	-6.16 ± 1.80	-0.66 ± 2.95	82	-6.46 ± 1.94	-1.81 ± 4.13
Total	161	-2.73 ± 4.30	-1.89 ± 4.43	121	-3.45 ± 4.29	-4.28 ± 4.49	210	-2.83 ± 3.69	-0.28 ± 3.21	195	-2.73 ± 3.91	-1.65 ± 3.98

	$\Delta20\text{-}B^c$	t(a)	$\Delta20\text{-}B^c$	t(a)	$\Delta20\text{-}B^c$	t(a)	$\Delta20\text{-}B^c$	t(a)
Normal	-1.83 ± 4.32	-4.09[d]	-4.06 ± 4.09	-7.82[d]	0.07 ± 3.55	N.S.	-1.51 ± 3.54	-4.53[d]
Low	4.49 ± 4.18	8.88[d]	2.43 ± 5.75	3.25[d]	5.50 ± 3.37	15.99[d]	4.65 ± 4.55	9.25[d]
Total	0.84 ± 4.44	2.40[d]	-0.90 ± 5.92	N.S.	2.55 ± 4.40	8.40[d]	1.08 ± 5.02	3.00[d]

	13 vs. 15	14 vs. 15	16 vs. 15
	t(b)	t(b)	t(b)
Normal	N.S.	-4.13[d]	3.36[d]
Low	N.S.	-2.46[d]	N.S.
Total	N.S.	-3.05[d]	3.12[d]

[a] N, number of subjects.

[b] B, mean ± SD for baseline evaluation; 20, ± mean SD for 20 months evaluation.

[c] Δ20-B mean ± SD change between evaluations; t(a), t value for change within community; t(b), t value for comparison with community 15 (control).

[d] Statistically significant.

PCV (Table V), although results are more variable. In general, adult males and females did not show significant changes in iron status with fortification since they were near normal values initially.

These results and preliminary interpretations are further substantiated when "normality" groups in HbU and PCVU are considered (Tables VI and VII). At this point in time it appears that it may be too early to detect clear changes in hematological condition in the fortified communities although a trend toward normalization is evident. This possibility has been complicated further, by an improvement in hematological conditions of the control community. This was not clearly noted in

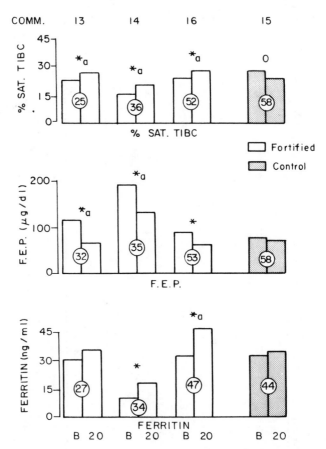

Fig. 3. Mean values of indicators of iron nutrition at the baseline and 20 months evaluations for adult females. * Significantly better; (0) significantly worse; (a) significantly better than community 15; (b) significantly worse than community 15; circled numbers indicate number of subjects.

previous evaluations. The reasons for these changes are not apparent but may be due to delayed effects of vitamin A fortifications which started one year before the initial evaluation of iron status (30). Further studies will most probably clarify this unexpected situation.

Iron Nutrition

Essentially the same type of analyses as those for Hb and PCV have been done for percent saturation TIBC (% sat TIBC), FEP, and ferritin. The mean values and their changes are presented for age-sex categories in Figs. 3 to 5 and for "normality" categories and total populations in Figs. 6 to 8.

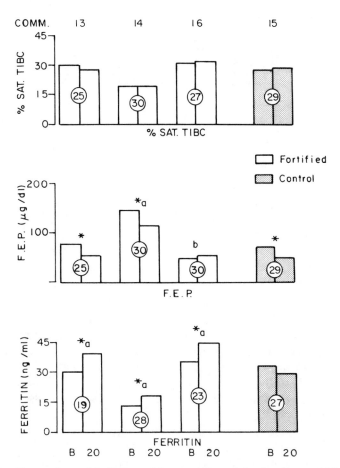

Fig. 4. Mean values of indicators of iron nutrition at the baseline and 20 months evaluations for adult males. See Fig. 3 for definition of symbols.

Fernando E. Viteri et al.

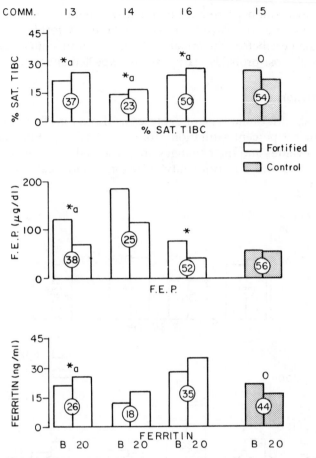

Fig. 5. Mean values of indicators of iron nutrition at the baseline and 20 months evaluations for children 5–12 years of age. See Fig. 3 for definition of symbols.

The changes observed with fortification follow a predicted pattern compatible with an improvement in iron nutrition: adult females significantly improve their iron transport (% sat. TIBC) as well as their iron availability during erythropoiesis (FEP), and iron reserves (ferritin) (Fig. 3). Adult males primarily improve iron reserve (ferritin) and iron availability for Hb synthesis (FEP), while iron transport is essentially unchanged (Fig. 4).

Children behave very similarly to adult females (Fig. 5). It is important to notice that the control community (No. 15) showed a slight and often not significant deterioration in iron nutrition in essentially all variables

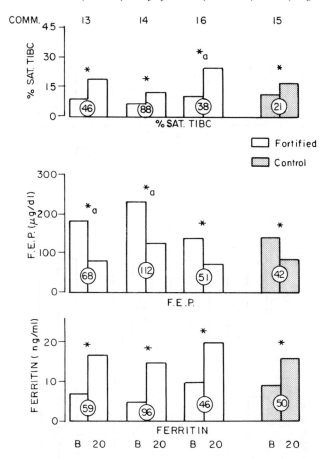

Fig. 6. Mean values of indicators of iron nutrition at the baseline and 20 months evaluations for deficient subjects.

measured, particularly in children and adult females, which constitute the "at risk" population. The results by "normality" groups present, again, what is expected. First, that naturally and due to the phenomenon of regression to the mean, the "defficient" population tends to improve, whereas the "normal" populations tend to deteriorate (31, 32). However, often the changes in the fortified communities reflect a greater improvement in the "deficient" group (Fig. 6) and less of a deterioration in the "normal" group than the control community (Fig. 7). The overall result is that clearly the iron nutrition of the fortified population appears significantly improved (Fig. 8).

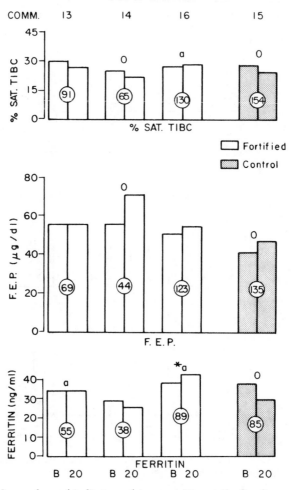

Fig. 7. Mean values of indicators of iron nutrition at the baseline and 20 months evaluations for normal subjects.

The magnitude of changes observed in iron nutrition were often greater than predicted, the opposite of what was observed in hematological condition. The fact is that there are no data with which to compare the sequential changes at the population level of fortification trials. It may be that the responses to very small increments in iron availability differ substantially from the responses to iron supplement which provide over 20 times more iron than food fortification. Interactions with other environmental factors such as repeated and/or chronic infections, vitamin A intake and compliance with the fortification are undoubtedly influenc-

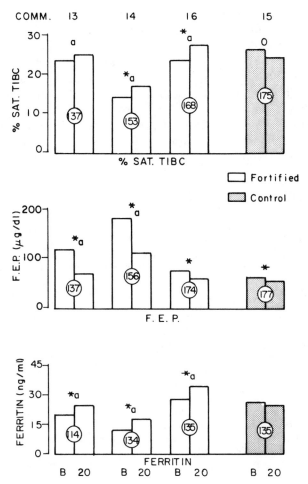

Fig. 8. Mean values of indicators of iron nutrition at the baseline and 20 months evaluations for the total population.

ing results. The continued observation and quantification of these and other variables for a longer time span of fortification will improve our appreciation of the series of phenomena which influence the response to small changes in dietary iron intake.

Finally, the evaluation of supplementation and fortification trials must consider two interrelated outcomes which demand different evaluative concepts. On the one hand, the effect of the intervention must be quantitated against the baseline situation of the population being studied, as well as against the "natural" changes which take place in "control" communities. The second aspect which must be evaluated is that of the efficacy of the intervention, that is, how effective the intervention is in bringing the population to an optimal condition. The comparison in this case is against a set of norms and distributions recognized adequate and characteristic of healthy populations. At 20 months of sugar fortification with NaFeEDTA at a level of 1:1000, the fortified communities are demonstrating a clear positive *effect* in iron nutrition. As expected the efficacy of fortification trials must be evaluated in long term programs. We expect that 3 years will allow us to estimate certain aspects of the *efficacy* of fortification.

ACKNOWLEDGMENTS

The authors wish to acknowledge the important contributions brought about by discussions with Drs. S. Baker and S. Greenhouse, consultants to the iron fortification projects in Guatemala. Sincere appreciation are expressed also to all the members of the communities in the study, the field and laboratory personnel, in particular to Luis Mejia, C. R. de Campos, S. Morales, and R. Funes and to the data clerks and statistical assistants, in particular Miss A. E. Leiva. This work was partially financed by the U.S.A.I.D., by WHO, and by the Government of Guatemala.

REFERENCES

1. Sood, S. K., Banerji, L., and Ramalingaswami, V. Occurence of nutritional anaemias in tropical countries. *Symp. Swed. Nutr. Found.* **6**, 36–49 (1968).
2. Roche, M., and Layrisse, M. The nature and causes of hookworm anemia. *Am. J. Trop. Med. Hyg.* **15**, 1031 (1966).
3. Dallman, P. R., Bentler, F., and Finch, C. A. Effects of non deficiency exclusive of anaemia. *Br. J. Haematol.* **40**, 179 (1978).
4. Viteri, B., and Torún, B. Anaemia and physical work capacity. *Clin. Haematol.* **3**, 609 (1974).
5. Pollitt, E., Viteri, F., Saco-Pollitt, C., and Leibel, R. L. Functional aspects of iron deficiency. *In* "Iron Deficiency: Brain Biochemistry and Behavior" (E. Pollitt and R. K. Leibel, eds.), p. 195. Raven Press, New York, 1982.
6. Chandra, R. K. Reduced tactericidal capacity of polymorphs in iron deficiency. *Arch. Dis. Child.* **48**, 864 (1973).
7. Steckel, A. Case study. *In* "Iron Deficiency in Infancy and Childhood," pp. 44–47. A Report of the International Nutritional Anemia Consultative Group (INACG). Nutrition Foundation, New York, 1979.
8. "Nutritional Evaluation of the Central American Population," 6 vols. INCAP-OIR, Public Health Ministries of the Central American Countries and Panama, 1969.
9. Viteri, F. E., and Guzmán, M. A. Haematological status of the Central American populations. Prevalence of individuals with haemoglobin levels below "normal." *Br. J. Haematol.* **23**, 723 (1972).

10. Viteri, F. E. "Hematological status of the Central American population: Iron and folate deficiencies," 12th Meet. Advis. Comm. Med. Res. Pan Am. Health Organ. Washington, D.C., 1973.
11. Viteri, F. E., Guzmán, M. A., and Mata, L. J. Anemias nutricionales en Centro América. Influencia de infección por uncinaria. *Arch. Latinoam. Nutr.* **23**, 33 (1973).
12. Bothwell, T. H., Charlton, R. W., Cook, J. D., and Finch, C. A. "Iron Metabolism in Man." Blackwell, Oxford, 1979.
13. Bulux, J., and González, H. H. Estudios sobre el efecto de la sumplementación con hierro y con hierro mas acido fólico en comunidades de la costa sur de Guatemala. M. D. Thesis, University of San Carlos, Guatemala, 1980.
14. Arroyave, G., Aguilar, J. R., Flores, M., and Guzmán, M. A. Evaluation of sugar fortification with vitamin A at the national level. Sci. Publ.—Pan. Am. Health Organ. **384**, 82 (1979).
15. Layrisse, M., Martinez-Torres, C., Renzi, M., Velez, F., and Gonzalez, M. Sugar as a vehicle for iron fortification. *Am. J. Clin. Nutr.* **129**, 8 (1976).
16. Pineda, O., and Viteri, F. E. Compatibility of vitamin A and iron fortification of sugar. (In preparation.)
17. Will, J. J., and Vilter, R. W. A study of the absorption and utilization of an iron chelate in iron deficient patients. *J. Lab. Clin. Med.* **44**, 499 (1954).
18. Jimenez, F. E., Jimenez, B. R., and Viteri, F. E. Tratamiento de la anemia ferropénica con nuevas sales de hierro. *Rev. Med. Hosp. Natl. Ninos (Costa Rica)* **10**, 105 (1975).
19. Viteri, F. E., García-Ibañez, R., and Torún, B. Sodium iron NaFe EDTA as an iron fortification compound in Central America. Albsorption studies. *Am. J. Clin. Nutr.* **31**, 961 (1978).
20. O'Donnell, A., Alvarez, E., and Viteri, F. E. Iron absorption from a typical Central American rural diet in the absence and presence of FeNa EDTA: Estimation by two methods. *Proc. Int. Congr. Nutr. 11th 1978* p. 480 (1979).
21. Layrisse, M., and Martinez-Torres, C. Fe (III)- EDTA complex as iron fortification *Am. J. Clin. Nutr.* **30**, 1166 (1977).
22. Vohra, P., and Kratzer, F. D. Influence of various chelating agents on the availability of zinc. *J. Nutr.* **82**, 249 (1964).
23. Suso, F. A., and Edwards, H. M. Influence of various chelating agents on absorptions of ^{60}Co, ^{59}Fe, ^{54}Mn, and ^{65}Zn by chickens. *Poult. Sci.* **47**, 1417 (1968).
24. Oberleas, D., Muhrer, M. E., and O'Dell, B. L. Dietary metal complexing agents and zinc availability in the rat. *J. Nutr.* **90**, 56 (1966).
25. Batres, R., Rose, D., Solomons, N. W., Pineda, O., and Viteri, F. E. Absorción de zinc con una dieta de maíz y frijol. Interacción de diversas dosis de hierro en forma de sulfato ferroso o de NaFeEDTA. *Inf. Anu. INCAP, 1980* (in preparation).
26. Solomons, N. W., Jacob, R. A., Pineda, O., and Viteri, F. E. Studies on the bioavailability of zinc in man. Effects of the Guatemalan diet and of the iron fortifying agent NaFeEDTA. *J. Nutr.* **109**, 1515 (1979).
27. Viteri, F. E., Christensen, A., and Batres, R. Estudios de la absorción y metabolismo de hierro y EDTA radioactivos en ratas. *Inf. An., INCAP, 1979* (in preparation).
28. Food and Drug Administration (U.S.A.) "Safety of EDTA (ethylene-diamino-Fetraacetate) as a Food Additive." Internal Report. FDA, Washington, D.C., 1977.
29. Viteri, F. E., de Tuna, V., and Guzmán, M. A. Normal haematological values in the Central American population. *Br. J. Haematol.* **23**, 189 (1972).
30. Mejía, L. A., Hodges, R. E., Arroyave, G., Viteri, F. E., and Torún, B. Vitamin A

deficiency and anemia in Central American children. *Am. J. Clin. Nutr.* **30**, 1175 (1977).

31. Buss, A. R. Toward a unified framework for psychometric concepts in the multivariate developmental situation: Intraindividual change and inter- and intraindividual differences. *In* "Longitudinal Research in the Study of Behavior and Development" (J. R. Nesselrode and P. B. Baltes, eds.), pp. 41–59. Academic Press, New York, 1979.

32. Garby, L., and Yeo, G. Interpretation of results of supplemental trials. *Am. J. Clin. Nutr.* **31**, 1515 (1978).

27 Prevention of Iron Deficiency in Infants by Milk Fortification

ABRAHAM STEKEL, MANUEL OLIVARES,
INES LÓPEZ, MIRNA AMAR, FERNANDO
PIZARRO, PATRICIA CHADUD, SANDRA
LLAGUNO,AND MARISOL CAYAZZO

Iron deficiency in infancy is highly prevalent in most countries of the world and represents an important cause of morbidity. Studies in Santiago, Chile, (see Ríos et al., Chapter 24, this volume) have shown that about one-third of infants of low socioeconomic condition develop iron-deficiency anemia during the first 2 years of life, and a higher percentage presents iron-deficient erythropoiesis or latent iron deficiency. Considering this high prevalence and the fact that iron deficiency at an early age may represent the beginning of a long-lasting condition of deficiency in the individual, it seems clear that preventive measures in infants and children should have high priority. Systematic programs of prevention, however, are rare.

Food fortification has been recommended as the best method of preventing iron deficiency in a community (1) (see Cook, Chapter 25, this volume) because the oral administration of medicinal iron is impractical and parenteral iron is potentially hazardous. Cereals and milk appear to be the foods most practical for fortification in infancy and when appropriately performed, fortification of these products is effective in preventing iron deficiency (2–4). However, the type, the quantity, and method by which cereals are given to infants, vary widely, whereas the consumption of cow's milk is much more constant and universal. Infant formulas or powdered milk can be easily fortified during processing,

NUTRITION INTERVENTION STRATEGIES IN NATIONAL DEVELOPMENT
Copyright © 1983 by Academic Press, Inc.

and because milk often provides most of the calories in the diet, the level of fortification can be accurately calculated.

In Chile, a large part of the milk consumed by infants is distributed free by the National Health Service (NHS). Under this National Program of Supplementary Feeding (NPSF), in recent years about 30 million kilograms (kg) of powdered milk or milk substitutes have been distributed each year to infants, preschool children, and pregnant and lactating women. Each infant, or the nursing mother, receives 3 kg of powdered milk from 0 to 6 months and then 2 kg until 2 years of age. Breast-feeding in Chile is of short duration, and solid foods are introduced into the infant's diet at about 4 months of age.

A few years ago, investigators at INTA began studying the possibility of fortifying the milk used in the national program with iron. Even though the use of highly modified and rather expensive milk-based infant formulas fortified with iron was known to be effective in preventing iron deficiency, little experience existed concerning the simple addition of iron salts to powdered milk. At the time, a powdered low-fat milk was being distributed to infants by the NHS. Isotopic studies showed that when ferrous sulfate was added to this milk in the proportion of 15 mg of elemental iron per 100 g of powder (or 1 liter of reconstituted milk) the geometric mean absorption of the iron was 3 to 4%.

A field trial with the fortified low-fat milk was started in 1972 in three NHS clinics (Fig. 1). Infants were given the fortified or a nonfortified control milk for 1 year starting at 3 months of age. Each home was visited by a nurse every 15 days in order to encourage consumption of the fortified milk and to perform a dietary survey. Infants consuming

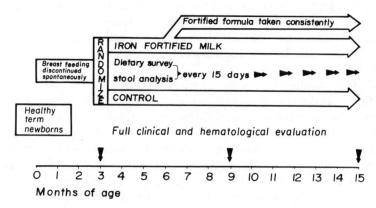

Fig. 1. Experimental design of field trial with low-fat milk fortified with ferrous sulfate.

the fortified milk were identified by serial determinations of iron in their stool. Milk distributed through the national program is sometime sold or shared with other members of the family. Studies in our laboratory have shown that infants fed fortified milk consistently excreted more than 15 mg iron per 100 g of stool.

A total of 603 infants entered the field trial; 382 were studied at 9 months of age and 314 at 15 months. At 9 and 15 months, there were significant differences in hemoglobin concentration between the groups. Anemia (hemoglobin below 11 g/dl) was present in 27.7% of the control infants at 9 months and in 34.6% at 15 months of age (Fig. 2). Corresponding figures in the iron-fortified group were 20.7 and 12.7% at 9 and 15 months, respectively. The group of infants consuming the fortified milk consistently had a higher hemoglobin concentration, but anemia still existed in 14.8% of them at 9 months and in 9.9% at 15 months of age. Differences between the groups in transferrin saturation and free erythrocyte protoporphyrin were small, even in infants who were shown to have consumed the fortified milk. The fortified low-fat powdered milk was initially delivered in polyethylene bags and later in tin cans. Preservation in both cases was excellent. No appreciable organoleptic changes occurred in up to 2 years of storage at room temperature under temperate climatic conditions.

It was concluded that even though fortification of low-fat milk with

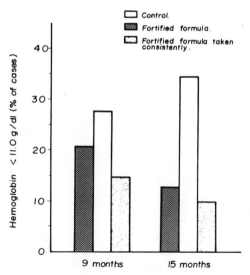

Fig. 2.   Anemia at 9 and 15 months of age in infants and children receiving nonfortified milk (control) or low-fat milk fortified with ferrous sulfate (see text).

ferrous sulfate was a simple, safe, and inexpensive way of improving iron nutrition, not enough iron was absorbed from this product. The incidence of anemia and iron deficiency was high even in infants known to have taken the fortified milk consistently. The most likely cause of these findings was the relatively low absorption of fortification iron in milk. The mean absorption of iron from fortified formulas reported in infants with adequate iron nutrition was about 4% (5, 6). Figure 3 summarizes the results from isotopic studies of absorption of fortification iron in milk conducted at INTA. These studies were done in children under 2 years of age in whom iron deficiency was prevalent. Geometric mean absorption ranged from 3 to over 10%. The main factor explaining the differences in absorption seemed to be the presence or absence of ascorbic acid. Double isotope studies in our laboratory demonstrated that absorption increased by a mean factor of 1.8 and 2.8, respectively, when 100 or 200 mg/liter of ascorbic acid was added to milk containing 15 mg/liter of iron as ferrous sulfate (7).

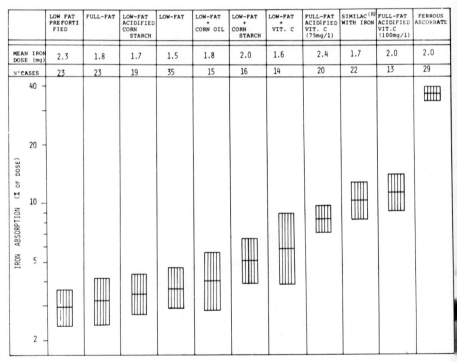

Fig. 3.   Absorption of fortification iron in milk. Formulas contained 10 to 15 mg/liter of iron as ferrous sulfate. Infants received 100 to 250 ml of milk extrinsically labeled with [59]Fe.

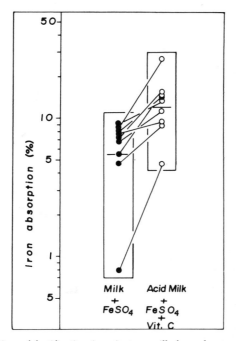

Fig. 4. Absorption of fortification iron in two milk formulas compared by a double isotope technique. Infants received on day 1 low-fat milk fortified with ferrous sulfate (●) and on day 2 acidified milk plus ferrous sulfate and ascorbic acid (○).

A new milk formula was developed as a result of these studies. The full-fat (26%) powdered milk presently used by the NPSF was fortified with 15 mg of iron as ferrous sulfate and 100 mg of ascorbic acid per 100 g of powder (or 1 liter of reconstituted formula). The product was also slightly acidified in order to discourage its consumption by other members of the family. Compared with the low-fat fortified milk, iron absorption from this formula was higher by a factor of 2.7 (Fig. 4). Storage of the product for 1 year at room temperature did not produce significant changes in organoleptic characteristics or iron bioavailability.

A field trial with this new formula was started in 1976 in three urban communities. The experimental design was similar to the first trial (Fig. 1). Two hundred and eighty infants received the fortified milk; 278 infants received the regular unfortified milk and served as controls. Laboratory studies at 3 months of age showed no differences between the groups. At 9 and 15 months there were highly significant differences between the two groups in hemoglobin, transferrin saturation, free erythrocyte protoporphyrin, and serum ferritin (Fig. 5). Figures 6 and 7

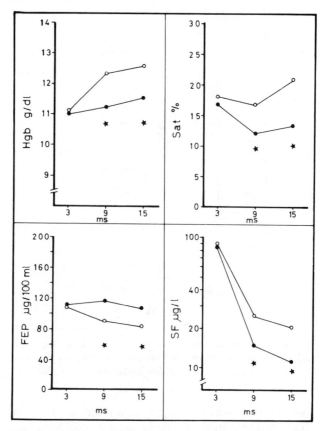

Fig. 5. Mean values of hemoglobin (Hb), transferrin saturation (Sat), free erythrocyte protoporphyrin (FEP), and serum ferritin (SF) at 3, 9, and 15 months of age in infants receiving acidified milk fortified with iron and ascorbic acid (○) or nonfortified milk (●). Asterisks indicate a *p* value of < .001.

show the cumulative frequency distribution of some of these laboratory parameters. Anemia (Hb < 11.0 g/dl) was present in 7.5% of infants in the fortified group at 9 months and in 1.6% of these children at 15 months. Corresponding figures in the nonfortified controls were 34.7 and 27.8%, respectively. Marked differences also existed in the proportion of infants in each group having a transferrin saturation below 9% or a free erythrocyte protoporphyrin over 100 μg/100 ml RBC.

Acceptance of the acidified formula was good. Survey information indicated that 94% of infants weaned to acidified milk were still consuming it at 12 months and 89% at 15 months of age. Similarly, stool analysis

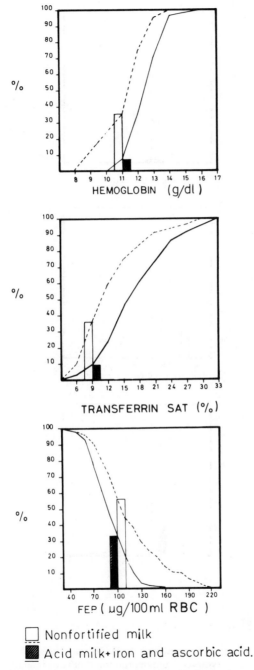

Fig. 6. Cumulative frequency distribution of individual values of hemoglobin, transferrin saturation, and free erythrocyte protoporphyrin (FEP) at 9 months of age in infants receiving two different milk formulas. The height of the columns indicates the percentage of infants with hemoglobin < 11 g/dl (top), transferrin saturation < 9% (middle), and FEP > 100 μg/100 ml RBC (bottom) in each of the two groups.

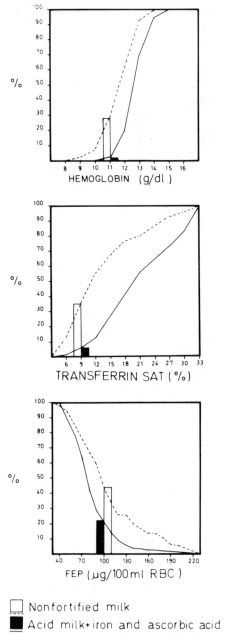

Fig. 7. Cumulative frequency distribution of individual values of hemoglobin, transferrin saturation, and free erythrocyte protoporphyrin (FEP) at 15 months of age in children receiving two different milk formulas. The height of the columns indicates the percentage of children with hemoglobin < 11 g/dl (top), transferrin saturation < 9% (middle), and FEP > 100 μg/100 ml RBC (bottom) in each of the two groups.

showed that 94% of infants receiving the fortified milk had a mean iron concentration in stools over 15 mg% and, therefore, had a high probability of actually consuming the fortified formula consistently. The results of this study confirmed under field conditions the high iron bioavailability of the formula containing ascorbic acid. All laboratory indices indicative of iron nutrition were improved and anemia was essentially eradicated. Since milk distribution programs in Chile cover a high proportion of the infant population, it is concluded that if the unfortified milk presently used by the NHS could be replaced by the fortified formula, iron deficiency would be prevented in the vast majority of Chilean infants.

ACKNOWLEDGMENTS

Supported by grants from Consejo Nacional para la Alimentación y Nutrición (CONPAN) the Research Corporation and the United Nations University.

REFERENCES

1. Report of a WHO Group of Experts. Nutritional anaemias. *W. H. O. Tech. Rep. Ser.* **503** (1972).
2. Marsh, A., Long, H., and Stierwalt, E. Comparative hematologic response to iron fortification of a milk formula for infants. *Pediatrics* **24**, 404 (1959).
3. Andelman, M. B., and Sered, B. R. Utilization of dietary iron by term infants. *Am. J. Dis. Child.* **111**, 45 (1966).
4. Moe, P. M. Iron requirements in infancy. Longitudinal studies of iron requirements during the first year of life. *Acta Paediatr. (Stockholm), Suppl.* **150** (1963).
5. Ríos, E., Hunter, R. E., Cook, J. D., Smith, N. J., and Finch, C. A. The absorption of iron as supplements in infant cereal and infant formulas. *Pediatrics* **55**, 686 (1975).
6. Saarinen, U. M., and Siimes, M. A. Iron absorption from infant formula and the optimal level of iron supplementation. *Acta Paediatr. Scand.* **66**, 719 (1977).
7. Stekel, A., Olivares, M., Amar, M., and Pizarro, F. Effect of ascorbic acid on the absorption of supplementary iron in milk. *Proc. Int. Congr. Hematol., 16th, 1976* Abstract 3–12 (1976).

28 Interventions for the Prevention of Endemic Goiter

JOHN B. STANBURY AND JOSIP
MATOVINOVIC

No programs of nutritional intervention have been so spectacularly successful as those which have been directed toward the prevention of endemic goiter. Since the first demonstration of the efficacy of iodine in Akron, Ohio in 1923 by Marine and Kimball, (1), addition of iodine to table salt in many countries throughout the world has resulted in a virtual disappearance of endemic goiter and endemic cretinism wherever a consistant program has been achieved. Thus, significant endemic goiter has vanished from the United States (2) and most European countries. Remarkable success has also been achieved in Guatemala (3) and in several other Latin American countries, in New Guinea (4), in Thailand (5), and in the endemic regions in The Peoples Republic of China (6).

Safe, effective, feasible, and inexpensive prophylaxis is available. The tragic irony is that endemic goiter continues to afflict an estimated 200 to 400 million persons. There are perhaps 200,000 cretins in the world. In addition, there is a strong suspicion that there are in addition, large numbers of persons whose mental and physical development has been delayed by a deficiency of iodine that was not sufficiently severe to cause the gross defects of the readily recognized cretin. Major foci of endemic goiter and cretinism are found today in the Andes and in the central plains of South America, in a vast belt extending across central Africa, in the Himalayas extending from the middle east to Thailand, and in Indonesia and New Guinea (see Fig. 1). In some of these regions, villages may be found where 7.6% of the population show the extreme retardation characteristic of the endemic cretin and where virtually the

NUTRITION INTERVENTION STRATEGIES IN NATIONAL DEVELOPMENT
Copyright © 1983 by Academic Press, Inc.
ISBN 012-709080-0

entire adult population has significant enlargement of the thyroid gland (7).

Why do endemic goiter and endemic cretinism continue to exist? The reasons are several, but are principally geographic, economic, and political. There have been those who have objected to iodization programs on the grounds that effectiveness had not been established or that the occasional minor complication of iodine-induced thyrotoxicosis (Jod Basedow) outweighed the advantage of preventive programs. The principal reason, however, has been apathy on the part of governments. There are a number of countries which have legislated the iodization of salt for the prevention of goiter, but have not implemented these programs for economic, political, or other reasons. Other programs have been less than successful because the technique of the distribution programs has not been technically adequate to the task.

There remain a number of places in the world which are cut off from the modern world by reasons of geography, poverty, or both and where regular channels for the distribution of iodine are difficult or impossible. One answer to this problem has been the use of iodized oil by injection. This technique needs to be extended into these regions until such time as they may enter the modern commercial sector.

Among students of endemic goiter, there is a consensus that iodine deficiency is both a sufficient and a necessary cause of the disorder and of cretinism as well. In addition, there is evidence that environmental goitrogens in certain instances may have had a role in enhancing the contribution of deficient iodine intake. Gaitan (8) has found sulfur-containing low molecular weight organic substances in drinking water in the Cauca Valley of Colombia, which may be responsible for persistent mild goiter in that region. Ermans *et al.* (9) have made a strong case for a cyanogenic glycoside in cassava as a contributing cause in the endemic region of Zaire. There is evidence for a goitrogen in the milk of cows in Finland (10). Nevertheless, disappearance or a sharp diminution of goiter has occurred whenever a prophylactic program has been implemented, even when a goitrogenic factor has been identified.

METHODS OF INTERVENTION

Iodization of Salt

The use of salt as a carrier for iodine was first suggested by Boussingalt in 1831 in what is now Colombia (11). This method received its principal impetus from the already cited studies of Marine and Kimball in 1923 and is now by far the most important method for the general distribution of iodine as a prophylactic measure (1). The iodine may be added to salt as it is prepared for commercial distribution, either by wet spraying or by dry blending (12). The calcium, potassium, and sodium salts of iodide and iodate have been used. At present sodium or potassium iodate is most commonly employed in some countries because it is considered to be more stable under warm humid conditions. The metabolic fate of iodide and iodate are precisely the same, in that iodate is reduced to iodide after ingestion.

Countries vary widely in the level of iodide in iodized salt from 1 part in 10,000 to 1 part in 200,000. Assuming a mean intake of 5 g of table salt daily this translates into an ingestion of 25 to 500 μg daily. Given the wide variability in salt intake it would appear that a concentration of less than 1 part in 50,000 is too low and 1 part in 10,000 exceeds ordinary needs. It is generally conceeded that an adult requires more than 50 to 80 μg of iodine daily if he is to avoid significant hyperplasia of the thyroid.

Intervention by the iodization of salt has proved to be highly effective (Table I). Nevertheless, certain problems have arisen. As with any program of iodine supplementation, a certain number of susceptible individuals develop thyrotoxicosis (14, 20–22). This presumably is in those persons in the community who have a tendancy to thyrotoxicosis which is held in abeyance by the iodine deficiency prevailing prior to the prophylactic program. Their numbers are small and the thyrotoxicosis engendered is generally mild and transient. Three instances were identified among nearly 1000 persons injected with iodized oil in a program in Ecuador (23). Only one was found in a program of similar size in Peru (14), whereas, three were found among 97 persons given iodized oil given for nodular goiter in Western Argentina (25). The rate of thyrotoxicosis rose by a factor of nearly 4 in Tasmania when iodide was introduced prophylactically whereas no cases were found in the extensive trials of iodized oil in Papua–New Guinea (26). The symptoms and findings may be subtle. There may be weight loss and heat intolerance together with tachycardia. Manifestations have been mild, and the disorder easily managed with antithyroid drugs. It is probably a transient phenomenon, but the existence of Jod Basedow after preventive programs is an established fact and requires that programs be monitored for its occurence.

Iodated Bread

Since bread is almost universally consumed, the use of iodine in bread making has been employed as a technique for the distribution of iodine. Iodide has the additional advantage of catalyzing the cross-linkage of

TABLE I

Goiter Prevalence Rates[a] as Affected by Phrophylaxis Programs

Country	Before prophylaxis program	After prophylaxis began (years)	Method of prophylaxis	Subjects	Reference
Guatemala	38	5.2 (10)	Salt iodization	General population	13
Peru	68	12 (1½–2)	Iodized oil	Years 6–45	14
Papua–New Guinea	38 (saline control)	5.3 (5)	Iodized oil	General population (females)	15
Argentina (Mendoza)	46	3.2 (15)	Salt iodization	School children	16
Zaire (Kivu)	49	16 (1)	Iodized oil	General population	17
Argentina (Nequen)	82[b]	39 (1–2)	Salt iodization	School children	18
Colombia Cauca Valley (Candalaria)	86	21 (5)	Salt iodization	School children	19

[a] Methods of estimation of prevalence rates vary among studies.
[b] Selected subjects, numbers calculated from available data.

gluten and, therefore, of improving the quality of the baked bread. Iodized bread has been used for goiter prophylaxis in Holland, Tasmania, and Australia and has been employed widely in the United States as a conditioner rather than as a technique for goiter prevention. Indeed, in the last instance the addition of iodide to bread has been partly responsible for the increased consumption of iodine well beyond any estimate of optimal daily intake.

The iodization of bread in Tasmania was followed by an interesting and well documented increase in the incidence of thyrotoxicosis in hospitals in that country (20, 22, 26). This increase persisted for approximately a decade and now is said to be declining. There is no reason to believe that iodization of bread has any particularly deleterious or unwanted effects by comparison with other methods of iodide distribution.

The iodization of bread has not been widely adopted as a prophylactic measure. The principal problem is the difficulty in controlling the distribution because of widely varying levels of consumption of bread by the population participating in the program.

Other Methods of Distribution through Ingestion

Several other techniques of prophylaxis have been employed. Iodine has been given as candy containing iodate to school children (27). It has been incorporated in candies such as licorice which have been distributed to schools. It has been employed in the water supply with the dual purpose of purifying the water and supplying the iodine to the population. All these methods are less than satisfactory for logistical and economic reasons. For example, less than 1% of water is customarily used for drinking purposes and accordingly the distribution of iodine in drinking water is highly uneconomical.

Iodized Oil

The use of iodized oil by injection as a public health measure was introduced by McCullagh (28) in New Guinea as a result of the observation that lipiodol, a highly iodinated poppy seed oil persists for months in the chest after bronchography. Iodized poppy seed oil usually contains 37% iodine by weight. McCullagh did a controlled study in the Huan Peninsula of New Guinea in 1957. Follow-up disclosed that the measure was effective and that a single dose was adequate for up to 4.5 years in causing a subsidance of established goiter (29). Additional studies in New Guinea established that endemic cretinism is also prevented if the injection is given before pregnancy (30). This observation has been confirmed in highland Ecuador and in central Africa (31, 32). These observations have led to the extensive employment of iodized oil by injection in several major foci of endemic goiter and endemic cretinism. This prophylactic measure has been employed elsewhere in Papua–New Guinea, in Peru, Ecuador, Western Argentina (18), and in Zaire.

The pharmacology of iodized oil has been extensively studied. It disperses slowly from the injection site and is lost from the body with a half-life of approximately 6 months. Pretell has calculated that a 1 ml dose would meet minimum daily requirements of 50 μg per day for 20 months, and a 4 ml dose for 36 months (14). Since the iodide disappears from the injection site faster than it appears in the excreta, the conclusion may be drawn that it is stored elsewhere in the body, perhaps in the body lipid. Iodide derived from the injected iodized oil appears quickly in the thyroid gland.

The injections are well tolerated. Local reactions occur rarely and are trivial. The only complication appears to be the rare occurrence of Jod Basedow, as already described. It may be a phenomenon which is largely observed in older persons with preexisting nodular goiter. Idiosyncratic reactions to iodized oil injections have not yet been reported.

The use of iodized oil is pecularily advantageous in those settings where the economy does not support the uniform distribution of iodized salt or where there are multible entries for salt into a country in ways which make iodization difficult or impossible. Iodized oil may be used advantageously for remote groups which are difficult to reach. Roving medical teams can administer injections at widely spaced intervals. We are unaware of any satisfactory cost-effectiveness studies of iodized oil by comparison with iodized salt, but such a study might be less than useful since iodized oil is customarily used only where geographical, political, or social factors make the iodization of salt impractical or impossible. There can be no question that either technique is highly cost-effective in terms of prevention of disease and improvement in economic productivity (33).

Concurrent Administration of Other Supplements

There is no compelling reason for not considering other supplements along with iodide. Salt may be fortified with iron or with vitamin A or both where there is a general need for those supplements. Conversely, where other techniques or vehicles for vitamin A or iron are employed, iodine can be added as one of its salts. We are unaware that one of these various combinations has in fact been tried. The possibility that vitamin A or iron might be administered in combination with depot oil has not been explored to our knowledge. The advantage of giving iodine as iodinated oil is that the requirement for iodine is so small that sufficient iodine for long-term residual storage can be covalently linked with the oil. The requirements for vitamin A iron are much higher and could be beyond the carrying capacity of an amount of oil which would be reasonable for an injection. A more serious constraint in the case of vitamin A, however, is that oily solutions are not mobilized from the injection site and, therefore, are ineffective. Water-miscible vitamin A injections are effective. This multiple nutrient approach through a common carrier might be worth exploring, nevertheless.

Prophylactic programs need to be monitored for several reasons. Possible complications should be identified and treated as necessary. The phenomenon of Jod Basedow is established and is a potential complication of any prophylactic program. Although patients with this disorder have been readily and easily treated, a lengthy episode of thyrotoxicosis is undesirable and at least theoretically can be dangerous. Programs should be monitored for effectiveness. This may be done by examining standardized samples of persons at risk, such as school children. Surveys are relatively meaningless unless they are conducted by trained observers using a standardized format under conditions as nearly identical as possible and conducted on highly comparable population groups. Surveys should be conducted every 6 months to 1 year. Failure to attain the objectives of the program would signal trouble. Thus, while a sufficient amount of iodine might be added to salt, consumption patterns, or loss of iodine from the packaging, failure of the iodizing process, or other elements in the chain from manufacture to consumption might have failed and contributed to the lack of response. In addition, it is desirable to keep the manufacturing and distribution of iodized salt under scrutiny. There have been too many instances of breakdown.

There are other levels of sophistication which can be employed in the monitoring process, but are perhaps unnecessary for large-scale programs. These would include physiological assessment of the patients in the program. Measurements of urinary excretion of iodine can indicate the quantity of iodine in the diet. The function of the thyroid as reflecting the changed iodine intake resulting from the program can be assessed by measurements of radioactive iodine uptake, or measurements of blood concentration of thyroid hormones or thyrotropic hormone. Lack of resources for doing these tests should not be an impediment to implementation of goiter prevention programs.

Case Study: Iodized Oil in Ecuador

Taking its lead from the successful studies on the use of iodized oil in the prevention of goiter in Papua–New Guinea, an intensive study of iodized oil was begun in 1966 in two villages north of Quito, Ecuador (23, 31). This program has been under the general direction of Dr. Rodrigo Fierro since its inception. Prior to 1966, Dr. Fierro and colleagues had made careful inventories of the population of the two villages for incidences of goiter, frequency of cretinism, clinical aspects of these disorders, prevalence of deaf-mutism, genetic characteristics of the population, nutritional status and their social and economic conditions (Table II).

The villages lie close to one another at an altitude of approximately 3000 m. The population of one, Tocachi, is approximately 1000, and the other, La Esperanza, is approximately 2500. The inhabitants are of Spanish–Indian origin, are extremely impoverished, isolated, and socially deprived. Their diet is monotonous, largely vegetable in origin, and marginal in calories and protein. At the time of the beginning of the study, goiter was extremely prevalent, deaf-mutism was commonplace, and many people could be found who conformed to the classic description of endemic cretinism. There were no significant differences be-

TABLE II

Certain Features of the Equadorian Iodized Oil Study Population (1966)[a]

	Tocachi	La Esperanza
Population	1100	2500
Altitude (meters above sea level)	2952	2883
Infant mortality (%)	43	29
Annual income per persons (U.S. dollars)	90	85
Iodine content of water, soil, and urine		
Iodine in water ($\mu g/g$)	1.00	0.85
Iodine in soil ($\mu g/$liter)	7.00	23.00
^{127}I urinary excretion (μg per 0.9 g creatinine)	10.4	17.7
General goiter (%)	69.7	52.8
Nodular goiter (%)	41.1	23.4
Diffuse goiter (%)	28.6	29.3
Endemic cretinism (%) (mental deficiency and severe impairment in hearing and speech)	7.4	5.5
Endemic cretinism (%) (mental deficiency and severe impairment in hearing and speech and short stature and motor abnormalities)	0.8	0.5

[a] From ref. (23).

tween the two villages which are only a few km apart. Initially, all the villagers who were available in the smaller of the two towns were injected with iodized oil in a dose related to age. All from the very young to the very old were injected. The neighboring village of La Esperanza served as a control. Administration of the oil was carried out by technical persons working in teams under medical supervision. Later many of the residents of La Esperanza also received iodized oil as part of an expanded study program. The injections were readily accepted by the villagers. There were virtually no refusals. This perhaps is a testament to the carefully nurtured good relationships between the villagers and the medical teams.

The results of the program have been measured in terms of the changing prevalence of goiter, the characteristics of goiter, the physical and osseous development of children, the appearance of retardates in the population, and neural and intellectual development. No local or constitutional reactions have been encountered. Three subjects out of the initial group developed overt thyrotoxicosis. These were older women with large nodular goiters. The thyrotoxicosis was readily controlled by routine medical measures.

There was little change in either the incidence or size of goiter in subjects who were over the age of 40, but in younger persons there was a substantial and gratifying reduction in goiter size, and frequently in children, the goiter had disappeared (Table III). Goiters hardly ever appeared in children whose mothers had received iodized oil. In some instances there was an apparant slight increase in the nodularity of goiter, but this was probably due to shrinkage of a hyperplastic glandular mass which had masked the nodules at earlier examinations.

TABLE III

Evaluation of Goiter in a Population of Patients Each of Whom Was Given Iodized Oil Prophylactically[a]

Time (months)	Nodular goiter (%)			Diffuse goiter (%)			Total (%)
	Male	Female	Total	Male	Female	Total	
Control	33.9	50.3	41.1	29.4	27.9	28.6	69.7
6	41.2	59.8	51.6	4.6	9.4	7.3	58.9
20	25.4	36.7	31.0	6.4	13.9	10.3	41.4
25	31.9	43.6	38.2	3.9	9.9	7.1	45.3

[a] From Fierro-Benitez *et al.* (23).

There was no evidence of an effect on linear growth or maturation of bones. On the other hand, administration of iodized oil appeared to have some effect on IQ scores if given before age 8. Intelligence quotients were assessed by standard methods which were modified for the local context. It appeared that children born of mothers who had been injected developed their motor functions earlier than those whose mothers had not been injected. Although there was evidence for an improvement for IQ scores for children of injected mothers, these did not reach the levels of children in a nearby urban center.

Correction of iodine deficiency prior to conception appeared to result in some improvement in language development and in the aquisition of word recognition. Correction of iodine deficiency prior to conception appeared to have beneficial effects in preventing speech disorders. Although the numbers were small, there appeared to be fewer deaf-mutes born in the injected population.

It is apparent that correction of iodine deficiency did not solve all the developmental problems of the children in these villages. In searching for collateral factors, observations are now in progress on the effects of dietary supplementation with lysine and tryptophan. These essential amino acids are deficient in maize, the principle dietary staple.

Preliminary and partial results are now available on 217 children in the program. The mothers of some of these received tablets of lysine– tryptophan in amounts calculated to satisfy their minimal daily requirements. A companion group serving as a control received tablets containing equicalorie amounts of glycine. A third group received no amino acid supplement. It appears that lysine–tryptophan conveyed no significant benefit in perinatal mortality or postnatal development. If these impressions are borne out by further analysis, it will be necessary to look further for contributing factors. The possibility that choline may be involved is being explored. The choline content of maize is low. Also, the methionine content of the diet is probably low, since dietary surveys have indicated a marginal or submarginal protein intake. Methionine furnishes the methyl groups for the intrinsic synthesis of choline. Thus, choline may be in short supply for the fetuses and newborn in this region, and choline is an essential substance for the growing nervous system.

The following conclusions seem to be warranted from the Ecuadorian program.

1. The administration of iodized oil by injection to large and remote population groups is an effective way of distributing iodine to a population at risk for endemic goiter and its attendant disabilities. Large popu-

lation groups can be quickly covered by small teams of trained technicians working under the guidance of medical personnel.

2. The technique is relatively inexpensive by comparison with the benefits achieved, and the rate of side effects and their severity are acceptable.

3. Iodized oil is effective as a preventive measure for endemic goiter, endemic cretinism, and endemic deaf-mutism.

4. At least in the Ecuadorian setting, administration of iodized oil has little beneficial effect on stature, but may have some effect on intellectual and neural development. Nevertheless, it is incompletely effective for full restoration of intellectual growth. It is possible that other dietary items such as protein or specific amino acids or important lipids such as choline esters are necessary in addition to iodine.

COMPONENTS OF A SUCCESSFUL INTERVENTION PROGRAM FOR ENDEMIC GOITER

In order that a program of intervention for endemic goiter be successful, it is necessary that the dimensions of the problems be established. This implies a survey of the whole population or of a statistically valid sample for the prevalence of goiter, disagregated according to size and nodularity. It is desirable also that cretins, deaf-mutes, and other retardates be tabulated. The techniques of examination and the criteria for categorization are well established. It is highly advantageous if the survey includes quantitative estimates of iodine metabolism in the population. This can be done by measurement of iodine excretion in 24 hr urine collections, or more readily by simply measuring the iodine-to-creatinine ratios in statistically valid samples of morning urine collections.

In addition to establishing the prevalence of the disease and complications, it is important that continuing surveillance guide the program in order to ensure effectiveness. If goiter does not promptly diminish then flaws must be sought in the program.

In order to be successful a goiter intervention program must be simple, easily administered, reach the bulk of the population, be inexpensive, and be free of a significant number of side effects. It is probably impossible to institute any program of goiter prophylaxis without encountering an occasional patient with Jod Basedow. This must be expected and looked for in order that patients may be promptly identified and treated. The program must be consistent with local economic factors and accepted by the population. An iodized salt program will not work until the economy supports wide distribution of commercial salt. An

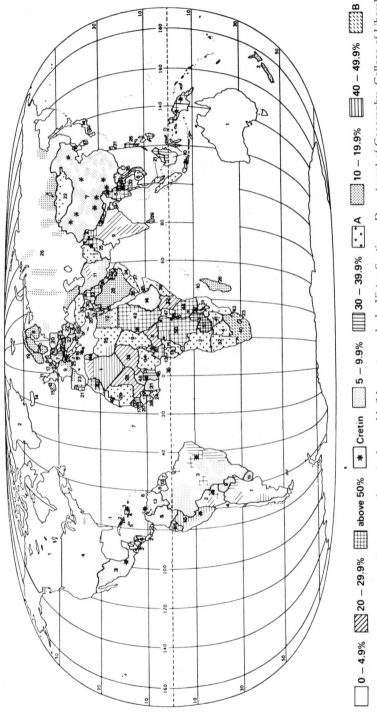

Fig. 1. Geographic map of goiter prevalence in the world. (Map cartography by Victor Santiago, Department of Geography, College of Liberal Arts, University of Michigan.)

0 – 4.9% 20 – 29.9% above 50% ★ Cretin 5 – 9.9% 30 – 39.9% A 10 – 19.9% 40 – 49.9% B

iodized oil program will not work if the population is not prepared to accept a program of intramuscular injections. An iodized bread program cannot be successful in a community where a population of subsistence farmers prepares its own grain and bakes its own bread.

Successful programs will usually have governmental support. Governments or ministries of health must pressure salt manufacturers to iodinate their salt. Often governmental subsidies are required. It is essential also that some responsible government agency monitor the iodization of salt in order to ensure that the iodine reaches the consumer. For a regional iodized oil programs, it is essential that local health authorities participate in the planning and execution of the program or at the very least that they give it their full support.

The ingredients of successful intervention programs for the prevention of endemic goiter thus are readily attainable and intervention programs are demonstrably successful in preventing a widespread disease which has implications far beyond the appearance of a swelling in the neck. The continued existance of endemic goiter is an international disgrace. We are long past the time when this disease should have been eliminated.

GEOGRAPHIC MAP OF GOITER PREVALENCE IN THE WORLD COMPILED IN 1981 (FIG. 1)

In this figure the states are grouped geographically and labeled numerically in alphabetical order. The legend indicates goiter prevalence in percentage of population.

Key to Symbols

A = Endemic goiter area, prevalence not known. B = Goiter prevalence probably below 10%, or probably reduced below 10% by prophylaxis. (*) = Endemic cretinism present. c = Goiter prevalence established mostly or only by surveys in children.

Sources

Publications on goiter prevalence with references on goiter surveys and studies.

1. Kelly, F. C., and Snedden, W. W. "Prevalence and Geographical Distribution of Endemic Goitre." World Health Organization Monograph No. 44, pp. 27–233. Geneva, 1960.

2. De Maeyer, E. M., Lowenstein, F. W., and Thilly C. H. "The Control of Endemic Goitre." World Health Organ., Geneva, 1979.
3. J. B. Stanbury and B. S. Hetzel, (eds.) "Endemic Goiter and Endemic Cretinism. I: The Present Status of Endemic Goiter As A Problem of the Public Health. pp. 1–153. John Wiley and Sons, Inc. New York, 1980.
4. Ma Tai, Lu Ti-Zhang, Tan Yu-Bin, and Chen Bing-Zhong Zhu Xian-Yi (H. I. Chu) "The Present Status of Endemic Goiter and Endemic Cretinism in China," Tian-Jin Medical College, Institute of Clinical Endocrinology, Tian-Jin, China, to be published.

Sources are identified by four numbers in parenthesis after each state, with letter "c" added as explained above. Zero indicates that a source was not available.

The Americas
North America: Canada (3), Greenland (1), Mexico (3), United States of America (3).
Central America: Belize (0), Costa Rica (3), El Salvador (2), Guatemala (3), Honduras (3), Nicaragua (2), Panama (3).
West Indies: Bahamas (0), Cuba (3c), Dominican Republic (2), Haiti (2) Jamaica, Trinidad and Tobago (2).
South America: Argentiana (3c), Bolivia (3), Brazil (3c), Chile (3), Colombia (2, 3), Ecuador (3), French Guiana (1), Guiana (1), Paraguay (2), Peru (3), Uruguay (2), Surinam (0), Venezuela (3c).

Europe
Albania (1), Austria (3c), Belgium (3), Bulgaria (3), Czechoslovakia (2,3), Denmark (3), Federal Republic of Germany (3), Finland (1,3), France (1,3), German Democratic Republic (3), Great Britain (1,3c), Greece (3), Hungary (3), Iceland (3), Ireland (3), Italy (3), Luxembourg (3), Netherlands (3), Norway (1,3), Poland (3), Portugal (1), Romania (3), Spain (3c), Sweden (1,3), Switzerland (1,3), USSR (1,3c), Yugoslavia (1,3c).(1,3c).

Africa
Algeria (3), Angola (1), Benin (0), Botswana (1), Burundi (0), Cameron (3), Cape Verde (0), Central African Empire (2), Chad (1), Comoros (0), Congo (1), Egypt (3), Equatorial Guinea (0), Ethiopia (2), French Territory of Afroes & Issa (1), Gabon (0), Gambia (0), Ghana (2), Guinea (1), Guinea-Bissay (1), Ivory Coast (3), Kenya (2), Lesotho (0), Liberia (1), Libya (2), Madagascar (1), Malawi (1), Mali (2), Mauritania (1), Morocco (3), Mozambique (1), Nambia (1), Niger (2), Nigeria (2), Ruanda (0), Sao

Tome and Principe (0), Senegal (2), Sierra Leone (1), Somalia (1), South Africa (2), Southern Rhodesia (2), Sudan (2), Swaziland (1), Tanzania (2), Togo (0), Tunisia (2), Uganda (1), Upper Volta (0), Western Sahara (0), Zaire (2), Zambia (2).

Asia

Afganistan (1,2,3), Bahrain (0), Bangladesh (2), Bhutan (0), Burma (3), Cambodia (3), China (1,3,4), Cyprus (3), India (3), Indonesia (2,3), Iran (1,2), Iraq (1,3), Israel (1,3), Japan (1,2), Jordan (2,3), Korea (North) (2), Korea (South) (1), Kuwait (3), Laos (3), Lebanon (3), Malaya (1), Mongolia (1), Nepal (3), Oman (3), Pakistan (3), Philippines (2), Qatar (3), Saudi Arabia (3), Sri Lanka (3), Syria (3), Taiwan (3), Thailand (2), Turkey (1,3), United Arab Emirates (3), Vietnam (3), Yemen (3), Yemen, Peoples Democratic Republic of (3).

Oceania
Australia (3), New Zealand (3).

REFERENCES

1. Marine, D., and Kimball, O. P. The prevention of simple goiter in man. *JAMA, J. Am. Med. Assoc.* **77,** 1068 (1921).
2. Trowbridge, F. L., Hand, K. A., and Nicaman, M. Z. Findings related to goiter and iodine in the Ten States Nutrition Survey. *Am. J. Clin. Nutr.* **28,** 712 (1975).
3. DeLeon, R., and Retana, O. G. Eradication of endemic goiter as a public health problem in Guatemala. *Sci. Publ.—Pan Am. Health Organ.* **292,** 227 (1974).
4. Hetzel, B. S. The epidemiology, pathogenesis, and control of endemic goitre and cretinism in New Guinea. *N. Z. Med. J.* **80,** 482 (1974).
5. Suwanik, R., Nondasuta, A., and Nondasuta, A. Endemic goitre in Thailand. *J. Med. Assoc. Thailand* **60,** 79 (1977).
6. Ma Tai, personal communication (unpublished).
7. Thilly, C. H., Delange, F., Ramioul, L., Lagasse, R., Luvivila, K., and Ermans, A. M. Strategy of goitre and cretinism control in Central Africa. *Int. J. Epidemiol.* **6,** 43 (1977).
8. Gaitan, E. Goitrogens in the etiology of endemic goiter. *In* "Endemic Goiter and Endemic Cretinism" (J. B. Stanbury and B. S. Hetzel, eds.), p. 219. Wiley, New York, 1980.
9. Ermans, A. M., Mbulamoko, N. M., and Delange, F. "Role of Cassava in the Etiology of Endemic Goitre and Cretinism." Int. Dev. Res. Cent. (no date).
10. Peltola, P. The role of l-5-vinyl-2-thio-oxazolidone in the genesis of endemic goiter in Finland. *In* "Current Topics in Thyroid Research" (C. Cassano and M. Andreoli, eds.), pp. 872–876. Academic Press, New York, 1965.
11. Boussingault, J. B. Recherches sur la cause qui produit le goitre dans les Cordillieres de la Nouvelle-Grenade. *Ann. Chim. Phys.* **48,** 41 (no year).

12. DeMaeyer, E. M., Lowenstein, F. W., and Thilly, C. H. "The Control of Endemic Goiter." World Health Organ., Geneva, 1979.

13. Leon, J. R., and Retana, O. G. Eradication of Endemic goiter as a public health problem in Guatemala. *In* "Endemic Goiter and Cretinism: Continuing Threats to World Health" (J. T. Dunn and G. A. Medeiros-Neto, eds.), Publ. No. 292, p. 227. World Health Organ., Geneva, 1974.

14. Pretell, E. A. The optimal program for prophylaxis of endemic goiter with iodized oil. *Adv. Exp. Med. Biol.* **30**, 267 (1972).

15. Hennessy, W. B. Goitre prophylaxis in new Guinea with intramuscular injections of iodized oil. *Med. J. Austr.* **1**, 505 (1964).

16. Perinetti, H., Staneloni, L. N., Nacif-Nora, J., Sanchez-Tejeda, J., and Perinetti, H. A. Results of salt iodization in Mendoza, Argentina. *In* "Endemic Goiter and Cretinism: Continuing Threats to World Health" (J. T. Dunn and G. A. Medeiros-Neto, ed.), Publ. No. 292, p. 217. World Health Organ., Geneva, 1974.

17. Delange, F., Thilly, C., Pourbaix, P., and Ermans, A. M.: Treatment of Idjwi Island endemic goiter by iodized oil. *In* "Endemic Goiter" (J. B. Stanbury, eds.), Publ. No. 193, p. 118. World Health Organ., Geneva, 1969.

18. Watanabe, T., Moran, D., Tamer, E. E., Staneloni, L., Salvaneschi, J., Altschuler, N., Degrossi, O., and Niepominiszcze, H. "Iodized oil in the prophylaxis of endemic goiter in Argentina." *In* "Endemic Goiter and Cretinism: Continuing Threats to World Health" (J. T. Dunn and G. A. Medeiros-Neto eds.), Publ. No. 292, p. 231. World Health Organ., Geneva, 1974.

19. Gaitan, E., Wahner, H. W., Correa, P., Bernal, R., Jubiz, W., Gaitan, J. E., and Llanos, G. Endemic goiter in the Cauca Valley. 1. Results and limitations of twelve years of iodine prophylaxis. *J. Clin. Endocrinol. Metab.* **28**, 1730 (1968).

20. Vidor, G. I., Stewart, J. C., Wall, J. R., Wangel, A., and Hetzel, B. S. Pathogenesis of iodine-induced thyrotoxicosis: Studies in northern Tasmania. *J. Clin. Endocrinol. Metab.* **37**, 901 (1973).

21. Stanbury, J. B., Brownell, G. L., Riggs, D. S., Perinetti, H., Itorz, J., and Del Castillo, E. B. "Endemic Goiter." Harvard Univ. Press, Cambridge, Massachusetts, 1954.

22. Connolly, R. J., Vidor, G. I., and Stewart, J. C. An increase in thyrotoxicosis in an endemic goitre area after iodization of bread. *Lancet* **1**, 500 (1970).

23. Fierro-Benitez, R., Ramirez, I., Estrella, E., Jaramillo, C., Diaz, C., and Urresta, J. Iodized oil in the prevention of endemic goiter and associated defects in the Andean region of Ecuador. 1. Program design, effects on goiter prevalence, thyroid function, and iodine excretion. *In* "Endemic Goiter" (J. B. Stanbury, ed), Publ. No. 193, p. 306. World Health Organ. Geneva, 1969.

24. Pretell, E. A., Moncloa, F.- Salinas, R., Guerra-Garcia, R., Kawano, A., Gutierrez, L., Pretell, J., and Wan, M. Endemic goiter in rural Peru: Effect of iodized oil on prevelence and size of goiter and on thyroid iodine metabolism in known endemic goitrous populations. *In* "Endemic Goiter" (J. B. Stanbury, ed.), Publ. No. 193, p. 419. World Health Organ., Geneva, 1969.

25. Watanabe, D. T., DeGrossi, O. J., Santillan, C., Tamer, E. E., Sotorres, A., Altschuler, N., and Forcher, H. Profilaxis del bocio endemico utilizando aceite yodado. *Rev. Argent. Endocrinol. Metab.* **17**, 83 (1971).

26. Hetzel, B. S., Thilly, C. H., Fierro-Benitez, R., Pretell, E., Buttfield, I., and Stanbury, J. B. Iodized oil in the prevention of endemic goiter and cretinism. *In* "Endemic Goiter and Endemic Cretinism" (J. B. Stanbury and B. S. Hetzel, eds.), p. 513. Wiley, New York, 1980.

27. Stacpoole, H. H. Prophylaxis of endemic goitre in Mexico. *Bull. W. H. O.* **9**, 283 (1953).

28. McCullagh, S. F. The Huon Peninsula Endemic. I. The effectiveness of an intramuscular depot of iodized oil in the control of endemic goitre. *Med. J. Aust.* **1**, 769 (1963).

29. Buttfield, I. H., and Hetzel, B. S. Endemic goiter in New Guinea and the prophylactic program with iodinated poppyseed oil. *In* "Endemic Goiter" (J. B. Stanbury, ed.), Publ. No. 193, p. 132. World Health Organ., Geneva, 1969.

30. Connolly, K. J., Pharoah, P. O. D., and Hetzel, B. Fetal iodine deficiency and motor performance during childhood. *Lancet* **2**, 1149 (1979).

31. Ramirez, I., Fierro-Benitez, R., Estrella, E., Gomez, A., Jaramillo, C., Hermida, C., and Moncayo, F. The results of prophylaxis of endemic cretinism with iodized oil in rural Andean Ecuador. *Adv. Exp. Med. Biol.* **30**, 223 (1972).

32. Delange, F. Endemic goitre and thyroid function Central Africa. *Monogr. Paediatr.* **2** (1974).

33. Correa, H. A cost-benefit study of iodine supplementation programs for the prevention of endemic goiter and cretinism. *In* "Endemic Goiter and Endemic Cretinism" (J. B. Stanbury and B. S. Hetzel, eds.), p. 567. Wiley, New York, 1980.

29 The Use of Food Fortification to Prevent Folate Deficiency

NEVILLE COLMAN

The poor nutritional status of certain populations in South Africa has spurred attempts to initiate nutrient specific intervention. The clinical manifestation of one such deficiency, namely that of folate, was the frequent presentation of megaloblastic anemia among pregnant and lactating Black women from rural areas of South Africa. This finding led us to conduct a number of studies on the possibility of fortifying food with folic acid (1–8). The population group subject to frequent megaloblastic anemia is characterized by many factors implicated in the development of folate deficiency, and common to many developing countries, such as poor socioeconomic conditions (9), adverse diets (10), high parity (11), and prolonged breast feeding (12). Prior to our studies, it had been demonstrated that many had subclinical folate deficiency, as judged by folate clearance studies (13), an observation that was confirmed using other techniques during our food fortification study.

The frequency of megaloblastic anemia among the Black pregnant and lactating women in South Africa occurred despite the fact that orally administered folic acid tablets are extremely effective in preventing this condition and that concerted efforts were made to deliver this prophylactic treatment to women at risk. This failure of an effective prophylactic program is consistent with both a lack of adequate antenatal facilities in the areas concerned and with inadequate utilization of facilities where these do occur. We noted in our *first* report that a prior survey of pregnant women in New York City indicated that almost one-half received no effective antenatal care (14). A further likely contributing factor to this high incidence is the reluctance of pregnant women to take

NUTRITION INTERVENTION STRATEGIES IN NATIONAL DEVELOPMENT
Copyright © 1983 by Academic Press, Inc.
ISBN 012-709080-0

tablets, a factor common in studies of iron prophylaxis in pregnancy (15). Iron itself may be responsible for some of these problems because it discolors the stool and can cause gastrointestinal symptoms. This effect is probably also important with the use of iron–folate combinations, which account for almost all prophylactic hematinics given in pregnancy. The combination of these and perhaps other factors led Metz to comment on the "insurmountable difficulties" of such prophylaxis, in which "many of the patients failed to take the tablets issued to them; many first attend antenatal clinics late in pregnancy, so that supplementation begins only in the last trimester . . . folic acid supplementation during pregnancy failed appreciably to reduce the incidence of anemia at term" (16).

Much of the inspiration and guidelines for our studies came from a WHO publication detailing principles of food fortification and summarizing the recommendations of the Joint FAO/WHO Expert Committee on Nutrition (17), which was published at the time we were attempting to solve these problems. These guidelines recommended that, when it was impossible to change the dietary habits of malnourished populations rapidly, anthorities should "improve the quality of the food supply immediately, without necessarily changing food habits, by adding nutrients directly to the food." At that time, although it was known that cooking destroyed natural folate (18), its effect on synthetic folic acid had not yet been reported.

The sequence of studies embarked upon was based upon the FAO/WHO recommendations. These consisted of selecting a site by initiation of a small pilot survey of pregnant women in rural hospitals, progression to a preliminary trial of food fortified with folic acid, subsequent systematic evaluation of the properties of folic acid relevant to food fortification, the characterization of the area's population to identify target groups for folate deficiency, trials of food with different levels of folic acid fortification in pregnant women, demonstration that folic acid-fortified food was effective in the treatment (and thus the prevention) of megaloblastic anemia, a home-based trial of folate-fortified maize, and finally, a cost analysis of food fortification.

PILOT SURVEY OF FOLATE DEFICIENCY (8)

Certain rural South African hospitals lend themselves particularly well to the type of intervention study that we had proposed, because they are not only located in an area where folate deficiency was common, but also are compelled to admit healthy pregnant women to their lodging facilities after the 36th week of gestation to avoid the risk of travelling long hours once labor commenced. A pilot survey conducted among pregnant women revealed that, at the Charles Johnson Memorial Hospital in Nqutu, 40% of apparently healthy pregnant women had clinical evidence of folate deficiency as manifested by low serum and erythrocyte folate concentrations, hypersegmented polymorphs in the peripheral blood, and peripheral erythrocyte changes suggestive of megaloblastic hemopoiesis. Based upon this survey, it was considered valid to proceed to a controlled clinical trial of folate-fortified maize meal in pregnant women.

PRELIMINARY TRIAL OF FOLATE FORTIFIED MAIZE MEAL (1)

The preliminary trial included all pregnant women admitted to the lodging facilities at the hospital during a 3-week period in midwinter who were judged to be less than 37 weeks pregnant, had no known medical illnesses or complications of pregnancy, had not received folate or antibiotics, and had hemoglobin concentrations of at least 11 g/dl as measured at the hospital using a field visual hemoglobinometer. As dictated by hospital policy at the time, the patients all received iron supplementation from the date of their first antenatal visit, and they were assigned to test and control groups on a random-number basis.

The vehicle for the folate supplement was maize meal, the staple food of most South African Blacks. Patients randomized into the test group received a daily helping of 30 g (dry weight) of maize meal, containing 1 g of crystalline folic acid (33 ppm) mixed in a homogenous fashion with a pharmaceutical Y blender. Each helping was cooked for 30 minutes in boiling water on a gas stove to provide at least as vigorous heat exposure as occurred in the home environment, and was then served as a soft porridge with milk and sugar.

Evaluation of results was based on a total of 268 blood samples collected from 18 control and 20 supplemented patients before the supplement was given and weekly until delivery, each sample being taken at 11 A.M. with meals arranged so that there was a period of 28 hours between the last dose of supplemented food and venipuncture.

The baseline data on these patients confirmed the preliminary survey in that, although only patients with hemoglobin below 11 g/dl were excluded from the study, presumably excluding those with folate deficiency anemia, 37% of the remaining patients had red cell folates in the deficient range. Red cell and serum folate levels were statistically similar in the control and supplemented groups at the time of admission to the study, but there was a highly significant difference at the time of delivery ($p < .001$). In general, serum folate levels fell to the deficient range in unsupplemented patients and rose to the normal level in the other group after 2 weeks of supplementation. Erythrocyte folate levels fell to the deficient range in a further 22% of unsupplemented patients and rose to the normal range in all but 5% of patients receiving at least 2 weeks of supplementation. The results showed that food fortification could be used to correct folate deficiency, in that women receiving supplemented maize showed a marked and statistically significant rise in serum and red cell folates, whereas control group erythrocyte folates fell at an average rate of 7.5 ng/ml per week. Linear regression analysis of the rise in patients receiving supplements suggested an initial lag period of 4 days, which was interpreted as reflecting the time taken for newly formed erythroid cells to be released from the marrow.

Although the FAO/WHO Expert Committee on Nutrition stressed the value of a fortification vehicle selectively consumed by the target group, it was clear to us that the obstacles to finding such a vehicle would prove insurmountable. Hence, it was necessary to consider the effects of fortifying foods to be consumed by the entire population. This prospect was not unattractive because, as previously mentioned, nonpregnant women in similar populations had been reported as having subclinical folate deficiency (13), and there was evidence that the vitamin had a definitive role to play in the prevention and treatment of kwashiorkor (19), a disease common in Black South African children.

The study then progressed to evaluation of the properties of folic acid that were relevant to food fortification.

PROPERTIES OF FOLIC ACID RELEVANT TO FOOD FORTIFICATION (2,8)

Primary factors considered important by the Joint FAO/Who Expert Committee on Nutrition were the effects of the micronutrient on the color, odor, flavor or cooking properties of the meal. These subjective effects were not identified as problems by either the investigators or the subjects of the study. The stability of the vitamin activity in the maize was tested by preparing three concentrations of folate-fortified maize and assaying their folate content after 6–18 months of storage under conditions conventionally used by commercial marketers. There was no significant alteration in the folate content of the maize over these periods of time, indicating that the folate activity was stable for periods much longer than those encountered in conventional distributions.

In view of the heat lability of various forms of food folate (20) and the possibility that synthetic folic acid added to food might be destroyed during the process of preparation, a number of experiments were carried out to assess the effect of conventional cooking and baking practices on the stability of folic acid used in the studies. To test potential degradation by boiling foods containing folic acid, 20 ml aqueous solutions of folic acid in five concentrations up to 1 ng/ml were assayed for folate after being immersed in boiling water for seven different time periods between 10 minutes and 2 hours. When expressed as a percentage of the unheated control solutions, the calculated recovery for all concentrations at each cooking time ranged from 96 to 103%, consistent with the known variations of the microbiologic assay ($\pm$ 5%). There was no correlation between the period of boiling and recovery of folic acid ($p > .1$), and the mean recovery at each time during the experiment was not significantly different from the control. When similar bottles containing the solutions were baked in an electric oven at 230°C (the temperature used for baking bread), there was a significant reduction in the recovery of folic acid at all time periods after 1 hour. It should be noted, however, that bread baked at this temperature begins to blacken at 45 minutes and is certainly burnt by 90 minutes, the time at which the first significant fall in folate concentration was noted.

The effect of different foods on availability of folic acid used for fortification was studied by sequential absorption tests carried out on seven healthy volunteers who ate similar amounts of folate-fortified foods in a randomized sequence after prior saturation with 15 mg folic acid daily for 3 days. The test materials used for these comparative absorption studies were water, maize meal porridge, rice, and bread. Each food was boiled or baked after the addition of 1 mg folic acid per helping, with care being taken to achieve adequate homogenization to ensure an even distribution. Beginning 36 hours after the last saturating dose of folic acid, and after a 12-hour fast, subjects were given one of the four test materials on each of 4 consecutive days. With each test, the baseline folate level of serum taken before administration of the food was subtracted from that in the specimens taken at 1 and 2 hours, and the sum of the remaining values was used for comparison between the absorption of folic acid and each of the folic acid-fortified foods. This modification of the conventional folate absorption test (21) was used to minimize the possible distortion of events caused by the effect of the food vehicle on gastrointestinal motility and the rate of absorption of folic acid in the duodenum and jejunum.

The results (Fig. 1) indicated that despite the fact that the summated increase in serum folate concentration after administration of folic acid

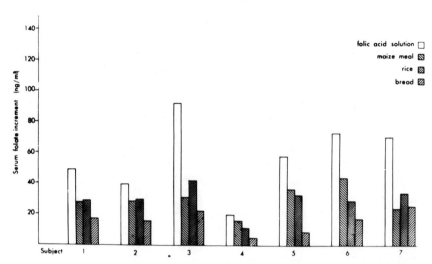

Fig. 1. The absorption of folic acid from fortified staple foods (S. *faecalis* assay). Sum of rise in serum folate 1 and 2 hours after ingesting 1 mg folic acid alone or cooked with food.

solution varied widely in the different subjects, ranging from 37 to 146 ng/ml, the mean percentage of absorption after each of the staple foods was fairly consistent, averaging 52.7% for fortified maize, 57.6% for fortified rice, and 38.3% for fortified bread, based on a control value of 100% for the summated increase after folic acid solution in the same subject.

In summary, this phase of the study indicated that folic acid in fortified maize was stable in storage under conventional conditions for periods much longer than those experienced in commercial use, that it was stable to boiling and baking for periods used in conventional cooking, and that it did not effect the color, odor, flavor, or cooking properties of the maize meal. Absorption studies indicated that the amount of folate available from fortified foods would be sufficient to allow these foods to be used as vehicles in food fortification programs. To ensure that nutritional requirements are met in most members of the population, it would be necessary to take into account not only the mean percentage absorption but those at the lower limits of the range of absorption. The lower limits of absorption observed in our study suggested that folate requirements in some subjects would only be met if the folic acid added to fortified maize and rice was 3 times the required dose and that added to bread it was 5 to 7 times the required dose.

To examine a specific potential hazard of folic acid in fortified foods, we assayed the sera in these absorption studies using not only L. *casei* but also *S. faecalis.* The results using the former organism always exceeded those using the latter, probably excluding the risk of significant absorption of pteroic acid, a degradation product of folic acid that has no biologic value for man or *L. casei* but that does stimulate the growth of *S. faecalis* (22). As indicated below, the results of these absorption studies were subsequently supported by other studies in which the availability of folic acid in fortified maize and bread compared with folic acid taken alone was measured by calculating incorporation of the vitamin into erythrocyte folate.

We noted that prior knowledge of the highly labile nature of food folate might have discouraged investigation into the fortification of food with this vitamin. Our study indicated that the fortification of staple food, namely maize meal porridge, rice, and bread, with folic acid was feasible and that any of the three foods investigated would be a suitable vehicle for a folate supplementation program. Availability might be slightly better in foods that are usually boiled, such as maize and rice, rather than those that are baked, such as bread, because of the risk of destroying folic acid with baking.

We then conducted a further and more extensive clinical trial of folic acid-fortified maize meal.

EFFECTS OF DIFFERENT LEVELS OF FORTIFICATION IN PREGNANT WOMEN (3)

Since the preliminary study, described above, had indicated that large increases in blood folate content were rapidly apparent in subjects receiving 1000 μg added folic acid daily, the effect of two lower levels of fortification were studied. Therefore, 500 and 300 μg of folic acid were added daily, each administered in an identical fashion to the 1000 μg previously described. A final group of subjects received tablets containing 300 μg folic acid administered under supervision in a single daily dose. It should be noted that all subjects in the study received the same diet, including the breakfast helping of maize meal porridge, differing only in the presence and level of fortification.

The mean red cell folate of women entering the study was 201.2 ng/ml and was statistically similar for each of the five groups. The mean for each of the groups receiving folic acid supplements was significantly higher than the control group mean at the time of delivery ($p < .01$). Regression analysis of the weekly red cell folates in the different groups indicated that the rise in red cell folate with time was significant by comparison with the fall in the control groups and that the rate of rise in the group receiving 300 ug folic acid tablets was similar to that in the group receiving 500 ug folic acid in maize.

The regression lines for erythrocyte folate in each group are shown in Fig. 2. Statistical analysis of the regression lines for each supplemented group, compared with the baseline for the unsupplemented group, revealed a "corrected rate of rise" of 13.4 ng/ml per week when 300 ug were given daily in maize, 23.2 ng/ml per week when the same dose was given in tablets, and 21.5 and 28.6 ng/ml per week when 500 and 1000 µg, respectively, were given in maize daily. The rate of increase in the group receiving 300 µg in maize was 57.5% of that receiving the same dose in tablets. This observation based on rate of incorporation of folate into erythrocytes is in close agreement with our previous observation based on summated rise in serum folates.

Similar techniques used to calculate the efficacy of these forms of fortification in maize indicated that the 300 and 500 µg daily doses were utilized with similar efficiency, whereas the additional amount of folic acid present in 1000 µg doses was only utilized one-third as well. It was concluded that single doses of folic acid tablets in excess of 300 µg would be inefficiently utilized, since the 500 µg dose in maize was similar in effect to the 300 µg tablet and was at the upper limit of efficient utilization.

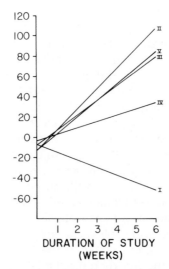

Fig. 2. Changes in erythrocyte folate (regression lines) in five groups of pregnant women receiving folic acid supplements in different forms. (I) no supplement, (II) 100 µg daily in maize, (III) 500 µg daily in maize, (IV) 300 µg daily in maize, (V) 300 µg daily as tablets. From Colman *et al.* (3) with the permission of the *Amer. J. Clin. Nutrition.*

In a subsequent supplemental study of the effect of folic acid fortified bread administered under similar conditions, the rate of rise in subjects receiving a daily dose of 900 μg folic acid in bread was similar to that in women receiving 300 μg folic acid tablets (7). This further observation on the availability of folic acid in fortified bread again confirmed the excellent predictive value of folic acid absorption tests based on summated serum folate levels as a measure of the availability of folate for incorporation into erythrocytes.

The efficacy of each regimen of folate supplementation was estimated separately from the rate of rise by grouping subjects according to whether erythrocyte and serum folate levels rose, fell, or remained unchanged. Based on this method of analysis, the highest doses of folate in maize and the folic acid tablets were no more effective than 300 μg folic acid in maize in preventing the progression of folate deficiency, as judged by the proportion of subjects whose levels rose, fell, or remained unchanged. In contrast, as expected, the unsupplemented group differed significantly from all other groups.

An unexpected observation in these studies was that, although there was no significant alteration in the mean hemoglobin concentration in subjects during this study, the number of subjects in whom hemoglobin levels rose, fell, or remained unchanged as analyzed by the chi-square test was significantly different in the unsupplemented group as compared with the supplemented groups ($p < .001$), indicating that the number of subjects in whom hemoglobin levels fell during the trial was statistically much greater in the unsupplemented group. This was particularly unexpected because the subjects selected had hemoglobin levels of 11 g/dl or greater and were studied for only a few weeks. The difference in hemoglobin levels suggests that hemopoiesis in these subjects was limited by folate deficiency and was considered additional evidence that the supplementation of food with folic acid in these populations should be regarded as a matter of priority.

A nutritional survey of the population was then conducted to determine the incidence of folate deficiency and potential target groups for future supplementation.

TARGET GROUPS FOR A FOLATE FORTIFICATION PROGRAM (4)

The population served by the hospital in which these studies were conducted was surveyed for evidence of folate deficiency. A particular interest of ours was the incidence of folate deficiency in apparently healthy nonpregnant adults because there had been no reported surveys of this incidence despite the numerous reports and reviews of folate deficiency in pregnancy, infancy, and malnourished children. The factors assessed in our survey were folate status, vitamin B_{12} status, family consumption of maize meal, income, and family size. The sample comprised 469 healthy Black adults, corresponding to 1 in 170 of the total population of the district enumerated, and therefore a greater proportion of the adult population.

There were three groups studied. The first was comprised of 144 women in the third trimester of pregnancy, including many subjects who had participated in the clinical trials. These comprised a selected group in that they only included individuals whose measured hemoglobin was greater than 11 g/dl and who had no complications of pregnancy or medical illnesses. Their mean age was 23.5 years (range 16–45 years), and they had had an average of 1.4 previous viable pregnancies (range 0–13). The remaining subjects were men and nonpregnant women aged at least 16 years who were approached at random in the areas surrounding the outlying clinics affiliated with the hospital and surrounding the hospital itself.

The sample also included 185 nonpregnant women who had not been pregnant or lactating within the prior 6 months, with an average of 44.1 years (range 16 to 79 years) and an average parity of 4.5. There were 140 men studied with an average age of 46.2 years (range 16 to 82 years). There was a very high incidence of folate deficiency in all the groups studied.

Two important facts emerged about the incidence of folate deficiency, and both are apparent in Fig. 3, which shows the frequency of low red cell folate in men and women of different ages. As perhaps expected, folate deficiency was extremely common in women of childbearing age, being observed in 45% of those 16 to 40 years of age, whereas it was present in only 14% of men under the age of 60. There was striking evidence that this difference was attributable to the effects of pregnancy and lactation, in that 51% of women who had been pregnant or lactating 6 to 24 months prior to study were folate deficient, whereas only 18% of nulliparous women and 26% of those pregnant or lactating more than 2 years prior to study were deficient.

The second observation was that both men and women over the age of 60 had a marked increase in the frequency incidence of folate deficiency compared with those 40 to 60 years old. There was no significant difference between the sexes and the combined incidence rose from 12.5% in the 40 to 60 year olds to 34% in those over 60. These results confirmed prior impressions (12) that the improvement in folate nutrition after pregnancy was short-lived in populations whose dietary folate

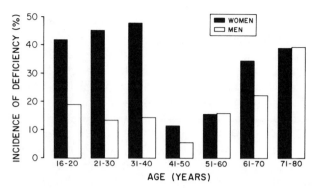

Fig. 3. The incidence of folate deficiency in rural South African Black adults grouped according to sex and age. Folate deficiency was defined as an erythrocyte folate below 160 ng/ml. From Colman *et al.* (4) with permission of the *Amer. J. Clin. Nutrition.*

intake was suboptimal, and they suggested that it took 2 to 3 years before folate stores in this population returned to normal after cessation of lactation. Thus, many women were entering pregnancy with depleted folate stores, a situation that could be prevented by food fortification.

Although this was the first population survey that reported widespread folate deficiency in adult males and females, there was unpublished data at that time suggesting that widespread folate deficiency may be common in the United States. This data was gathered during the Ten State Nutrition Survey (23) in the United States from 1968 to 1970 but was not made available in the report thereof which listed only quartile distributions and not the incidence of low values. However, the incidence of deficiency was assessed in the report of the Massachusetts section (24) of the Ten State Survey that was not published in the literature but to which we did subsequently gain access through the courtesy of the Massachusetts authorities. This report revealed that, in the low income districts surveyed, the incidence of folate deficiency as assessed by low red cell folate was 26% of all subjects, reaching a peak of 31% in women and 28.4% in men over the age of 60.

The maize consumption survey that we conducted revealed an average intake of 400 grams per adult per day, confirming a prior survey in another part of the country. We calculated that, in order to provide an effective dose of 200 μg folic acid in 400 μg maize meal, it would be necessary to add 350 μg folic acid to each 400 μg maize at the time of mixing. At this level of fortification, the adults in 90% of the families studied would have received an effective dose of 100–400 μg folic acid daily, with 5% receiving less than 100 μg daily and 3.6% receiving

400–500 μg daily. The families of 1.5% of the sample bought maize in quantities such that an effective dose of up to 800 μg folic acid would have been present in the daily adult allotment if all was used to make porridge which was eaten. None of the 431 subjects studied had serum vitamin B_{12} concentrations significantly below the lower limit of normal, although two fell in the range suggestive of deficiency (below the mean ± 2 SD but above the mean ± 3 SD lower limits). Neither of these subjects had additional evidence of vitamin B_{12} deficiency, consistent with prior reports in this population suggesting that vitamin B_{12} deficiency was rare. Thus, despite the potential hazards of giving folic acid to subjects with vitamin B_{12} deficiency, it was unlikely that any deleterious effect would result in this population, because the effective dose was less than 0.4 mg daily in 95% of the subjects studied, with this dose being the lowest at which reticulocyte responses in vitamin B_{12} deficiency have been reported (25). The survey illustrated that the dangers of folic acid fortification were infinitesimally small, since no subject with unequivocal vitamin B_{12} deficiency were observed, and very few would receive an effective dose of folic acid greater than 400 μg daily. It should be noted that the effective dose of 200 μg daily at which this program would be aimed, corresponding to an actual dose of 350 μg daily received in maize, was as effective as any other dose in preventing the progression of folate deficiency in our controlled clinical trials.

THE ANTIMEGALOBLASTIC EFFECT OF FOLATE-FORTIFIED FOODS (6)

Although the studies discussed above documented that folic acid-fortified maize meal causes a rise in serum and red cell folates of pregnant women as assessed by activity for *Lactobacillus casei*, this did not conclusively prove that the folate provided was biologically available to humans. For this reason, the efficacy of folate-fortified maize meal as a therapeutic agent in patients with megaloblastic anemia due to folate deficiency was evaluated. Five adult women with severe megaloblastic anemia of lactation were studied. After admission to hospital, the women continued to nurse their infants and were carefully observed for 4 to 8 days until the diagnosis of folate deficiency was established by appropriate laboratory investigations. This control period also ensured that the diet in this particular urban hospital did not induce a reticulocyte response, a finding which had been documented in several previous studies. Standard hematologic methods were used to assess the response to folic acid-fortified maize meal, and this response was interpreted on the basis of numerous prior studies of optimal reticulocyte responses.

The meal fed to one patient contained 100 μg folic acid daily, that fed to two contained 300 μg daily, and that fed to the final two patients contained 500 μg folic acid daily and was followed after 10 days by a course of 15 mg folic acid plus 240 mg iron in an attempt to elicit a secondary hematologic response. The course in one of the last named is shown in Fig. 4. The three criteria used to estimate optimal hematologic response were attainment of the reticulocyte peak between days 5 and 8 after therapy (26), the attainment of certain reticulocyte levels (27), and the rise in red cell count at a specified rate (28). All subjects demonstrated a reticulocyte response with elevation in hemoglobin, but the patient who received only 100 μg folic acid in maize meal daily had a suboptimal reticulocyte peak and suboptimal rate of rise in the red cell count. The remaining four subjects all had optimal responses, and no

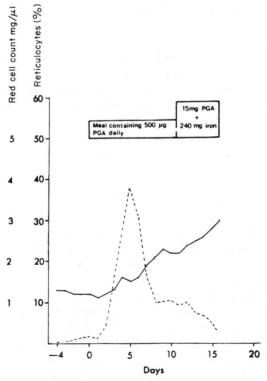

Fig. 4. Reticulocyte response (broken line) and rise in red cell count (solid line) in a patient with folate-deficient megaloblastic anemia after eating maize meal fortified with 500 μg folic acid per day. There was no secondary reticulocyte response to pharmacological doses (15 mg/day) of folic acid. From Colman *et al.* (6) with the permission of the *South African Med. J.*

secondary reticulocyte response to large doses of folic acid and iron were noted. This portion of the study indicated that cooking folic acid in the presence of maize meal did not alter its biological efficacy as an anti-megaloblastic agent in humans.

PILOT FIELD TRIAL OF FOLATE-FORTIFIED FOOD (5)

The hospital-based clinical trials discussed above were conducted using folic acid-fortified meal cooked at the hospital and administered under supervision. To prove conclusively the value of a food fortification program, it was considered necessary to demonstrate an improvement in nutritional status in populations that stored, cooked, and ate the fortified food in the home environment in accordance with their local customs. It was considered that this investigation would reveal whether any aspect of local custom that had been unaccounted for in the hospital-based trial might interfere with the efficacy of such a food fortification program.

In this investigation, the effect of the maize meal in the home environment was examined by giving folic acid-fortified meal to selected families for home use and by studying six index patients (5 healthy women in the 28th week of pregnancy and one lactating woman 8 weeks after parturition). The oldest member of each family was also studied to assess the effect of the fortified food on members of the age group in which the incidence of pernicious anemia was highest. The pregnant women were all given iron supplements from the start of the study and the lactating subject had received iron during pregnancy. Based upon the average consumption of maize in the population, which was partly corrected for age, the families were given enough fortified maize meal to last for 6 weeks. Five of the six families consumed this maize meal within 5 to 7 weeks, corresponding to an average adult intake of 500 μg folic acid as fortification per day, or 50% more than the ideal intake of 350 μg daily that we later calculated from responses to different levels of fortification. One family consumed only approximately 60% of the predicted amount, corresponding to about 300 μg folic acid per adult per day. The change in erythrocyte folate in each subject is shown in Fig. 5. Although hemoglobin and serum vitamin B_{12} remained essentially unchanged in all subjects throughout the study, red cell folates increased significantly through the course of the study in all of the index subjects (5 pregnant and 1 lactating) and 5 of the 6 older subjects. Red cell folates rose by 39 ng/ml per week in the pregnant subjects receiving fortified maize and at a greater rate in the lactating subject. In contrast, the rate of

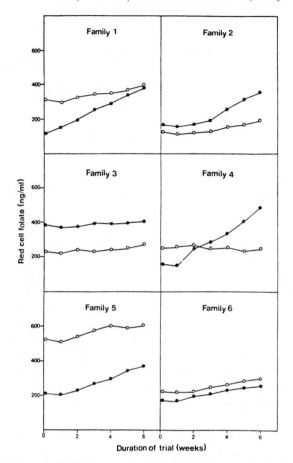

Fig. 5. Weekly red cell folate concentrations in families supplied with folic acid-fortified maize meal (closed circles, index subjects; open circles, oldest members of family). From Colman *et al.* (5) with permission of the *South African Med. J.*

rise in erythrocyte folate in the older subjects was significantly less than that in the younger subjects, an observation presumably attributable to decreased intake and/or decreased absorption of folate by the older subjects. This observation suggests that it may be valuable to study folate uptake in older subjects.

The results of this study were important for a further reason relevant to the possible harmful effects of fortification of food with folic acid. As previously indicated, the lowest dose of folic acid that had been reported to cause response in vitamin B_{12} deficiency was 400 μg daily, whereas the effective dose for prevention of folate deficiency in pregnancy was one-half that amount (200 μg daily). This study suggested that lactating women would be even better protected at this level of fortification and that older subjects, in whom almost all cases of vitamin B_{12} deficiency would have an even greater margin of safety because they either ate less of the fortified staple food or had less effective absorption of folic acid.

POSSIBLE HAZARDS OF FOOD FORTIFICATION WITH FOLATE (28, 29)

As indicated above, there is an extremely low probability that the very rare patient with pernicious anemia would be adversely affected by low level fortification of foods with folate. This is true because the consumption of staple foods in this population appear to fall within a relatively narrow margin, with less than 5% of subjects consuming amounts potentially in the danger zone and with the older subjects prone to pernicious anemia consuming relatively less than the average. There is no data in any study that would indicate that the low levels of folic acid delivered by these food fortification programs would in any way be connected with a possible neuroleptic effect of folate (28) or the suggested hazards of precipitating neuropathy in pernicious anemia (a suggestion that has little support in the literature, even when megadoses of folic acid are administered). Because the purpose of food fortification is to raise the dietary folate levels of large undernourished populations to the level enjoyed by more affluent groups and to levels approaching the Recommended Dietary Allowances (RDAs), there is no rational reason to withhold fortification in anticipation of potential hazardous effects of administering a normal dietary nutrient in the diet. Indeed, there is no evidence in any study that hazardous effects attributable to folic acid are specific to this, the parent compound, rather than shared among all folates that by definition share most structural and biological characteristics (29).

TECHNOLOGICAL AND ECONOMIC CONSIDERATIONS (8)

An important effect of any food fortification program must be the stage in processing of the vehicle food to which the nutrient can be added. In South Africa, the production, processing, and marketing of maize is controlled by law through the Maize Board, which reported that during the 1973 season, the commercial millers accounted for more than 98% of all maize milled in South Africa. Because there were 310 commercial millers registered in that year, the most effective means of fortification was considered to be a pre-mix. This achieved satisfactory results in a field trial of maize meal fortified with riboflavin and nicotinamide (31) in which 70 g of pre-mix were added to each 100 kg of maize. The annual cost of a food fortification program in 1971 would have averaged less than 1.5 U.S. cents per adult per year if added to a fortification program proposed for other vitamins that had been accepted in theory by the South African government. If fortification with folic acid alone were initiated, the additional cost of equipment and supplies would have increased the cost of the program to 2.5–3.5 cents per adult per year. It should be noted, however, that the direct costs of such a fortification program might well be partly offset by the economic benefits of improved health of a population that currently suffers from a very high incidence of folate deficiency. These economic benefits may include increased labor productivity, improved scholastic performance, and decreased demands on medical services (32). Added to this is, of course, the intangible benefit resulting from improved health of a population, a concept that must be viewed as the motivating force for all preventive medicine programs.

Although the studies described above were completed in 1973 and published by the end of 1975, they have assumed new relevance because nutritionists in various scientific and administrative roles have broached the issue of possible food fortification with folate in the United States. A publication addressing the need and feasibility aspects of this issue, as well as other matters related to folate deficiency, has recently been published as part of a contract with the Food and Drug Administration (33).

ACKNOWLEDGMENTS

Supported in part by the South African Medical Research Council, the South African Atomic Energy Board, the Medical Research Service of the Veterans Administration and by USPHS Grant #HD14837 from the National Institutes of Health.

REFERENCES

1. Colman, N., Barker, M., Green, R., and Metz, J. Prevention of folate deficiency in pregnancy by food fortification. Am. J. Clin. Nutr. 27, 339–344 (1974).
2. Colman, N., Green, R., and Metz, J. Prevention of folate deficiency by food fortification. II. Absorption of folic acid from fortified staple foods. Am. J. Clin. Nutr. 28, 459–464 (1975).

3. Colman, N., Larsen, J. V., Barker, M., Barker, E. A., Green, R., and Metz, J. Prevention of folate deficiency by food fortification. III. Effect in pregnant subjects of varying amounts of added folic acid. *Am. J. Clin. Nutr.* **28,** 465–470 (1975).
4. Colman, N., Barker, E. A., Barker, M., Green, R., and Metz, J. Prevention of folate deficiency by food fortification. IV. Identification of target groups in addition to pregnant women in an adult rural community. *Am. J. Clin. Nutr.* **28,** 471–476 (1975).
5. Colman, N., Larsen, J. V., Barker, M., Barker, E. A., Green, R., and Metz, J. Prevention of folate deficiency by food fortification. V. A pilot field trial of folic acid-fortified maize meal. *S. Afr. Med. J.* **48,** 1763–1767 (1974).
6. Colman, N., Green, R., Stevens, K., and Metz, J. Prevention of folate deficiency by food fortification. VI. The antimegaloblastic effect of folic acid fortified maize meal. *S. Afr. Med. J.* **48,** 1795–1799 (1974).
7. Margo, G., Barker, M., Fernandes-Costa, F., Colman, N., Green, R., and Metz, J. Prevention of folate deficiency by food fortification. VII. The use of bread as a vehicle for folate supplementation. *Am. J. Clin. Nutr.* **28,** 761–763 (1975).
8. Colman, N. The use of food fortification to prevent folate deficiency in poorly nourished populations. Ph.D. Thesis, University of the Witwatersrand, Johannesburg, 1974.
9. Kahn, S. B., Fein, S., Rigberg, S., and Brodsky, I. Correlation of folate metabolism and socioeconomic status in pregnancy and in patients taking oral contraceptives. *Am. J. Obstet. Gynecol.* **108,** 931 (1970).
10. Edelstein, T., Stevens, K., Brandt, V., Baumslag, N., and Metz, J. Tests of folate and vitamin B_{12} nutrition during pregnancy and the puerperium in a population subsisting on a suboptimal diet. *J. Obstet. Gynaecol. Br. Common.* **73,** 197 (1966).
11. Hibbard, B. M., & Hibbard, E. D. Anaemia and folate status in late pregnancy in a mixed Asiatic population. *J. Obstet. Gynaecol. Br. Common.* **79,** 584 (1972).
12. Metz, J. Folate deficiency conditioned by lactation. *Am. J. Clin. Nutr.* **23,** 843 (1970).
13. Metz, J., Stevens, K., Krawitz, S., and Brandt, V. The plasma clearance of injected doses of folic acid as an index of folate deficiency. *J. Clin. Pathol.* **14,** 622 (1961).
14. Schoeneck, F. J. Prenatal care in New York City. *N.Y. State Med. J.* **64,** 557 (1964).
15. Bonnar, J., Goldberg, A., and Smith, J. A. The efficacy of prophylactic iron supplements in pregnancy. *Lancet* **1,** 457 (1969).
16. Metz, J. "The Proceedings of a Symposium on Folic Acid." Glaxo Laboratories, Middlesex, U.K., 1966.
17. FAO/WHO Expert Committee on Nutrition. Food fortification. *W.H.O. Tech. Rep. Ser.* **477** (1971).
18. Herbert, V. Megaloblastic anemia as a problem in world health. *Am. J. Clin. Nutr.* **21,** 1115 (1968).
19. Kamel, K., Waslien, C. I., El-Ramly, Z., Guindy, S., Mourad, K. A., Khattab, A.-K., Hashem, N., Patwardhan, V. N., and Darby, W. J. Folate requirements of children. II. Response of children recovering from protein-calorie malnutrition to graded doses of parenterally administered folic acid. *Am. J. Clin. Nutr.* **25,** 152 (1972).
20. Herbert, V. A palatable diet for producing folate deficiency in man. *Am. J. Clin. Nutr.* **12,** 17 (1963).
21. Chanarin, I., Anderson, B. B., and Mollin, D. L. The absorption of folic acid. *Br. J. Haematol.* **4,** 156 (1958).
22. Herbert, V., and Bertino, J. Folic acid. *In* "The Vitamins: Chemistry, Physiology, Pathology, Methods" (P. Gyorgy and W. N. Pearson, eds.), 2nd ed., Vol. 7, p. 243. Academic Press, New York, 1967.

23. U.S. Dept. of Health Education and Welfare. Ten-State Nutrition Survey 1968–70. *DHEW Publ. No. (HSM)* **72-8132** (1972).
24. Edozien, J. C. National Nutrition Survey, Massachusetts. Report of the Survey Director to the Commissioner for Public Health, Commonwealth of Massachusetts, May 1972, cited by V. Herbert, N. Colman, M. Spivack *et al.*, Folic acid deficiency in the United States; folate assays in a prenatal clinic. *Am. J. Obstet. Gynecol.* **123,** 175 (1975).
25. Herbert, V. Current concepts in therapy: Megaloblastic anemia. *N. Engl. J. Med.* **268,** 201 (1963).
26. Chanarin, I. "The Megaloblastic Anemias." Blackwell, Oxford, 1969.
27. Sturgis, C. C., and Isaacs, R. Pernicious anemia. *Hand. Hematol.* **3,** 2231 (1938).
28. Bethell, F. H. Personal communication, cited by Sturgis and Isaacs (27).
29. Colman, N.: Folate deficiency in humans. *Adv. Nutr. Res.* **1,** 77–124 (1977).
30. Colman, N., and Herbert, V. Folate metabolism in brain. *In* "Biochemistry of Brain" (S. Kumar, ed.), pp. 103–124. Pergamon, Oxford, 1979.
31. Du Plessis, J. P., Wittman, W., Louw, M. E. J., Nel, A., van Twisk, P., and Laubscher, N. F. A field trial of fortification with riboflavin and nicotinamide. *S. Afr. Med. J.* **45,** 530 (1971).
32. Popkin, B., and Lidman, R. Economics as an aid to nutritional change *Am. J. Clin. Nutr.* **25,** 331 (1972).
33. Anderson, S., and Talbot, J. "A Review of Folate Intake, Methodology and Status; Folate Deficiency in the United States." FASEB Life Sci. Res. Off., Bethesda, Maryland, 1981.

30 Interventions for the Prevention of Vitamin A Deficiency: A Summary of Experiences

JOHN I. MCKIGNEY

Xerophthalmia is the term used to describe the clinical manifestations in the eye of vitamin A deficiency. Although the syndrome was known to be diet related from biblical times (1), only in the last 2 decades has it received growing attention as a problem of public health significance that is preventable. The lack of awareness of the true magnitude of the problem and it's cost to society was due to a variety of factors, including:

1. Affected children are mainly in families of low socioeconomic status, often living at great distance from health facilities.
2. The onset of eye lesions is insiduous in the susceptible age group.
3. The onset of xerophthalmia is frequently associated with protein–energy malnutrition and/or measles or diarrhea, thus often overlooked.
4. Health and nutrition staff have traditionally not received training in the diagnosis of eye disease.
5. High mortality rates among postxerophthalmic children have hidden the actual numbers of blind children and deaths due to vitamin A deficiency.

EVENTS LEADING TO COORDINATED INTERVENTION

A worldwide survey of xerophthalmia by the World Health Organization (WHO) in 1962–1963 documented the widespread geographic dis-

NUTRITION INTERVENTION STRATEGIES IN NATIONAL DEVELOPMENT

tribution and high mortality rate associated with the disease. The survey results suggested that xerophthalmia was the most important cause of blindness in young children, affecting an estimated 100,000 annually. Subsequently, more detailed prevalence surveys in several countries confirmed the seriousness of vitamin A deficiency as a major nutritional problem (2,3). WHO prepared a tentative list of 72 countries where vitamin A deficiency was suspected to be a problem of public health magnitude (4). It was proposed (5) that for prevention of xerophthalmia high level doses of vitamin A be administered as a prophylactic to women at delivery and infants at risk of deficiency. This proposal stimulated field testing in several countries (2) leading to acceptance of a standardized 200,000 IU oral dose for both prophylactic and therapeutic use. During this same period, use of synthetic vitamin A in the form of stable microencapsulated beadlets to fortify supplemental foods for international donation programs was initiated (6).

These concurrent developments led to extensive discussion of vitamin A deficiency at the 1974 World Food Conference, emanating in a recommendation that there be a concentrated and coordinated attack on this worldwide problem by affected countries and international donor agencies. Shortly thereafter, WHO and the United States Agency for International Development (USAID) jointly convened a meeting in Jakarta, at the invitation of the Government of Indonesia, for this purpose. In discussing priorities for research and action programs, the participants agreed on an international classification of xerophthalmia, criteria for diagnosis of xerophthalmia and vitamin A deficiency, treatment and prevention protocols, listing of intervention strategies, and research needs (2). This landmark meeting also led to the establishment of the International Vitamin A Consultative Group (IVACG), which provides a forum for exchange of experiences, consultation, guidance and coordination of activities by governments and donor agencies participating in the attack on nutritional blindness.

SELECTION OF INTERVENTION STRATEGIES

The following strategies have been identified as meriting consideration for vitamin A intervention programs:

1. High level dosing: intermittent oral delivery at specific time intervals of vitamin A, usually a 200,000 IU dose at 6-month intervals.
2. Nutrification (Fortification): addition of vitamin A to one or more foods widely consumed by the population.
3. Horticultural approaches: encouragement of the production of

fruits and vegetables rich in precursors of vitamin A at the community or family level (micro) or at the national level (macro), leading to the greater consumption of these by the population at risk.

4. Nutrition education: an instructional program conducted through both formal and informal channels, designed to improve food consumption practices as they relate to health concerns and vitamin A nutriture in particular.

5. Socioeconomic approaches: governmental policies/actions to increase the effective demand and utilization of food sources of vitamin A, such as improved marketing or a more even income distribution.

6. Public health: health programs devised to alleviate environmental factors which contribute to the inadequate utilization of the vitamin.

7. Combined interventions: utilizing more than one of the above strategies to accomplish the goal. The major characteristics of each individual strategy are summarized in Table I.

The distinctive characteristics of each intervention strategy result in it having greater or lesser potential for improving vitamin A nutriture in a given situation. Table II summarizes the conditions under which each strategy would normally be indicated. The reader is referred to other documents (2,7–10) for more detailed discussion of vitamin A intervention strategies. However, it must be stressed that consideration of intervention strategies is premature unless there has been an adequate assessment of the vitamin A problem in terms of its magnitude, causitive factors, and geographic distribution. Likewise, those strategies selected should be complementary to, or at least consistent with, the broader context within which they will be applied, such as governmental structure and policies, other health and nutrition-related activities, and socioeconomic trends which can be predicted to impinge on vitamin A status over the intermediate/long term. Also, planning of each intervention should incorporate a mechanism for its evaluation. It can be assumed that in all countries the ultimate goal will be for all members of the population to consume adequate vitamin A in the form of natural foods.

SUMMARIZATION OF EXPERIENCE IN VITAMIN A INTERVENTIONS

Periodic Massive Dosing

The initial pilot trials of this approach were carried out in Guatemala, Jordan, and India based on individual doses of between 100,000 and

TABLE I

Characteristics of Vitamin A Intervention Strategies[a,b]

Strategy	Population coverage	Time to achieve benefits	Focus	Initial cost	Continuing cost	Public participation	Personnel	Expertise	Initial effort	Continued effort	Ease of system monitoring
Massive dosing	Individually targeted	Very short (days)	Single or multi-nutrient limited	H	H	L-p	H	L	H	H	D
Nutrification	General population or targeted segment	Short (months)	Single (vitamin A) or multinutrients	M	L	N	L	H	M	L	S
Macro-horticultural approach	General population or targeted segment	Long (years)	Multinutrients	H	M	H-a	H	H	H	M	M
Micro-horticultural approach	General population or targeted segment	Medium (months/years)	Multinutrients	M	L	H-a	M	M	H	M	D
Nutrition education	General population or targeted segment	Long (years)	Multinutrients	M	M	M-a	V	H	H	M	D
Public health	General population or targeted segment	Medium (years)	Program dependent	V	V	V	V	H	V	V	D
Socioeconomic change	General population or targeted segment	Long (years)	Program dependent	V	V	M-a	V	H	V	V	M

[a] By permission from Ref. (7).
[b] Key to abbreviations: H, high; M, medium; L, low; V, variable; H-a, high (active); M-a, medium (active); L-p, low (passive); N, none; D, difficult; S, simple.

TABLE II

Situations and Indicated Potential Interventions[a]

Situation components of problem[b]						Interventions range[c,d]		
(1)	(2)	(3)	(4)	(5)	(6)	Short	Intermediate	or long
Yes	Yes	No	No	Yes	Yes	I, II	IIIb	IIIa, IV, VI
Yes	Yes	No	No	Yes	No	I, II	IIIb	IIIa, IV
Yes	Yes	No	No	No	Yes	IIIb, II	IV	IIIa, VI
Yes	Yes	No	No	No	No	IIIb, II	IV	IIIa
Yes	No	No	No	Yes	Yes	I, II	IV	VI
Yes	No	No	No	Yes	No	I, II	IV	IV
Yes	No	No	No	No	Yes	II	II	VI
Yes	No	No	No	No	No	II	IV	
No	Yes	Yes	No	Yes	Yes	I	IIIb, VI	IIIa, VI, V
No	Yes	Yes	No	Yes	No	I	IIIb, V	IIIa, IV
No	Yes	No	Yes	Yes	Yes	I	IV, IIIb	IIIa, VI
No	Yes	No	Yes	Yes	No	I	IV, IIIb	IIIa, IV
No	Yes	Yes	No	No	Yes	II	VI, V	IV, IIIa
No	Yes	Yes	No	No	No	IV	IV	V, IIIa
No	Yes	No	Yes	No	Yes	IV	IIIb	VI, IIIa
No	Yes	No	Yes	No	No	IV	IIIb	IIIa

[a] From Ref. (7), with permission.
[b] Key to numbers: (1) Lack of natural food vitamin A sources; (2) potential for increasing natural food vitamin A sources; (3) improperly distributed and consumed by different sectors of population; (4) improper intrafamilial distribution and consumption (especially affecting the small child); (5) important incidence of severe clinical and biochemical signs; (6) important secondary contributing factors (diarrhea, infections, poor overall diet).
[c] Key to Roman numbers: (I) Massive dosing; (II) nutrification; (IIIa) macro-horticulture; (IIIb) micro-horticulture; (IV) nutrition education; (V) socioeconomic approaches; (VI) public health approaches.
[d] Time also has a connotation of priority.

330,000 IU of oily or aqueous vitamin A palmitate. The standard dose used at the present time in all countries, except India, is an oral gelatin capsule provided by the United Nations Children Fund (UNICEF) containing 200,000 IU of retinyl ester and 40 IU of vitamin E in an oil solution. India produces and uses an orange-flavored oil solution in which 200,000 IU of vitamin A are administered by measured oral doses. All countries have established a maximum of 6 months intervals between doses; most include children 1–5 years of age in the mass distribution program. It has been established that 30–50% of the dose of vitamin A is stored by the body (2), providing a protective period of approximately 180 days for a growing child.

Massive dosing programs have been instituted on a regional or national basis in a number of countries, including India, Bangladesh, Indonesia, Haiti, Philippines, Sri Lanka, El Salvador, Thailand, and most recently, Tanzania and Malawi. The largest of these programs is in India (25 million children targeted), Bangladesh (15 million targeted), and Indonesia (5 million targeted).

Indonesia is targeting different intervention strategies to specific geographic areas, based on the results of a comprehensive 3-year research program on the etiology of vitamin A deficiency, which included a national prevalence and dietary pattern survey. Thus, capsule distribution is being carried out through four different types of community outreach programs in that country.

Evaluation, although rarely incorporated into program design from the outset, has been done on an ad hoc basis in several countries. It has generally been found that high coverage is achieved initially, with a progressive reduction through successive cycles to a plateau, usually at 60–65% of targeted individuals reached. As might be expected, protocols calling for distribution to the home achieve greater geographic coverage than clinic distribution, but at greater staff time and effort cost. The documented reduction in coverage appears to be associated with delays in repleting stocks of capsules both at the port of entry and inland distribution points, method of delivery, inadequate recording and review of operations, lack of initial or refresher training of personnel, and inadequate incentives for or recognition of personnel. Thus, problems in maintaining coverage levels seem to reflect deficiencies in program management rather than any inherent weakness in the intervention strategy. Massive dosing programs have been found to be associated with major reductions in the prevalence of blindness and conjunctival signs of vitamin A deficiency. For example, the prevalence of blindness in children 0–6 years of age was reduced from 27 per 10,000 (0.276%) to less than 4 per 10,000 (0.038%) during 8 years of capsule distribution in Bangladesh (11). Rigidly controlled evaluations required to demonstrate a reduction in corneal lesions (which occur much less frequently) have not been completed in any country as yet but are under way in India and Indonesia.

Fortification

The first example of food fortification was the addition of a cod liver oil concentrate to margarine in Denmark during the World War I. Replacement of butter in the Danish diet with vegetable margarine had resulted in an epidemic of xerophthalmia (12). Fortification stopped the

TABLE III

Changes in Distribution of Serum Retinol Levels in Preschool Children in the Philippines (1979–1981)

| Serum retinol μg/dl | Fortified provinces | | | | Control | |
| | Marinduque | | Nueva Viscaya | | Cebu | |
	Initial	Final	Initial	Final	Initial	Final
Mean	26.6	31.4[a]	27.4	32.4[a]	29.3	30.8[b]
Percentage with values						
< 10 μg/dl	26.7	4.8	14.9	6.7	22.0	14.5
< 20 μg/dl	80.7	82.9	72.5	77.9	79.4	73.1
> 20 μg/dl	18.2	17.1	27.6	22.1	20.6	24.8
n	591	608	565	683	591	557

[a] $p < .005$.
[b] $p < .01$.

1. Initial dilution of fortified MSG while the stock of unfortified product in the distribution chain (manufacturer–wholesaler–retailer–consumer) was used up.

2. The problem of "caking" of the fortified MSG within the packet associated with use of the new form of vitamin A concentrate for this study.

3. Leakage of unfortified MSG from neighboring provinces into the experimental provinces.

4. Reduction in proportion of small (fortified) versus large (unfortified) packets purchased during the study—in Marinduque: from 70 to 55%, in Nueva Viscaya: from 79 to 40%.

5. Loss experienced in potency of the new form of vitamin A concentrate, from the original level of 15,000 IU/packet to mean value of 7200 IU/packet sampled at consumer level.

6. Widely publicized criticism from some members of the Philippine medical community that MSG is toxic and of the dangers of hypervitaminosis A.

It is worth noting that most of the difficulties experienced during the Philippines study are either (a) technical in nature and presumably could be resolved without great difficulty or (b) problems which could be avoided by strong government commitment to support this intervention approach. An extremely important advantage (at least in the Philippines) to use of MSG as a vehicle for delivery of vitamin A is that it is essentially a *no* cost intervention.

INDONESIA—MONOSODIUM GLUTAMATE

In late 1976, the Government of Indonesia and Helen Keller International initiated a major research project to determine the prevalence, incidence, and etiology of xerophthalmia and to find the means whereby vitamin A status in Indonesia might be improved (19). This included a national prevalence survey of children through 5 years of age, during which nutritional status, breast feeding and weaning practices, family eating practices, and food purchase information was obtained. These data identified wheat, sugar, and MSG as potential vehicles for fortification in some areas of the country. Feasibility indicated that the annual cost per child would be (US) $0.06 for fortification of MSG, as compared to $0.44 for capsule distribution, $0.47 for wheat flour and $1.83 for sugar. Fortification of MSG has therefore been pursued, and a large pilot study based on distribution through normal commercial channels is to be initiated in the near future. The Indonesian investigators have maintained close liaison with their Philippine colleagues and believe that they have resolved the technological problems and can largely avoid the operational problems encountered in that country (20).

HORTICULTURAL APPROACH

The Food and Agriculture Organization (FAO) has developed information from food balance sheets showing that in those areas of the world where vitamin A deficiency is prevalent, vegetable products are the main dietary source of the vitamin (21). They provide 86% of the dietary vitamin A in Africa and Asia, 65% in the Near East, and 53% in Latin America. The FAO data describe the situation at the regional level. Consideration of inequalities in distribution by countries within region and income groups within countries would indicate even higher percentages for low income groups, particularly in Latin America. Intrafamily disparities in distribution of vitamin A activity food sources make the children of these families especially vulnerable. The very low intake of animal products by low income groups in these areas (thus low intake of preformed vitamin A) and associated low fat intake from both animal and vegetable sources undoubtedly also contribute to the vitamin A deficiency problem. Conversion of carotene (pro-vitamin A) from plant sources to vitamin A in the body is more efficient when there is adequate fat in the diet to facilitate absorption. Economics dictate that increases in the proportion of animal products and fats in the diets of low income families will, at best, occur very slowly. Promotion of production and consumption of low cost, carotene-rich vegetables and fruits should therefore be an important strategy in these countries.

Unfortunately, the body of relevant knowledge and experience is not sufficiently developed to plan and implement horticultural promotion activities in many areas with certainty that they will be successful. Some of the reasons include:

1. Most horticultural research has been directed toward varieties which produce high yields, have standardized color/shape, and withstand handling in marketing channels, rather than considering nutritive content.

2. Likewise, horticultural research has been directed to production for cash crop rather than for home/village use.

3. Promotion has often encouraged use of vitamin A-rich foods widely used in developed countries rather than traditional food sources.

4. Promotion has often not considered the sociocultural setting or food preferences of the area.

5. Imported seeds have often been inappropriate for local crop conditions.

6. Extremely little effort has been addressed toward understanding which foods are or are not grown/purchased or consumed by the family or by intrafamilial distribution.

7. There has been little dissemination of field experience into the total body of knowledge.

Nevertheless, there has been substantial effort addressed to this approach, particularly by those who considered it to be the most sustainable means of overcoming vitamin A deficiency and/or by those concerned with the health and nutritional well being of populations where no other intervention was available. A recent publication "Tropical Leaf Vegetables in Human Nutrition" (22) describes the very large number of green leafy vegetables which can be used in the family diet for the prevention of vitamin A deficiency in tropical areas throughout the world and lists previous publications on this subject. Dr. Oomen, the senior author, promoted use of leafy vegetables for this purpose in rural areas of Indonesia for many years. Another physician, Dr. G. Venkataswamy of Tamil Nadu, India, has promoted feeding of leafy green vegetables to young children among low-income Indian families by demonstrating how their use in feeding xerophthalmic children results in rapid and complete recovery at essentially no cost to the family or society, as compared to rehabilitation in a hospital. This approach is currently being extended to all states of India under a blindness prevention project supported by the British Royal Commonwealth Society for the Blind (RCSB) (23). For many years, UNICEF has supported the promotion of home and school gardens in developing countries as a feasible means of improving the nutritional status (including vitamin A) in the community. UNICEF has recently sponsored the printing of a home garden handbook (24) which is receiving widespread distribution by donor agencies. UNICEF has also funded research in Africa to determine the effects of a variety of ways of cooking, storage, and preservation of green leafy vegetables on their acceptability and vitamin A content (25).

The Asian Vegetable Research and Development Center (AVRDC), with funding from the Agency for International Development, is promoting home gardens through agricultural research/extension channels. After orientation visits to determine vegetables and fruits currently used, and food preferences of low income families in each Asian country, AVRDC seeks a mix of plants which, grown in 4 × 4 meter area, will contribute the largest amount of nutrients with minimal requirement for fertilizers, insecticides, and labor and will also be culturally acceptable.

Once suitability of the garden is determined in the target country, AVRDC's outreach program will work with government officials to assure adequacy of quality seeds and promote the gardens through extension programs. Vegetables which are rich sources of carotene are accorded high priority in designing the garden for each country in view of the importance of vitamin A deficiency throughout Asia.

A series of WHO-USAID sponsored preliminary assessment surveys and more comprehensive surveys in areas of three countries by the Office pour la Recherche Scientifique et Technique Outre Mer, and Organisation Regionale pour l'Alimentacion y la Nutricion en Afrique (ORSTOM-ORANA) have confirmed that vitamin A deficiency is an important problem in several countries of Africa. Representatives of these countries met in Nairobi, Kenya, in November, 1981, to review the survey results and begin planning of vitamin A strategy. They recommended that encouragement of local growing, preservation and consumption of vitamin-A rich foods should be a priority activity (11). Thus, it is likely that there will be emphasis placed on the horticultural strategy in vitamin A programs on that continent as country programs get under way.

Nutrition Education

The vitamin A program in any country should have a nutrition education component, if for no other reason than the need for families to be aware of the cause of vitamin A deficiency and the special nutritional needs of young children. However, most countries have also selected this as one intervention strategy in keeping with the concept that the ultimate resolution of xerophthalmia lies in each family achieving an adequate intake of vitamin A from locally available foods, together with the control of factors which impair its utilization. In some countries, this will represent only placing special emphasis on vitamin A within existing, broadly based health and nutrition activities carried out by several sectors of government. In other countries, it might be deemed necessary to mount a separate nutrition education effort addressed specifically to vitamin A. In any event, the messages must be built on an understanding of local social, cultural and economic conditions.

At an early stage of the coordinated worldwide attack on vitamin A deficiency, it became clear that in many countries, it would be necessary to also provide training and educational materials to the professional and intermediate level personnel who would be responsible for the country program and implementation of the selected intervention strategies. Accordingly, the donor agencies have sponsored the preparation of a number of materials for this purpose. These include:

1. Under a USAID grant, Helen Keller International and the Nutrition Foundation prepared (a) a series of prototype training aids for training of physicians, public health workers, and nutritionists, (b) prototype nutrition education materials, and (c) a Field Guide to the Detection and Control of Xerophthalmia which has been printed by WHO (26).

2. An IVACG report on Guidelines for the Eradication of Vitamin A Deficiency and Xerophthalmia (7).

3. An IVACG report on Recent Advances in the Metabolism and Function of Vitamin A and their Relationship to Applied Nutrition (27).

4. A WHO Report on Guidelines for Programmes for the Prevention of Blindness (28).

5. An IVACG report on The Safe Use of Vitamin A (6).

6. An IVACG report on the Symptoms and Signs of Vitamin A Deficiency and Their Relationship to Applied Nutrition (29).

7. An FAO, USAID, University of the Philippines at Los Banos report on Food, Nutrition and Agriculture Guidelines for Curriculum Content for Agricultural Training in Southeast Asia (30).

8. A two volume IVACG manual on Biochemical Methodology for the Assessment of Vitamin A Status (31).

9. The UNICEF Home Gardens Handbook (24).

10. The International Center for Epidemiologic and Preventive Ophthalmology, Johns Hopkins University, with WHO and USAID funding is developing xerophthalmia recognition/treatment booklets for use by primary health workers in Asia. They have been field tested in five languages used widely in Bangladesh, India, Indonesia, and the Philippines, and will be modified for use in Africa as country programs get under way on that continent.

11. Although not a technical guideline document or training manual, the Xerophthalmia Club Bulletin, funded by RCSB and IVACG, is distributed biannually to all persons worldwide who are concerned with xerophthalmia. Its purpose is to keep all level of individuals from the government planner, to the scientist, to the nutrition field worker informed of developments in the vitamin A field. The Bulletin thus provides an important ongoing educational service.

The nature and scope of nutrition education activities used for vitamin A intervention purposes in a few countries will now be described:

1. *Bangladesh:* A flip book developed in 1979 has been distributed to nearly 13,000 primary health workers who distribute vitamin A capsules. The flip book is used in emphasizing to mothers the importance of breastfeeding, weaning foods, feeding during illness, and of increasing consumption by young children of cheap and abundantly available green leafy vegetables. Posters with a similar message are displayed in health centers, eye clinics, and primary schools. A color film is displayed on national television, at 210 cinema houses in the country, and by mobile film units in rural areas. Xerophthalmia and its prevention are also stressed in the media: periodicals, newspapers, radio, television (11).

2. *Haiti:* Emphasis on training of medical, health, and nutritional personnel has been given priority since initiation of the national vitamin A program. As a result, xerophthalmia has been integrated into the nutrition curricula of training programs for these personnel, and particularly in all major instructional materials disseminated to the rural health sector. Articles appear in journals and newspapers, and a program has been televised. Messages are broadcast by radio frequently and a series of cassettes have been developed specifically for this purpose. A flip book with illustrations by a Haitian artist has been developed and is widely used at the local level to facilitate nutrition communication between the health or nurse auxiliary and mothers (8, 11).

3. *India:* Although each state in the country has its own educational program, the National Institute of Nutrition, Hyderabad, and the Vol-

untary Agency for Health Planning, New Delhi, have prepared educational materials for national distribution. The RCSB- assisted national program will establish a community based project in each state where there is a high prevalence of xerophthalmia. Each project will have a nutrition rehabilitation center patterned after the program developed at the Government Erskine Hospital in Madurai. Thus, mothers of affected children will receive comprehensive nutritional instruction, as well as all at-risk families in the community (11, 23).

4. *Indonesia:* The Directorates of Health, Education and Nutrition of the Ministry of Health collaborate closely with reference to the nutrition education component of the national program. The overall strategy involves participation of the agricultural, health, and religious sectors, women's organizations, voluntary agencies, etc. Posters, flip books, and other visual aids are especially designed for both village and urban use. Mass media campaigns have accompanied the initiation of capsule distribution in new areas of the country (8).

A unique aspect of the nutrition education component in this country is that of utilizing findings of the comprehensive research project to tailor nutrition messages more precisely to the current child rearing and dietary practices. These findings (10, 32) are strongly supportive of the need to be knowledgeable about the community and culture where educational messages are to be applied.

5. *Philippines:* Vitamin A education is directed to many levels of society and through a wide array of measures, ranging from the mass media, to small group orientations, to the interpersonal approach. The National Nutrition Council (NNC) and the Nutrition Center of the Philippines (NCP) report on vitamin A developments in their newsletters which are distributed at the national and local level. NCP has produced a vitamin A information leaflet for similar distribution. Special emphasis has been placed on preparation of educational materials for use by all teachers in the country. Barangay Nutrition Scholars (selected residents who are trained to deliver basic nutrition and health services in the community) are the primary link with individual families. A novel educational approach in the Philippines is that of delivering nutrition education through comic books which utilize popular heroes from Philippine folklore (8).

Socioeconomic Approaches

The need for adequate nutrient intake is now generally accepted as a basic human right and part of the purpose of development. Additionally, most governments consider that improved nutrition among low income groups is both a political necessity and contributory in itself to the development process. Therefore, government policies and development plans almost universally include improved nutrition as a goal. This has been one of the traditional justifications for allocation of funds for health, education, and water supply programs.

In recent years, governments (with active encouragement and support by multi- and bilateral donor agencies) have addressed increasing amounts of attention and resources to decisions and activities which should have a more rapid and direct nutritional impact on the most at-risk groups of the population. These include (a) incorporating nutritonal considerations in food policy, agricultural policy, agricultural research/ extension programs, and agricultural development projects and (b) re-distribution of income through food, housing and marketing subsidies, and food stamps or food distribution to targeted groups. A decision by government to fund fortification of a staple food item with vitamin A would be an example.

Although relatively few critical evaluations of such policies and activities have been carried out as yet, the available evidence indicates that improvement in nutritional status accompanies more equal distribution of income and that a strong political commitment by a government can result in a measurable reduction in malnutrition (33). With reference to vitamin A, general economic development and government-mandated fortification of vegetable ghee with vitamin A and carotene in Jordan resulted in a reduction in clinical symptoms of deficiency from 4.1% in 1962 (34) to 0.15% in 1977 (35). Similarly, economic development combined with a sugar fortification program brought about a very significant reduction in the prevalence of low and deficient serum levels of retinol in Costa Rica, between 1966 and 1978 (16). Presumably, the significant increase in mean serum retinols experienced in Cebu, the control province in the 1979–1981 Philippines study (18), was also associated with generalized nutritional improvement and economic development.

Public Health

In practice, the large dose intervention has frequently been superimposed on an existent health delivery system. In such cases, the health system provides the base for a direct attack on vitamin A deficiency. However, the public health approach by definition is based on indirect means of attack. This refers to health measures which are taken as a means of improving the environment so as to reduce or eliminate those conditions associated with an increased need for vitamin A. For example, an improved water supply should result in a reduced incidence of acute diarrheal disease, chronic and systemic infections. A measles immunization program is a similar example. Extension of health services into a previously unserved area of the country is a third example. As indicated in Tables I and II, the beneficial impact of these interventions on vitamin A status—with the possible exception of measles immunization—is usually intermediate or long term in nature and difficult to assess.

COMBINED INTERVENTIONS

Since the various vitamin A intervention strategies discussed previously are, as a rule, complementary to one another, it is to be expected that more than one should be implemented concurrently in each country. This is the case in most countries with national vitamin A programs. However, it should be noted that at the current time most resources and attention are being addressed to those interventions which produce an immediate or short-term impact, although providing only a temporary and partial solution. This is understandable in those areas where a serious clinical problem exists. Fortunately, several countries are consciously selecting and testing a variety of short and longer term interventions in their national programs. As more experience is gained with each strategy individually and with programs wherein there is phasing of different strategies, this more comprehensive approach to vitamin A interventions may be expected to become the norm.

SUMMARY

As indicated throughout this chapter, major intervention programs have been initiated in several countries and substantial momentum has been achieved in a coordinated worldwide effort to bring about a major reduction in nutritional blindness and its accompanying social and economic toll. Credit for this impressive progress is due to (a) the international, bilateral, and private donor agencies who have drawn attention to the worldwide problem and provided much of the resources needed to demonstrate the effectiveness of various interventions and to (b) the developing countries who have responded to the challenge and made national commitments to protect young children from this preventable scourge.

Current intervention and prevention efforts are based primarily on estimates made in the early 1970s of 100,000 cases in developing countries annually of blindness in early childhood caused by xerophthalmia.

Since then, new epidemiologic evidence indicates that as many as 250,000 children are blinded annually in Asia alone. Also, recent preliminary assessment surveys indicate that vitamin A deficiency is sufficiently prevalent in several African countries to undertake further assessment and control measures (11). The extent of the problem in that continent has yet to be determined.

Relatively little attention has been addressed to a long known additional dimension to the problem—that of extraocular effects of vitamin A deficiency. In the early 1900s (37), a substance (later identified as vitamin A) was shown to permit resumption of growth and reproduction of rats receiving a purified diet devoid of fat. The etiology of this growth retardation effect was not documented until 1979 (38). Vitamin A deficiency has also been implicated as the cause of skin lesions, increased susceptibility to infections, anemia, reduced plasma volume, increased cerebrospinal fluid pressure, adverse reproductive effects and perversions of sensory function (taste, smell, vestibular balance) (29). Additional research on the total health, social and economic implications, and physiologic processes involved in the extraocular effects of vitamin A deficiency can be expected to provide even stronger justification for adequate support of intervention programs and may coincidentally identify means for earlier diagnosis of vitamin A deficiency.

REFERENCES

1. Wolf, G. A historical note on the mode of administration of vitamin A for the cure of night blindness. *Am. J. Clin. Nutr.* **31**, 290 (1978).
2. Report of a Joint WHO/USAID Meeting. Vitamin A deficiency and xerophthalmia. *W.H.O. Tech. Rep. Ser.* **590** (1976).
3. McLaren, D. S. "Malnutrition and the Eye." Academic Press, New York, 1963.
4. Anonymous. Vitamin A enrichment of donated foods. *PAG Bull.* **6** (4), 1 (1976).
5. McLaren, D. S. Xerophthalmia: A neglected problem. *Nutr. Rev.* **22**, 289 (1964).
6. A Report of the International Vitamin A Consultative Group. "The Safe Use of Vitamin A." Nutrition Foundation, New York, 1980.
7. A Report of the International Vitamin A Consultative Group. "Guidelines for the Eradication of Vitamin A Deficiency and Xerophthalmia." Nutrition Foundation, Washington, D. C., 1976.
8. Report of a Joint WHO/UNICEF/USAID/Helen Keller International/IVACG Meeting. Control of vitamin A deficiency and Xerophthalmia. *W.H.O. Tech. Rep. Ser.* **672** (1982).
9. Arroyave, G., Aguilar, J. R., Flores, M., and Guzmán, M. A. Evaluation of sugar fortification with vitamin A at the national level. *Sci. Publ.—Pan Am. Health Organ.* **384** (1979).
10. Sommer, A. "Nutritional Blindness: Xerophthalmia and Keratomalacia." Oxford Univ. Press, London and New York, 1982.

11. Report of 1981 IVACG Meeting. Unpublished document (1982).
12. Blegvad, O. Xerophthalmia, keratomalacia and xerosis conjunctivae. *Am. J. Ophthalmol.* **7**, 89–117 (1924).
13. Anderson, A. J. C., and Williams, P. N. "Margarine." Pergamon, Oxford, 1965.
14. Food and Nutrition Board, National Research Council, National Academy of Sciences. "Proposed Fortification Policy for Cereal-Grain Products." Nat. Acad. Sci., Washington, D. C., 1974.
15. Report of a PAHO Technical Group Meeting. Hypovitaminosis A in the Americas. *Sci. Publ.—Pan Am. Health Organ.* **198** (1970).
16. Valverde, V., Arroyave, G., Guzmán, M., and Flores, M. Overview of nutritional status in the western hemisphere: Central America and Panama. *Proc. West. Hemp. Nutr. Cong., VI, 1980,* pp. 271–282 (1981).
17. Solon, F. S. Vitamin A deficiency in the Philippines. A study of xerophthalmia in Cebu. *Am. J. Clin. Nutr.* **31**, 360–368 (1978).
18. Latham, M. C. "Evaluation of a Fortification Program to Control Vitamin A Deficiency in the Philippines," Final report from Cornell University to Office of Nutrition, Agency for International Development for Contract AID/DSAN-C-0009 (unpublished document), 1982.
19. Government of Indonesia and Helen Keller International. "Characterization of Vitamin A Deficiency and Xerophthalmia and the Design of Effective Intervention Program," Final report to Office of Nutrition, Agency for International Development for Contract AID-ta-C-1321 (unpublished document), 1980.
20. Muhilal, personal communication.
21. Perisse, J., and Polacchi, W. Geographical distribution and recent changes in world supply of vitamin A. *Food Nutr.* **6**, 21–27 (1980).
22. Oomen, H. A. P. C., and Grubben, G. J. H. "Tropical Leaf Vegetables in Human Nutrition," Dep. Agric. Res. Commun. 69. Koninklysk Institute Voor de Tropen, Amsterdam, 1977.
23. Krishnamurthy, K. A., Venkataswamy, G., Moorthy, O. K., Arora, S., and Pinto, J. "Project for the Prevention of Blinding Malnutrition." Bull. Nutrition Foundation of India, 1982.
24. The United Nations Childrens Fund. "The UNICEF Home Gardens Handbook for People Promoting Mixed Gardening in the Humid Tropics." United Nations, New York, 1982.
25. Gomez, M. I. Carotene content of some green leafy vegetables of Kenya and effects of dehydration and storage on carotene retention. *J. Plant Foods* **3**, 231–244 (1981).
26. Sommer, A. "Field Guide to the Detection and Control of Xerophthalmia." World Health Organ., Geneva, 1978.
27. International Vitamin A Consultative Group. "Recent Advances in the Metabolism and Function of vitamin A and their Relationship to Applied Nutrition." Nutrition Foundation, New York, 1979.
28. World Health Organization. "Guidelines for Programmes for the Prevention of Blindness." World Health Organ., Geneva, 1979.
29. International Vitamin A Consultative Group. "The Symptoms and Signs of Vitamin A Deficiency and their Relationship to Nutrition." Nutrition Foundation, New York, 1981.
30. Food and Agriculture Organization, United States Agency for International Development, University of the Philippines at Los Banos. "Food, Nutrition and Agriculture Guidelines for Curriculum Content for Agricultural Training in Southeast Asia." FAO, Rome, 1981.

31. International Vitamin A Consultative Group. "Biochemical Methodology for the Assessment of Vitamin A Status." Nutrition Foundation, New York, 1982.
32. Tarwotjo, I., Sommer, A., Soegiharto, T., Susanto, D., and Muhilal, O. Dietary practices and xerophthalmia among Indonesian children. *Am. J. Clin. Nutr.* **35,** 574–581 (1982).
33. Berg, A. "Malnourished People—A Policy View." World Bank, Washington, D.C., 1981.
34. A Report by the Interdepartmental Committee on Nutrition for National Defense. "The Hashimite Kingdom of Jordan Nutrition Survey." U.S. Govt. Printing Office, Washington, D.C., 1963.
35. Hizazi, S. S. "Child Growth and Nutrition in Jordan." Royal Scientific Society Press, Amman, 1977.
36. Sommer, A., Tarwotjo, I., Hussaini, G., Susanto, D., and Soegiharto, T. Incidence, prevalence and scale of blinding malnutrition. *Lancet* **1,** 1407 (1981).
37. McCollum, E. V., and Davis, M. Observations on the isolation of the substance in butter fat which exerts a stimulating effect on growth. *J. Biol. Chem.* **19,** 245 (1914).
38. Anzano, M. A., Lamb, A. J., and Olson, J. A. Growth, appetite, sequence of pathological signs and survival following the induction of rapid, synchronous vitamin A deficiency in the rat. *J. Nutr.* **109,** 1419 (1979).

VII *Nutrition Education*

31 Why Teach Nutrition and to Whom?

ABRAHAM HORWITZ

Although both questions are sequential, some may believe that the answers are so obvious that there is no need for any discussion. And yet, providing human beings with energy and essential nutrients for normal performance is a complex problem that becomes even more complex when it is approached as a condition of societies facing actual and potential risks of malnutrition. It then appears to be more than just a biochemical or medical dysfunction, but reflects a maladaptation to a changing environment. It is, thus, a problem of ecology and development.

Treating the determinants and/or the symptoms of chronic undernutrition involves an analysis of biologic, economic, behavioral, social, and political factors related to the production, consumption, and utilization of food. Each one includes a series of variables whose analysis, in varying degrees, should form the basis for governmental food and nutrition policy and for translating planning into specific programs and projects. From such an examination, malnutrition emerges as a problem of development, being of a multisectoral and multidisciplinary nature.

In defining food and nutrition policy a government must clearly state what it wants to change in order to prevent and control malnutrition and how it intends to go about it. To this end the role of the specialists in nutrition becomes paramount. For they are to sensitize convincingly all decision-makers between and within sectoral agencies on the significance of the problem both for the economy and for the well-being of the people. In turn, specialists should understand the criteria used for establishing priorities and allocating resources for national development. Thus, they must present their proposals—and alternative options—not

NUTRITION INTERVENTION STRATEGIES IN NATIONAL DEVELOPMENT

exclusively in humanitarian terms but based on evidence that shows that malnutrition impairs health, intellectual activity and adaptive behavior, education, productivity, well-being, and induces death, and that these ill effects will continue as long as its incidence remains high.

Without rational strategies, therefore, the prospects for marshalling investments—both national and external—seem dim. Governments must recognize that development has both an economic and a social dimension and act accordingly. To the extent that policies take human beings and their basic needs into account as their primary purpose, the probability of reducing malnutrition and of improving patterns of food consumption will be proportionately greater. In the words of Mahbub Ul Haq: "We were taught to take care of our GNP, as this will take care of poverty. Let us reverse this and take care of poverty, as this will take care of the GNP" (1).

These considerations determine the scope of the process of educating and training human resources to improve the nutritional status of the people and reduce malnutrition. It establishes the framework to determine the number and type of professionals and paraprofessionals needed and the content of the curricula.

In organizing the educational system we start with some premises:

1. That food and nutrition must be accepted as a distinct field of knowledge, learning, research, technology, and practice. Professionals, therefore, are to be recognized in their own right.

2. That in view of the multisectoral and multidisciplinary nature of chronic undernutrition there is a need to form and inform different categories of scientists involved in social and economic development on the dimensions, determinants, consequences, and remedial actions of the problem.

3. That among the constraints governments face nowadays for formulating and implementing food and nutrition policies, the lack of human resources seems the most pressing.

4. That the attempts of physicians and public health workers to instruct their patients and population groups in nutrition are seldom appropriate to the need. The fault lies in the inadequate instruction offered by most schools of medicine and of public health. The erroneous concept, still held by the former that nutrition is dietetics, and hence should not dignify the medical curriculum, is in urgent need of correction. In schools of public health an equally fallacious concept exists that nutrition is the province of the specialists instead of being a necessary ingredient in the training of every public health worker. And it also should be, to some extent at least, part of the training of every university graduate who, as a professional, will deal with socioeconomic development.

5. That it should be emphasized that nutrition educators are in intense competition for the minds of men in both technically underdeveloped and developed regions. The competition may be with ingrained ignorance and superstition in some areas and with profit-inspired commercial television in others. Nonetheless, the competition is keen, and the antagonists resourceful. The nutrition educator cannot, therefore, live in an ivory tower. He must cope with the realities of his environment, but in so doing he must always bear in mind his ultimate goal and the principles on which his training has been based (2).

The questions are posed: Why should nutrition be taught? To whom? The following reasons can be offered:

1. Nutrition is vital to all human beings and to the societies that they comprise—for the biological development of the former and for the economic development of the latter.

2. Malnutrition, given its high incidence (it is estimated to affect, depending on the indicators, between 500 and 1000 million people) and given its role as an underlying or associated cause of death in vulnerable groups, has become a grave social problem in many countries of the world.

3. The prevalence of nutritional deficiencies has a direct relationship to poverty, privation, economic marginalization, and social abandonment—precisely the determinants that identify those groups at greatest risk.

4. Nutrition can have an effect on resistance to disease, infections in particular, as well as on intellectual development, learning ability, and labor productivity—all of which in turn have bearing on production and well-being. Moreover, malnourished mothers tend to have low birth weight babies, and these babies, if they survive, again bring into play the same chain of factors mentioned.

5. Programs for building manpower to deal with the problem lag far behind the clearly evident need in almost all parts of the developing world. The Pan American Health Organization reports that 95% of all the region's graduates in nutrition are concentrated in but four countries of Latin America (3).

6. Despite the notable progress achieved in the current century, reflected in the discovery of essential nutrients, we are still far from understanding the relationships between food intake and normal productive social performance, and there is therefore an increasing need for operational research, which can only be carried out by those who study the problem in depth.

7. From the gates of the hacienda to the mouth of the consumer, to

use Aylward's expression (4), a myriad of functions intervene—food storage, control of losses, distribution, industrialization, supply—that call upon specialized technology and human resources.

8. Development policies, programs, and projects are usually unmindful of the consequences they entail, in terms of an adequate and balanced diet, for the entire population. For example, there are fiscal and monetary policies, which affect the purchasing power of low-income groups—nothing being more sensitive to price fluctuations than poverty—and agricultural production and food export programs, which do not allow for social considerations or provide for food imports in order to meet the biological requirements of the population. Policies relative to foreign credit and the importing of agricultural inputs for increased food production usually fail to take the small farmer into account and thus impair his income and his family's diet. Policies for the social sectors— health, education, food, housing—are neither sufficient nor efficient in their coverage. The availability of services is far below the evident demand. In Latin America 40% of the population is without minimum health care. Moreover, the resources, scarce as they are, are not channeled toward alleviating the most widely prevalent problems, and they do not always benefit those who are most greatly in need.

9. In the world today there is greater awareness of nutrition's important role in putting the principle of equity into practice, expanding the range of opportunities available, stimulating social mobility, and redistributing income more rationally. The primary health care system, whose significance has been recognized by all the Governments, is a means of introducing nutrition within rural development schemes and programs aimed at reaching poor communities in the cities.

10. International banks and capital-exporting countries are now requiring good nutrition projects in order to make decisions on the corresponding investments and yet the personnel to design them properly are not available.

11. In sum, action is the fruit of knowledge, and each must nourish the other.

These, then, are some reasons *why* nutrition should be taught; they tell us, correspondingly, *to whom* it should be taught. We must start from the basic fact that no developing country has sufficient manpower for formulating and implementing economic and social development programs with quantifiable objectives in order to improve food consumption and reduce the deleterious effects of malnutrition.

It is not surprising that the concept of nutrition is said to be diffused and imprecise, difficult to bring into focus, because it does not seem to belong to any one sector of development. Thus priority is given in the national budget to food in the sense of production and not to nutrition understood as mere consumption. However, for those to whom man is the end and the means of everything, nutrition belongs to all the sectors of development, for it affects everyone, either directly or indirectly.

There is a hard and urgent task ahead: to form and to inform.

It will be necessary to form:

1. Those who formulate and evaluate policy, programs, and projects in the field of nutrition, as well as those who carry out the activities in institutions and communities.

2. Those who teach students and prepare graduates in the health sciences.

3. Those who investigate the basics and the dynamics of the problem in its differing ecological settings in search of suitable technologies.

4. Those who advise consumers to choose balanced and adequate diets that take customs into account and yet moderate the influence of superstititions, myths, and popular beliefs.

5. Those who work in food technology to improve the quality and increase the availability of products.

6. Those who, as leaders, must have an overall understanding of all aspects of the problem—food production, consumption, and utilization.

It will be necessary to inform:

1. Those who are responsible for development policy in general so that nutrition will be duly incorporated.

2. Those who make policies and programs that bear on food production, including exports and imports, so that priority will be given to the biological needs of the population.

3. Those who plan and carry out comprehensive projects for rural development, so that nutritional goals will be part of them.

4. Those responsible for the educational system at all levels.

5. Those who set fiscal, monetary, price, trade, and other related policies, so that possible harmful effects on the diet of the people can be taken into account.

As to how all this should be done will be discussed by other distinguished colleagues.

REFERENCES

1. M. Ul Haq, M. A new perspective on Development. *In* "International Development, 1971" (A. E. Rice, ed.), p. 65. 1972.
2. Horwitz, A. Food and protection of health. *Fed. Proc., Fed. Am. Soc. Exp. Biol.* **20**(1), Part III, 401 (1960).

3. Pan American Health Organization. "Methodologies for the Formulation of National Food and Nutrition Policies and Their Intersectoral Implementation," Tech. Discuss., Doc. CD23/DT/1 (Eng), Table 20. Pan Am. Health Organ., Washington, D.C., 1975.
4. Aylward, F. Food conservation and utilization in developing countries. *In* "Progress in Human Nutrition." (S. Margen, ed.), pp. 53–67. Avi Publ., Westport, Connecticut, 1971.

32 Some Problems in the Implementation and Evaluation of Food and Nutrition Education Programs

RAFAEL E. FERREYRA

Among the many questions that could be asked when discussing nutrition education programs carried out in various countries are as follows:

1. What problems usually appear during their implementation?
2. How does one evaluate such programs?
3. Are they worthwhile to continue as a mean of reducing problems of malnutrition?

This chapter will only point out some of the challenges that educators must face in attempting to answer questions of the relationship between implementation and evaluation of food and nutrition education programs.

Too often it is noticed that the evaluation of educational programs is conceived and begun too late, i.e., after the fact when the implementation is already finished. The conception of implementation and evaluation as sequential instead of concomitant processes prevents the collection during implementation of the necessary data to readjust the program and improve its on-going efficiency and renders impossible verification of the basic assumptions of the causal model, seldom explicit, on which the design of the program is based.

The problem of retrospectively planned evaluations may have its origin in the misconception that evaluation is associated almost exclusively to the final effects of the programs, ignoring the mechanisms which led

NUTRITION INTERVENTION STRATEGIES IN NATIONAL DEVELOPMENT
Copyright © 1983 by Academic Press, Inc.

to the attainment of those effects. Every program includes a set of elements and processes which must interact during implementation to produce the causal process leading to the desired final effect. Many educational program designers tend to consider as trivial the theoretical causal model on which the program is based and, therefore, underestimate the importance of making it explicit. The failure to make explicit the causal model to be implemented from the beginning makes subsequent evaluation and adjustments difficult.

Food and nutrition education programs have as their ultimate aim the modification or adoption of habits and the attainment of knowledge, abilities, and values related to the food and nutritional welfare of people. Professionals know the kind of knowledge, abilities, values, and general habits they hope to develop in the beneficiaries of educational programs. Most will surely agree that identification of program contents is a relatively simple problem. The challenge consists in designing and implementing programs which effectively reach the targeted population groups and produce the desired behavioral changes.

It is easy to reach students through the formal education system. Teachers are prepared for the transmission of information in classrooms settings, especially when texts and other appropriate materials are available. Even when not available the technology and the experience exists for the development of appropriate instructional materials and for the training of teaching personnel. Therefore, the transmission of specific knowledge of food and nutrition in schools is not likely to be a major problem. The same cannot be said about the translation of this information into development of abilities and values that lead to appropriate and lasting desired food and nutrition behaviors. This is precisely the challenge to be faced by educators belonging to the formal system.

Those human groups most vulnerable and in need of food and nutrition education generally are not found in the schools but in the community. Their level of education is generally low and reaching them with suitable methods and materials is the great challenge for nonformal education.

This challenge requires that professionals be creative in developing efficient operative models, of tested and proved validity, and in the implementation of those models through effective new program approaches. When a new program is designed, it is expected that it will initiate a process leading to an explicit desired outcome which, in this case, means new behaviors, abilities, and habits. To design improved programs we must monitor and explore deeply the elements involved in the process.

Experience has taught that too often designers and implementers of programs deemed to have had the desired effect will be satisfied and will not be interested in finding out in detail the elements of the process that led to success. This kind of evaluation is critical to extracting fundamental elements transferable to other program designs. For example, when the desired effect is not achieved by a program or only partially attained, there is a need to detect deficiencies and correct them guided by transferable experiences gained from successful programs. It should be noted that program failure may be caused by an inappropriate causal model or by failure in the implementation process or both.

Reasons why a program does not produce the desired effects cannot be found if impact is evaluated only after implementation is completed. In such a case all that is known is outcome. The information required both to improve the program during implementation and to reformulate ideas about its operation is lacking. This is the reason for linking evaluation to implementation. To establish the linkage requires an explicit theoretical causal model of the inputs and processes intervening to attain the desired effect. For example, let us assume a program with the objective of promoting production and consumption of some green vegetables in a certain rural area. The strategy is to reach the target population through an existing literacy program. Instructional materials especially designed for the new program will be needed. Inputs such as tools, seeds, booklets, and other materials for implementation will be required, as well as the training of promoters, instructors, and community leaders and the support of the mass media, etc. All these elements will operate in a predetermined sequence and time period until the target population acquires the ability to produce and the habit to consume the green vegetables promoted. The causal model is the chain of events which should occur from the beginning of the program implementation until the habits have been acquired. In this particular case the model will surely include among the intervening factors, knowledge of the relative advantages associated with the consumption of green vegetables, their acceptance by the population as suitable food for the family diet, the acquisition of the necessary production techniques and related knowledge, the knowledge of food recipes using the products and the abilities to prepare them, the cultural and social acceptance of the new dishes, or other combinations, by the population, etc.

The model is a working hypothesis in which a sequence of processes is established as well as the mixture of elements of the processes which are thought necessary to produce the desired effect in a determined period of time. Such a model must allow identification of those variables to be measured and when and what intermediate goals are to be attained during the different stages of implementation and after the predetermined time.

As mentioned before, many educational program designers do not perceive how important it is to make explicit the theory and the assumptions on which they operate. Changing habits and behaviors is not a trivial problem and is often oversimplified. For example, failure may be caused by the assumption that food habits of the population will be changed through conferences and the distribution of booklets. This process must be carefully designed and tested as any scientific hypothesis. The model must permit the explanation of the phenomenon, the identification and measurement of the variables to be used in evaluating intermediate processes during the implementation, and making appropriate and timely decisions to reorient those processes towards the attainment of the desired effects.

The challenge to professionals responsible for food and nutrition education programs is to design and test efficient models which produce the desired outcomes and at the same time are adaptable to the needs, circumstances, and characteristics of the specific targeted population groups. This requires the use of evaluation procedures suitable to correct, not only the programs during their implementation, but also our ideas about the causal processes on which the programs have been designed. Only in this way, will we accomplish our duties as educators and to contribute to the development of more efficient programs, by which food and nutrition education may play its important role in the improvement of the people's welfare.

33 Nonformal Education: An Instrument for Nutrition Intervention

RICARDO UAUY AND MARTíN MIRANDA

INTRODUCTION

Terms coined following the "non" prefix are usually poorly defined; nonformal education is not an exception. The true meaning and justification of nonformal education is the failure of the traditional school system to meet the knowledge needs of a community. Customarily it is used in reference to education directed for adults or others who have already ended their contacts with the schooling system. It can also serve as a way to continue educating throughout life. For the developing world and specifically for Latin America, nonformal education means trying to bypass the intrinsic constraints of the formal educational system, reaching all those regardless of age who require knowledge with methodologies that consider the local environment and specific needs of a given community. The experience acquired over the last 20 years is filled with new ideas on how to establish meaningful links between those who possess knowledge and the underprivileged who most need it. A change of focus from the educator and his methods to the learner and his needs has been occurring. By now most people agree that there is no education until learning has taken place.

The need for nonformal nutrition education is clearly established since relevant nutrition knowledge is virtually absent in most school curricula. The vast majority of the population in the developing world has very limited access to schooling or have high rates of failures after the initial stages of primary education. During the late 1970s in Latin America, one

NUTRITION INTERVENTION STRATEGIES IN NATIONAL DEVELOPMENT

out of four children never entered school, more than one-half of those who entered failed before completing the primary cycle, one of three finished their high school and only one in twenty entered the university (1). These data represent mean figures for the region and are comparable to those from other parts of the developing world. Undoubtedly there are marked differences between and within countries. The nutritionally vulnerable low socioeconomic strata groups are also selectively marginated from the school system.* Nevertheless the whole educational system is directed and aimed at trying to make a potential university student out of every child. The failure of this approach can be documented throughout the world by measuring practical nutrition-related knowledge within the community and observing virtually no improvement in those with formal education (2–4). From this analysis of the problem, it is tempting to conclude that education is the main conditioning factor for malnutrition. Undoubtedly this would represent an over simplification as damaging as excluding education as an intervening variable in the multifactorial causation of hunger and malnutrition.

The consequences of poor food and nutrition education for a given community potentiate the effect of low income, heavy food losses, infection, and diarrhea acting synergistically to self-perpetuate poverty and malnutrition. Nonformal nutrition education, if effective, can help break this cycle. The challenge in this process is to modify attitudes, habits, beliefs and to produce lasting changes in people's actions. Man has accumulated considerable knowledge on how to change the physical environment, limited knowledge on changing the social habitat; but has yet to learn how to best change himself and others through education.

CONCEPTUAL BASIS

The purpose of any given educational process can be solely the dissemination of knowledge. In this case the objective will be accomplished if the population acquires the information on food and nutrition as programmed by the educator. This goal has dominated most of the traditional nutrition education efforts through either the formal or nonformal systems (3). What is usually called "nutrition education" in most cases is the transfer of information at the individual or group level through different types of lectures. This turns out to be highly ineffective if the outcome is an expected behavioral change. The information transfer mode in education is not only characteristic of nutrition educational

---

*Their access to schooling is more restricted and failure rates are higher.

practices but concerns the whole educational tradition which assumes that the acquisition of knowledge is the basis from which behaviors develop. The key issue in traditional education is the selection of subject content. This is undoubtedly important for information transfer but will not answer the challenge we posed earlier in the introduction (i.e., to modify attitudes, habits, beliefs and produce lasting changes in people's actions).

The weakness of this premise has been demonstrated by human behavioral scientists. They have shown that man's planned actions occur only after he has understood, analyzed, and internalized a problem (5). In so doing he will make responsible decisions within the context of his personal and social background. According to this concept, the educational process must not only transfer information, but must also promote creativity in the diagnosis and solution of a given problem. It should develop problem solving abilities and establish desirable conducts based on a socially acceptable standard. The definition of these objectives necessarily has a specific orientation given by those who design a given educational program. Implicitly or explicitly they are defining what they would like to obtain through the educational process. The answer to the challenge of nutrition education lies in the integration of the learner's previous experiences with the educator's message. This implies a close identification between people's need and the nutrition educational contents. Table I compares the traditional and integrated educational process in theory and practice.

Considering this conceptual basis, we can tentatively define general objectives for nutrition education efforts. It starts with the identification and description of factors which affect food consumption. This obviously must be specific for a given local reality which determines the nutritional needs to be satisfied. It requires that educational efforts be centered on those members of the community or the family which make decisions relating to food and nutrition problems. A second overall objective is the identification of nutritional problems observed in that community. What are the determining factors and how does food consumption affect their food and nutrition-related problems. Examine the present and long-term consequences of a set of nutritional problems for the specific community. After a good understanding and analysis have taken place, the problem becomes internalized. At this stage we can expect that the action oriented toward the third objective can be considered appropriately. It should include designing and carrying out actions which can help improve life quality, of which food and nutrition are fundamental and essential components. This approach should adopt concrete forms by which changes of attitudes and habits at the indi-

TABLE I

Comparison of Two Models for Nonformal Education

	Traditional education	Integrated education
Purpose	Acquire knowledge	Integrate personal experiences
Focus	Teacher and his message	Learning by the group
Educator's role	Lecture on the topic	Facilitate the learning process
Student's role	Passive receptor with memory	Active participant in search of knowledge
Objectives	Defined by nature of the discipline	Arise from a diagnosis of problems and needs of the community
Contents	Based on scientific theory and principles	Based on the interaction of science and local culture
Method	Information transfer of subject matter	Sharing diverse experiences to promote integrated learning
Evaluates	Specific knowledge	Complete process and resulting behavior

vidual or group level can help alleviate nutritional problems. It is also of utmost importance that the learner participate in the evaluation of both the educational process and the impact it may have on a given reality.

Each of the general objectives proposed should be accomplished if the right educational activities are developed. This requires defining a set of specific objectives and didactic resources. For operational purposes each specific objective should be directed at a given desired conduct providing the concrete bit of knowledge necessary to support it. An example of this will be presented in the case study.

METHODOLOGICAL ASPECTS

The nutrition problem necessarily exists within an ecological setting. The thrust of the educational efforts must be centered on the family or the community where general application is likely and not at the individual level where greater variation is expected. The dietary history is determined at the family level mainly by food availability and by cultural factors affecting food habits. If we accept that the family should be the primary focus of our education and that the adults are the primary food decision makers, our efforts will be centered on them. The adult members of the family, especially women, establish food habits and behavior. A more precise definition of our target group will come by incorporating economic, geographic, and demographic factors. We should typify our target group as well as possible in order to design the right type of educational program.

Multiple efforts using various types of teaching devices have shown that person-to-person interaction is still one of the most powerful didactic resources available. Mass media such as television and radio have the advantage of widely disseminating the message but their ability to significantly improve food habits is limited (6). This is true especially if the same communication vehicle is used to promote consumption of dispensable foods items with marginal nutritional benefits. There are presently vast segments of the target population with minimal exposure to these media to make them broadly effective. There is a need to improve our use of mass media to better serve the basic requirements of people. Mass media can support educational efforts by increasing people's awareness of issues, but such information or publicity is not by itself a true educational alternative.

The most successful didactic resources in nonformal education is the untapped potential within the community itself. The vocation for teaching by community members is one of the bright spots in this otherwise frustrating effort. The multiplicative effect of a group of well learned community leaders has been a constant finding in most cases where evaluation of nonformal education has taken place (7–13). The best way to obtain a multiplicative effect at the community level is to use well structured and simple messages which can be transmitted verbally. A good example of this method are religious prayers and rituals which depend predominantly in nonwritten communication. This also assures that the message will not be modified on passing from one person to another. A set of objectives can be assembled in a unit which should be focused on a given problem. The efforts placed on providing community leaders not only with specific knowledge but also with simple group dynamic techniques will be rewarding. The effective use of the human voice can be reinforced with sign language using the hands or objects to dramatize the message. These methods are available under all conditions, do not require fancy equipment and are undoubtedly very powerful to induce behavioral change (9–13).

The structured unit should include a group dialogue to elicit what are the answers arising from the community for a given problem. The teacher should stimulate the participants to provide their own experiences. After all have expressed their views, he should incorporate the scientific knowledge on the issue. Finally, the group should arrive at a synthesis where a relevant and feasible behavior or action is agreed upon.

There are four necessary steps in designing effective teaching units. The first step is identification of the problem, its determining factors and the knowledge required to improve this situation. A set of specific objectives is assembled into a unit including appropriate didactic resources and activities. The unit should then be validated or redesigned and tested with a sample representative of the target population. The unit should then be evaluated in a pilot project introducing the necessary adaptations and measuring the impact in a controlled way. Finally after the unit has been tested and modified it can be implemented on a wider basis.

Many experiences have been carried out following some of these general principles yet few have been reported or evaluated adequately. Some common pitfalls in these efforts observed by the authors in their experience are due to a lack of respect for the community. The educator imposes answers which have not been well analysed with the people. The message is part of a political control scheme where the educator is an agent for or against a given ideology. Furthermore, the educational effort may be viewed as part of a government's program to expand primary services and the learner is expected to become part of that service.

It may not be readily apparent that the community leader who enters the service system may loose contact with his group and may no longer be able to criticize that system. It is very tempting to use well trained community leaders to expand services, but this will be short lived unless they are given rights, not duties. They should be respected as evaluators of the system and given some control as long as they remain representative of their community. Unless community participation is incorporated nonformal education becomes easily a vehicle for indoctrination.

CASE STUDY

Protein Energy Malnutrition (PEM) continues to be an important nutritional problem in Chile. Close to 12% of children under 6 years of age suffer from some degree of PEM by weight/age criterion (10). Over the last 40 years a progressive decrease in the age of onset of PEM has occurred coupled to a decline in the prevalence and duration of breast-feeding. Significant progress in decreasing mortality figures has been made with the help of supplementary feeding programs provided to children as part of their primary health care. Nevertheless the problem of marasmus in the first year of life still prevails. Powdered milk provided by the National Health System reaches 85% of the total infant population and covers over 95% of the at risk group. Each infant or nursing mother receives 3 kg per month of full fat powdered milk for the first 6 months and 2 kg thereafter until age 2. In spite of this and other PEM preventive programs, which include inmunizations, family planning and extension of primary health services, marasmus remains a relevant problem. It affects predominantly infants who have been weaned very early or not breast fed at all. Less than 50% breast feed beyond the first month and only 10% for more than 6 months (11). Having recognized that under the prevailing environmental conditions the promotion of breast feeding is probably the most important measure to reduce marasmus in the first year of life. Instituto de Nutricion y Tecnologia de los Alimentos (INTA) since 1977 is developing practical ways of prolonging breast-feeding among the urban poor. This task has been approached by nutritional supplementation of pregnant and lactating women and by nonformal education.

Educational efforts have focused on the health team, the pregnant women, and the community at large. A pilot project was carried out during 1980 to evaluate the role of educating women community leaders in promoting sound breast feeding practices (12). The specific objectives were:

1. The selection and training of volunteer women as leaders in the promotion of breast feeding in their community
2. Develop with the participation of community women leaders educational material for the training of other mothers
3. Evaluate the impact of the educational intervention by women leaders on breast feeding practices
4. Contribute to a better understanding of the sociocultural and biodemographic factors which condition the success or failure of breast feeding amongst the urban poor.

This study was carried out in "población El Cortijo" a poor district in periurban Santiago. The actions undertaken can be summarized in 6 steps:

1. Diagnosis: Information of knowledge, myths, beliefs, and attitudes of pregnant mothers regarding breast feeding was collected. This served as a basis to evaluate factors associated to successful breast feeding.
2. Selection of leaders from those mothers with a positive attitude and with a history of successful breast feeding experiences. We selected 18 as potential leaders. Based on previous community roles, completion of primary school, stable male partner, not having a mar-

asmic child, and a minimum of teaching skills, seven were invited to participate in the study.

3. Training of leaders using "learning by doing" methods meaning sharing previous experiences following the program contents. They would later use this same method for educating other mothers. This process took 8 weekly 2-hour sessions. The leaders also became familiar with the educational activities carried out by the health team.

4. Design of the educational program and teaching materials. These activities were done in parallel with the training of the leaders. The researchers proposed a program and materials to the leaders. They analyzed and modified contents and methods to make them more adequate for that community. A final configuration for the program was achieved after much interaction. From this step researchers realized that breast feeding for the community leaders could not be separated from pregnancy, delivery, and infant rearing practices. The leaders argued that the integrated approach needed coherence and that the focus could not be breast feeding alone, but it should also answer other concerns of the pregnant and lactating mothers, which undoubtedly affect breast feeding.

5. The multiplicative action. After the leaders completed their training, they initiated the training of other mothers under the supervision of the research team. Two leaders were in charge of educating 10 mothers each. Evaluation of this transfer by the researchers included interviews with mothers prior to their training to explore myths, beliefs, attitudes, and knowledge regarding breast feeding and to detect changes after the program. The research team also observed the sessions to validate the material and methods and to evaluate the interaction between the leaders and the learning mothers.

6. Evaluation of results. This step was carried out jointly by community leaders and researchers. All mothers were interviewed after their delivery and their breast feeding practices followed. Results are availabile for the initial 6 months.

Table II illustrates the results obtained in 30 pregnant women who were trained by community leaders to improve breast feeding practices. In addition all mothers reported preparing their nipples for successful breast feeding and answered correctly the need for more food during pregnancy and lactation.

Our observations on the use of educational methodology by the leaders showed that in some instances they chose to play a directive role for the group. This was associated with a progressive deterioration in the

TABLE II

Pre- and Posttraining Knowledge of Pregnant Women Trained by Community Leaders

Content	Pretraining (% correct answers)	Posttraining (% correct answers)
Will you continue to breast feed if your milk is "thin"	8	100
How early should breast feeding be started	48	100
The importance of colostrum	0	81
Need for additional fluids	15	100
Satisfaction of nutritional needs from breast milk	8	87
Breast feeding schedules	48	100
Breast feeding and contraception	36	100

motivation of the learning mothers. The greatest interaction and lowest desertion or absenteeism from the teaching sessions was observed when the leaders played a facilitating role permiting the free exchange of ideas and problems. The leaders that assumed a directive role were quick at providing the educational content without elliciting an intense response regarding previous experiences and beliefs.

Presently available data for the initial 6 months postpartum show that of 30 mothers trained by the leaders only one failed to breast-feed beyond 4 months. More detailed results will be reported after the efficacy of community leaders is tested under less supervised conditions.

This case report does not permit conclusive interpretations; it merely serves to illustrate the potential of the integrated educational methodology applied to nonformal nutrition education. It also underscores the need for action-oriented research to explore the best ways to link community experiences and scientific knowledge.

CONCLUSIONS

Nonformal education education is an important instrument for nutritional improvement. There are fundamental differences in both theory and practice between traditional education and the integrated educational process required for good learning. Nutrition education must be focused on the learner and his life experience. It must be seen as a way to enhance community participation and also as a transfer of power, not just knowledge. Its goal should be a change in people's awareness on the nature of food problems and how to solve them.

ACKNOWLEDGMENTS

The authors express their appreciation to Sonia Olivares, Juliana Kain, and María Teresa Guzmán for their review and suggestions and to Ms. Genoveva Escobar for secretarial assistance. Many of the ideas presented in this paper reflect the experience of one the authors (RU) who worked for 5 years in community health and nutrition education projects under Dr. Vicente Silva Moreno. His inspiring unpublished work has oriented many community based nonformal education efforts in Chile and Latin America.

REFERENCES

1. UNESCO. "Statistical Year Book." UNESCO, Paris, 1980.
2. Griffin, A., and Light, L. "Enseñanza de la nutrición, idoneidad y adaptación de los programas de estudio," Estud. Doc. Educ. No. 18. UNESCO, Paris, 1975.
3. Whitehead, F. E. "Nutrition Education Research Project." Office of Nutrition, AID, Iowa, 1970.
4. Biolley, E., Lerou, I., and Olivares, S. Conocimientos alimentarios y nutricionales de alumnos que ingresan a la Universidad de Profesores de Enseñanza Básica y Media en Chile. Nutrition M.S. Thesis, Instituto de Nutrición y Tecnologia de los Alimentos, INTA, Santiago, Chile, 1980.
5. Bloom, B. *et al.* "Como Aprender para Lograr el Dominio de lo Aprendido." Ateneo, Buenos Aires, 1974.
6. Manoff, R. The effective use of mass media in nutrition education. *PAG Bull.* **4,** 12 (1978).
7. Drake, W., and Fajardo, L. F. "The Promotora Program in Candelaria." Community Systems Foundation, Ann Arbor, Michigan, 1976.
8. Drummond, T. "Using the Method of Paulo Freire in Nutrition Education: An Experimental Plan for Community Action in Northeast Brazil," Cornell Int. Nutr. Monogr. Ser. No. 3. Cornell University, New York, 1975.
9. Lemmers, C., and Toro, H. Programa integral de salud mental en alcoholismo. *Cuad. Med. Soc.* **21,** 66 (1980).
10. González, N., Infante, A., and Mardones, F. "Análisis del Impacto de la Atención primaria de salud, sobre los indicadores de Salud y Nutrición, Chile 1969–1978," Apartado Docente 164/79. Instituto de Nutrición y Tecnología de los Alimertos, Santiago, 1979.
11. Mardones, S. R. Historia y situación actual de la lactancia materna en Chile. *Rev. Med. Chile* **107,** 750 (1979).
12. Miranda, M. *et al.* "Evaluación del impacto de la acción educativa de madres voluntarias, organizadas para promover la lactancia materna en su comunidad," Inf. Final. INTA, Santiago Chile, 1980.
13. Rohde, J. E., and Northrup, R. S. "Mother as the Basic Health Worker: Training Her and Her Trainers." Rockefeller Foundation, Yogyakarta, Indonesia, 1977.

Index